D0594182

bow's End

ift Of

itcher

PIVOTAL MOMENTS
IN AMERICAN HISTORY

Series Editors

David Hackett Fischer

James M. McPherson

James T. Patterson

Brown v. Board of Education:
A Civil Rights Milestone and Its Troubled Legacy

Rainbow's End

The Crash of 1929

Maury Klein

OXFORD•
UNIVERSITY PRESS
2001

OXFORD
UNIVERSITY PRESS

Oxford New York
Athens Auckland Bangkok Bogotá
Buenos Aires Cape Town Chennai Dar es Salaam Delhi
Florence Hong Kong Istanbul Karachi Kolkata
Kuala Lumpur Madrid Melbourne
Mexico City Mumbai Nairobi Paris São Paulo Shanghai
Singapore Taipei Tokyo Toronto Warsaw

and associated companies in
Berlin Ibadan

Published by Oxford University Press, Inc.
198 Madison Avenue, New York, New York 10016

Oxford is a registered trademark of Oxford University Press

Library of Congress Cataloging-in-Publication Data
Klein, Maury, 1939–.
Rainbow's end : the crash of 1929 /
Maury Klein.
p. cm. — (Pivotal moments in American history)
Includes bibliographical references and index.
ISBN 0-19-513516-4
1. Depressions—1929.
2. Depressions—1929—United States.
3. Stock Market Crash, 1929.
4. New York Stock Exchange—History.
5. United States—Economic conditions—1918–1945.
I. Title. II. Series.
HB3717 1929 .K588 2001
338.5'4'097309043—dc21   2001036069
KLEIN

1 3 5 7 9 8 6 4 2

Printed in the United States of America
on acid-free paper

Once again, to Kathy, with love . . .

Contents

Editors' Note

This volume is part of a series called Pivotal Moments in American History. Each book in this series examines a large historical problem through the lens of a particular event and the choices of individual actors. The design of the series reflects the current state of historical writing, which shows growing attention to the experiences of ordinary people, increasing sensitivity to issues of gender, class, and ethnicity, and deep interest in large structures and processes. We seek to combine this new scholarship with old ideas of history as a narrative art and traditional standards of sound scholarship, mature judgment, and good writing.

Many scholars have searched for the cause of the Great Crash. They have produced a large literature, and much of it is intelligent, deeply informed, and highly inventive. But nobody has been able to find an explanation that most other scholars accept.

Economists seek to understand this event in terms of theoretical propositions that take the form of "if x . . . then y . . . ." Even when they share the same neoclassical frame, as most do, their explanations of this puzzling event have been very different. Monetarists of the Chicago School (Friedman, Schwartz, et al.) have concluded that monetary policy had been too tight. Others, of the Austrian School (Hayek), believed that monetary policy was too easy.

Many economists at the time attributed the Crash to the growth of excess capacity in American industry. Others followed Schumpeter in thinking that the root of the problem was underconsumption. Keynes believed that the cause was a contraction of investment. Kindleberger thought it was a decline in foreign trade. Eichengreen suggested that it was the "golden fetters" of the bullion standard. Galbraith preferred to think in terms of institutional dysfunction. Others have argued for "diminished expectations" from the impending Smoot-Hawley tariff or other sources.

Many economists have combined two or more of these theoretical propositions within a single neoclassical model, but none has been able to put the pieces together in a way that is thought to be generally satisfactory.

Historians have studied the Crash in a different way. They are trained to think in terms of problem-solving rather than theory-testing. They also seek to understand events in their particulars. Maury Klein's *Rainbow's End* is a good example of that approach. It begins by assuming that the Great Crash is analytically distinct from the Great Depression, and it studies its origins as a sequence of contingencies.

The book poses large causal questions, but in historical terms. Was the Crash the end of an era, in which the American economy had suffered similar collapses with remarkable regularity since 1819? Or was it the product of a new era that began in the early twentieth century? Is something similar happening again in the twenty-first century? Was the Crash a great aberration, or did it expose a deep systemic flaw in the American economy, or both?

Rainbow's End offers new answers to all of those questions. At the same time, it also has another historical purpose: to understand the event as experience. One of its strongest contributions is its study of a distinct mentality that fed the great euphoric boom, and then turned into panic and despair. It suggests that the psychology of the Crash, perhaps more than its economics, made it the pivotal moment that it became.

This book presents its findings not as a monograph or research report, but as a vivid narrative that can be read for pleasure and instruction by anyone with an interest in its subject.

David Hackett Fischer
James M. McPherson

Introduction: The Crash as Historical Problem

The crash of 1929 is both a pivotal moment in American history and a great mystery. More than 70 years later it remains high on the list of national traumas for Americans, who wonder apprehensively during every bull market whether that calamity is about to be repeated. Like other pivotal moments in our past, such as the firing on Fort Sumter in 1861 or the dropping of the first atomic bomb in 1945, the stock market crash became a symbol for the end of one era and the beginning of another. It brought to a stunning halt a decade that had witnessed the greatest economic prosperity and most profound cultural changes yet known and ushered in a decade blighted by the longest and deepest depression Americans had ever endured.

The crash also ranks high on the list of unsolved puzzles for scholars, who have yet to come up with convincing answers to the two crucial questions of what caused the crash and what role, if any, it played in bringing on the grinding depression that followed. As David M. Kennedy observed, "The disagreeable truth . . . is that the most responsible students of the events of 1929 have been unable to demonstrate an appreciable cause-and-effect linkage between the Great Crash and the Depression."[1] Neither have they put forward a persuasive explanation for why the crash occurred. Through the years many historical questions have engaged scholars in sharp, long-running debates over the best answer, but few have left them unable to supply even the semblance of a satisfactory explanation after so long a time.

Contrary to popular belief, the Great Crash was not the event of one day but a series of events that stretched initially across the week from Wednesday, October 23, through Thursday, October 31. During these eight frantic sessions a total of nearly 70.8 million shares were traded— more than had changed hands in any *month* prior to March 1928. The

Dow Jones average fell 53 points from 326.51 to 273.51 and the *New York Times* combined average 50.21 points from 280.21 to 230.[2] In broader terms the crash extended until November 13, when the Dow hit 198.69 and the *Times* average 166.15. Of the seven abbreviated trading sessions during those bleak November days, only one registered a gain.[3] Although the drama of the October sessions remains the popular image of the crash, contemporary observers paid almost as much attention to the following two weeks as a harbinger of what the crash meant for the future.

If these figures seem tiny by the standard of today's market, it must be remembered that the population, the economy, and the stock market itself were much smaller in the 1920s. Put another way, the Dow fell 39 percent and the *Times* average nearly 41 percent between October 23 and November 13. The volume of trading, which did not surpass the 100-million-share monthly total mark until November 1928 or the 10-million-share mark in a single day until October 24, 1929, also seems small compared with today's. At the time, however, both these figures were considered colossal. Moreover, this flood of trading overwhelmed the available technologies for handling it far more than was the case in more recent declines of the stock market.

Popular belief has also tended to view the depression as occurring immediately after the crash and therefore as being caused by it in some way. Actually, the depression did not begin to fasten itself upon the nation until the autumn of 1930. Between December 1929 and March 1930 the market bounced back solidly; the Dow regained 74 percent and the *Times* average 63 percent of what had been lost since the beginning of the crash. This recovery brought prices back to levels well below the euphoric highs of the summer of 1929 but comparable to those at the end of 1928, a record-setting year in itself. During the first half of 1930 it was the economy rather than the stock market that failed to show vigor, and its growing sluggishness sent the market tumbling again in late spring. The real question, then, is not what effect the crash had on the stock market itself but rather what impact it had on the behavior of the economy—and there the mystery deepens.

The market has long been regarded as a harbinger of the economy in the sense that price movements anticipated and discounted broader trends within the economy and their effect on individual companies. Many historians and economists have described the height of the great bull market as a time when stock prices severed their connection with

Wall Street and the New York Stock Exchange building.   (Brown Brothers)

economic realities and flew upward on the wings of an illusion that a
"New Era" had arrived in which prices would march inexorably upward
and be immune to ruinous collapses. In this interpretation, New Era euphoria took command of the market by the summer of 1929 or perhaps
earlier. Yet during the first three quarters of that year the economy itself
performed at a record-setting pace that began to slow somewhat only in
the fall. While many observers doubted that the economy could maintain this pace, few believed that it would do anything more than cool
down into the usual seasonal or cyclical recession for an uncertain but
probably short duration.

In short, both the stock market and the economy can be seen as
overheated during 1929 and therefore due for some kind of adjustment.
Then came the crash, which sent the market reeling and plunged the
nation into several complex and interrelated levels of uncertainty. As
the *Magazine of Wall Street* aptly observed in November 1930, "Uncertainty is worse than knowing the truth, no matter how bad."[4] No one
recognized the dangers posed by this miasma of uncertainty more
clearly than President Herbert Hoover, who responded with swift, vigorous action. Among other things he invoked a chorus of confidence
about the future led by himself and sung lustily by corporate and financial leaders, businessmen of all stripes, government spokesmen, media
representatives, and hosts of ordinary people. This positive attitude remained dominant through the first months of 1930 and only began
crumbling in earnest during the late spring of that year.

From this basic scenario emerged a host of questions for which 70
years of debate have produced no definitive answers. Were stocks
greatly overpriced or not? Was any part of the New Era doctrine valid?
How well or poorly did the stock market reflect the underlying realities
of the economy? Was the economy really in trouble? If so, what were its
problems, and how serious were they? Why did the economy fail to recover during the first half of 1930? Could some vigorous action by the
government or elements of the private sector have averted the crash
and/or the onset of depression? If so, what was that action, and who
should have undertaken it? Did people really believe after the crash that
things would get better, or were they just whistling in the dark to ward
off their fears? These are but a few of the questions raised by the crash
and its aftermath. This book cannot provide final answers to them, but
it does seek to illuminate all of them.

For writers the crash poses another kind of problem, one very much like another national trauma that I have treated elsewhere: the national crisis that led to the firing on Fort Sumter.[5] Everyone knows the ending of the story; the interest lies not in the conclusion but in the tangled chain of circumstances that brought all parties to such a pivotal moment. There is one important difference: after the firing on Sumter everyone knew that war had come, whereas after the crash no one knew exactly what was to come. Nevertheless, to fathom the crash, one must look past the event itself to the context from which it sprang. That context has its roots in the American experience during World War I. Four times in American history—in 1781, 1865, 1918, and 1945—the fighting of a major war has brought forth a new nation irretrievably altered from the one that entered the conflict. The United States emerged from World War I radically changed at home and with a radically changed role abroad. Not surprisingly, the nation was slow to grasp, let alone respond to, these altered conditions.

Perhaps the most striking aspect of this strange new world was that change, that most characteristic catalyst of the American experience, came faster and in more varied forms than ever before. The transformation that it wrought separated the postwar generation from their parents in everything from values to behavior to dress to beliefs with a suddenness that shocked traditionalists. What came to be called modernism had been developing in American life since the turn of the century, but in postwar America it exploded onto the scene at the same time that far-reaching changes in the economy—spurred also by the wartime experience—drove productivity to new heights and fashioned a dazzling array of new consumer goods. A host of key technologies—most notably electricity, the automobile, motion pictures, and radio—spread rapidly and reshaped the daily lives of millions of Americans.

Change was nothing new in American life, but never before had so much of it come so quickly to so many people. It created a milieu in which change itself became a way of life. Many of the tenets by which Americans had long guided their lives were eroded or rendered seemingly extinct. A people taught to value work as the center of life discovered the pleasures of play. The timeless doctrine of scrimping and saving gave way to a new imperative to spend and enjoy, even if it meant going into debt. The strictures of religion, which resigned people to the troubles of this life in exchange for the consolation of a better one in the next, were recast to emphasize the good life to be had in the here and now. Habits and tastes once denounced as scandalous and obscene became routine pleasures first for the young and then for their parents. The ethos of scarcity was fast giving way to the delights of abundance and consumption.

From this welter of change emerged the amorphous set of beliefs and attitudes that came to be known popularly as the New Era. Never a developed or full-blown theory or philosophy, it was rather a concept vague and slippery enough to be applied to whatever need its advocates might require. But it did embrace one consistent theme: that the striking changes wrought in so many sectors of American life had created conditions in which past rules no longer applied, whether in business, industry, finance, religion, personal behavior, or traditional values. A corollary to this theme proclaimed that change promoted progress and was therefore nearly always for the better. Readers alert to the connection between the past and present will notice distinct echoes of the New Era experience in the contemporary hosannas to the New Economy.[6]

The first chapters of this book portray the emergence of this postwar world and the forces that shaped it. Without this context the crash makes little sense. It cannot be satisfactorily explained from the narrow perspective of a technical approach that views it as merely a financial phenomenon. Neither can it be explicated by a mathematical model or theoretical construct that focuses on monetary policy or some other aspect of the crisis. Rather it evolved within a context that saw more Americans than ever before attain a standard of living that enabled them to invest in the market or to see their future as somehow linked to its performance. Enchanted by the comforts, conveniences, and entertainments of this new material civilization, exhilarated by the prospects for the future promised by the slogans of the New Era, they came increasingly to view the market as the key to the pot of riches awaiting them at the rainbow's end.

By the late 1920s the bull market had outgrown its financial boundaries and assumed a new role as potent symbol for the success story that was America. As economist John Kenneth Galbraith wrote, "The striking thing about the stock market speculation of 1929 was not the massiveness of the participation. Rather it was the way it became central to the culture."[7] In truth we don't know how many people actually invested in the market, but even in small towns people put money into it or heard stories of it or knew someone who knew someone who had made a killing in it. The lure, as always with a rainbow, was the promise of quick, easy wealth with little effort as opposed to a lifetime of toil to eke out a living. The fact that the new consumer economy offered so many more things to buy spurred the desire for a fast fortune. Money became the new messiah in more ways for more Americans than ever before.

There was something almost mystical in popular attitudes toward the bull market. It was as if people willed it to go higher, and it would continue to go up as long as they believed it would. In a bizarre sense this notion contained at least a modicum of truth. If there is a common thread in the literature seeking to explain the crash and its aftermath, it is the importance of mood and the power of illusion to influence people's behavior. Writer Frederick Lewis Allen, one of the earliest and most astute students of the subject, expressed in 1931 a view that many later writers would develop in a variety of ways:

> Prosperity is more than an economic condition; it is a state of mind. The Big Bull Market had been more than the climax of a business cycle; it had been the climax of a cycle in American mass thinking and mass emotion. There was hardly a man or woman in the country whose attitude toward life had not been affected by it in some degree and was not now affected by the sudden and brutal shattering of hope. With the Big Bull Market gone and prosperity now going, Americans were soon to find themselves living in an altered world which called for new adjustments, new ideas, new habits of thought, and a new order of values. The psychological climate was changing; the ever-shifting currents of American life were turning into new channels. The Post-War Decade had come to a close. An era had ended.[8]

This insightful observation is all the more remarkable for having come so soon after the crash. But Allen was not alone in grasping the crucial role of psychological factors in economic and financial affairs. Eight months before the crash a *Wall Street Journal* columnist made an astute appraisal of the role of mood in language that might have come from a current issue of the paper. "The market as well as business is more or less a state of mind," he wrote in February 1929. "The people have been in an optimistic state of mind for several years. . . . That has been the basis for the longest period of prosperity in history and the longest bull market in history. If the people begin to lose confidence prosperity will ebb with it and so will increased earnings . . . production . . . dividends . . . high wages and a healthy market. Sentiment is something dangerous to trifle with."[9]

The enduring quality of this emphasis on the role of confidence—or, in broader terms, mood and illusion—can be seen in numerous recent articles stressing the same point in explaining the economy's sluggishness. "What's driven this economic boom has been confidence in the boom itself," wrote Robert J. Samuelson in *Newsweek* on December 18, 2000. "People have acted as if it could go on forever, and they have spent accordingly. But we are now seeing the first signs of fraying confidence. . . . If confidence unravels, the mild economic slowdown that's now unfolding could deteriorate quickly into a nasty slump."[10]

The problem for historians, of course, is that mood cannot be measured or gauged with any degree of accuracy. Moreover, it is but half of the equation—the other half being the events that shape and color mood. It is one thing to itemize the key events that affect mood, that sustain or jar illusion, and quite another to measure or even estimate their precise effect. Aware of this limitation, this book attempts to convey at least a sense of the interplay between the shifting mood of Americans during these years and the key events that influenced them, as viewed through the eyes of many different key players in the unfolding drama. Only in this way can one begin to comprehend what was involved in this pivotal moment in American history and what it meant to people at the time.

It may be that in the end the best way to understand the crash and the depression that followed is one that satisfies neither historians nor economists. Both the crash and the depression can be viewed as aberrations, and their relationship as the product of an unlikely and unpredictable sequence of events—the random coming together of a confluence of unfortunate forces. The accumulated effect of these forces not only created the crisis but prolonged and deepened it, much like the strengthening of a routine storm into a killer hurricane or blizzard when a variety of unfavorable factors, each one unpleasant but not lethal in itself, combine on rare occasions to forge the worst-case scenario. In short, the crash and its aftermath was the perfect storm.

Rainbow's End

Prologue:
The Summer of Fun, 1929

T he summer of fun came to its regularly scheduled conclusion on Labor Day weekend. For the well-to-do based in New York City, it marked the season's end for a social ritual that had endured for decades in their migration to such fashionable resorts as the Hamptons on Long Island, Newport, Rhode Island, Bar Harbor, Maine, Saratoga, New York, and scattered colonies on the Jersey shore. One student of this pageant of pleasure, R. L. Duffus, described it as "an attempt to build up a make-believe world grander than the real one." After a final fling of teas, dinners, parties, dances, sailing, golf, and other pleasures, the wealthy and their entourage of servants packed up for their return to the city. In recent times the habit had spread on a more modest scale to middle-class folk, who vacated the city for the Catskills, the Adirondacks, Atlantic City, or some smaller resort village with a boardinghouse. Some even had their own cottage on a nearby lake or river. Even those of modest means could find refuge by taking a boat to picnic at Coney Island (which Duffus called a "bargain-counter paradise"), Long Beach, or the Rockaways.[1]

For the tens of thousands fleeing the city on this last summer weekend, fun meant travel to some source of pleasure. "If names were ever more than polite handles concealing the truth," noted a journalist, "Labor Day would promptly be rechristened Travel Day." Many people, laden with suitcases, lunch baskets, golf bags, fishing rods, and other impedimenta, climbed aboard the hundreds of special trains put on for the sole purpose of hauling vacationers out of the city on Friday and bringing them back sometime Monday evening. Others poured out of the city in their automobiles, heading in all directions for a day's drive in the country, a visit to the seaside or the mountains, or a stay at one of the many resorts located within a 300-mile arc of the city.[2]

More people than ever before ventured out of the city to enjoy themselves this holiday weekend. For this last escape into summer's delights, large numbers of them paid a steeper price than usual on the return journey. A relentless heat wave baked the East Coast as the record number of vacationers flowed back into New York City on Monday evening—or tried to. The sweltering 92-degree heat had driven massive numbers of people to the beaches—an estimated 900,000 at Coney Island, 500,000 at Long Beach on Long Island, 400,000 at the Rockaways, and 200,000 at Staten Island—and not all of them made it home that night. Police reported that as many as 5,000 men, women, and children spent the night on Coney Island's beach alone. The line of cars waiting to board the ferryboats at Staten Island stretched back over a mile.[3]

Those who did return clogged every mode of travel like the straggling remnants of a broken army. At midnight long lines of traffic still choked the overworked bridges, ferries, and tunnel leading into the city. From the north some 16,000 vehicles streamed across the Bear Mountain bridge. The roads of Long Island and Westchester County overflowed with automobiles crawling toward their destination, but their ordeal paled before that of travelers piling up beyond the Holland Tunnel. On three New Jersey roads that converged on the tunnel, the crush of overheating cars stretched back five miles. Packed three to five abreast, they inched forward while their weary, sweating drivers muttered curses. Some saw no hope of the congestion easing before dawn and ended their vacation weekend on an inglorious note: they parked their cars in Newark or Jersey City and trekked with their luggage to the subway or train for the last leg of their journey home.[4]

Things were little better at the cavernous rail stations, where passengers gushed from a steady stream of trains late into the night. Police estimated that half a million travelers passed through Grand Central and another quarter million through Pennsylvania Station, their ranks swollen by armies of children returning from summer camps in groups that sometimes numbered 400. The New York Central had put on 40 extra trains and the New York, New Haven & Hartford 65, making the latter's total 185 for the weekend. Some of the 400 buses arriving at the Waldorf Astoria's terminal ran five hours late, and long lines of cars jammed the West Shore Railroad's nine ferryboats that ran to West 42nd and Cortlandt streets until 10:00 that night. Thus did the summer of fun end not with a bang but with a traffic jam.

It had been a summer like no other since the return of what President Warren G. Harding had called "normalcy" in 1920. After the brief but severe recession of 1920–21 the United States had marched steadily onward into the New Era proclaimed by President Calvin Coolidge late in 1927. Since then, riding the coattails of a booming economy, it had surged forward with a force as irresistible as a tidal wave.[5] By the torrid summer of 1929 everything seemed to be soaring. The economy was as hot as the weather and setting some new record almost every day. Batting averages in the major leagues were up more than 50 points, giving rise to charges of a doctored or "rabbit" ball.[6] Skyscrapers, especially in Manhattan, thrust ever higher toward the honor of being tallest, and hemlines continued their titillating rise above the knee despite futile efforts by some Parisian designers to restore interest in the long skirt.[7] Even ordinary people were scaling new heights as a fad for flagpole sitting swept the nation.

Daring aviators, inspired by the enormous popularity (and publicity) generated by the transatlantic flight of Charles A. Lindbergh two years earlier, dominated the headlines with their attempts to set every kind of record. One band of St. Louis flyers managed to remain in the air for a record 420 hours and 21 minutes. The majestic *Graf Zeppelin* arrived in New York after a 93-hour flight from Germany, then set out on a round-the-world flight that covered 19,000 miles in 21 days and 7 hours. Women no less than men flocked to the skies, but the best-known among them were foreign. "It is humiliating to admit," sighed one American aviatrix, the wife of a Tiffany vice president, "that at present there seems to be no American girl who can successfully compete." Amid the craze for flying, one scientist aimed highest of all. Robert H. Goddard, inventor of the rocket, fired his latest steel cylinder a quarter of a mile into the sky, a modest step in his quest to reach and study the still unknown region beyond the earth's atmosphere.[8]

The only thing seeking greater heights than Goddard's rocket that summer was the stock market, which soared into regions once considered as remote and fantastic as the moon. In August the Dow Jones industrial average swept beyond 380, nearly 47 points greater than in June and 63 points above its January high. A year earlier, amid the boom of 1928, it had stood at 240. The *New York Times* combined average of 50 industrial and rail stocks hit a record high of nearly 305, a gain of 40 points since June and nearly 70 since January. In August of 1928 it had not yet reached 204. Brokers' loans, that barometer of borrowings for use in the securities markets, also rose to record heights month after month and stood at a breathtaking $6.2 billion at the end of August, nearly $2 billion above the figure for that same month in 1928.

And no end was in sight. Business was humming as it never had during the usually sluggish summer months. Two indices regarded as key measures of economic health—steel production and railroad freight car loadings—exceeded all expectations. For a time the mills churned out steel products at a rate exceeding 100 percent of capacity, while railroad income set new records. Fall business and mercantile prospects looked glowing.[9] Consumer confidence remained high; America had been on a gigantic spending spree that showed few signs of slowing down. "Everything indicates that business continues to make progress with production at a new high record," reported the *Wall Street Journal* in mid-July. "And there seems to be nothing in sight to check the upward trend. It will probably be the best summer in earnings and production general business has ever experienced. This is the real basis for the continuance of the bull market. And . . . there is no inflation."[10]

Late in August a survey by Dominick & Dominick concluded that "basic industrial conditions continue to be unusually favorable. Production in fundamental industries is establishing new high records, and it is evident that earnings for the year . . . will be exceptionally large."[11] Even agriculture, long the Achilles heel of the economy, had rallied during the summer from a June scare in which the price of wheat fell below 95 cents a bushel, a level not seen since 1923. However, just when "dollar wheat," long a benchmark minimum, seemed threatened, a wild rally in the commodities market pushed the price back above a dollar in a single day. By mid-July estimates of the wheat crop had been revised downward and wheat jumped 50 cents above its earlier low price amid talk that it might go to $2 a bushel. "The continued climb of grain prices," declared the *New York Times*, "is undoubtedly the most important development of the month."[12]

During August wheat began slipping downward again, losing 21 cents from its earlier high by the 25th, but few observers seemed worried. "A slump in grain prices might have had demoralizing results years ago when the country was not as wealthy as it is today and industry not so widely diversified," noted the *Wall Street Journal*, adding that "no one line of industry, no matter how large, can force the country into a general depression." Moreover, in June President Herbert Hoover had signed into law the Agricultural Marketing Act, which created a Federal

Farm Board designed to help farmers stabilize prices and production. "The farm," he proclaimed, "is more than a business; it is a state of living." For months Congress, called into special session by Hoover, had been grappling with a controversial tariff bill. Whatever the outcome, Hoover was adamant that it favor the farmer. "The first and most complete necessity," he emphasized, "is that the American farmer have the American market. That can be assured to him solely through the protective tariff."[13]

The president and his wife spent the holiday weekend relishing the solitude of their fishing camp at the headwaters of the Rapidan River in Virginia, where they had also gone on August 10 to celebrate his 55th birthday. "I have discovered why Presidents take to fishing, the silent sport . . . ," he explained. "Fishing seems to be the sole avenue left to Presidents through which they may escape to their own thoughts and may live in their own imaginings and find relief from the pneumatic hammer of constant personal contacts." Yet even there he could not resist mixing a little philanthropic business with pleasure. When the scant education of children in the mountain area around his retreat was brought to his attention, he promised to head a committee to raise funds for a school.[14]

Barely five months in office, Hoover basked in the apparent good fortune of being the right man in the right place at the right time. A trained engineer and self-made millionaire, he embodied the bedrock American virtues of rugged individualism, hard work, and unquenchable faith in the future. He had ridden to victory on a tidal wave of prosperity and vowed to maintain its surge. At the time of his election on November 6, 1928, the *New York Times* average reached a record high. The stock market boasted a closing average twice that of 1924 and three times that of 1918.[15] Business was active, production climbing, agricultural prices rising, and factory payrolls reaching new heights. "Hoover prosperity" they dubbed it, and the president intended to make its perpetuation his legacy.

In accepting the nomination Hoover had proclaimed, "We in America today are nearer to the final triumph over poverty than ever before in the history of any land. The poorhouse is vanishing from among us. . . . We shall soon with the help of God be in sight of the day when poverty will be banished from this earth." No man seemed better equipped or more competent to make this dream come true or handle the burdens of power. "We were in a mood for magic . . . ," recalled writer Anne O'Hare

McCormick of the inauguration; "the whole country was a vast, expectant gallery, its eyes focused on Washington. We had summoned a great engineer to solve our problems for us; now we sat back comfortably and confidently to watch the problems being solved. The modern technical mind was for the first time at the head of a government. . . . Almost with the air of giving genius its chance, we waited for the performance to begin."[16]

It began with a flourish. Hoover had signed the farm bill and summoned a sullen Congress to thrash out the tariff riddle. A strong devotee of the balanced budget, he predicted in June that the federal government would run a surplus of $110 million. Foreign affairs, too, showed signs of progress. Two issues left over from the war, the huge debt owed the United States by its allies and the reparations demanded by them from Germany, had poisoned international relations for an entire decade. Although bitter wrangling continued, a resolution seemed near that summer with the signing in June of an agreement creating a Bank for International Settlements. At the end of August the reluctant Germans accepted certain compromises embedded in a plan devised by American negotiator Owen D. Young, the brilliant head of General Electric and RCA who had just been voted "the one outstanding American businessman" by students at the Harvard Business School. Negotiations were also under way for a conference to scale down and balance the navies of the major powers.[17]

During the tedious months of negotiations in Paris, Young had as his partners David Sarnoff of RCA and banker J. P. Morgan Jr., but Jack Morgan had neither Young's patience nor his finesse at this form of diplomacy. He could scarcely conceal his intense dislike of the Germans and complained that the conference impinged on his plans for a Mediterranean cruise aboard his yacht. At one point he simply quit the negotiations and sailed to the Mediterranean with his friend the Archbishop of Canterbury. "If Hell is anything like Paris and an International Conference combined," he wrote a friend, "it has many terrors, and I shall try to avoid them." Eventually he returned to the table, but when the conference wrapped up he looked forward eagerly to his annual fall pilgrimage to the Scottish highlands for grouse shooting.[18]

Trouble spots still lingered elsewhere. The French led 38 nations in protesting the tariff bill under consideration. Smoldering tensions between the Soviet Union and China erupted in July when the USSR severed relations with its giant neighbor and prepared to send troops into

Manchuria. Riots raged in Jerusalem, and 12 Americans were slaughtered in Hebron as savage fighting broke out throughout Palestine. But those conflicts seemed far away and unimportant to most Americans during the summer of fun. To New Yorkers in particular, far more relevant was the news that Mayor Jimmy Walker had decided to run for another term. The dapper, jovial Walker looked and acted like the perfect politician to preside over good times in a city that had come to be the center of world finance and tended to regard itself as the center of the known universe.[19]

One element of that civic supremacy was slipping badly. The New York Yankees, who had dominated the decade even longer than the bull market, were faltering in the face of a brash new dynasty put together by Connie Mack in Philadelphia. Over the holiday weekend, the Yankees lost three straight games to Philadelphia, and manager Miller Huggins glumly conceded the pennant. The old Murderers' Row of Babe Ruth, Lou Gehrig, and Bob Meusel had given way to one composed of Mickey Cochrane, Al Simmons, and Jimmy Foxx in a city where brotherly love did not extend to New Yorkers. This shocking development came at a time when baseball seemed headed into a new era of unabashed hitting. The ball seemed to be flying out of parks everywhere. By late July, outfielder Chuck Klein of the Philadelphia Phillies had already equaled Ruth's 1919 record of 29 home runs. There was little doubt that the advantage had passed to the hitters or that small boys who once longed to grow up and be Christy Mathewson or Walter Johnson now looked to Babe Ruth or Rogers Hornsby as their models.[20]

As batting averages soared, so did the skylines of American cities with new skyscrapers. As always, New York led the procession. In 1912 some 1,048 of its 92,749 buildings were 10 stories or higher; by 1925 another 552 buildings exceeded 10 stories. Wall Street was slow to join the parade. As late as 1912 nearly half its buildings rose no more than five stories, but after the war its skyline followed the bull market upward. During the construction boom of the 1920s a flock of new buildings, many of them in the popular art deco style, joined the club exceeding 20 stories. Few were more striking than the 24-story black, gold-trimmed American Radiator Company Building (1924), which one writer has called "one of the decisive events in the evolution of the Art Deco skyscraper." Others soon dwarfed it in size if not in appearance as one building after another pushed past the 30-story mark. By 1929 no fewer than 78 buildings reached above 20 stories, and 19 of them towered 40 stories or more.[21]

Since 1913 the 792-foot Woolworth Building had owned the honor of being the tallest building in the world, but two structures under construction, the Chrysler Building and the Bank of Manhattan, were eager to usurp the title. The former was a monument to himself by Walter P. Chrysler, the latest automobile titan whom *Time* had named its Man of the Year in 1928 for putting together a company that seemed poised to challenge the industry leaders, General Motors and Ford. Another automobile magnate, the indefatigable John J. Raskob, conceived an even more audacious project: he would tear down the old Waldorf-Astoria Hotel and erect a skyscraper towering 80 or more stories high. In August he recruited former New York governor and failed presidential candidate Alfred E. Smith to head his Empire State Building Corporation. It was a natural connection for Raskob, who was also national chairman of the Democratic party.[22]

Some ordinary citizens reached new heights and headlines on a more modest scale. Of all the fads that raced across the nation like the flu during the 1920s, none was more bizarre than the epidemic of flagpole sitting. The primary spreader of the virus was Alvin "Shipwreck" Kelly, whose nickname echoed his past as both sailor and untalented boxer. After perching atop a Hollywood flagpole for 13 hours and 13 minutes in 1924 and receiving more attention than he had ever dreamed of, Kelly discovered his mission in life. He journeyed from city to city demonstrating to the citizenry "the hardihood of the American posterior by sitting for extended periods on flagpoles."[23]

When Kelly took his act to the normally staid city of Baltimore in 1929, he left behind a serious infection among the young. After Kelly had set another world's record and gone his way, a brief notice appeared in the paper that one Avon Foreman, age 15, had mounted a flagpole and intended to stay until he had broken the "juvenile record." His father, an electrician, helpfully rigged up some spotlights to illuminate his perch for the crowds who came day and night to watch his "performance." No one knew exactly what the juvenile record was, but "Azey," as he was called, manned his platform for 10 days, 10 hours, 10 minutes, and 10 seconds before descending to loud acclaim. Mayor William F. Broening, never one to overlook a crowd or a bromide, showed up to present an autographed testimonial inscribed with the city's seal and to hail the achievement as a shining example of "the pioneer spirit of early America."[24]

Here was a call to arms no one could have foreseen. Within days backyards and vacant lots were dotted with new poles ranging from 10 to 20 feet high, each one manned by a determined contender for the hitherto unknown Juvenile Flagpole Sitting Championship of the World. Some children rose to new heights without parental knowledge and came quickly down when found out; others had the enthusiastic support of star-struck mothers or fathers. "My boy is sunburned and the exposure to fresh air will benefit him," explained one proud dad. "I want him to make a real record and I've promised him a reward of 50¢ a day for each day over 20 he stays aloft." An eager mother placed her 20-month-old son in a box atop a seven-foot pole and left him there for one hour to claim the "infant record." Two children suffered broken legs and another a broken arm, but fresh recruits eagerly took their places.

Official Baltimore responded to this outbreak of mass elevation by requiring that poles be approved for safety by city engineers and that sitters obtain a permit costing one dollar. While the epidemic raged, Mayor Broening dutifully visited the contestants, assuring them that "stamina and grit are essential in the great struggle of life." An unimpressed critic took a less patriotic view of what had turned into a commercial ritual, observing that "when a boy, through the simple expedient of installing himself in a coop at the end of a pole can bring the Mayor to call on him, cause a minister of the Gospel to hold services with sermon at the foot of the pole and be the central occasion for a brass brand, scores of popcorn vendors, offers of free dentistry for a year and a 'write-up' in the newspapers, parental authority . . . avails very little. . . . The corner druggist pays a dollar or two for the right to advertise his business on the sacred totem."

Fads seemed to be coming ever faster from an ever widening range of sources, some of them hard to detect. People started drinking sauerkraut juice for no apparent reason, and broccoli returned to the dinner table after a long absence. Marathon dancing absorbed some hardy souls; one couple staggered to victory at Milton Crandall's Eternity Hop after 534 numbing hours on the dance floor. "Americans are crazy people," concluded newspaper cartoonist Ralph Barton. "They drink too much, do everything too much. They like something for fifteen minutes, then turn about and like something else. They are faddists. They idolize some hero of the hour beyond all sensibility, then leave him flat for some one else."[25]

Psychologist and fashion authority Elizabeth B. Hurlock predicted that "the more rapidly the fads are copied and adopted by the masses, the shorter will be the life of each fad and the more rapid will be the changes." By contrast fashion lasted longer, affected more people, and was taken more seriously, but it too was undergoing profound changes. For women the most obvious of these was the amount of clothing they no longer wore and the availability of styles of all kinds even to those with modest means. Social critic Stuart Chase listed three sights that made the streets of New York and other large cities in 1929 different from those before the war: "skyscrapers, motor cars, and skirts. . . . Women are wearing about half as much clothes." He may have overestimated; by one calculation the average woman's outfit in 1928 consumed only 7 yards of cloth compared with 19¼ yards in 1913.[26]

Chase was also impressed with how clothes had ceased to be a badge of social status. "Only a connoisseur can distinguish Miss Astorbilt on Fifth Avenue from her father's stenographer or secretary . . . ," he noted. "So eager are the lower income groups to dress as well in style, if not in quality, as their economic superiors, that class distinctions have all but disappeared." Hurlock saw another influence at work: "A large percentage of the people who conform to fashion do so not because they want to imitate their social superiors, but because they fear social disapproval. . . . Youth is ruled by this tendency far more than is age." Two trends were, however, undeniable: hemlines kept creeping higher, and fashion had become as volatile as it was popular. "Never in history has fashion held such power as it does today," admitted Hurlock. "Never have fashions been so varied and fleeting. Never has fashion's sway been so universal that to be out of fashion might literally be interpreted to be 'out of the world.' . . . Americans are perhaps the most ardent votaries of fashion that the world has ever known."[27]

The fads for flying and flagpole sitting, as well as the flights of fashion fancies, proved to be worthy emblems for the summer of fun. Devotees of them tended to ignore a truth that was at once a law of nature and a harsh reality of human affairs: that what goes up must eventually come down.

It was a truism that applied no less to the economy and to Wall Street, which had learned this bitter lesson over and over only to forget it in the next rush of enthusiasm. "Probably the question most frequently heard around Wall Street is 'How high can stocks go?' . . . " reported one analyst. "Professional Wall Street admits that there must be a maximum point for all stocks, but usually adds that it is difficult to determine what that point is in view of the fact that many issues now active are selling at twenty to thirty times earnings." Only a year earlier

John J. Raskob had dismissed the traditional maxim that a stock should sell at no more than 10 times earnings and asserted that 15 times earnings was a more apt figure for modern times. Now few speculators blinked at stocks selling as high as 30 times earnings.[28]

The ebullient Raskob had a more compelling message for ordinary investors. In May he had unveiled a plan that would enable even ordinary people to buy stock on the installment plan. Three months later, in a magazine article entitled "Everybody Ought to Be Rich," he proclaimed that anyone who invested $15 a month and let the dividends and rights ride would have a fortune of at least $80,000 in 20 years and from it an income of $400 a month. "He will be rich," Raskob insisted. "And because income can do that I am firm in my belief that anyone not only can be rich but ought to be rich." He did not trouble the reader with minor details like how a man earning $100 or $120 a month could save $15 of it to invest, or how he could be certain to pick the right stock. Nor did he go into the crucial assumption behind all the calculations: that the market would continue its rise for decades to come.[29]

To sneering skeptics Raskob insisted that his only desire was to help others. "I have all the money I want," he declared, "and now I want to help other people make some." He also offered the opinion that "many stocks are not too high even at their present level." As usual, his remarks had behind them other agendas. If he had all the money he wanted, it was partly because he had been quietly liquidating his stock holdings and getting out of the market. That summer, too, he had joined broker Mike Meehan to help their fellow Irish-Catholic high roller Joseph Kennedy unload some of his Pathé Pictures stock by engineering a pool to elevate the stock's price through the time-honored device of spreading a rumor that the group was deeply interested in buying the company.[30]

In the summer of 1929 much of America was on an artificial high. It was a high born not of drugs but of an illusion that the prosperity and the good times then being enjoyed were made of new miracle ingredients that would last forever. As one chronicler of the age explained, "The New Era . . . meant permanent prosperity, an end to the old cycle of boom and bust, steady growth in the wealth and savings of the American people, continuously rising stock prices." It also meant steady employment, rising wages, and shorter workweeks, enabling even ordinary people to enjoy the good things of life while keeping the vast and intricate machinery of the new consumer economy humming smoothly. Nowhere was New Era thinking more evident than in the stock market.

"Every crash of the past few years had been followed by a recovery," recalled Frederick Lewis Allen, "and . . . every recovery had ultimately brought prices to a new high point. . . . What the bull operators had long been saying must be true. . . . This was a new era. Prosperity was coming into full and perfect flower."[31]

Records of all kinds were being set, and not only atop flagpoles or in the stock market. In August the American Gas and Electric System, one of several mammoth power holding companies, proudly threw a switch placing in operation the last link in the longest power transmission line in the world under single ownership. The new line carried a load of 100,000 horsepower across 980 miles from Lake Michigan to the Virginia–North Carolina border, where connections with other systems extended it to points south. The feat was cheered as one more symbol of progress in an economy that thrived on record numbers. That same month Henry Ford watched Model A number 2,000,000 roll off the assembly line less than seven months after number 1,000,000 had made its debut. Other figure-happy individuals noted that 75 percent of the world's radios bore the inscription "Made in America" and that an estimated 10,900,000 passengers rode one of Manhattan's 28,104 elevators every day.[32]

Progress was measured not only by numbers but by new amenities and conveniences as well. "The day is not far off when the casual motorist in New England will have a new joy," reported *Time* that August. "He will drive up to a handsome colonial edifice set in a little park with poplar trees about it and there he will satisfy both his machine and himself. For the machine there will be gasoline and oil; for the man there will be hot dogs."[33]

In America during the New Era anything was possible. The stock market had demonstrated in its repeated comebacks an ability to turn the despair of the moment into ultimate triumph. Like the movies that enthralled rapt audiences across the nation, it transformed even mistakes into happy endings. No one better exemplified this spirit than Amandus J. Paulsen of Santa Cruz, California, a despondent quadriplegic who tried earnestly that August to kill himself by somehow turning on the gas, maneuvering himself into a tub of water, and struggling to cut his throat. Despite this dogged effort, he was discovered in time and rushed to the hospital. Not only was his life spared, but he awoke from his ordeal to find that his paralysis was gone.[34]

Even some leading bankers, normally the most cautious of souls, subscribed to the doctrine of the New Era. One of the most prestigious bankers in America, the urbane Thomas W. Lamont of the House of Morgan, saw virtue in its tenets despite the skepticism of some of his colleagues. No one worshiped more ardently at the altar of the New Era or better exemplified the sheer energy behind it than Charles E. Mitchell, head of the powerful National City Bank. So potent and positive was his faith that he was known as "Sunshine Charley," and never had the sun shone brighter for him than during the summer of fun. The bank had enjoyed record earnings this year and last, fetching Mitchell each time more than $1 million. Now the handsome, genial banker stood at the pinnacle of his career. National City had just opened its first office in Mexico, number 100 in its stable of foreign branches that extended from China to South America. Mitchell himself was busy negotiating a merger with the Corn Exchange Bank that would make National City the largest bank in the world and also planning a new office building that he hoped would be the tallest in the city.[35]

The chorus of bulls on prosperity and the market, which had been gathering volume through the ups and downs of a particularly hectic year, built a beguiling crescendo through the summer. Sunshine Charley's strong and influential voice rose above the choir. "General situation looks exceptionally sound with very few bad spots," he cabled an inquiring Bernard Baruch in mid-August, adding, "I doubt if anything that will not affect business can affect the market, which is like a weather-vane pointing into a gale of prosperity." The *New York Times* conceded that "to the speculating public, the picture has apparently come to be that of a continuous rise in prices which nothing can interrupt more than momentarily." On Labor Day afternoon the voice of one who had gained peculiar notoriety for predicting the market reassured thousands of radio listeners: asked her view of the market's future by a reporter from station WJZ, astrologist Evangeline Adams replied, "The Dow Jones could climb to Heaven."[36]

Major business figures had sung this hymn lustily all year long. Many of them shared the view of Alfred Sloan Jr. of General Motors, who had said in January, "Personally I believe it is going to be a very prosperous year—I do not see how it could be otherwise." Tom Watson of IBM agreed that "we may look forward to the progress of business in 1929." Prominent professors, notably Irving Fisher of Yale and Charles Amos Dice of Ohio State, chimed in with arguments that the soaring bull market was rooted not in reckless speculation but in sound economic fundamentals. Fisher noted that corporate earnings in the first nine months of 1929 had increased 20 percent compared with 1928, a comparison he found "eloquent in justification of a heightened level of common stock prices."[37]

These reassurances were music to the ears of the "minnows," as notorious speculator Jesse L. Livermore called them—the legions of small-timers and outsiders who eagerly followed the market leaders for what they hoped would be a nonstop ride upward. No longer was the stock market merely the playground of the rich, the ambitious, and the professionals. For the first time it seemed as if anybody could play the Wall Street lottery in the hope of quick, effortless riches. "Smaller participants . . . were investing their savings in the expectation that the market was going indefinitely higher and . . . they would never have another chance to buy at such low prices . . . ," wrote one historian. "They had seen fortunes made in the market. They or their friends had indulged in this trading for several years without substantial loss. . . . They were assured on the highest authority that they were merely sharing in the lasting prosperity of the country."[38]

Earlier in the year steel magnate Charles Schwab had observed that "as long as the people remain enthusiastic and interested the market will hold up." During the summer of fun, interest had elevated into obsession as stocks became the chief topic of conversation everywhere. "Literary editors whose hopes were wrapped about American Cyanamid B," noted Frederick Lewis Allen, "lunched with poets who swore by Cities Service[;] . . . the artist who had once been eloquent only about Gauguin laid aside his brushes to proclaim the merits of National Bellas Hess." The market seemed to be everywhere. During the U. S. amateur golf championship at Pebble Beach, California, the E. F. Hutton brokerage firm erected a temporary office in a tent near the 18th green so that the spectators—and players—could follow their favorite stocks and execute orders. Thanks to Mike Meehan, who had just put branch offices aboard select ocean liners, the market even accompanied vacationers heading overseas.[39]

Market madness sometimes invaded even the citadel of illusion, the movie lot. That spring the Marx Brothers were hard at work filming *Cocoanuts* in the mornings and afternoons while performing *Animal Crackers* every evening at a Manhattan theater. On occasion a weary Groucho found himself spouting lines from one show during the other, but he always found time to slip off the set to call his broker for the latest word on the market. All the brothers had caught stock market fever, but in

Alexander Dana Noyes, financial
columnist of the *New York Times*.
(The New York Times Studio;
© 1934 *New York Times*)

many ways it hit the peripatetic Groucho, by far the most conservative
of the brothers, harder than the others. When summer came on and *Animal Crackers* went into mothballs for the season, he rejoiced in having
more time to devote to the market.[40]

The mania also extended to small towns in the hinterland. Alexander
Dana Noyes, the financial maven of the *New York Times*, was struck by
what he called "a wholly new phenomenon. Workingmen whose imagination or covetousness had been aroused by the 'New Era talk,' and to
whom easy facility for speculating on a margin was offered by country
banks or by the country-wide network of branch offices set up by Wall
Street commission houses, had joined in the great speculation." The
vice president of a utilities company noticed the same thing upon his return from several months abroad. "Every vice president, every head of
department, every clerk, male and female," he reported, had loaded up
on the company's stock and were basking in "pleasing paper profits."
The same pattern held true elsewhere in his building. "The elevator
man, the barber, the bootblack, the engineers, the porters, the news-
stand man, and the help in the drug store were long of our stock."[41]

The spectacle disturbed Noyes as much as it fascinated him. He
knew the patterns and behavior of Wall Street better than most, having
been financial editor of the *Times* since the autumn of 1920 after nearly
30 years in the same position at the New York *Evening Post*. Long experience and close observation had given Noyes a keen nose for the market

and its vagaries—the nose of a great chef capable of detecting the slightest wrong odor or ill-mixed ingredient. He might not always uncover its source, but he could sense its presence and ruminate over its possible effects. Noyes made no claim to the gift of prophecy; unlike most younger, brasher heads, who had no sense of history or chose to ignore what little they had, he ransacked the past for comparisons or clues, believing that finance and the Street, like most human affairs, were governed by certain basic and immutable principles. "Interest in the older financial picture never flags," he insisted, based as it was "on the teaching of experience that human nature does not change and that even financial history repeats itself."[42]

For many months something had smelled wrong to Noyes, one of only a few voices that chose not to sing in the all-bulls' choir. He sneered at the calculations of Fisher and the pronouncement of Dice that "old standards are not only futile; they are childish." The extravagant illusions endorsed by businessmen who knew better made him uneasy, as did the claptrap of widely read books that explained how "it was a sensible citizen's duty to 'cash in' on the country's impregnable financial future." It distressed him that even professional speculators who had been through the cycle of illusion and collapse many times seemed to have succumbed once more to the siren's call. Some had distrusted the general public's enthusiasm and sold short or closed out their speculative lines and taken their profits, only to plunge back in on a more extravagant scale than before.[43]

Noyes's suspicions gave the *Times* financial section a tone of skepticism that contrasted sharply with the *Wall Street Journal*, which had made itself the official cheerleader of the bull market. Going against the grain proved as thankless as it had in 1901, when he had played a similar role in another runaway market. "It was not in all respects an agreeable task to point out . . . what seemed to be the very visible signs of danger," he recalled. "Even friendly readers . . . would often write to say that they had accepted my judgment, had sold their stocks in 1928 or early in 1929, and had thereby missed their chance of making a fortune." But he shrugged off such criticism. Long ago George Cary Eggleston of the New York *Commercial* had taught him a valuable principle: "Choose your original position with the utmost care . . . but having chosen it, hold to it unswervingly until it is no longer tenable; because . . . if you follow that principle you can never be wrong but once, but if you follow any other, you may be wrong a dozen times."[44]

The prim, bespectacled Noyes had followed that ideal throughout his career, and he was not about to let the summer of fun lure him away from it. The market resembled a game of Hot Potato in which speculators kept tossing high-priced stocks back and forth, hoping not to be the last holder when the reckoning came. During the long Labor Day weekend, with the markets closed, Noyes paused to survey the overall situation. "Labor Day . . . marks the ending of Summer play-time . . . ," he observed, "but it rarely introduces any immediate change to Autumn activities in finance and trade." However, this year was like no other in his experience. The stock market had reached new heights in August, with the *Times* industrial average soaring more than 80 points and the rails 34 points. During the past week alone many leading stocks had burst through their former highs, a sign to many professional traders that the list was destined to go higher still. Brokers' loans, too, had smashed every record in their steady climb upward.[45]

What bothered Noyes most about this performance was the "failure of the trading community to take serious alarm at portents which once threw Wall Street into a state of alarm, bordering on demoralization. In particular, the recent disregard of the . . . brokers' loans astonishes the older school of market operator. Undoubtedly the heavy margins required . . . have done much to build up this assurance. Traders . . . now feel confident that they can ride out any storm." Moreover, the market's ability to rebound after every drop had "engendered a spirit of indifference to all the old-time warnings." Noyes wondered whether this attitude had not itself become a kind of danger signal. He was far from alone in this concern. "Do you still feel as I do," New York governor Franklin D. Roosevelt wrote a friend on August 5, "that there may be a limit to the increase of security values?"[46]

The economy itself presented more puzzling questions. Usually economic activity relaxed somewhat during the summer, yet this year the season began and ended "with practically all industries working at high pressure and with . . . steel production close to its maximum." Normally that signaled either some extraordinary influence or recovery from a downturn, but neither was at work here. "Industrial profits have reached a wholly exceptional level for the season," Noyes conceded, and there existed "practically no labor disturbances and no congestion on the railways. Consumers' demand for goods and investors' demand for securities have seemed all but unlimited. Even the agricultural situation . . . has been completely altered. The farmer . . . is getting 20 cents a bushel

more for his new wheat than . . . a year ago." Did this abnormal activity
mean merely the early filling of requirements for goods that would usually come later, or did it signal a rising curve of demand that would
reach even greater heights in the fall?

Still more puzzling to Noyes was the reaction to these conditions in
the trade journals. Despite so rosy a picture, several writers voiced skepticism that it would stay that way, and even on Wall Street "the prediction
is heard that a severe reaction is a possibility of the future to be reckoned
with." To be sure, there were always some disciples of gloom, and Noyes
readily conceded that "these misgivings may be superfluous. . . . Yet it is
worth while to inquire why such should be entertained at all." Was there
a snake in the garden? If so, what was it? Noyes attributed the undercur-
rent of pessimism largely to concerns over the credit situation; he also
pointed to the decline in construction contracts during August, an excess
of oil output, and the effects of a drought on wheat production as damp-
ening influences on the economic future. But these factors brought him
no nearer to a definitive answer or even a satisfactory explanation.

What did it all mean? "Even in this era of unbounded speculative enthusiasm, prediction in all these matters is reserved," he admitted. It
seemed to him that three different stances had been taken over what the
future held. "One is that we have now discovered positively the existence of a new financial and industrial era in which old rules are wholly
abrogated and past experience has no lessons worth considering." The
second took the opposite view: that the economic and financial boom
could not last and that "its reversal, when it comes, may be severe in
proportion to the violence of the movement which is interrupted," but
no one could fix the time and circumstances for the change. The third
possibility, which he thought was probably the majority view, reflected
his own uncertainty and frustration. "Reasoned judgment has been discredited so often in the past three years," he sighed, "that it may as well
be suspended for the present and that, whatever underlying convictions
may be entertained, it is just as well to go with the stream, while watching the longer horizon carefully."

In the steamy heat of that holiday weekend, neither Noyes nor any
of those who had relished the highs of the summer of fun suspected
how drastically the horizon was about to shift.

1

America

the Bountiful

The state of the world after the Great War . . . was . . . half-blind, half-deaf, and chronically dazed. . . . It was shell-shocked besides. . . . Some of what had occurred was fundamental alteration from which we would never go back.

—Mark Sullivan[1]

*I*f it is true, as historian Jacques Barzun once observed, that "whoever wants to know the heart and mind of America had better learn about baseball," the 1920 season serves as a revealing emblem of both the country's past and its future.[2] The game was in disarray and disrepute, wracked by internal bickering and reeling from the infamous Black Sox scandal in which eight members of the Chicago White Sox had been charged with accepting bribes to throw the 1919 World Series to the Cincinnati Reds.[3] It had also been stunned by tragedy that summer when Cleveland Indians shortstop Ray Chapman died after being hit by a pitched ball—the first and only major leaguer killed by an injury on the field.

Yet in the midst of deep gloom there were clear signs of a new era dawning. Babe Ruth had opened the age of the slugger by smacking an astounding 54 home runs; the National League leader, Cy Williams of the Philadelphia Phillies, hit only 15. The dismal Black Sox headlines failed to dampen a thrilling World Series between the Indians and the Brooklyn Dodgers, which included one memorable, almost surrealistic game in which three rare "firsts" were recorded. Outfielder Elmer Smith of the Indians hit the first grand-slam homer in a World Series game, and his teammate Jim Bagby became the first pitcher to hit a Series homer. These impressive feats were dwarfed by that of Indians second baseman Bill Wambsganss, who in the fifth inning pulled off the first unassisted triple play. A month after the Indians won the Series, baseball took a giant step to restore its credibility by appointing Judge Kenesaw Mountain Landis as its first commissioner. Landis displayed his new authority by issuing a controversial order banning the eight White Sox players from baseball for life even though a jury acquitted them of charges.

The nation, like its favorite sport, was steeped in gloom during 1920 and reeling from a series of shocks that in six short years had turned the world upside down. The outbreak of war in Europe during the summer of 1914 caught nearly all Americans by surprise. The immediate financial turmoil forced the New York Stock Exchange to shut down for the first time in its history and remain closed for more than four months. An already sluggish economy sagged even more from the dislocations wrought by war until a rising tide of orders from the allied nations in need of food, war materials, and other supplies propelled it into a boom from which manufacturers and farmers alike prospered. Then came American entry into the war in 1917, which led to drastic measures that reshaped the American economy, and ultimately society as well, to an unprecedented extent. Only then, as historian Preston Slosson observed, "did mine and factory, farm and home, school and laboratory, become so many cogs in a single war machine."[4]

The wartime mobilization organized, standardized, and centralized American life as never before. Every male in America between the ages of 18 and 45 had to register for the army; the 4.7 million who were called to service learned firsthand the virtues and vices of regimentation. Businessmen were summoned to Washington to take charge of the economy through such new centralizing agencies as the War Industries Board headed by Bernard Baruch. This service enabled them to redeem reputations that had been blackened by attacks from Progressive reformers and muckrakers since the new century opened. A Division of Planning and Statistics introduced Americans to the possibilities not only of statistics but of government planning as well. The Committee on Public Information, which produced propaganda in support of the war effort, trained a generation of bright young minds in techniques that were later applied to politics, business, advertising, and a promising new field called public relations.[5]

The controls placed on American industry exceeded anything known before. The War Industry Board exerted broad powers over manufacturing, priorities, conversion of facilities, price fixing, and other areas. Two other bodies, the National War Labor Board and the War Labor Policies Board, handled labor matters. Another agency, the Food Administration, organized the food industries; its dynamic leader, Herbert Hoover, emerged as the best known of the wartime managers. The War Finance Corporation took charge of financing war industries as one of several government corporations created to handle specific problems. This first extensive use of government-owned corporations, like so many other wartime measures, provided important precedents in later years. When the nation's railroads gridlocked under the pressure of wartime traffic, President Woodrow Wilson nationalized them and created a government agency to run the roads as a coordinated national system.[6]

Drastic measures were imposed to stimulate production, establish priorities, and standardize many types of goods for more efficient output. The variety of automobile tires was slashed from 287 types to 9, steel plows from 312 to 76, and buggy wheels from 232 to 4. Expenditures for new manufacturing plants and equipment rose from $600 million in 1915 to $2.5 billion in 1918. Valuable German patents, especially in dyes and chemicals, were confiscated and became sources of great profit to American firms, many of which emerged as giants during the conflict. "The lesson of the war," noted historian David Noble, "was that large-scale continuous operation and extensive organized research and development were the essentials of financial success in the chemical industry, and that these demanded big companies, corporate organization, and stable markets." Firms in other industries learned the same crucial lesson and applied it vigorously after the war ended.[7]

Wartime demand also generated runaway inflation, an experience unknown since the Civil War. Consumer prices doubled between 1914 and 1920, and wholesale prices shot up 126 percent. Those who lived on fixed incomes or salaries found themselves becoming what Mark Sullivan called the "new poor," while those who owned land, goods, or securities benefited. The rise in land values and commodity prices, along with huge wartime demand, proved a bonanza for long-depressed farmers. As the price of wheat and cotton nearly tripled between 1913 and 1919, farmers eagerly planted record crops and bought more land on credit. Farm mortgage debt increased 79 percent between 1914 and

1920. Overall, this experience implanted a fear of inflation that remained deep within American memories during the postwar years.[8]

To pay the enormous cost of the war, the government imposed a graduated income tax along with new forms of taxation and increased rates on existing types—including an excess profits tax on both corporations and individuals. But these devices raised only about $10.7 billion of the $31.5 billion spent on the war (including $9.5 billion in loans to the Allies). Between 1917 and 1919 the federal government borrowed about $23 billion, mostly through the sale of bonds conducted through a series of vigorous public campaigns. The national debt, a paltry $1.2 billion in 1916, mushroomed to $25.5 billion by 1919. The four Liberty Loan and one Victory Loan drives combined patriotism, publicity, public spectacle, and peer pressure to goad every citizen into buying as many bonds as possible. This experience, too, would have huge repercussions after the war. As one historian put it, the loan drives "taught people to buy securities. More than 22 million individuals had discovered the magic of coupon-clipping and the desirability of bonds as a form of wealth."[9]

The goal of all these efforts was to place the American economy on the most efficient possible footing for winning the war. However forced and fumbling it sometimes became, the attempt at wholesale organization marked the first time that massive central planning and economic management had been applied to a national purpose. The war also set in motion major changes in American society. It closed the great floodgate that had fed a steady stream of European immigrants into the American population since the 1880s. During six months of 1917 alone it also sent more than 600,000 blacks (and even more southern whites) northward in search of jobs—the first major shift in traditional American racial demography.[10]

Scarcely had this mighty machinery of national mobilization sprung to life than the war came to an end in November 1918, leaving in its wake a ghastly spectacle of ruin. The known world of 1914 had been blasted into oblivion, scattering shards of devastation, chaos, bitterness, and fear of the unfamiliar forces at work amid the debris. Two of the Four Horseman of the Apocalypse, war and death, had already trampled across the face of a prostrate civilization. During the months just before the war's end the other two, famine and pestilence, began to spread their misery across the globe. Hunger stalked the war-ravaged regions of Europe, but its effects were mild compared to those of disease. During 1918 and 1919 a pandemic of influenza, the worst ever known, killed an estimated 21 million people, including 675,000 Americans, in only a few months.[11]

The old world had died, and the new one struggling to be born bore little resemblance to it. The war had lasted 1,563 days, taken the lives of 10 million soldiers, wounded 20 million others, and squandered more than $300 billion of the world's resources. Its outcome hurled empires and dynasties alike into oblivion. Gone were the Hohenzollerns in Germany, the Hapsburgs in Austria, the Romanovs in Russia. Europe entered the war with 17 nations and emerged from it with 26. New regimes claimed power in St. Petersburg, Berlin, Vienna, Warsaw, Budapest, Prague, and Dublin, some of them fueled by revolutionary doctrines. The Bolsheviks in Russia especially disturbed Americans because their alien ideology attacked the three principles dearest to our national credo: private property, freedom of religion, and individual freedom.[12]

The disorder wrought by war went still deeper to the basic structure of the international order. For a century Great Britain had been the center of world finance and had provided nations a system of trade through its currency, its navy, its mercantile fleet, and its enforcement of international law. But Great Britain and its European allies were physically and financially exhausted from a war that proved for them a Pyrrhic victory. The British no longer had the power or the will to rule the waves or even (as the old joke went) to waive the rules. Nor could they maintain the gold standard, which had stabilized international trade for decades. All the major trade routes had been disrupted or paralyzed; every belligerent nation had borrowed heavily to fight the war and was deeply in debt. Our "associates" (we never called them allies) spent some $19.8 billion on American goods and loan servicing during the war. Much of the purchasing had been on borrowed money, and the status of these loans became a raging controversy once the war ended.[13]

Here was a power vacuum begging to be filled. The war had completely transformed America's position in world affairs. Having already emerged as the largest industrial power, the United States in 1918 was the only major power left standing in almost every sense. Americans had suffered little loss of life and treasure compared to that of other countries, and no physical damage. Where other economies lay exhausted from the demands of war, the American productive engine continued to hum at high speed. Most significant of all, the United States had gone from being a debtor to a creditor nation. Throughout the nation's history foreign investment had underwritten its economic development. On the eve of war in July 1914 American debts to foreigners still exceeded those of foreigners to Americans by nearly $3.7 billion. By the end of 1919, however, a stunning reversal had occurred: the balance had shifted in favor of the United States by $12.56 billion.[14]

This historic change required rethinking of the American role not only in trade but in the broader realm of world affairs. With all the major European powers physically, economically, and morally spent by the Great War, the United States was the logical choice to assume a leadership role in rebuilding fractured world relationships. President Wilson recognized this when he made the bold decision to lead the American delegation to the peace negotiations. Sailing to France in December 1918, he became the first American president to cross the Atlantic while still in office.[15] Wilson hoped to use his influence to create a new world order based on his Fourteen Points and embodied in the League of Nations. But his mission turned to ashes. The Versailles Treaty that emerged in the spring of 1919 did contain provisions for the League, but it was a harsh, bitter, punitive document that perpetuated rather than solved the problems underlying the war and its outcome. In David Kennedy's words, it "sowed the wind that would eventually lash the world with gale fury."[16]

In 1917 Wilson had sold the conflict to Americans as a great national crusade, the war to end all wars and make the world safe for democracy. That vision turned sour in 1919 as the treaty became a political football. When opposition in the Senate threatened its defeat, Wilson undertook a speaking tour to rally public support. The effort strained his already fragile health; a severe stroke in October immobilized him for two months. The treaty died in the Senate, leaving the United States out of the League and technically still at war. Instead of exerting leadership in a new world community, a distracted and disillusioned nation retreated from the world stage to tend its own affairs. The crippled, embittered Wilson yielded his office to Warren G. Harding, who had proclaimed in May 1920 that "America's need is not heroics but healing; not nostrums but normalcy; not revolution but restoration . . . not surgery but serenity."[17]

Normalcy may have been urgently needed, but it was hard to come by. The momentum built up by the national mobilization crusade could not be slowed or shifted as quickly as the war had ended. The conversion effort produced serious dislocations. Government agencies canceled $2.5 billion in outstanding contracts at a time when a quarter of the civilian labor force was engaged in making war-related goods. Within six months after the Armistice 2 million discharged servicemen were thrown onto the job market of a contracting economy. The elaborate system of government controls and agencies created to push the war effort was dismantled as quickly as it had been put together in a zealous effort to restore the "normalcy" of as little government control over business as possible.[18]

Despite these moves, economic conditions remained deceptively calm until the spring of 1919, when consumer and business spending increased sharply along with demand for exports. Sparked by a brief worldwide boom, the economy seemed back in high gear again by autumn, and a speculative mania seized the stock market. This brief euphoria sent wholesale prices up 25 percent by May 1920; then the economic roller coaster suddenly plunged downward as the demand for both manufactured and farm products withered after the initial postwar surge to replace depleted inventories. Within a year the wholesale price index dropped 45 percent, with farm products and raw materials taking the hardest hit. While manufacturers quickly cut production to keep their prices from falling as severely, farmers could not control their output and depended on high prices to pay the mortgages they had incurred during the war.[19]

"What happened," recalled Alexander Noyes, "was simply that demand for goods by the larger consuming public suddenly stopped . . . at the moment when the extraordinarily high prices had greatly stimulated supply." He had watched inflation send prices of clothing, fuel, and household goods in 1920 soaring 40 to 70 percent above November 1918 levels. The impact literally hit home for Noyes; in September 1920 the lease on his New York apartment expired and the rent of $2,500 a year, which he had paid for six years, was hiked to $4,500. Throughout the nation consumers reacted to what they called HCL (high cost of living) by boycotting purchases and organizing "old-clothes clubs." Noyes believed the organized resistance helped "put a stop very soon to rising prices."[20]

The depression that followed lasted well over a year. During 1920-21 the gross national product fell 6 percent, stocks lost a quarter of their value, manufacturers cut their workforce by 25 percent, unemployment soared to 4 million, half a million farmers lost their homesteads, and 100,000 businesses went bankrupt. The purchasing power of farmers fell about 25 percent and never recovered. Although the price of manufactured goods remained 66 percent above the levels of 1913, the drop was severe enough that even giant corporations struggled to survive. General Motors wrote off an appalling $85 million in inventory losses, while Henry Ford averted disaster by forcing his dealers to buy cars they could not sell. Montgomery Ward took a loss of nearly $7.9 million for 1920 and in 1921 wrote off $5.6 million as "loss on inventory, loss on accounts receivable, and depreciation." Julius Rosenwald of Sears kept that company from default only by dipping into his personal fortune.[21]

Society was no less out of joint. The froth of hatred and intolerance whipped up by wartime propaganda could not be turned off like water from a spigot. The rabid campaign against all things German fanned other forms of prejudice against people and things foreign or different. The volatile new racial mix in northern cities unaccustomed to large black populations triggered a series of bloody race riots during the summer of 1919. The Ku Klux Klan rose from the grave of history with a more ecumenical message of bigotry. Centered more in the lower Midwest than in the deep South, the "new" Klan denounced not only blacks but Jews, immigrants, Catholics, radicals, and anyone or anything it deemed not "100 percent American."[22]

Labor unrest gripped the nation as workers, hurt by prices that had risen faster than wages, demanded pay increases and went on strike in record numbers. A series of unexplained bombings in the spring of 1919, coupled with a record number of strikes, escalated existing fears over bolshevism into an ugly bout of public hysteria that swept the nation like the flu during 1919-20. The "Red Scare" turned into a sweeping assault on labor militants, radicals, and foreigners, who were an easy target as the source of all things and ideas considered un-American. Then, like the flu pandemic, the Red Scare departed as abruptly as it had come, leaving in its wake a bitter legacy of bigotry.[23]

Ironically, the bloodiest single event came after the hysteria had subsided. At noontime on September 16, 1920, amid the lunchtime crowds, a wagon filled with iron sash weights pulled up outside the offices of J. P. Morgan & Company at 23 Wall Street. Suddenly it exploded, hurling iron like shrapnel in all directions and blowing out windows within a half-mile radius. Thirty-eight people were killed and 300 wounded. Inside the House of Morgan one employee lay dead, another fatally injured, and dozens more seriously hurt. On Wall Street the blast knocked to the ground a young passerby named Joseph P. Kennedy. At the New York Stock Exchange shards of glass burst through the heavy silk curtains, sending traders into an unfamiliar kind of panic. The New York Curb Exchange, which still operated outdoors on Broad Street only a couple of hundred feet from the site of the blast, found its place of business transformed into a battlefield strewn with stunned and wounded brokers.[24]

In later years the fortress-like exterior of the House of Morgan wore its blast scars like battle ribbons. The source of the explosion remains a mystery, though many suspected then and later that it was the work of an anarchist sending a message to the inner circle of Wall Street. None of the Morgan partners was hurt. Four of them—Thomas W. Lamont, Dwight Morrow, George Whitney, and Elliott Bacon—were in conference on the second floor away from the blast. With them was a French general who happened to be there as Morrow's guest. As the blast died away and smoke billowed skyward in the street amid the tinkle of still falling glass, the general asked his hosts politely, "Does this happen often?"[25]

Mercifully it did not. Nevertheless, the war to make the world safe for democracy had failed even to make the United States safe for democracy. Victory had brought not elation but relief tinged with bitterness at having wasted so much time and energy on a fool's errand that most Americans vowed never to repeat. "The average man," observed Mark Sullivan, "felt . . . a discontent with the post-war commotion . . . a wish for settled ways . . . for routine that remained set, for a world that 'stayed put.' " Small wonder, then, that so many people embraced Harding's siren call for normalcy. The problem was that so much had changed in the postwar world that no one knew what was normal anymore. By any measure it could be labeled a new era, even if no one could figure out exactly what that meant.[26]

To most eyes the tensions and hysteria of 1920 and the depression of 1921 showed few signs of brighter times ahead. Yet the change came with unexpected swiftness. From the depths of gloom and depression Americans moved into what Frederick Lewis Allen called "the seven fat years," a golden age of business prosperity that in many ways marked the beginning of the modern era. With only brief interruptions in 1924 and 1927, the economy performed at unprecedented levels, bringing a new standard of living—and a new lifestyle—to more Americans than ever before.[27]

During the seven fat years (1922–28) the index of industrial production rose 70 percent, gross national product nearly 40 percent, and per capita income about 30 percent. New miracles of productivity increased output per factory man-hour by 75 percent. Every worker was producing much more, yet the economy expanded enough to absorb workers displaced by new technologies. Unemployment scarcely existed, real earnings of wage earners rose about 22 percent, and the workweek shrank, giving workers more leisure time to enjoy their improved income. The wartime horrors of inflation vanished entirely as both wholesale and retail prices remained stable for the entire decade.[28]

Here truly was a new era, and its ramifications went far beyond the economic transformation. No one could have foreseen the changes that reshaped American life during these years or predicted the wide array of forces and conditions that came together to produce them. Once past the dislocations and readjustments wrought by the war, the economic fundamentals were not only sound but glowing with potential. As Stuart Chase observed, "The war helped American business. With Europe flat on its back . . . a vigorous, unscarred, highly industrialized nation could hardly go elsewhere than forward."[29]

One key source of this spurt in productivity was the rapid spread of electric power, which gave manufacturers a flexibility of organization never before possible. By 1929 about 70 percent of manufacturing plants used electricity. The output of electric power tripled, making electric utilities a major new industry in itself, and its use extended beyond the factory to the home. By one estimate, 63 percent of the population lived in dwellings with electricity in 1927, compared to only 16 percent in 1912. As more and more residences were wired, a vast market arose for a wide range of new products that used electric power: toasters, irons, stoves, refrigerators, washers, dryers, vacuum cleaners, radios, and a host of others. These appliances became a staple of the new consumer economy.[30]

Two other industries lay at its heart: automobiles and construction. Residential construction gave the moribund economy an immediate jolt, jumping more than $1 billion between 1921 and 1922 under conditions that could not have been more favorable. The war had created an acute housing shortage, rents remained high, prices of building materials had fallen, labor was plentiful, and the high level of savings wrought by the war had as yet nowhere else to go but into mortgages. Gradually business and commercial construction gave their own boost to the construction industry, as did a rush of business from an unexpected source: roads and highways. For that bonanza the industry could thank the automobile.[31]

The undying American love affair with the automobile began in earnest during the 1920s. In 1900 the nation had 8,000 registered horseless carriages, mostly playthings of the wealthy; by 1929 the number surpassed 23 million cars along with more than 3.5 million trucks and nearly 34,000 buses. That worked out to one automobile for every 5.3 Americans. No other possession came so quickly to be coveted so deeply by so many people. "We'd rather do without clothes than give up the car," insisted one midwestern mother of nine children. Another woman asserted that she would "go without food before I'll see us give up the car." A small-town banker agreed that "the paramount ambition of the average man a few years ago was to own a home and have a bank account. The ambition of the same man today is to own a car." This kind of demand created an unprecedented market for carmakers. As Walter Chrysler marveled, "We were making the first machine of considerable size in the history of the world for which every human being was a potential customer."[32]

In many respects the automobile did for the 20th century what the railroad had done for the 19th. It not only created an enormous new industry but in the process fueled a host of other industries such as rubber, plate glass, steel, and lead. The internal combustion engine also rejuvenated the giant petroleum industry by giving it a huge new market at a time when the use of oil for illumination had faded. By 1929 the passion for automobiles had also planted rich crops of other new businesses across the landscape, notably filling stations, public garages, and car and truck dealers, along with motels, restaurants, and tourist attractions. It had also given rise to a portentous sign of things to come: expansive new suburbs encircling every major city.[33]

Like the railroad, too, the automobile drastically reconfigured the American landscape and its demographics. Where the iron horse had crisscrossed the land with corridors of steel and created cities and towns where none had existed, the horseless carriage brought with it endless ribbons of asphalt and concrete that connected cities and lured large numbers of people into new settlements on their perimeters or deeper into the countryside. Some commuters were already driving 20 to 40 miles to work. "The small cities of the nation are tending to become suburban to nearby larger centers," concluded the Research Committee on Social Trends created by President Hoover to examine every facet of modern American life, "or, if remote from large cities, to assume the role of embryonic metropolises to surrounding villages."[34]

Roads underwent a metamorphosis in both mileage and quality during the 1920s. In 1904 the United States had nearly 2.2 million miles of road (excluding city streets), of which less than 7 percent were surfaced and a meager 144 miles paved to some degree. Automobiles, it seemed, needed smoother surfaces than did horses. An ingenious penny-per-gallon tax on gasoline, first adopted by Oregon in 1919, spread to every other state by 1929 and provided funds for massive road-building programs. Congress passed two acts to promote a national road system. The first, in 1916, enabled states to organize highway departments, while the second, in 1921, earmarked 200,000 miles of road as "primary" and thereby eligible for federal funds on a matching basis. It also created a Bureau of Public Roads to plan a highway network that would connect with every city having a population of 50,000 or more. As a result the total mileage grew to more than 3 million by 1929, of which 23 percent had some form of surface and 4 percent was paved.[35]

Two men did much to push the automobile to the center of American economic and social life. Of the two, Henry Ford is by far the better known and was already a national icon by 1922. What Ford did above all else was to give the era its most crucial working concept: mass production allowed high volume output at low cost, thereby transforming what had once been a luxury into a necessity that almost anyone could afford and enjoy. "I will build a motor car for the great multitude," Ford vowed in 1907, "constructed of the best materials, by the best men to be hired, after the simplest designs that modern engineering can devise . . . so low in price that no man making a good salary will be unable to own one—and enjoy with his family the blessings of hours of pleasure in God's great open space."[36]

After starting his own company in 1903, it took Ford five years and eight models to deliver on what seemed an impossible promise. In October 1908 he produced the first Model T, which sold for $850, or about $250 more than Ford had hoped. By 1920 a Model T rolled off the production line every minute and every other car in the world was a Ford. He accomplished this miracle of productivity by building one car in one style with one color as cheaply and efficiently as possible—and improving it steadily over the years. By forcing the price of motoring relentlessly downward, he democratized the automobile. In 1907 the average sales price for all cars had been $2,123; by 1916 it had dropped to $820. After the war a decent car could be bought for $500 to $600 and a superior one for $1,000. Without realizing it, Ford had changed American life forever; the "Tin Lizzie" was not only the most famous car ever built but arguably the most influential piece of technology to appear since the printing press.[37]

No such lasting glory attached itself to William Crapo Durant, yet in some respects he epitomized more of the era's essential forces than did Ford. For a time Durant, too, became something of a folk hero, though in a very different way than Ford. No one bounced across more points in the pinball machine that was the early automobile industry. Between 1903 and 1926 no fewer than 181 companies tried their hand at producing cars, and it sometimes seemed as if Durant played some part in most of them. Of that number, only 44 remained alive in 1926, and only 11 of them had survived the entire period. More than a few of the casualties had known Durant's touch somewhere along the way—and an almost shocking number of the survivors as well.[38]

Billy Durant, as he was known to his close friends, was born in Boston eight months after the firing on Fort Sumter, the son of a mother whose own father, Henry Howland Crapo, achieved prominence as a merchant, mayor, and ultimately governor. But after Durant's father abandoned the family when Billy was 11, they moved to Flint, Michigan. There Billy grew up and launched a business career that was as erratic as it was spectacular. After a brief stint at the family lumber mill he took a second job selling patent medicines and discovered his true calling: salesmanship. In 1886, at the age of 25, he left a secure job to become a partner in the Flint Road Cart Company with an investment of $1,500. By 1902 the firm had been recapitalized at $150,000 and added seven new divisions. Having grown rich and outgrown Flint, Durant moved to New York in search of greater challenges.[39]

In 1904, however, a group of former associates asked him to return home and help them salvage the automobile firm of David Buick, an inventor who had produced a promising car but was floundering in debt and frustration. Durant accepted the challenge and flung himself into this promising but treacherous new industry. His insight at this early date was uncanny. As biographer Bernard Weisberger observed, Durant "quickly grasped the pattern that would govern the infant industry, and his ultimate success would be incomprehensible and miraculous to those who did not also see the elements of the pattern." What Durant

saw was a cluster of automobile firms emerging in Detroit and another
in Lansing. "Michigan was in full procession into the automotive future.
And Flint . . . was behind the parade."[40]

Durant jumped into the parade by demonstrating his slant on the industry's destiny. The Flint men had cautiously reduced capitalization of
the Buick Motor Company from $100,000 to $75,000. Durant signed
his agreement with them on November 1, 1904, and upped the capitalization to $500,000 in less than three weeks. Early in January 1905 he
went off to the annual automobile show in New York and returned to
Flint with orders for 1,108 Buicks, which was 1,071 more than had been
produced the entire past year. In September he tripled the company's
stock to $1.5 million. Within four years Buick shot to the top of the
sales charts. When a financial panic struck the nation in 1907, Durant
did not cut back production but plunged boldly ahead in the belief that
the financial spasm was temporary and not the opening of a serious depression. Events proved him right, and when the clouds parted, Buick
dealers had cars to sell while their competitors struggled to catch up.
"He was one hell of a gambler," marveled industrialist Charles Stewart
Mott, one of many important businessmen who found themselves
pulled into Durant's orbit.[41]

A small, intense, dynamic man, Durant seemed always to be in motion and seldom in need of sleep. He belonged to the sunshine school
of men like Charley Mitchell, who saw the future only as opportunity.
His amiable, jolly personality never showed anxiety and rarely displayed its darker side. "I cannot hope to find words to express the charm
of the man . . . ," Walter Chrysler said of him. "He could coax a bird
right down out of a tree." Durant was a risk taker by nature, and his success with Buick only whetted his appetite for greater challenges. One
night in 1906, after having dinner with close associates Charles Nash
and Josiah "Dallas" Dort, Durant waxed rhapsodic over the future of the
automobile, predicting that the day would come when one company
would sell 10,000, 20,000, 50,000—even 100,000 or more cars a year.
His friends looked at one another. "Dallas," said Nash, "Billy's crazy."[42]

That day was approaching faster than anyone realized, thanks primarily to Ford and Durant. Where Ford sought the perfect machine,
Durant envisioned an organization capable of overseeing the production of cars on a gigantic scale. Not that he possessed any special talent
as an organizer; the lack of such talent would in fact prove his undoing.
What he grasped was the need for combination, something that would

do for the still adolescent auto industry what United States Steel had done for the steel industry. In 1908 he made a first attempt to combine with Benjamin Briscoe (who had the Maxwell), Ransom E. Olds (who had left his name with his successful namesake company in 1904 and formed a new firm to produce the Reo), and Henry Ford. An agreement seemed near until Ford and Olds demanded payment in cash rather than stock in a new joint company, and no bankers would put up the $6 million to $8 million needed.[43]

Undeterred, Durant formed a new holding company, named it General Motors (GM), and gave it a capital stock of $12.5 million as ammunition for acquiring other companies. After folding into GM his own Buick firm and the struggling Oldsmobile company, he launched an orgy of acquisition beginning with the Oakland Motor Car Company, which later took the name of its Michigan home, Pontiac. In 1909 he pulled off an impressive coup by persuading Henry Leland to sell GM his Cadillac Motor Company, a leader in the high-priced field. Then, in rapid succession, Durant swept up the Marquette, the Reliance Motor Truck, the Welch, the Elmore, the Randolph, and the Cartercar, an innovative vehicle that proved a complete bust. He made another pass at Ford and came within a whisker of consummating the deal only to be thwarted again by the refusal of bankers to lend the necessary cash. What the future of the automotive industry would have been had he succeeded can only be imagined.[44]

Still Durant did not stop. GM became the warehouse for a menagerie of firms. By 1910 it housed 25 companies that produced automobiles, taxis, trucks, parts, and accessories. One of them became the foundation for General Motors of Canada; another, which produced spark plugs under Albert Champion, became AC Spark Plug. Through his use of what Weisberger called "fiscal gymnastics," Durant assembled an empire that employed 14,000 workers and turned out 20 percent of the nation's automobiles. Most of it was accomplished through stock exchanges, leaving the parent firm with serious cash flow problems. Nor was it well built. GM was a mosaic composed of pieces that did not fit well together and were of strikingly different value. At its top sat Durant, a human whirlwind who was reluctant to share power and lacked the patience to organize and systematize the giant he had thrown together. He seemed actually to prefer crisis to planning. As a friend once remarked, "W. C. is never happy unless he is hanging to a window sill by his finger tips."[45]

It was vision that drove his frenetic pace, and charm that captured those men pulled into his orbit who had to make sense of the debris left in his wake. "There are no harsh lines in his face," noted a reporter, "no note of autocrat in his speech or act. . . . His smile . . . is as innocent as a child's and as philosophic as a sage's. . . . Mr. Durant is a man of heart and very attractive human failings." Another reported that "Durant sees—actually sees—90,000,000 people just aching to roll along the roads of this country in automobiles . . . and he wishes to fill that void." But like so many visionaries, he reckoned without the intrusion of harsh reality. A sudden drop in car sales during 1910 transformed the cash flow problem into a full-blown crisis. In desperation Durant turned reluctantly to the investment bankers who had shunned his initial merger proposals.[46]

The bankers obliged on terms that awarded generous profits to themselves and decreed that Durant leave the company. Bitterly he accepted their terms and turned his "baby" over to men who proclaimed that they had rescued a wrecked company suffering from "lack of management." Boston banker James J. Storrow took charge of GM, quickly pruned away many of the weak companies Durant had acquired, installed a management of order and system rather than one-man rule, and placed the organization into the hands of two managers capable of realizing his goals: Charles W. Nash and Walter P. Chrysler. The vision of these three men could not have been more different from that of Durant. They believed in management by committee with responsibility at the top. Above all, Storrow despised debt and Durant's freewheeling style that had produced so much of it. He ran a tight ship—too tight in the minds of some directors, even though it proved profitable. "Your board," declared the 1915 annual report flatly, "does not believe in running into debt." This cautious approach turned GM into a sound but stagnant company. In five years the company's share of the automobile market shrank from 20 percent to 7.8 percent.[47]

During those years Durant wasted no time brooding over his loss, painful as it was to him. In 1911 he formed three new companies, one of which, Chevrolet, turned into a gold mine after a disastrous start. In 1914 his engineers produced two models, the Baby Grand and the Royal Mail, which became instant hits. By 1917 Chevrolet sales surpassed even Durant's sunny predictions, reaching 125,882. The whole industry was surging, as Durant had predicted it would; total production soared from 63,500 in 1908, when GM was formed, to 1,525,578 in 1916. Once again Durant's vision turned expansive. Using friendly bankers, he merged the various Chevrolet companies into one capitalized at $12.5 million.[48]

The constant dealing in securities had given Durant a taste for the stock market and its potential for making money as well as controlling enterprises. For decades railroad stocks had dominated the major stock markets, as most industrial enterprises remained firmly in private hands. But more and more corporations, as they grew larger through mergers and expansion, had not only gone public with their stock but also resorted increasingly to new issues for raising money or completing mergers rather than borrowing from bankers. Gradually the industrial, utility, and other nonrail companies came to dominate the growing list of equities on stock exchanges, and their presence of necessity gave corporate officers a keen interest in the doings of the stock market for both personal and company reasons.

Durant took a keener interest than most. Gradually he came to regard the market less as a means and more as an end in itself. What began as a business tool for realizing his audacious schemes to build giant firms turned into a passion in its own right—one devoted to making money rather than making cars or anything else. Boldly he laid plans to reacquire GM through his own purchases of stock and support enlisted from other key stockholders. In the proxy fight that ensued, Durant was obliged to compromise by sharing power in the management with Pierre du Pont and John J. Raskob, du Pont's close associate, who were to serve as the "middlemen" between the Durant and Storrow factions. Finally Storrow and his banker allies quit the board in June 1916, leaving Durant back in the saddle and eager to ride.[49]

Although he did not have an entirely free rein, Durant plunged eagerly into the thicket of acquisitions. A new company, United Motors, was formed and became the home for several new parts and accessories companies, including Delco and the Hyatt Roller Bearing Company. These two firms brought GM two other prizes in the form of a brilliant inventor named Charles F. Kettering and an executive who would exert profound influence over GM's destiny. Alfred P. Sloan was a thoughtful man who brought to the roisterous automobile industry the rational, orderly mind of a creative librarian. Of all the contributions Durant made to GM, the quality of men added by his acquisitions may have been his greatest.[50]

These were the best of times for Billy Durant. As GM prospered, his own income soared, exceeding $3.4 million in 1916 and nearly reaching $5 million the next year. He bought a mansion, Raymere, on the New

Jersey shore. In 1918 he happened upon a machine by an obscure inventor—an electric icebox he called a "Frigerator." The father of one of Durant's friends had poured money into it without success, and his son appealed to Durant for help. He looked into it and saw at once the possibilities. Casting about for a suitable name, Durant came up with a winner: "frigid air," or Frigidaire. Within a year the new company was thriving, and Durant sold it to GM for little if any profit to himself.[51]

It did not take long for Durant's freewheeling style to perplex and annoy Pierre du Pont, a tidy, meticulous man who had turned his own giant family firm into a model of organization and efficiency. Du Pont thrived as much on order and rational planning as Durant did on motion and improvisation, but he knew nothing of the automobile industry. The man who mediated between them, John J. Raskob, had more in common with Durant but owed his place in life to du Pont. The son of an Alsatian immigrant, Raskob had lucked into a position as stenographer to du Pont and turned the opportunity into a Horatio Alger success story. "Mr. Raskob was brilliant and imaginative," observed Sloan, "where Mr. du Pont was steady and conservative." His pushy, impatient style complemented du Pont's more retiring personality in ways that proved useful to them both.[52]

Raskob got along well with Durant because of their similarities. The feisty, diminutive Raskob subscribed to the sunshine school of business; like Durant, he was a bull on the market and on America, as well as an indefatigable go-getter. But he worked with figures rather than production lines, liked to enlarge existing enterprises rather than start new ones, and preferred the safe haven of working for the du Ponts to going it on his own. He was loyal to Pierre du Pont, who demanded systematic management and was distressed by Durant's way of ignoring the board and paying scant attention to procedures. When American entry into World War I sent stocks plummeting in April 1917, Durant rashly undertook on his own to sustain the price of GM through buying on margin. Pushed to the brink that summer by falling prices, he was obliged to ask du Pont and the board for a $1 million loan. They refused but voted him a salary boost that provided the funds.[53]

Wartime prosperity soon resolved the crisis, but not the tension between Durant and du Pont. Unable to curb Durant's maverick tendencies, du Pont moved gradually to increase his holdings of both GM and Chevrolet stock. Raskob came up with a plan late in 1917 by which E. I. du Pont de Nemours & Company invested half of its $50 million surplus in GM and Chevrolet. His memorandum predicted that "ultimately the Du Pont Company will absolutely control and dominate the whole General Motors situation with the entire approval of Mr. Durant." The plan was approved, and a new holding company was created to hold the 97,875 shares of General Motors (about 24 percent of the total) and 133,690 shares of Chevrolet stock purchased for $25 million.[54]

Durant never saw the Raskob memorandum, but after his market fiasco he had little choice but to go along. The plan was to leave Durant at the head of the company but to keep him on a leash through control of the finance committee headed by Raskob and backed by the support of the Du Pont Company, which had become the second largest holder of the stock. Everyone agreed that future expansion should be financed from within and not on borrowed funds. But Pierre du Pont was preoccupied by the family company, and Raskob hesitated to make major decisions on his own. None of the Du Pont people in GM understood the intricacies of the automobile business, and in hitching themselves in tandem with Durant, they soon found themselves galloping along at a speed more suitable to him than to them.[55]

The new arrangement began early in 1918, when GM was still working through wartime uncertainties. As part of the deal Durant also agreed to merge Chevrolet and United Motors into the parent company. Chevrolet became a division of GM, although Durant kept his own stock in the company. Completed in December 1918, the merger placed for the first time all of Durant's empire under one corporate roof. But legal unity and administrative coordination proved very different creatures, and the gap between them grew even greater with the abrupt end of the war in November 1918.[56]

In the minds of both Durant and Raskob, the coming of peace meant a surefire mushrooming of demand for vehicles of all kinds. Hurriedly they drew up an expansion program that Raskob estimated would cost about $52.8 million. Earnings could contribute less than half that amount; Raskob advised raising $21.6 million through sale of stock and suggested that the Du Pont Company take most of the new issue. Du Pont did so and nearly doubled its investment in GM. With this money Durant and the finance committee went on a buying binge, scooping up two car manufacturers, a steel plant, a die-casting firm, companies to build housing for GM workers in five cities, and Frigidaire. More funds went to set up the General Motors Acceptance Corporation and the General Motors Export Division, and in September 1919 the largest single outlay, $26.7 million, went to acquire 60 percent of Fisher Body Company.[57]

Far from harnessing Durant, the finance committee and the board joined heartily in creating a monster company, the basis of the modern GM. By the end of 1919 they had in haphazard fashion increased their investments in other companies by $50.5 million, spent another $47.7 million for real estate, plant, and equipment, and acquired via consolidation $12.7 million worth of property. GM joined United States Steel as a billion-dollar corporation with net earnings that exceeded half a billion dollars. As national car sales soared to 1,905,560 in 1920, everyone looked forward eagerly to the first 2,000,000 sales year. But some of the financing had not gone smoothly, and Pierre du Pont was not alone in fretting over the lack of system in the management of GM or Durant's poking into the smallest details rather than developing a sound central organization.[58]

By 1919 GM was no longer Durant's offspring but a super-corporation that had begun to overwhelm even his capacity for keeping up with everything. His personal style of management faltered under the avalanche of demands made on it. He bounced unpredictably from subordinates needing urgent answers to his huge battery of telephones (10 by Chrysler's count, 20 by Sloan's) that linked him to plants, offices, and especially his brokers. He seemed never without one or more of the receivers in hand. "In the same minute he would buy in San Francisco, sell in Boston . . . ," sighed one observer. "It seemed to me he was trying to keep in communication with half the continent." Even his top lieutenants had to cool their heels. Walter Chrysler, whose time Durant had once valued at $10,000 a week, wasted four days waiting to see the boss before giving up and going back to his factory. In March 1920 he resigned from GM, leaving behind the belief that Durant had cost the company one of its best officers.[59]

During the winter of 1920 a financing plan for the expansion program flopped, leaving Raskob with the need to raise $60 million. The best source, he and Pierre du Pont agreed, was the House of Morgan, the same firm that had rejected Durant's original merger efforts in 1908. Although most of the men he had dealt with—and J. P. Morgan himself—were by then in their graves, Durant still objected to the idea and to the price the bankers would exact. But the need was urgent, and he had little choice but to go along. The bankers raised the necessary funds and as part of the agreement gained seats on the GM board.

Pierre du Pont welcomed Morgan partner Edward Stettinius with a flattering letter and was told in reply that the House of Morgan had deigned to enter GM only because of the du Pont presence. The giant company had become a house of giants, none of whom particularly cared for William C. Durant.[60]

Scarcely had the new arrangement been completed when the economic roller coaster plunged sharply downward, leaving GM with huge inventories of cars built at inflated prices for which no buyers could be found. Durant had projected an output of 876,000 cars for 1920; in June sales slumped to 47,000 units and kept falling to a mere 12,700 in November and a record low of 6,150 in January 1921. Burdened with unsold cars and warehouses crammed with parts and supplies ordered for increased production, and with prices dropping relentlessly, GM ended the dismal year by writing off nearly $85 million in inventory as dead loss.[61]

For Durant the disaster was even more cataclysmic. A syndicate led by the House of Morgan was formed that summer to support the price of GM stock as the market fell. The members—including Durant as president of GM and Chevrolet—had pledged not to deal in GM stock on their personal account during the life of the syndicate. But Durant could not leave the market alone. As he had in 1917 during a less severe crisis, he bought GM stock heavily until by autumn every drop of a point in the stock cost him nearly $2 million. Desperately he shoveled more funds into the campaign until by November he had little left to give. Alarmed by rumors of Durant's activities, Pierre du Pont arranged a meeting with Durant and Morgan partner Dwight Morrow to clear the air.[62]

Gradually it came out that Durant owed various bankers and brokers the staggering sum of $34 million. With the price still falling, margin calls threatened the stock deposited as collateral. This posed the danger that it would be dumped on the market and drive the price down even more, thereby undoing all the syndicate's efforts. A stunned Pierre du Pont turned to Raskob, who once again came up with a plan. Another new company, Du Pont Securities, was formed to buy Durant's stock. The Morgan firm would raise $20 million and the Du Pont Company $7 million to pay off Durant's most pressing debts and receive in return the underlying GM stock, which became an asset of the Du Pont Securities Company. In addition, Du Pont loaned Durant $1.17 million to meet his most immediate margin calls.[63]

One other stipulation was included in the deal: Durant had to leave the management of GM, to be replaced as president by Pierre du Pont.

Raskob remained chairman of the finance committee and assumed the role of company spokesman. Later it would be charged that the du Ponts and their Morgan allies conspired to trap Durant and oust him from the company, but no proof exists. As Weisberger noted, "It was clear enough from his history that he was entirely capable of ensnaring himself." The final Morgan figures left Durant with a balance after paying off debts of only $7,865.54 on his GM stock worth more than $24 million. No one disputed his later estimate that the episode ultimately cost him about $90 million, as well as the emotional pain of being thrown out of the company he had created—for the second time.[64]

Durant left GM on December 1, 1920, a week before he turned 59, but he was far from finished in business. In mid-January he organized yet another car company, Durant Motors, capitalized at $5 million, and promised to build it in Flint. Subsidiary companies were created in Indiana, Michigan, California, and Canada. Much of the money for these ventures came from an odd little company he had created in October 1920. The Durant Corporation had sought to enlist an army of small investors into the ranks of GM stockholders by selling them shares with time payments, a 50-share maximum, and even passbooks to keep track of their purchases. After leaving GM, Durant redirected the company's buying toward Durant Motors. Within two years the expanding investment firm had offices in 35 states, 3,000 salesmen, and 146,000 participants whose small checks sometimes totaled $1 million in a single day for their stake in Durant Motors and other select companies in lots of no more than 20 shares per person. Their buying helped push Durant Motors stock from $10 to $27 by the end of November 1921.[65]

Funded largely by this "financial children's crusade," a scheme that anticipated plans promoted later by Charley Mitchell and others, Durant went into production again. The old magic still seemed to be there. But something had changed, and the expansion of the Durant Corporation revealed it more than most people realized. For most of his adult life Billy Durant had shown a passion for the automobile industry, and he had given America some of its most famous and enduring brands. But the company he had created was now a colossus far beyond his reach, ruled by administrators and bankers who seemed to be taking over much of the American business landscape. "Mr. Durant was a great man with a great weakness—he could create but not administer," observed Alfred Sloan, and administrators seemed to be what giant enterprises like General Motors most needed.[66]

Durant's love for the automobile did not die, but it had cooled. More important, it had been replaced by a new passion in an arena where creativity and improvisation still counted for something. Durant Motors became his company and his business identity, but more and more his attention was drawn into the stock market. He was not alone in this ardor among automobile men; the seven Fisher brothers, having sold their body company to GM, used their new fortunes to become high rollers in the market. But few men plunged into speculation with Durant's zeal. As Weisberger put it, "The market was an old flirtation kindled into an autumn love, to which he seemed eager to give all that was left in him." As events revealed, Billy Durant still had plenty left to give.[67]

2

The Club

and the Street

The great private bankers . . . did perform necessary functions. But the manner of their performance and the terrific concentration of power in their hands from many sources were no less threatening. . . . The bankers were neither a national asset nor a national danger—they were both.

—Ferdinand Pecora[1]

Wall Street was a world apart from the rest of the city, and its denizens were worlds apart from each other. To outside eyes the Street seemed a tight, narrow community where men expert in arcane financial skills swam endlessly in treacherous, unpredictable currents, seeking their fortunes by dubious means. Those who made their living there found something very different: a sort of apartheid born less of money than of class. To be sure, the very rich segregated themselves from the merely rich and the latter from everyone else, but there was as pronounced a caste system among the very rich as there was between them and their financial lessers.

The first line of demarcation separated the club from the street. The club consisted of that small band of investment bankers who dwelled in an exclusive aerie atop the leading firms on Wall Street. Foremost among them was the House of Morgan, which had held its privileged place for nearly four decades. The towering figure they called Jupiter, J. P. Morgan, who had transformed himself from a banker into both a legend and an institution, had died in 1913, leaving the firm in the hands of his namesake son, "shy, awkward, shambling Jack who had cowered

Wall Street, looking west toward Trinity Church.   (Brown Brothers)

in the corners of Pierpont's life." Standing six foot two, with broad shoulders set on a burly frame and a generous nose, Jack bore an uncanny resemblance to the father who had largely ignored him until the last years of his life. Some said they even walked and talked alike. Both were also "high strung, thin-skinned, moody, and prone to melancholic self-pity. Deeply emotional, they feared their ungovernable passions."[2]

In stepping into his father's shoes, Jack seemed to emulate him in so
many areas of his life as to reflect some inner desire to become him.
"His similarity to his father in thought and outlook," remarked a columnist, "is almost weird." He shared virtually all his father's interests except
his appetite for women; Jack remained devoted to and deeply depen-
dent on his wife, Jesse. Although he could never dominate the financial
world or even the House of Morgan as Jupiter had, a quirk of fate gave
it unprecedented wealth and influence in his time. Three generations of
business and emotional ties to Great Britain had made the Morgans
equally at home in that country. Early in the war, as the Allies sought
supplies from the United States, the strong Anglo-American complex-
ion of the House of Morgan prompted the British government to rely
on it as agent for wartime banking and purchasing needs. To everyone's
surprise, this business ultimately amounted to a staggering $3 billion,
from which Morgan gleaned a 1 percent fee of $30 million as well as in-
valuable political and business contacts. The firm also handled more
than $1.5 billion in Allied loans and credits.[3]

From this windfall the House of Morgan emerged from the war
richer and more powerful than ever before. Some said it was the only
bank with its own foreign policy; certainly it had become an important
factor in the government's overseas dealings, especially in the postwar
climate, where financial issues loomed over every negotiation. In 1924,
for example, the firm successfully floated a bond issue of $110 million in
New York as part of the Dawes Plan to alleviate the German financial
crisis. One role Jack would never have to play was that of surrogate central bank as undertaken by his father during the gold crisis of the 1890s
and the Panic of 1907. The Federal Reserve System had been created in
1913 to coordinate the American banking system. Although still young
and feeling its way—critics blamed it for bringing on the nosedive of
1920—the Fed was improving its ability to manage monetary policy
under the tutelage of Benjamin Strong, whose influence went well beyond his position as governor of the New York Reserve Bank.[4]

Nor did Jack have to play his father's once domineering role within
the firm. Like his father, whose interest in business increasingly took a
backseat to his passion for art after 1900, Jack relied on his senior partners to keep the wheels of progress and profits well oiled. Although no
one doubted his authority, he was by his own admission "a loafer, a stu-
dious amateur in the style of a British country squire" who loved "gar-
dening, yachting, reading detective fiction." At first the suave, magnetic

Thomas W. Lamont (left), senior partner of J. P. Morgan and Company.
(Collection of the Museum of Financial History)

Harry Davison assumed the role of top lieutenant, but he died while undergoing surgery for a brain tumor in 1922. In his place came the debonair Thomas W. Lamont, who quickly became the brains and the voice of the House of Morgan, a position that made him the most powerful man on Wall Street. On the Street it was said that "Mr. Morgan speaks to Lamont, and Mr. Lamont speaks to the people."[5]

A short, slim man with rounded shoulders, Lamont was the son of a poor parson who had parlayed his contacts at Phillips Exeter Academy and Harvard into a brilliant career. He played the role of aristocrat as if to the manor born, with a smooth, unflappable, and unfailingly congenial style that masked a shrewd, appraising mind and a voracious appetite for work. His smiling eyes and cheerful nature drew people to him. No man made more friends more easily or exercised more influence in more circles than Thomas Lamont, and no one made prodigious exertions look more effortless. His son once said that he had never seen his father angry; scarcely anyone admitted to seeing him even flustered.

Partners' Row at the House of Morgan. (Collection of the Museum of Financial History)

The other Morgan partners were all cut from the same mold: white, Anglo-Saxon (and strongly Anglophile) Protestants of old American stock—what John Brooks called "the old Yankee trader gone high-brow." They tended to be tall, slender, handsome men with fair skin and generous amounts of hair gone prematurely white. As a group they were men of culture, taste, and propriety, acutely conscious of their role as leaders of the Establishment and careful to avoid any act that might compromise the dignity and reputation of "the Corner," as it was called. The House of Morgan had no sign on its outer door and needed none. Its partners were *the* club; everyone else belonged to something else.[6]

The second most powerful firm on Wall Street dwelled in quite another world. Kuhn, Loeb actually did as much business as the House of Morgan, or even more, and had its own "well cultivated air of breathtaking superiority," but it could not hope to compete in the area of influence and prestige. Kuhn, Loeb was the flagship firm of the German Jews in Wall Street, the most successful of whom grew quite as rich as their WASP rivals but were shunned socially. Anti-Semitism had been a way of life on Wall Street since the arrival of the first Jews and tended to become rampant during panics, when scapegoats were needed. The magisterial Jacob Schiff had transformed Kuhn, Loeb into a dominant house by making it the leader in railroad financing. He also managed to develop a pleasant, cooperative working relationship with the Morgans that continued after Schiff's death in 1920 when leadership of the firm passed to the elegant, magisterial Otto Kahn, who became the nation's foremost patron of the arts.[7]

But that pleasant relationship did not extend to society, which systemically froze the Jews out of its institutions. Not all the WASPs on Wall Street snubbed the Jews in their midst, but their clubs, hotels, and social institutions banned their presence, and few parlors or parties offered them admittance. The Morgan partners worked with Kuhn, Loeb but retained a strong streak of anti-Semitism, none more so than Jack Morgan himself. The war exacerbated these feelings, pitting Morgan's Anglophile ardor against Schiff's German roots. The sinking of the *Lusitania* by a German submarine in 1915 prompted Schiff to visit 23 Wall to offer his regrets. Jack Morgan greeted him with harsh words and stalked off, leaving a crushed Schiff to walk away in dejection. When the other partners protested this breach of Wall Street etiquette, a contrite Jack conceded that he had gone too far and went off to Kuhn, Loeb to apologize.[8]

Apart from the coterie of Jewish firms, the other major investment banking houses on Wall Street followed the Morgan pattern. "Wall Street is a school of manners," observed Frederick Lewis Allen. "Go into one of the luncheon clubs where the men of the Street gather and you will note . . . that most of them have the air of gentlemen." Allen's profile of 50 leading Wall Street men revealed remarkable similarities apart from their dress and demeanor. Unlike an earlier generation of Wall Street men, 40 of them had attended college, mostly in the East, not so much to get an education as to meet the right people. They nested on the Upper East Side of Manhattan, belonged to the same clubs, had country places on the north shore of Long Island or in New Jersey, and favored such sports as golf, sailing, and horse racing. Most were what John Brooks called "lapsed Protestants" and rigidly excluded from their social and business ranks not only Jews but Catholics as well.[9]

They were the heart of the Wall Street Establishment, the men who ruled the rhythms of finance. Outsiders studied their words and deeds like scripture for clues. The tightest, most exclusive circle among them belonged to the investment bankers, whose firms were individually impenetrable to each other and collectively impenetrable to the outside world. They operated by what writer Ron Chernow called the "Gentleman Bankers Code," a business ethic imported by the Morgans from London and adapted to Wall Street. "Under this code, banks did not try to scout out business or seek new clients but waited for them to arrive with proper introductions. They had no branch offices and refused to take on new companies unless the move was first cleared with the former banker. The idea was not to compete, at least not too openly, which meant no advertising, no price competition, and no raiding of other firms' clients."[10]

The code still prevailed as the 1920s opened, although its ritualistic courtesies often masked vicious underlying rivalries. The commercial bankers had nothing like it. They were a far more varied and numerous lot, with the largest of them beginning to dwarf the investment bankers in size and strength if not in influence or prestige. One of them belonged to the club and was unique in many respects. The First National Bank at 2 Wall Street was a family institution dominated by George F. Baker and his namesake son. Long a close ally of the Morgans, it did a limited, almost exclusive business, but its short list of clients included the cream of major corporations. The rumor was that a company had to maintain a minimum balance of $500,000 to get in the First National's door. It was an old-fashioned bank where the officers sat alongside each other behind ancient roll-top desks on a mezzanine floor and each set his hat (usually a derby) on top of his desk. This signaled everyone below that he was in; a hatless desk indicated that the officer was out.[11]

The congeries of trading houses had practices and customs but no strict code of behavior. They were a varied group that often specialized in one or more functions. Some (like Brown Brothers, and Heidelbach, Ickelheimer & Co.) did a large international business; others (such as Lehman Brothers; Goldman, Sachs & Co.; and Lazard Frères & Co.) concentrated on underwriting. The stock exchange or brokerage houses (like Clark, Dodge & Co.; Dominick & Dominick; Post & Flagg; J. S. Bache & Co.; and Merrill, Lynch) did some underwriting but devoted themselves mainly to buying and selling securities. Some firms also did a large business in commodities and owned seats on the Chicago Board of Trade and the New York Cotton Exchange. A small group specialized in bonds, and a still smaller cluster dealt in foreign exchange.[12]

Each house had its own style and reputation that was guarded zealously in the gossipy realm of Wall Street. In size and stature they ranged from large, well-established brokerage firms, many of them with close ties to the major investment bankers, to the disreputable "bucket shops" that had long dwelled in the shadows of the financial world, feeding like scavengers on its droppings until they either died of malnutrition or grew fat enough to become respectable. This netherworld existed because only members could trade on the New York Stock Exchange, and only stocks that met criteria established by the Exchange could be listed and traded on its floor. Complaints from the legitimate firms led to periodic cleaning up of the disreputable bucket shops, but they soon reappeared in some new location.

The major institution on Wall Street with a formal set of rules and regulations was the New York Stock Exchange, and it too was a closed universe. A "seat," or membership, on the Exchange could be obtained only by buying one of the 1,100 already belonging to brokerage houses or individuals. In that way the Exchange remained a private, exclusive world wholly outside government control. As a federal prosecutor later noted, "It was operated as a strictly private gentlemen's club, and an extremely select one. . . . There was . . . an elaborate system of committees, rules, and regulations by which the Exchange was supposed to exercise 'self-discipline,' but no outside power could set foot within its walls." However lax or faithful the members were in their duties, they resented even the slightest hint of outside interference in their rituals. The Exchange in 1920 was, according to John Brooks, "so newly risen to such power that it had not yet mellowed into responsibility," and "probably in a more arbitrary and arrogant mood than at any time before or since."[13]

The men who dominated the Exchange were pale imitations of the Morgan mold. They came largely from Yankee stock, had gone to the best New England schools, where they majored in sports and making the right connections, were more shrewd than bright, thrived on urban club life, and tended to be snobs despite their general ignorance of art, literature, music, history, and world affairs. Their overriding interests, which they made no attempt to disguise, were making money and climbing the social ladder. They were as narrow as they were venal and made little attempt to mask their ambitions.[14]

Farther down the Street could be found the smaller and less haughty Curb Market, which had come a long way since the days when it operated like an outdoor bazaar at William and Beaver streets. In 1902 it moved to Broad Street just below the Stock Exchange and continued to operate outdoors, its uproar providing amusement for tourists and consternation for the tenants of nearby buildings who protested the din.

A New York Curb
Exchange trader placing
an order by phone on
the floor of the
Exchange, 1929.
(Collection of the Museum
of Financial History)

Not until 1921 did it move indoors at 86 Trinity Place, but the old name
lingered until 1929, when it was changed to the New York Curb Exchange. Although lacking the traditions and reputation of the New
York Stock Exchange, the Curb grew in size and importance throughout the decade. Its traders were men who, socially and literally, had
come in from the cold. In addition, there existed an even more informal
"over the counter" market that dealt in unlisted shares.[15]

The money industry did not have Wall Street all to itself. Along this
crooked street that ran downhill a mere eight blocks from the doorstep
of Trinity Church on Broadway to South Street and the waters of the
East River could be found not only the financial heart of the nation (and
soon the world) but also an astounding array of related enterprises. Its
buildings housed the offices of 91 major banks and 25 trust companies,
the fiscal offices of 130 railroads, 57 life, 209 fire and marine, and more

than 100 other types of insurance companies, 15 safe-deposit firms, 20 cable and telegraph companies, 50 coal and iron companies, and hundreds of industrial corporations. Clustered around them were the produce, cotton, sugar, metals, and maritime exchanges as well as offices of some of the largest law firms in the country.[16]

For nearly its entire history Wall Street had been a small, insular world of professionals, speculators, insiders and outsiders, bankers and others who dealt in finance, and the army of workers who kept its machinery running. Alexander Noyes described the Street as "a centre of gossip, a whispering gallery of conjecture and information, such as probably exists nowhere else in American society — not even at Washington, which is saying a good deal." Rarely had the outside public intruded on its domain except as tourists or journalists in search of stories to titillate their readers. But that was changing, thanks to the war and especially to the bond drives that had given the general public a taste of investing and the larger commercial banks a doorway to new avenues of expansion.[17]

No one hurried through that doorway more enthusiastically than Charley Mitchell, whose own career had been one furious sprint toward success. A native of Chelsea, Massachusetts, he graduated from Amherst in 1899 and went to work for the Western Electric Company in Chicago. Moving to New York, he became assistant to the president of the Trust Company of America just before that institution nearly went down in the Panic of 1907. During that crisis Mitchell performed well, liquidating the Trust Company's investments skillfully and learning enough from the process to form his own firm in 1911. His work there attracted the attention of Frank A. Vanderlip, president of the powerful National City Bank, who in 1916 recruited Mitchell to take charge of the bank's key affiliate, the National City Company.[18]

Trouble had always preceded rather than followed Charley Mitchell's career, thereby opening doors of opportunity for him. National City was no exception to this happy pattern. By 1913 the velvety James Stillman had made National City the largest bank in the nation and a leader in both commercial and investment banking. Under Vanderlip the bank continued to grow, but it struggled against serious limitations. Its charter as a national bank did not allow it to have branches, perform trust services, or deal in securities. State-chartered banks and trust companies, being less heavily taxed and regulated, could both operate branches and provide a broader range of services. Vanderlip tried first to secure reform of the banking laws. When this effort failed, he created an affiliate company with a charter enabling it to do what the parent bank could not.[19]

National City Company was born in July 1911 under a state charter and acquired the large interests in numerous other banks held privately by Stillman and other stockholders. The new company thus began life with what amounted to a chain of banks, but the Pujo investigation of the "Money Trust" in 1911 prompted Vanderlip to sell off these stocks. Passage of the Federal Reserve Act in December 1913 further complicated the bank's future by inserting a new body, the Federal Reserve Board, between the government and the banks. Vanderlip predicted astutely that the act would "recast the methods of the banking business," and he lost little time seeking new possibilities. Nothing forbade investment banking by commercial banks or their affiliates. The outbreak of war in Europe encouraged Vanderlip to seek opportunities in this direction.[20]

The distinction was one that had long separated the club from the street. Investment bankers specialized in underwriting and distributing securities, mostly bonds, for corporations and governments. They did not deal with the general public or handle individual accounts except as a favor to very wealthy clients. Nor did they sell bonds to the public; they were wholesalers who used retail brokerage firms and banks for that purpose. Commercial banks accepted individual accounts but concentrated on a variety of services for business firms. National banks also served as depositories and agents for the federal government. In simple terms, a commercial bank existed to furnish short-term, self-liquidating credit for "the production and distribution of consumable goods." As banker Winthrop W. Aldrich explained, it could not take undue risks or tie up funds in long-term loans because of its "responsibility to meet its deposit liabilities on demand." Investment bankers had no such depositor responsibilities and therefore could assume larger risks to meet long-term funding needs.[21]

Stillman had expanded National City by moving it into underwriting, broadening its range of services for corporations that gave the bank their large accounts, opening a foreign exchange department, gaining control of a network of correspondent banks, and making it the federal government's premier bank. Vanderlip extended its underwriting and retail distribution roles and broadened its customer base. He launched an aggressive campaign to solicit accounts from smaller corporations and in 1914 opened the first foreign branch of any nationally chartered American bank. By 1917 he had created the embryo of a global network, its penetration of Europe interrupted only by the war. After the Federal Reserve Act, he had made National City "less a bankers' bank and more of a business bank, less a bank for Wall Street and more a bank for the nation."[22]

The American bond market was already growing when the war energized it beyond all past experience. Vanderlip was among the first to recognize the importance of tapping into a broader customer base that included people of more modest means. The war led him to push these efforts even more and to create a broader distribution system to reach such individuals. During the summer of 1916 he acquired the brokerage firm of N. W. Halsey, one of the few retail investment houses with a genuinely national distribution system. The firm was made part of the National City Company, and Vanderlip hoped also to acquire its best officer, Harold Stuart, to run the operation. But Stuart decided to form his own company, leaving Vanderlip with a nationwide bond operation and no one to run it. This need brought him to Charley Mitchell.[23]

Mitchell took hold of National City vigorously, but above him loomed a problem similar to the one that plagued Billy Durant at General Motors. For all their genius at banking, Stillman and Vanderlip had not created an efficient top management for the bank's sprawling empire. Despite ill health and deep affection for his protégé, Stillman refused to give Vanderlip a share in the bank's ownership equal to his own or yield his place. When Stillman died in March 1918, his majority holding of National City stock passed to his namesake son, who decided to claim the presidency for himself and pushed Vanderlip out in June 1919. This abrupt transition soon demonstrated that National City had outgrown the old style of personal ownership.[24]

James A. Stillman had his father's name but not his ability. The postwar economic roller coaster hit the bank hard and exposed certain investment weaknesses, notably in Cuba, where by 1920 it had opened 23 branches and funneled $79 million into the sugar industry. Confronted by the worst fiasco in National City history and harassed for months by a much publicized divorce suit, Stillman the younger resigned the presidency in May 1921 and retreated to his seat on the board. In his place the board elected the dynamic Charles Edwin Mitchell, who at age 43 found himself at the pinnacle of the commercial banking world in circumstances that would have unnerved even hardened bankers.[25]

Charley Mitchell did not flinch at the formidable task before him. With ruthless efficiency he purged the bank's portfolio of nonperforming loans, closed marginal overseas branches, and imposed stricter financial controls. He went to Cuba in January 1922 and concluded that the bank could best protect its investment by putting in more funds and going directly into the sugar business. Mitchell also fired all the men responsible for the Cuban debacle, revamped the organization of the bank, and tackled the thorny challenge of turning a family enterprise into an institution. In February 1923 he unveiled a bonus plan called the management fund, which "linked the pay of key officers to the actual earnings of the bank." It proved effective both in raising morale and in keeping good men focused on the bank's business. In all this work Mitchell set the pace and left no doubt who was in charge. "We are on our way to bigger things . . . ," he promised the bank's employees in 1922. "We have been going through a period of readjustment and a time of rebuilding. We are ready now to go ahead full speed."[26]

These words proved a prophecy. With his usual good luck Sunshine Charley caught almost perfectly the swelling wave of prosperity that rolled into the "fat years." The United States emerged as the dominant force in the world economy, which gave the dollar a growing role in international affairs. New York emerged as the headquarters of corporate America and the world's leading securities market, "the one place in the world where borrowers could raise capital in large amounts on short notice." In addition, wartime prosperity had increased the ranks of the American middle class, people making a comfortable living who found themselves for the first time with money to invest and no experience at how to go about it. Vanderlip had foreseen the role these new investors might play, and Mitchell had targeted them in his highly successful work at National City Company. Once at the head of both the bank and the company, Mitchell redoubled his efforts.[27]

Stillman had given National City a wholesale commercial and investment bank aimed at large domestic corporations and correspondent banks. Vanderlip had moved the bank onto the international stage and beckoned to smaller companies. Mitchell carried this vision still farther by extending the bank's reach to not only small firms but individual households; he vowed to make it the "bank for all." Under his leadership National City evolved into the nation's first financial department store with a line of financial goods that offered something for everybody. Paradoxically, he made the bank larger by making it more local. As a national bank with no branches, it could not compete for business in Manhattan outside of Wall Street. But the National Bank Consolidation Act of 1918 opened a window for expansion by allowing two banks that merged to keep whatever branches they had at the time. By late 1926 National City acquired through mergers 7 offices in Manhattan and 11 in Brooklyn.[28]

The real breakthrough came in 1927 when the McFadden Act allowed national banks to own full-service branches so long as they abided by state law. Mitchell pushed expansion vigorously; by 1929 the bank had 37 branches scattered throughout New York's boroughs. The capstone to this effort came that summer in his negotiations to merge with the Corn Exchange Bank, which had 67 branches, more than any other New York bank. This expanding network was important because Mitchell viewed each branch as a miniature bank offering a full range of retail services to the dynamic pool of a new type of customer he called the "small but developing capitalist." These services were shaped to fit a variety of smaller customers and depositors, who brought the bank an important new source of funds in the form of personal savings and a new outlet for their use in the form of loans to small businesses and individuals. By 1929 National City had secured more than 230,000 individual accounts.[29]

Despite occasional setbacks, Mitchell also persisted in developing rather than curtailing the overseas network. By 1929 National City owned 98 branches in 23 countries, making it by far the largest foreign network of any American bank. Altogether these branches had become almost as important as National City's original core activity, the domestic wholesale business serving corporations and correspondent banks. This business grew more slowly during the 1920s, partly because corporations came to rely increasingly on issuing their own securities for their long-term financing instead of borrowing funds.[30]

Mitchell responded to this decline in core business by finding new customers and going to where the action had moved—the handling of securities. Even before becoming head of the bank he had taken the lead in this area through the National City Company. In 1922 nearly 600,000 Americans already had annual incomes exceeding $5,000; their number would exceed one million by 1929. This level of income enabled people to live comfortably and put reasonable sums aside, but many did not know where to invest their money besides the traditional harbors of savings accounts, life insurance, and equity in one's own house. Aware that these eager but untutored savers knew little or nothing about investment, Charley Mitchell set out to win their business by educating them in the basics and pointing them toward National City in the process.[31]

Instead of a classroom Mitchell relied on advertising, a blizzard of it. He aimed to lift "the veil of mystery" over investment banking and "get the people to look upon securities as something they were themselves vitally interested in and could readily understand." If advertising could generate a large volume of business and thereby reduce unit costs, the bank could keep expenses low by spreading them over this volume and still earn large profits. "We felt that if we could take from the books of successful merchandisers and distributors, the country over," he explained, "those pages . . . that had to do with successful advertising, and those with successful education . . . we could then . . . lift this investment banking business to a level it had never reached before."[32]

To accomplish this missionary work Mitchell transformed the National City Company into a financial chain store. When he took charge in 1916, it had offices in four cities. By 1919 that number had increased to 51; a decade later it owned 69 branch offices in 58 cities, staffed with 1,900 employees and connected by 11,300 miles of private communication wire. This giant organization, declared Mitchell proudly, existed to "serve the public on a straightforward basis, just as it is served by the United Cigar Stores or Child's Restaurants." Besides teaching potential customers the ABCs of bond investing, salesmen and sales brochures stressed the "sharp distinction . . . between good bonds *as a class* and what may proved to be a good bond *for you*." The customer was encouraged to be "as frank and open in discussing his investment problems as he is in discussing legal problems with his lawyer or his health with a doctor."[33]

Sunshine Charley knew how to sell—admirers called him the greatest bond salesman who ever lived—and he expected his battalions of salesmen to march into battle with the same enthusiasm he brought to it. Bruce Barton, the celebrated advertising executive, recalled standing with Mitchell at a window in the Bankers Club. Every now and then, Mitchell mused, he brought one of his salesmen to the club for lunch after hearing him complain that no new customers could be found. He would lead the man to the window and tell him to gaze at the street below. "There are six million people with incomes that aggregate thousands of millions of dollars," Mitchell would say. "They are just waiting for someone to come and tell them what to do with their savings. Take a good look, eat a good lunch, and then go down and tell them."[34]

At center, Charles E. ("Sunshine Charley") Mitchell, president of National City Bank, who mass-marketed securities as never before.   (Brown Brothers)

It was an effective technique but far from his only one. Mitchell exhorted, bullied, and browbeat his salesmen to get results. He devised contests that shamed the losers while rewarding the winners, and always there loomed the threat of dismissal if quotas were not met. Peddling bonds, he insisted, was no different than selling the public so many pounds of coffee. To that public, however, he took care to portray the company, its agents, and the bank as sound, conservative counselors marketing only safe, choice bonds that had been carefully researched. Much of the product came from National City Company itself, which emerged as one of the top underwriters and originators of securities. During the 1920s the company participated in or originated $10.7 billion worth of bonds, or 21 percent of the total issued in the nation, more than any other bank. In keeping with its conservative image, it did not offer any common stocks to the public until 1927. The types of bonds underwritten by City Company ranged from railroad, utility, and

industrial corporations to federal, state, and municipal offerings as well
as those of foreign governments and companies. During the 1920s National City Company had a hand in more than 150 bond issues from 26
different countries.[35]

Mitchell also took National City into the lucrative trust business after 1919, when new legislation clarified the rights of national banks in
this area. This work involved managing assets for individuals, families,
and institutions. Aware that the bank lacked the long-standing relationships of older, established trust companies with wealthy families and
corporations, he again targeted the growing middle class neglected by
the older banks. Using the same sales philosophy as other departments,
National City tailored its products to the needs of this new class of customers and went after them with advertisements and personal solicita-
tions. After boosting the bank's managed assets from nearly $21 million
in 1923 to $81.9 million in 1928, Mitchell resorted to a swifter, surer
form of growth: merger. In April 1929 he took over the prestigious
Farmers' Loan and Trust, with which National City had a relationship of
long standing. This coup increased National City's managed trust assets
to more than $158 million.[36]

The renamed City Bank Farmers Trust Company became a third part
of the organization along with National City Bank and National City
Company. With this acquisition Mitchell fulfilled his vision of the great
financial department store. National City had become the largest bank
in the world, with assets exceeding $2.2 billion and net profits of $22.8
million in 1929 compared to a mere $900,000 in 1922. Each of its three
components held a leading position in its field; the National City Company had become "the largest agency in the world for the distribution of
securities." Charley Mitchell had created a giant, and in the process he
had become one of the best-known bankers in the country. To the public he was Horatio Alger transplanted into the New Era, the self-made
millionaire who embodied the values of self-help, rugged individualism,
and "go-getter" energy so cherished by the age.[37]

And the end was nowhere in sight. As the bank continued to grow,
Mitchell had no difficulty expanding his vision. Although he had grown
rich, he still thrived on hard work and was fiercely devoted to the bank.
He believed that for all the pomp, power, and prestige of the House of
Morgan and the rest of the club, National City and other giant com-
mercial banks represented the wave of the future. In 1929 the National
City Company sold more securities than were floated by Morgan and

Kuhn, Loeb combined, and ahead lay the merger with the Corn Exchange Bank.[38]

Mitchell's closest rival in the realm of commercial banking embraced a similar vision. Although Albert Wiggin of the Chase National Bank could not have been more different from Sunshine Charley in personality, their backgrounds seemed to have much in common. Nine years older than Mitchell, he too hailed from the Boston area (Medford) with modest roots as the son of a Unitarian minister. Both were shrewd, aggressive men intent on pursuing success with as few distractions as possible, but where Mitchell was ebullient and outgoing, Wiggin was reserved, reticent, and cynical. He was as quiet as Mitchell was loud, but in his own way even bolder in action. Starting in 1885 as a clerk in the Commonwealth Bank of Boston, Wiggin climbed the banking ladder steadily until he reached the vice presidency of a Boston bank in 1897. Two years later he jumped to the big leagues, taking the same post in the National Park Bank of New York.[39]

Once in New York, Wiggin impressed a growing circle of financiers with his ability and appetite for hard work. In 1903 two of the city's most powerful bankers, George F. Baker and Henry P. Davison of the First National Bank, asked Wiggin to assist them in organizing the Bankers Trust Company. A year later they rewarded Wiggin by helping him to get a vice presidency with the Chase National Bank. There he climbed the ladder even more quickly. Arriving in 1904 as the bank's youngest vice president, he ascended to the presidency in 1911 and to chairman of the board in 1917. For the next 13 years he dominated the Chase in one or both of these offices, following a pattern strikingly similar to, if less spectacular than, the one established by Charley Mitchell.

In 1904 the Chase was a medium-sized bank with less than $250 million in assets. Wiggin expanded its traditional services and in 1917 helped organize the Mercantile Trust Company to get Chase into that lucrative field. That same year the Chase created its own security affiliate, Chase Securities Corporation, in the mold of the National City Company. But Wiggin went even further by also creating several satellite companies such as the Metpotan and Chase Harris Forbes corporations. Like Mitchell, too, he opened local branches throughout the city and established Chase branches overseas. Even more than Mitchell he enlarged the bank through mergers, swallowing six major New York banks by 1929. During that year, while Mitchell negotiated the merger with the Corn Exchange Bank, Wiggin was engaged in planning the biggest of all his acquisitions, the Equitable Trust Company, which had assets of more than $1 billion.[40]

Wiggin drew support from a wide range of businessmen and corporations by putting them on his own board and gained influence by serving on the boards of 59 different companies. By the decade's end, his bank competed with National City for the honor of being the largest in the world, depending on which one had completed what merger at what date. Wiggin had achieved a stature, if not a notoriety, comparable to that of Mitchell even if he lacked Mitchell's presence and bubbly personality, which sought attention like a moth seeking flame. But he did something Mitchell did not do, did it so quietly and inconspicuously that few people other than some of the bank's officers knew about it. He organized no fewer than six corporations controlled entirely by himself or his immediate family. Three of them were chartered in the United States, the other three in Canada. During the fattest of the fat years, they would prove useful vehicles for swelling Wiggin's personal fortune through stock operations, often in his bank's own securities.[41]

3

Plungers

and Politicians

In a sense, the financial conflict is more bitter and ruthless than war
itself; in war, friend and foe can be distinguished.

—Barnie F. Winkelman[1]

Within Wall Street could be found yet another world, one far
more fluid and fickle than the institutions that gave it presence and solidity. The professional traders who dealt in
stocks were as mixed a lot as the American population itself, but their
ranks included one special breed: the lone wolf whose speculative exploits gave an otherwise drab financial world most of its color. These
operators dwelled in a twilight realm as insiders to the market but outsiders to most respectable banks and brokerage houses. They belonged
to no firm and enlisted other brokers to conduct their operations—taking care never to let the left hand know what the right was doing. In the
sunshine world of Wall Street they were creatures of the shadows; mystery was always their ally.

Professional speculators cared little for anything beyond the forces
or influences that might move the price of a stock up or down. They
differed from bankers or brokers in having no responsibility to anyone
but themselves. Their operations lived or died by price fluctuations,
which put a premium on their ability to manipulate the movement of
prices in the desired direction. Sometimes they served as Hessians to
major bankers or others who needed to "make a market" in a given security for a time. Their skills were admired and feared by the rest of the
trading profession, to whom the lone operators were at once models

and menaces. It was not a career for the faint of heart. Most of the top operators had made and lost fortunes several times, and it was an axiom of the Street that few of them ever walked away from the game with anything left in their pockets.

The basic elements of dealing in stocks seemed simple enough at first glance. A "bull" market was one going up, a "bear" market one going down. Bulls made money by buying stocks at one price and selling them on the rise, bears by selling at a lower price than they had paid for the stock. To do this, bears had to use a dangerous and complicated technique of selling stock they did not actually own. For a fee they borrowed enough shares to complete the transaction, then bought the stock later at a lower price to fulfill their contract with the lender. In effect they rented stock from a broker until they bought enough to cover their sale. The perils of selling short, as it was called, had been immortalized in a couplet usually attributed to one of the most artful early practitioners, Daniel Drew: "He who sells what isn't his'n/ Must either buy or go to prison."[2]

Conservative investors paid cash for stocks and hoped to realize two kinds of gains over time: dividends that the company might pay and/or a rise in the price of the stock. In both cases the value of the investment depended on the long-term performance of the company. Speculators took a short-term view in which a company's performance mattered only insofar as it had an immediate effect on the price of its stock. For their purposes anything that jiggled the price—rumor, innuendo, natural disaster, even outright lies—could be used to turn a profit on quick transactions or assist an orchestrated campaign to move the price level higher or lower. The speculator, looking only for short-term opportunities, moved in and out of stocks with a speed that made him an unsettling force in a volatile market. For an operator, timing was crucial.

So was volume. Since speculative profits came from transactions, the larger the amount of stock traded, the greater the profit (or loss). Operators therefore did not pay cash for stocks but gained leverage by buying on *margin*. That is, they paid only a portion of the price in cash—anywhere from 10 to 70 percent—and borrowed the rest from a broker, who in turn usually got the funds from a bank loan. The purchased stock served as collateral for the loan, and the buyer received all gains or losses in price. If the stock's price dipped below the amount needed to cover the loan, the margin became impaired, meaning that the buyer had to put up more margin to make up the difference. If he could not "cover" this additional margin, the broker could "sell him out"—in effect, foreclosing the loan and selling the stock used as collateral for whatever it would bring.

The loans were adjusted at the end of each business day to reflect changes in interest rates and the amount of margin needed. Unlike "time loans," which were contracted for specified periods of time, these could be called at the end of each day and so were known as "call loans." Normally such loans were renewed at whatever rate was prevalent that day—the "renewal rate." If the margin was 10 percent, an operator could buy $100 worth of stock with only $10 in cash and the rest in the form of a call loan; at a 50 percent margin he still needed only $50 cash to control $100 worth of stock. Buying on margin thus increased the scale of both potential profit and risk of loss.

Even a novice at investment could employ these techniques, but learning the moves was a far cry from knowing how to play the game. As in chess, it merely opened a doorway to realms of vast, unexpected complexity and nuance, where the cost of further education often came painfully high. On Wall Street the tuition took many forms, ranging from financial loss to unraveled nerves to obsessive behavior. The personalities of lone wolves ranged from bookworm to braggadocio, with some combining aspects of both extremes. Such a figure was Jesse Lauriston Livermore, whom John Brooks called "the éminence grise" and "invisible genie of the market" for the entire decade. One Wall Street banker pronounced him "the best man on the stock market tape the speculative world has ever known."[3]

"J. L.," as his friends called him, learned the moves earlier and better than most. Born in 1877, the son of a failed Massachusetts farmer, he found work at 14 as a board boy in a Boston brokerage for $6 a week. The endless stream of price quotations he chalked on the board soon revealed in him a remarkable facility for figures. He began to see patterns in their fluctuations and then to anticipate their movements. Intrigued by the game, he jotted his observations down in a little book and became a close student of the tape until he grew expert at its behavior while remaining cheerfully ignorant of the reasons behind the deviations. "I didn't ask the tape why when I was fourteen," he said later, "and I don't ask it today, at forty." One day an office boy claimed to have a hot tip and dared him to join in putting a few dollars on a stock in a bucket shop. Livermore checked his little book, saw that the stock was rising, and gave the friend all his cash. Two days later he received his first profit of $3.12.[4]

Shown in a 1936 photo, Jesse
Livermore, whose successes as a
speculator were legendary.
(Associated Press)

From this modest transaction sprang a spectacular career of speculative activity. Livermore began frequenting the bucket shops in Boston,
where modest sums could be wagered on stocks. Although appearing to
resemble brokerages, complete with price boards, the bucket shops
were more like bookies taking bets on movements in stock prices. No
shares were actually bought or sold; the action came from quotations
taken directly from the tape. Most shops cleaned up on fluctuations of
less than a point, which usually sufficed to "wipe" small gamblers, but
Livermore showed an uncanny ability to pick movements. At 15 he
made his first thousand dollars and earned the nickname of "Boy
Plunger" as one bucket shop after another banned him from the
premises for excessive winning. Having beat the game in Boston, he decided at 21 to make the hegira to New York with his accumulated stake
of $2,500.[5]

There he found a different game that pushed his education to another level. Always an attentive learner, Livermore discovered that his
skill at reading the tape was not enough. He had profited from fluctuations that depended on acting instantly to buy or cut a loss. This
worked fine in a bucket shop but not in a brokerage, where he had to
buy and sell actual stocks and the delay between order and execution on
the floor often meant a fatal variation in price. Having mastered the art

of reading the tape, he learned next the techniques of stock speculation. He went broke within six months, went to St. Louis to earn a fresh stake with $500 borrowed from a friendly broker, and returned to New York with $2,800 to resume his career. "The game taught me the game," he recalled. "And didn't spare the rod while teaching."[6]

By 1901 he had parlayed his stake into a fortune of $50,000 only to lose it all in the wild market that spring. From that loss and other experiences he absorbed yet another valuable lesson: "There is only one side to the stock market; and it is not the bull side or the bear side, but the right side." Concluding that what mattered was not the price of a stock but the direction of the broader market, he went back to Boston to raise another stake, then returned to Wall Street for a third try. This time he won more often than he lost. He played the market hard from 10:00 to 3:00 and after hours devoted himself to "the game of living my life." He was learning the ropes, the hardest of which on Wall Street was the act of grasping how and what to learn and sticking to that knowledge under fire.[7]

The education of Jesse Livermore, like that of Henry Adams, impressed its lessons on him in one unexpected arena after another. As the scale of his operations grew, he made one fortune after another only to lose them through some fresh miscalculation. He discovered that "suckers differ among themselves according to the degree of experience. The tyro knows nothing. . . . But the next . . . grade thinks he knows a great deal. . . . He is the experienced sucker who has studied—not the market itself but a few remarks about the market made by a still higher grade of suckers. . . . It is naturally the semisucker who is always quoting the famous trading aphorisms and the various rules of the game. He knows all the don'ts . . . excepting the principal one, which is: Don't be a sucker!"[8]

But learning from his mistakes did not keep Livermore from making new ones. In 1906 he cleaned up by going short on Union Pacific shortly before the San Francisco earthquake turned a rising market into a falling one—only to be wiped out the next year by mistiming his play. He recouped his losses later in 1907, earned his first million, and branched into trading commodities on a large scale. There too the pattern repeated itself: a killing in cotton earned him a fortune, which he soon lost through a fatal misplay in the same commodity. His personal life followed the same bouncing ball. He won a wife in Indianapolis and lost her through neglect. Winning fed the lavish lifestyle he had come to love and his appetite for showgirls, while losing forced him to sell the yachts and other fine things he bought in flush times. By 1911 times were anything but good for Livermore; the period 1911–14 became for him the "long lean years."[9]

It was, quipped one of his acquaintances, "the kind of market in which not even a skunk could make a scent." A bad losing streak left Livermore more than a million dollars in debt and discouraged for the first time. He endured the humiliation of bankruptcy, borrowed enough money for a small stake, and set out to repair his shattered fortune. The war provided the opportunity he needed; in 1916 alone he rode the bull market to profits exceeding $3 million. Livermore paid off his debts and resurrected his old lifestyle with a new yacht, new town house, and new wife. This time he put some funds into annuities for the next rainy day and set up trusts for his two sons when they came along. Devoted to his young wife, he even gave up philandering for a time. In 1920 he paid $5,000 for a seat on the Curb Exchange but rarely used it. He also bought an estate in Great Neck, which the happy couple named Evermore.[10]

By the early 1920s Livermore had restored, even enhanced, his old reputation as well as his comfortable lifestyle. Both his professional and personal lives seemed more settled. His reputation on Wall Street soared in 1923 when he managed a pool that routed a bear operation in Piggly Wiggly shares. This maneuver, the first of many spectacular struggles on the Exchange during the decade, established Livermore as a master manipulator and gained him a public following eager to catch any rumor of his next move and invest in it. Sitting on the brink of a major bull market, Livermore was poised to use this growing legion of minnows to full advantage.[11]

He also felt comfortable enough to share his wisdom with the public, at least in a roundabout way. In 1923 there appeared a curious book entitled *Reminiscences of a Stock Operator* written by well-known financial writer Edwin Lefevre and dedicated to Livermore. Cast in the form of an autobiography, it was actually Livermore's version of his own career penned with Lefevre's help. But the lively and engaging narrative revealed only what Livermore wished to show, and even then through the elusive screen of a character with the pseudonym of Larry Livingston. Even in flush times this lonest of lone wolves was not about to move far from the shadows in which he dwelled.

For all its insularity and strong sense of self-importance, Washington had not really counted for much since the Civil War. Congress had followed its usual pattern of talking much while doing little. For a brief time the presidency underwent a resurgence under Theodore Roosevelt and Woodrow Wilson, and its powers grew as they had always done in wartime, but the war's end saw a rapid dismantling of the centralizing apparatus and a hasty retreat to the hallowed tradition of a sedentary executive presiding over a bickering Congress. The nation had moved into a new era, but its political institutions remained firmly anchored to past practices and the conservative spirit reflected in Warren G. Harding's handy new term, "normalcy."

Most people seemed to prefer it that way, as if the familiar flavor of past politics provided a cushion against the jarring change experienced in other areas of life. While Americans moved in record numbers to the cities and suburbs, they elected to the presidency three small-town boys. One never wanted to be president; the second aspired to be the least president the country ever had and succeeded; and the third longed desperately to be president even though he disliked politics and having to deal with people. The Ohioan never really left home even in Washington, the Vermonter expanded his horizons as far as Massachusetts, and the Iowan saw more of the world than any other president, having circled the globe five times by the age of 33.[12]

Although differing widely in personality and ability, the three men shared more than their Republicanism. None of them felt at ease in the office. "If there is anything wrong with the White House," complained Warren Harding in 1922, "it is the inability to be a human being." Calvin Coolidge and Herbert Hoover seconded that sentiment. They also shared a devout belief in the primacy of business. Well before Coolidge uttered his famous remark in 1925, "The chief business of the American people is business," Harding made the same point even more emphatically. "The business of America is the business of everybody in America . . . ," he proclaimed. "This is essentially a business country. . . . We must get back to the methods of business." Hoover carried this credo one step further by seeking to make government itself a business conducted along the lines of sound business principles. In that sense he earned a reputation as a progressive compared to the hidebound conservatism of his predecessors. "Mr. Coolidge was a real conservative . . . ," Hoover once observed. "He was a fundamentalist in religion, in the economic and social order, and in fishing."[13]

The demands of businessmen on government were few but insistent. They wanted economy in government, a protectionist tariff, lower taxes, and freedom from government interference. Congress moved with unaccustomed diligence toward the first two goals with the Budget and Accounting Act of 1921 and the Fordney-McCumber Tariff of 1922. The first created two new offices, a director of the budget and a comptroller general; the second produced the highest tariff rates in the nation's history and, in the words of historian John D. Hicks, "did about all that tariff protection could do for American manufacturers." It also hampered the efforts of American farmers to sell their surpluses overseas and those of foreign nations seeking to relieve their war debt to the United States by selling goods here. The protectionist wall was to prove a costly obstacle in more ways than one throughout the decade.[14]

The quest for government economy got a boost from the first director of the budget, Chicago banker Charles G. Dawes, whose program enabled Harding to submit a budget for 1922–23 that made possible an annual surplus rather than a deficit. His efforts complemented those of Secretary of the Treasury Andrew W. Mellon, who emerged as the most important and enduring cabinet figure of the decade. He provided continuity through all the Republican administrations; later it would be said that three presidents served under him. No man was held in higher esteem by business leaders or wielded more influence with them. It helped that Mellon was one of the three wealthiest men in the nation and that he took a resolutely conservative position on most financial and economic issues. His Republican orthodoxy would have been right at home in the cabinet of Benjamin Harrison or William McKinley.[15]

That Mellon even found his way into the cabinet seemed a remarkable turn of events. The son of a wealthy Pittsburgh judge turned banker, he entered the family bank at 19 and was made owner of it at 27. Andrew displayed a gift for finding small firms with grand potential for growth, backing them, and following the family rule of plowing profits back into them. He supported chemist Charles M. Hall and his associates, who held a patent for the electrolytic manufacture of aluminum, and ended up as the major stockholder of the Aluminum Company of America (Alcoa). A loan to inventor Edward Goodrich Acheson led Mellon into becoming first a partner and then major stockholder in the Carborundum Company.

Mellon's business interests roamed far and wide. He played a key role in the founding of the Gulf Oil Corporation, established the Union Steel Company (later merged into United States Steel), created the Standard Steel Car and New York Shipbuilding companies, and transformed the small American firm of German inventor Heinrich Koppers into a giant corporation. He joined with two partners in starting Marshall-McClintic, a company that grew famous by constructing the Panama Canal, Hell Gate Bridge, George Washington Bridge, Waldorf-Astoria Hotel, and other high-profile buildings. In 1890 his father handed him control of virtually all his property. Having already founded the Union Trust Company with Frick, Andrew incorporated the family bank in 1902 as the Mellon National Bank and gradually pulled other Pittsburgh institutions into his banking orbit. His name adorned more than 60 corporations as officer or director.

Mellon possessed a huge business empire, yet prior to 1921 the public scarcely knew he existed. A slender man of medium size with a long narrow head and gray-blue eyes that kept people at a distance, he was soft-spoken and without a shred of magnetism or desire for public attention. He lived with his parents until 1900 when, at 45, he unexpectedly fell in love with a high-spirited British girl of 20 and married her. The marriage produced two children but lasted only until 1912, after which Mellon shunned social invitations and devoted himself to business, his growing art collection, and a relatively new interest: state politics. The art collection he ultimately donated to the federal government along with enough money to house it in a structure that became the National Gallery in Washington. The interest in politics led him down a road into public affairs that he had never expected to travel.[16]

Mellon and his money became vital cogs in the well-oiled Pennsylvania Republican machine. His legal counsel and close friend Philander C. Knox had been pivotal in getting Harding nominated and elected; when Harding began assembling a cabinet, Knox pushed him to name Mellon as secretary of the Treasury. Mellon accepted the position with unfeigned reluctance and entered office as the richest and least known of the cabinet members. He was 66 years old, and no one expected him to do anything more than bring his undisputed business expertise to an administration devoted to business. Certainly no one dreamed that he would occupy the office for eleven years and be hailed by some as "the greatest head of the Treasury since Hamilton."[17]

In the ballyhoo world of Washington politics, those who got to know Mellon came away impressed by what newspaperman Silas Bent called "his simplicity and dignity, his air of complete and unshakable sincerity. . . . Even those who disagree most violently with his policies admit his entire and disarming candor." Alexander Noyes found Mellon both accessible and enlightening. "His conversation," Noyes recalled, "over the in-

evitable Pittsburgh stogie, was quiet, often humorous, but always indi-
cating practical grasp of the Department's problems." The public soon
got generous doses of the brilliance and insight that had characterized
Mellon's business career. Confronted by the complex problems of war
debts, reduction of the national debt, taxation, and fiscal policy, he
showed a mastery of the issues seldom seen in public officials.[18]

The thorniest task was to reduce a national debt swollen by wartime
borrowing and also satisfy the business world's clamor for tax relief.
While Dawes rigorously slashed government expenditures, Mellon presented Congress with a tax reform program late in 1921 that outraged
progressives. He got only part of what he wanted. A divided Congress
repealed the wartime excess profits tax but cut the surtax only to 50 percent (Mellon asked for 40 percent) while raising the tax on net corporate profits from 10 to 12$1/2$ percent. To his critics Mellon professed
indifference at the effect of changes in the tax system on anyone other
than business or industry. He scoffed at the idea of using taxation to re-
distribute wealth, declaring that "I have never viewed taxation as a
means of rewarding one class of taxpayers or punishing another." In November 1923 he unveiled another tax reform plan that met a cold recep-
tion. Congress, its Republican conservative and progressive wings
bitterly divided and mindful of the approaching election, spurned Mellon's program. Instead, it left the surtax unchanged, doubled the maximum estate tax from 25 to 50 percent, created an inheritance tax, and
opened tax returns to the glare of full publicity. Grudgingly Coolidge
signed the act in June.[19]

Coolidge's landslide victory in 1924 left the congressional progressives weakened and demoralized with its sweeping affirmation of government of, by, and for business. Back came the patient Mellon with a
third tax revision plan, which in 1926 sailed through Congress with little opposition. The new act shaved the maximum income tax surcharge
and the estate tax maximum rates down to 20 percent and repealed the
gift tax. These changes benefited the wealthy, including Mellon himself, while offering little relief to ordinary taxpayers. For a person with
an income of $1 million the difference meant paying a tax of less than
$200,000 instead of $663,000; in two years rich Americans had seen
their tax load reduced by $700 million. Mellon viewed these windfalls
for the wealthy as gains for capital investment that would be a boon to
the nation. Later it would become clear that many of the wealthy had

other, less productive ideas on how to make their money earn the most handsome returns.[20]

While fighting for lower taxes, Mellon also battled to keep federal expenditures well below revenues. Most Americans applauded this effort; the balanced budget had long been a pillar of fiscal orthodoxy. With fine impartiality the secretary resisted any raid on the federal coffers as violating two of his prime objectives: minimizing the role of the federal government in economic life and building a budget surplus to pay off the national debt. On both counts he made great strides. The debt shrank from just under $24.3 billion in 1920 to $16.9 billion in 1929 despite the tax cuts. Prosperity, coupled with a decline in the federal budget from $6.6 billion in 1920 to less than $3.9 billion in 1929, enabled Mellon to run a surplus every year of the decade.[21]

The Revenue Act of February 1926 confirmed Mellon's place as the main man in the administration. Coolidge regarded him as his most trusted advisor on matters ranging far beyond fiscal matters and had a private telephone line installed to connect them. These two silent men liked and respected each other as much as they disdained personalities and styles that shouted. During the fat years Mellon's own fortune swelled even more than his reputation. The assets of Alcoa soared from $75 million in 1921 to $250 million by 1929; those of Gulf Oil, from $272 million to $761 million during the same period. His other enterprises also did well, making him one of the prime beneficiaries of the tax reductions he had sponsored. With the economy booming and the administration enormously popular, Mellon looked to a future that promised more of the same. For that to occur, he needed the cooperation of an institution he could influence but not control: the Federal Reserve Board.[22]

As the decade of the 1920s opened, the Fed was still new enough to be groping for an identity. It had been created in 1913 to provide some form of central bank for a financial system that had suffered dearly for lack of one. Despite the rapid growth of the economy between 1865 and 1910, the American banking system had remained unchanged since the National Banking Act of 1863. During these years two major problems plagued banks. The currency, which consisted mainly of bank notes, was inelastic; that is, it could not expand or contract as needs changed. National banks were required to back their notes with government bonds. Since the supply of these bonds was fixed, and the supply of other forms of money such as gold and silver varied little, the currency was too rigid to respond to large seasonal shifts in demand such as when farmers needed loans to harvest their crops and bring them to market.[23]

The second problem lay in the inability of a decentralized banking system to raise funds during a crisis. Normally country banks kept their idle cash in city banks, which in turn deposited their unused funds in larger New York banks. The New York banks put much of their cash into call loans in the stock market. Any economic downturn sent country banks scurrying to retrieve their funds, triggering a chain reaction. To meet these demands, the New York banks had to call in their stock market loans, but liquidating stocks on a falling market posed problems. In past panics, most notably the one in 1907, private bankers such as J. P. Morgan had stepped into the vacuum of authority by organizing a consortium of bankers to avert disaster. That episode, capping a dreary history of recurring panics and monetary contractions, finally spurred action to create some more permanent mechanism—under public rather than private control—to prevent future crises and provide an elastic currency system.[24]

The Federal Reserve Act created a three-tier system. At the top sat a seven-member Federal Reserve Board in Washington composed of the secretary of the Treasury and the comptroller of the currency, as ex officio members, and five members appointed by the president. To ensure their independence, the appointees were given 10-year terms and salaries equal to those of cabinet members. The next level divided the nation into 12 districts, or regions, and established a new Federal Reserve bank for each one. Each bank was to be governed by nine directors, three of them chosen from member banks in the region, three representatives of the Federal Reserve Board, and three from the ranks of business and agricultural interests in the district. The third tier consisted of member banks; every existing national bank was required to join the system or surrender its charter, while state-chartered institutions, which comprised 75 percent of all banks, had the option of joining.[25]

The district banks acted as "bankers' banks." They served as depositories for member banks, thereby concentrating reserves in only a few vaults instead of scattering them throughout the country. The Federal Reserve Board issued a new form of paper currency, the federal reserve note, to replace the old bank notes. The latter had been issued by individual banks and backed by the reserves of each one; if a bank failed, its notes became worthless. The new currency was backed by reserves, mostly in gold, held in the regional banks to an amount equal to at least 40 percent of the outstanding currency and at least 35 percent of total deposits. Although the reserve requirement placed an obvious upper limit on the amount of currency and expansion of credit, it provided far more flexibility than the old system.

The new plan also provided a more elastic credit system through what was called "rediscounting." When a member bank issued a loan to a businessman or farmer, it could transfer the note to the district reserve bank in return for either federal reserve notes or a credit on the reserve bank's books. Since the member bank charged a higher interest rate than the one it paid the reserve bank for the funds, it could make new loans before old ones were fully repaid. It was hoped that this process of rediscounting would automatically expand or contract the total amount of currency and commercial loans as the needs of business changed. More important, the Federal Reserve Board could use changes in the rediscount rate (the interest rate charged member banks) as a tool to encourage or dampen credit expansion.[26]

Born amid controversy, a child of mixed parentage with conflicting views, the new Federal Reserve System started life in November 1914 with more problems than prospects. From the first it was a prisoner of paradox: it was supposed to be firmly under public control yet free of political influence; and it was supposed to be free from dominance by private bankers, yet it was dominated by bankers. Who else, after all, understood banking? But few bankers approved of it at first; some denounced it as "authoritarian" and "socialistic," others merely as unworkable. The act offered only broad hints concerning its mission and was even more vague about the methods to be employed. Questions of scope, objectives, and techniques had to be worked out in practice.[27]

Worst of all, there existed that most fatal of flaws, a power vacuum. Nothing in the act defined the relationship among the board, the regional banks, and the member banks. Some viewed the board as a guiding hand, others as a mere coordinating entity for largely independent regional banks. Others emphasized the need to detach the system from the operations of the Treasury Department and resented the provision that the Treasury secretary was to chair the board. Here, too, experience would fill the vacuum, most likely in one of four ways: (1) each regional bank might go its own way; (2) the regional banks might act together to control policy, thereby neutralizing the board; (3) the board might assume control of the system; (4) Treasury might gain control of the system.[28]

If these problems were not enough, fate dealt the new system an unkind blow. The Federal Reserve Act had been conceived by men who assumed it would operate in the existing world of 1913 with its minimal governmental role in economic affairs, small governmental outlays and debt, world peace, a stable gold standard supported by the Bank of England, and an orderly international flow of goods and capital. Even under these conditions the Federal Reserve would have struggled to define itself and develop policies, but before its doors opened, the onset of war in Europe blew the established order of things out of existence. Foreigners bought huge amounts of goods in the United States and borrowed heavily to pay for them, sold American securities, and shipped unprecedented quantities of gold to American banks. Prices soared, and the Fed was helpless to control them. When the United States entered the war in 1917, the Fed became in effect an appendage of the Treasury Department in the all-consuming task of raising money to finance the conflict.[29]

At the war's end the gold standard was gone, and with it the old rules of international finance. With London no longer able to exert leadership, the United States found itself in possession of half the world's gold supply and a new role as its leading monetary power. Having spent its entire existence in the shadowland of wartime, the Fed had to define itself in new conditions where the old rules no longer applied and new ones had yet to be worked out. "We were a lot of 'greenhorns'," admitted banker Benjamin Strong, "with no guide or compass, no experience, no cohesion—with everything to learn, and frankly, everything to lose as the result of our inexperience." Nor did they have time to reflect or contemplate. The postwar boom with its inflationary spike demanded immediate attention. The stock market was rising, and so were brokers' loans.[30]

Sound leadership was urgently needed, but where to get it? The strongest figure on the Federal Reserve Board—and the only one with international banking experience—was Paul Warburg of Kuhn, Loeb, but his German roots put him at odds with Anglophile colleagues, and he left the board in 1918. No other member had comparable stature or experience, leaving a vacuum that was filled by someone from the most powerful and influential of the regional banks. Benjamin Strong had been appointed governor of the New York Reserve Bank in 1914 and soon made himself the dominant personality in the entire system. No

Benjamin Strong, governor of the
New York Federal Reserve Bank
and the most influential member
of the Federal Reserve System.
(Federal Reserve Bank of New York)

one did more to define the Fed or shape its operating policies and style
during the next decade.[31]

In most respects Strong resembled a member of the club and might
well have become a Morgan partner had his career not veered into the
Federal Reserve and his personal life not been stalked by tragedy. Born
into an old-line New York family that endowed him with every advantage except wealth, Strong went to work at 18 as a clerk in a financial
firm. In 1900 he quit his job to become secretary for a trust company.
When his firm merged into the Metropolitan Trust Company three
years later, Strong became secretary of the parent company. He had
married in 1895 and moved to Englewood, New Jersey, where his
neighbors included three men who were to profoundly influence his
life: Harry Davison, Thomas W. Lamont, and Dwight W. Morrow.
Eventually all three men became Morgan partners.[32]

Strong grew especially close to Davison, who in April 1904 offered
him the post of secretary with the Bankers Trust Company, which had
been organized a year earlier as a "bankers' bank" owned and controlled
by men affiliated with commercial banks. Strong accepted the offer and
in that position impressed other bankers with his work during the Panic
of 1907. While Morgan, George F. Baker, and other leading bankers

struggled to mobilize funds to keep hard-pressed banks afloat, Strong
was made head of a small committee to examine the collateral of banks
under duress and decide which institutions could be saved. His reports
served as the basis for Morgan's decisions; the experience also convinced Strong, as it did others, of the urgent need for banking reform.[33]

Before this crisis Strong had undergone an agonizing ordeal of his
own. In 1905 his wife committed suicide, leaving four small children. A
year later one of the two daughters died. Harry Davison stepped forward and took the remaining children into his own home, leaving
Strong to slake his grief with work. Two years later, at 35, he married
Katherine Converse, the shy, beautiful, 20-year-old daughter of the
president of Bankers Trust. This marriage lasted only until 1916, when
Katherine left him with their two young daughters in tow. That same
June, Strong learned that he had tuberculosis and was forced to leave
the bank until the following spring. He had lost two families and his
health, and was never to regain either of them. His only consolation
was work, into which he poured his imposing intellect and the remnants
of his energy. In this respect, as well as in his ability, he was well suited
to the demanding position of governor for the New York Federal Reserve Bank.[34]

He could not have occupied a better post, for the new order of
things after the war gave the New York bank a dominant place among
the regional institutions. It was the largest among them and located in
the city that had just become the center of global finance. Serving markets that were national and international rather than just local, the New
York bank held great prestige and exerted even greater influence. Moreover, Strong proved to be the most knowledgeable and talented man in
the system. "He was just a natural-born leader," said one admirer. "No
one else in the System was in his class." Another remarked that "wherever he sat was the head of the table." A wiry, athletic six-footer with a
long face dominated by a large nose, Strong radiated charm and
warmth, was a master of planning and organization, and understood
how to delegate responsibility and develop younger men. He also had
the courage of his convictions and the boldness to act on them.[35]

The postwar rush of events, coming on the heels of wartime abnor-
malities, tested the infant Federal Reserve System severely. Galloping
inflation and an expansive stock market convinced Strong and others
that the boom had to be punctured. However, the Treasury Department
was in 1919 trying to finance its last major bond issue, the Victory

Loan, and an increase in the rediscount rate could undermine this effort. As tension between the Treasury and the Federal Reserve Board mounted, Strong waited until November 3 for the New York bank to vote an increase in the rediscount rate from 4 to 4³/₄ percent. The stock market promptly crashed, and prices did not return to their October 1919 levels for four years. Wall Street speculators blasted the Federal Reserve, and some editors demanded that it be investigated.[36]

Undeterred, Strong argued vigorously for further rate hikes, but his health gave way. Early in 1920 he was forced to leave his post for 13 months. During his absence the board and the Treasury grudgingly conceded the need for higher rates. A series of increases pushed the rate to 7 percent by that spring. Soon afterward the inflationary spiral broke sharply and the economy plunged into a severe depression. More blame was heaped on the Fed even though other basic forces were at work. The fall election put Harding in the White House, and in March 1921 Andrew Mellon took charge of the Treasury. One of his first acts was to urge the reserve banks to lower their rate to 6 percent. The Boston bank did so within days, but Strong, just back on the job, held out until May 4, when New York reluctantly lowered its rate to 6¹/₂ percent after repeated nagging by the Federal Reserve Board. Three more reductions brought the rate down to 4¹/₂ percent by November.[37]

The economy turned around almost as quickly as it had collapsed. Between July 1921 and May 1923 the Fed's own index of industrial production rose 63 percent. During 1921 Strong brilliantly fended off a congressional inquiry about whether the Fed's various bodies had conspired to throw the country into deflation. He was less successful in explaining why the Fed had continued its tight money policy in the teeth of a depression. The basic reason was that Strong and his colleagues still thought in prewar terms and were just then groping toward some sense of what the Fed should be and do in the new postwar environment. There existed no precedent for either what the economy was enduring or what action the Fed should take. For Strong and his colleagues this ordeal was on-the-job training from which they learned much. As prosperity returned, they found themselves confronted by problems of quite another kind.[38]

Inflation remained a menace because of the huge inflow of gold from abroad, which increased reserve holdings and allowed more federal reserve notes to be issued. As reserves rose well above the legal minimum, Strong feared that they might generate political pressure for an easier monetary policy. He utilized several devices to prevent this from happening and managed to keep inflation at bay. As the economy improved, Fed officials turned to the broader question of defining what exactly it should do and what tools were at its disposal. By 1924 they had developed three objectives. The first was to promote high levels of business activity and employment while keeping prices stable. A second goal was to curb the excessive use of credit for stock market speculation, and the third was to assist in the reconstruction of monetary stability abroad.[39]

The most obvious tool to achieve these goals was manipulation of the rediscount rate, but during 1922 a promising new implement emerged almost by accident: the buying and selling of federal government securities in the open market. This function could not have been envisioned in 1914, when the national debt was less than $1 billion, but wartime borrowing had swollen the national debt to more than $25 billion, creating a large supply of government paper that was widely distributed in the hands of banks, institutions, and individual investors who had bought war bonds. At first individual banks purchased these securities simply to provide much-needed income, but Strong and others soon realized their potential as a positive instrument for regulating credit. Large purchases expanded credit by increasing the reserves of the banks that sold the securities; sales contracted it by drawing down those reserves.[40]

In 1922 the Reserve banks made their first deliberate effort to regulate credit through open-market purchases. That May they also created the so-called Governors Committee to coordinate their open-market operations. Lester V. Chandler has called the road to discovery of this tool "one of trial and error, of conflict and even at times of brilliant action taken for quite the wrong reasons." The practice promptly drew fire from Mellon, who complained of its adverse effects on Treasury operations. But Strong defended it and led a campaign to strengthen the role of the Governors Committee, which had its office in New York. He understood clearly that the New York Reserve Bank would play the lead role in the committee's work, not only because it had the most talented leadership but for the simple reason that the market for government securities was in that city. The landmark Tenth Annual Report of the Federal Reserve in 1923 made clear that open-market operations had become a regular and important tool.[41]

For Strong this triumph was short-lived. In February tuberculosis struck his throat, forcing him to take another leave until October. During this absence the Federal Reserve Board strengthened its position by asserting control over both changes in the rediscount rate and open-market operations. Helpless to take part in the heated debate that followed, Strong learned of the board's decision to dissolve the Governors Committee and replace it with the Open Market Investment Committee. "The Federal Reserve Board had no right to discharge the committee and wouldn't have done so had I had a crack at them . . . ," he wrote bitterly. "I'd see them damned before I'd be dismissed by that timid bunch."[42]

But the damage was done. "Every time the Board assumes some power like this," Strong added, "we approach nearer to actual management (instead of supervision) by a political body. And the Board will be wholly political within two years!" By 1923 one key aspect of the Fed's future was clear to Strong and to a few others as well. Ahead lay a continuing power struggle between the board and the regional banks—and especially between the board and the New York Reserve Bank. The ability of the bank to hold its own in this contest depended heavily on Strong's leadership, which in turn teetered on the state of his health. Nor did it help that Harding's appointees to the board were men lacking in both talent and banking experience. When Strong returned to duty, he prepared grimly for a long uphill struggle.

4

The Birth

of the Bull

Increasingly we enter a money and credit age. Pecuniary standards make headway over all other standards. . . . Above all, the period has witnessed the emergence of the business man as the dictator of our destinies. . . . He has ousted the statesman, the priest, the philosopher, as the creator of standards of ethics and behavior, and has become the final authority on the conduct of American society.

—Stuart Chase[1]

The politics of normalcy turned out to be the worst kind of business as usual. Warren Harding was not a bad man so much as one who was in over his head and knew it. He was by his own admission "a man of limited talents from a small town. . . . I don't seem to grasp that I am President." Nor could he grasp the complexities of the issues that confronted him. "I can't make a damn thing out of this tax problem . . . ," he once complained. "I know somewhere there is a book that will give me the truth; but hell! I couldn't read the book." One observer thought his most notable quality was the "sweetness of his nature," and he proved compassionate enough to commute the prison sentence of an aging Eugene V. Debs. In his own life, however, he was what one critic called morally slovenly. For 15 years he carried on an affair with the wife of a close friend; when that broke up, he took as a mistress a young girl of 20 who had been infatuated with him since her teens and who later bore him an illegitimate child.[2]

To the White House, Harding brought the baggage of his past in the form of cronies and sycophants who formed the Poker Cabinet and held key posts in the administration. Some were loyal and dedicated to the president; others used his trust in them to conduct graft on a scale ranging from the petty to the spectacular. Emboldened by Harding's inability to see or accept the obvious, they grew steadily more brazen until certain congressmen grew suspicious. By 1923 several investigations loomed and Harding was beset by his own financial woes. He had been playing the market heavily, using a "blind" account under an assumed name, and owed his brokers $180,000. As he left on a trip to Alaska in June 1923, clouds of scandal were fast gathering around his administration.[3]

At first Harding refused to believe the accounts of betrayal that reached him. As the evidence piled up, however, his spirits sagged. "My God, this is a hell of a job!" he lamented to William Allen White. "I have no trouble with my enemies. . . . But my damn friends . . . my God-damn friends, White, they're the ones that keep me walking the floor nights!" During the trip west, as the stream of bad news continued to swell, he stumbled lethargically through his schedule. Four days at sea revived neither his energy nor his faltering health. He fell ill, then died of an embolism on August 3. The eulogies that poured forth soon gave way to revelations of one scandal after another. The largest of them, Teapot Dome, dragged on through most of the decade. By then three of his cronies and two other participants (including oil magnate Harry F. Sinclair) had gone to jail; two others escaped jail on technicalities, one man went to the madhouse, three of Harding's cronies killed themselves, and two other men committed suicide.[4]

So sour a stench of scandal had not hung over the White House since the Grant administration. Fortunately, the man charged with clearing the air could not have been more suited to the job. Called a "Puritan in Babylon" by William Allen White, Calvin Coolidge took the oath of office in the middle of the night by the light of an oil lamp at the plain family homestead in Plymouth, Vermont. Later the contrast between this rustic scene of an earlier America and the booze- and poker-soaked saturnalias in the White House struck moralists as a harbinger of changes to come. However, they missed a more revealing omen of what the future held: after being sworn into the most important office in the land by his father, a notary public, Coolidge went back to bed.[5]

As president, Coolidge remained, in White's words, "the same shy, imprisoned soul who had puzzled men in Boston," as he had everywhere during his 24-year political career. No American ever advanced higher in station by saying less, doing less, and having less charisma. Blessed with a happy marriage to a woman he adored, Coolidge detested excess in anything—especially display, emotion, or words. He transformed the White House from a public spectacle into a private nest and drove the cook from her job with his austerity. He entertained even less often than he spoke, and with the elegance of an ascetic. His expression registered little and revealed less; a wag once quipped that he looked as if he had been weaned on a pickle. Like Ulysses S. Grant, he was living proof that still waters did not necessarily run deep.[6]

His silence was legendary but deceptive. At a social gathering Alexander Noyes tried to draw Coolidge into conversation but got only perfunctory "yes" and "no" responses even on everyday topics. When Coolidge was vice president a young woman seated next to him at dinner tried to lighten the mood by saying she had made a sizable bet that she could get him to say three words during the evening. "You lose," he retorted. Stories of his taciturn manner multiplied, yet Walter Lippmann was not alone in finding that "Silent Cal" could be quite talkative if the occasion and topic were right. Others learned that he was also a practical joker, the effect enhanced by his dry manner that made it difficult to know whether or not he was serious.[7]

Coolidge brought to the presidency changes of style rather than substance. He kept Harding's cabinet, which ranged from such heavyweights as Mellon, Charles Evans Hughes (State), Herbert Hoover (Commerce), and Henry C. Wallace (Agriculture) to deadweights like Edwin Denby (Navy) and the man who had elevated Harding to prominence and narrowly escaped prison, Harry M. Daugherty (attorney general). His political philosophy, like his values, was rooted steadfastly in another era. "It can hardly be said," wrote one observer, "that Calvin Coolidge had much to do with the twentieth century." His habits were so odd and old-fashioned that he became a public curiosity, but his belief in as little government as possible met with a groundswell of approval, especially from businessmen.[8]

Never a hard worker, Coolidge set a presidential pace unique in its inertia. After breakfast at eight he went to work at nine, lunched around half past twelve, returned to work at two or three, often took an afternoon nap, and called it a day more often than not in midafternoon. He knew how to delegate and was masterful at deflecting unwanted duties. His very manner discouraged those around him from bringing new tasks forward. Walter Lippmann took his measure with his usual acuity:

Mr. Coolidge's genius for inactivity is developed to a very high point. It is far from being an indolent activity. It is a grim, determined, alert inactivity which keeps Mr. Coolidge occupied constantly. Nobody has ever worked harder at inactivity. . . . Mr. Coolidge's inactivity is not merely the absence of activity. It is on the contrary a steady application to the task of neutralizing and thwarting political activity wherever there are signs of life. The White House is extremely sensitive to the first symptoms of any desire on the part of Congress or of the executive departments to do something, and the skill with which Mr. Coolidge can apply a wet blanket to an enthusiast is technically marvelous. . . . There has never been Mr. Coolidge's equal in the art of deflating interest.[9]

This "Puritanism de Luxe," as Lippmann called it, did much to shove the Harding scandals out of the public mind, aided by the steadily widening stream of prosperity. Above all else, Coolidge proved the perfect president for an age infatuated with business and hungry for material gain. He got the federal government out of the way of business and added his voice to the chorus of praise for the virtues of businessmen. Less than five months after taking office he uttered the first version of his famous aphorism "The business of America is business." Later he embellished this credo with what for him amounted to an outburst of poetic enthusiasm. "The man who builds a factory builds a temple," he said, "the man who works there worships there, and to each is due not scorn and blame, but reverence and praise."[10]

His approach to the highest office, Coolidge explained, was governed by "one rule of action more important than all others. It consists in never doing anything that someone else can do for you." Critics snorted and intellectuals howled in derision—no one was easier to lampoon or caricature than Coolidge—but the public loved it. He was nominated in 1924 and won in a landslide, but before the campaign had even started he suffered a personal loss from which he never fully recovered. In July one of his two sons, Calvin, died of blood poisoning contracted from a blister he got while playing lawn tennis. "If I had not been President," Coolidge mourned later in one of the few poignant passages he ever wrote, "he would not have raised a blister on his toe. . . . When he went the power and the glory of the Presidency went with him. . . . I do not know why such a price was exacted for occupying the White House."[11]

Americans loved numbers. A quantitative people who measured rather than evaluated greatness, they doted on figures of every kind, whether income or output, batting averages or stock prices, election returns or sizes of fortunes. Their sense of the present and vision of the future began with the assumption that more was better. By this criterion the fat years were indeed the golden age of better. Most of the numbers were good and growing steadily better; those that were not, it was believed, would soon improve. For a people in love with numbers, the 1920s produced numbers to love.

Unprecedented productivity fueled an expanding economy. From 1922 to 1929 the gross national product (GNP) grew at an annual rate of 4.7 percent from $75.8 billion to $104.4 billion. The combined output of agriculture, manufacturing, mining, and construction industries increased 34 percent between 1922 and 1929. While farm output grew 50 percent between 1900 and 1930, manufacturing output doubled and redoubled during that same period. Output per man-hour in manufacturing grew an astonishing 72 percent between 1919 and 1929. Between 1922 and 1929 the index of production for durable goods increased 63 percent, that of nondurable goods 39 percent. Investment in new plant rose from $11.1 billion in 1920 to $20.7 billion in 1929.[12]

New machinery run by electricity drove much of this surge in productivity. By 1929 electric motors powered 70 percent of machines compared to 30 percent in 1914. Between 1920 and 1929 net production of electric energy increased 106 percent as electricity reached many more homes and factories; while industrial and commercial use more than doubled, residential use more than tripled during the decade. Telephone use expanded about 70 percent. Two industries emerged as bellwethers of the expanding postwar economy: construction and automobiles. The estimated value of construction at current prices rose from $12.2 billion in 1919 to a peak of nearly $17.4 billion in 1928. At first a housing boom sparked the industry; when it faltered in mid-decade, commercial and industrial building picked up the slack. Automobile production rose from 1.5 million in 1921 to nearly 4.8 million in 1929. By the latter year motorcars accounted for 12.7 percent of all manufactures, employed 7.1 percent of all manufacturing workers, and paid 8.7 percent of all manufacturing wages.[13]

As productivity increased, so did income for nearly everyone except farmers. National income increased 47 percent from $59.4 billion to

Table 4.1   Comparison of Income Classes, 1927–1928 [14]

Income Classes	1927	1928
$3,000 under $5,000	1,209,345	3,114,489
$5,000 under $10,000	567,700	561,114
$10,000 under $25,000	252,079	265,438
$25,000 under $50,000	60,123	67,300
$50,000 under $100,000	22,573	26,838
$100,000 under $150,000	5,261	6,988
$150,000 under $300,000	3,873	5,605
$300,000 under $500,000	1,141	1,720
$500,000 under $1,000,000	557	971
$1,000,000 and over	290	496

$87.2 billion. Real income per capita rose 37 percent at a time when the cost of living remained stable. By contrast farmers saw their share of a rising national income drop from 57 percent in 1919 to 40 percent in 1928.[15] Prosperity still eluded an estimated 44 million people who did not earn more than $1,000 in 1926. However, the number of people with incomes above $10,000 more than doubled during the 1920s. A report by the Bureau of Internal Revenue showed impressive gains made at both ends of the income ladder between 1927 and 1928 alone (see Table 4.1).[16]

As the table indicates, the well off grew better off and the rich steadily richer. The craze for numbers found one predictable outlet in curiosity over how many millionaires the country had. As late as 1924 only 75 people reported incomes of $1 million or more. Varying estimates put the figure at 11,000 in 1926, 15,000 in 1927, and 20.000 in 1929. The Wall Street Journal reported in July 1929 that the natizn had "more multimillionaires than ever before . . . scores ot men who are now worth more than $50,000,000, dozens . . . in the $100,000,000 class, and one or more in the $1,000,000,000 class." Leading the field, in no particular order, were Mellon, Henry Ford, John D. Rockefeller Jr., and George F. Baker.[17]

For a few select people like Professor Irving Fisher, numbers themselves proved the key to a fortune. One of the most unique and versatile characters of the era, Fisher was gifted enough both to marry into

Professor Irving Fisher, the Yale economist who became one of the best known financial mavens of the era.   (Collection of the Museum of Financial History)

money and make it as well. Born in 1867, the son of a Congregationalist minister who had studied divinity at Yale, Fisher became a fixture at that institution first as a student and then as a professor. He studied both mathematics and political economy, which led him to write one of the first American works on mathematical economics and began his lifelong passion for economic measurement. His work in economic accounting and monetary theory, developed in a series of books between 1896 and 1910, earned him an enduring international reputation. No less a giant in the field of economics than Joseph Schumpeter hailed Fisher as one who would "stand in history principally as this country's greatest scientific economist."[18]

While later generations of economists revered Fisher for his pioneering work in quantification, Americans during the 1920s regarded him as a curious blend of genius and crank. He developed tuberculosis in 1898 and left Yale for three years. His recovery under the celebrated fresh-air regime of Dr. E. L. Trudeau in Saranac, New York, transformed him into an ardent disciple of healthy living. He wrote a best-selling health manual entitled *How to Live*, made regular pilgrimages to practice "biologic living" at J. H. Kellogg's famed sanitarium in Battle Creek, Michigan, became a devout prohibitionist, and urged people to regain their "pristine animal mode of living" by giving up tobacco, chewing their food thoroughly, and filling their houses with fresh air. The sophisticates in New Haven dismissed Fisher as a health faddist, but they could not treat his influence in other areas quite so lightly.

In 1893 Fisher had married Margaret Hazard, the daughter of a wealthy Rhode Island manufacturer of woolen goods, Rowland Hazard. The marriage enhanced Fisher's finances and brought him a wedding gift from Hazard in the form of a palatial house in New Haven. But Fisher was not one to rest on his good fortune. Since publishing a study called *The Purchasing Power of Money* in 1911, which presented his basic monetary equation, Fisher had measured and published each year all the relevant quantities for what he called an "equation of exchange." During the 1920s he turned part of the house into the home of his Index Number Institute, staffed by a professional economic statistician and a dozen assistants. The institute compiled a weekly report that went to newspapers throughout the world and helped spread Fisher's reputation.[19]

The institute also provided material for Fisher's 1922 study called *The Making of Index Numbers*. For the learned professor this work proved far more than an academic triumph. In 1912 he had developed a card-index system and marketed it through his Index Visible Company, which in 1926 was merged along with its chief competitor into what became Remington Rand. This business success brought Fisher considerable wealth, which he did not hesitate to pour into the many causes he took up. In 1925 he declared his primary causes to be "the abolition of war, disease, degeneracy, and instability in money." He threw himself into one campaign after another to improve the national health and even devised quantitative arguments to support his efforts. His chief weapon against degeneracy became eugenics, which led him to organize the American Eugenic Society and crusade tirelessly on behalf of "race betterment." Amid all his other work he churned out no fewer than three books on Prohibition alone.[20]

To most Americans who paid any attention to Fisher, however, he remained the numbers man—a brilliant, respected economist whose views on money, the economy, and later the stock market were worth knowing. Like many experts, he also had a talent that went unappreciated until it was too late: a gift for making predictions that seemed reasonable at the time but turned out to be spectacularly wrong. An early example surfaced in the summer of 1914, when Fisher warned that a long war in Europe would wreck the American economy. From this miscalculation Fisher moved cheerfully on with little loss of face or fortune; later mistakes would not treat him so gently.[21]

———————

The gold rush was on again, but not to California. People were still going west, and the moviemakers in particular fled to the coast, where they concocted their own world of illusion and, in the words of Robert Sklar, "gave form to a platonic conception of themselves called Hollywood." In the 1920s, however, the rainbow formed first not in the West or over the canyons of Wall Street but above the land of sunshine. As hordes of ordinary fortune seekers moved south, their motive power was not a team of sturdy oxen but the internal combustion engine. Their motive remained the same: a hunger for quick riches to turn a failed life around or transform it into a storybook chapter. They rode not in covered wagons over dusty trails but in Model T's and buses over newly paved roads. The prize they sought was not gold but land—not for anything that grew or lived on it but simply for where it was, in the newly crowned playground of America, sunny Florida, "the fair white goddess of states," as one advertisement proclaimed.[22]

For most of its history Florida had slept in splendid isolation from the rest of the nation, virtually inaccessible except by boat and later by train. Its economy depended on agriculture and a sprinkling of tourists, mostly well-off people who could afford the journey and the stay. As late as 1900 the population was only 529,000 people. By 1920 it had increased 52 percent to 968,000, and during that decade it climbed another 52 percent to 1,468,000, thanks in large part to the land boom that drew a steady stream of seekers after fortune and something else: an easier life than the one they had known. "For the first time in the national life," noted historian George Mowry, "masses of Americans sought not opportunity but indulgence . . . [spurred by] a desire to escape the harsher features of their old homes."[23]

This vision of a softer life in the sun blended nicely with the hope of striking it rich. Speculation in land was a fine old American tradition and the source of more fortunes than any other activity. Like the flu, it struck in recurring waves over the years, the virus mutating from one form to another in changing times. During World War I it had infected farmers, who overbought and overproduced until the collapse left them mired in debt and depressed prices. After the postwar recovery it spread to the suburban sprawl around nearly every city, turning fields into housing tracts, then marched downtown to send land prices spiraling upward amid the skyscraper craze. As early as 1921 the land mania reached Florida, though it did not reach epidemic form until 1924–25.[24]

New roads and improved older ones made Florida accessible to the growing legion of automobile owners yearning to visit distant, warmer places. During the winter of 1920–21 they began streaming southward from the Northeast and the Midwest, their cars crammed with tents, bedding, canned goods, and other necessities. At DeSoto Park in Tampa one flock gathered to organize the "Tin Can Tourists of the World." Gainesville, too, got a cluster of Tin Can Tourist camps, as did other towns unprepared for so large an influx of visitors. To the surprise of many people, however, the real estate epidemic struck hardest at the re-mote backwater town of Miami in Dade County, where the assessed value of property mushroomed from $63.8 million to $421 million be-tween 1922 and 1926, and building permits went from a value of around $4.5 million to more than $58.6 million.[25]

Prior to the rush, little development had taken place south of Tampa on the west coast and Jacksonville to the east. During the 1880s Henry M. Flagler, one of the Standard Oil giants, caught the Florida fever. Af-ter transforming sleepy St. Augustine into "the Newport of the South," he extended rail lines north to Jacksonville and south along the coast to Daytona and then to Palm Beach. St. Augustine drifted back into obscu-rity as Flagler built new hotels in Palm Beach and built from scratch a new playground for the wealthy called West Palm Beach. Palm Beach, with its fabulous Royal Poinciana and Breakers hotels, soon became a favorite winter resort both for the wealthy and for middle-class social climbers. Although reluctant at first, Flagler extended his rail line south-ward to Miami and built the Hotel Royal Palm there in 1896, along with an electric lighting plant and a water and sewage system.[26]

Eight other hotels helped make Miami another winter haven for the growing number of well-to-do "snowbirds," but its population of 5,471 in 1910 hardly qualified it as a boom town. By 1920 it had grown to 29,571. On the eve of World War I it was still so much a winter resort that, as one wag put it, "from Easter to Thanksgiving you could swim bare-assed in the bay." South Bay Shore Drive developed into a million-aire's row, and Palm Beach remained an exclusive bastion of old money hostile to the brash young men who had grown rich in the automotive industry and other new fields. One of them, Carl Fisher, who created the Indianapolis Speedway among other feats, set out to provide the faster new-money set with its own playground. He succeeded so well that Will Rogers dubbed him the "midwife" of Florida and said he had "rehearsed the mosquitoes till they wouldn't bite you until after you bought."[27]

In 1913 Fisher put up the money to complete a bridge from Miami to a narrow strip of land that separated Biscayne Bay from the Atlantic Ocean. He began to develop properties there and in 1915 swept them together in a new town called Miami Beach. Unlike Flagler, who favored old-money exclusivism, Fisher wanted a faster, livelier town. To promote his developments he used high-pressure advertising and concocted gimmicks such as the Miami Beach bathing beauty contest and two elephants that gave rides to children. He also became the driving force behind construction of the Dixie Highway, a north-south artery that ultimately linked Florida to Chicago and other northern centers. Fisher filled the mangrove swamps to make Biscayne Bay suitable for boating and then dredged enough mud to fill it with artificial islands, leading Rogers to quip, "Today the dredge is the national emblem of Florida." He built giant hotels, including the Flamingo, and hawked real estate especially to those with new fortunes in the auto industry. By 1920 Miami Beach counted only 644 residents, but it had become a magnet for future development.[28]

What Fisher did for Miami Beach, George Merrick did with more taste for an elegant suburb west of Miami called Coral Gables. Having made a success of his family's fruit and vegetable plantations, Merrick turned to real estate development in 1914. After developing some small subdivisions around Miami, he conceived a plan for a model city "wherein nothing would be unlovely" and spent the next decade creating it. Starting with 1,600 acres southwest of Miami, Merrick began selling lots in November 1921. The infant boom struck him early; within two years he did well enough to expand his holdings to 10,000 acres and form the Coral Gables Corporation with sales offices in New York and Chicago. Under his supervision Coral Gables developed into a meticulously planned town with wide avenues, charming residences, a 26-story hotel, a country club, golf courses, and beautiful landscaping. Even the quarry that provided rock for construction became an attraction in the form of a colorful Venetian pool.[29]

A 1923 publicity shot staged by developer Carl Fisher to attract attention to his Miami Beach properties. (Florida State Archives)

Like Fisher, Merrick excelled at promotion. He reportedly spent $3 million one year for advertising, hired a fleet of buses to haul buyers to his "perfect city," and entertained them with celebrity events. For a brief time the aged William Jennings Bryan, who had moved to Miami in 1922, used his golden voice to extol the virtues of the city. Speaking from a platform on the Venetian Pool, Bryan rhapsodized of Miami as "the only city in the world where you can tell a lie at breakfast that will come true by evening." At other times Paul Whiteman's or Jan Garber's band serenaded the prospects or Gilda Gray, the original "shimmy girl," gave the spectators her version of the shakes. Merrick sent his buses as far afield as New York, Chicago, and even San Francisco. By 1925 some 500 homes in gorgeous settings graced Coral Gables. No promoter in the madness that followed created a more impressive settlement.[30]

As the boom gathered momentum, Merrick no less than Fisher stepped up his efforts, enlisting an army of 3,000 salesmen to surround the prospects brought in free of charge by the fleet of 76 buses. Other coastal towns entered the promotional sweepstakes, each with its own catch phrase. Fort Lauderdale billed itself as the "Tropical Wonderland," Hollywood the "Golden Gate of the South," Orlando the "City Beautiful," Winter Park the "City of Homes," St. Petersburg the "Sunshine City," Sebring the "Orange Blossom City," and Fort Myers the "City of Palms." As Frederick Lewis Allen observed, "The whole strip of coast line from Palm Beach southward was being developed into an American Riviera; for sixty-odd miles it was being rapidly staked out in fifty-foot lots."[31]

In Tampa a developer named D. P. "Doc" Davis studied the rising fervor in Miami and introduced the game there by dredging and bulldozing his "Davis Islands" into existence from the marshes of Tampa Bay. On one October Saturday in 1924 he sold 300 lots within three hours for more than $1.6 million even though most of them were still under water. By the end of 1925 Davis had sold out his entire development for $18.1 million. Even snobbish Palm Beach got into the act when the brilliant if bizarre Addison Mizner envisioned the most gaudy project of all at a small place called Boca Raton south of the town. His original plans called for a 219-foot-wide highway with 20 lanes, a "Venetian canal" with powered gondolas, the usual grand hotel, an airport, golf courses, and a yacht basin. The goal was to make Boca, in the blunt words of Mizner's publicist, a "platinum sucker trap."[32]

Even these efforts paled before the madness in Miami. At the peak of the boom in 1925 some 75,000 people clogged its overcrowded streets, including 25,000 agents working out of 2,000 real estate offices. Stories of overnight fortunes trickled into city and rural newspapers, especially in the Midwest, and were followed by lavish advertising and buses emblazoned with the name of the subdivision sent to fetch prospects from Mobile, Atlanta, Columbia, or Jacksonville, where the steamboats landed loads of northerners. Long lines of Model T's—what writer C. P. Russell called the "National chariot"—streamed down the Dixie Highway in a "National hegira" that, he mused, might be the start of a "National shift in population scarcely less important in American history than the rush to California."[33]

Russell paused at a roadside grove in North Carolina to visit a caravan of 14 cars, ranging from Fords to shiny limousines, bound for the new promised land. Some were couples with children, others older folk who had sold everything to settle in sunny Florida. Many of them had never ventured far from home; this was their "Great Adventure." Some said frankly they had failed and hoped to start over again, though none admitted that they were looking to get rich quick by dealing in land. In this overland trek Russell saw a new Oregon Trail, littered not with bleached bones on barren prairie but with discarded inner tubes and empty tin cans. It was, he concluded, "the first time in history that a hegira has been carried out on pneumatic tires, upholstered seats, and patented gasoline stoves. . . . By carefully selecting their routes they are able never to be long out of sight of ham and eggs or a quart of medium oil."[34]

Another writer, Gertrude Mathews Shelby, also joined the passing parade to learn what was going on. She sniffed at once "the smell of money in Florida," which "became ripe and strong last spring. The whole United States began to catch whiffs of it. Pungent tales of immense quick wealth carried far." From it flowed a pilgrimage like no other, travelers as thick as "army ants or the seasonal flight of . . . blackbirds." On the Dixie Highway she counted license plates from 18 states from Massachusetts to Oregon. Where the gold rush had drawn lone prospectors, Florida attracted whole families with grandparents and the family dog, all crammed into the Ford for the long journey south. Discomfort mattered little to those seeking the pot at the end of the Florida rainbow.[35]

It was the stories that drew them on, and the stories were everywhere. One man picked up ocean frontage for a quarter an acre and sold it for a million; another reluctantly took 1,200 worthless acres on a debt and couldn't sell it at $10 an acre until the boom delivered him a whopping $1.2 million. A returning soldier traded his overcoat for 10 worthless acres near the beach and soon found it worth more than $25,000. A poor woman who had bought a Miami lot back in 1896 for $25 sold it during the boom for $150,000. Shelby admitted that "an old and trusted friend turned loose upon our family a colony of Florida boom bacilli." The friend had been down on his luck until he went to Florida in November 1924 and returned the following June with $100,000. His associates did even better, making $600,000 by securing remnants of coastal properties at $22 an acre and selling them quickly for an average of $200 per acre. Since the sale, the land had gone 10 times higher in price.[36]

Once on the scene, Shelby found it hard to keep her perspective. "Again and again I declared that I had no intention to buy, but nobody let me forget for an instant I was a prospect." But how to resist an epidemic? "At home I do not even play penny ante. Buying stocks on margin would never occur to me. Yet, like thousands of others, I suddenly became feverish to speculate." Within a month she had made $13,000 on a small purchase. At one point a reputable firm offered her a city lot for the surprisingly low price of $1,000. She looked into it, found a large hole in the form of a rockpit, and reflected "on the credulous millions who buy lots from plats without ever visiting the land!" One salesman, surprised by her questions about a $3,500 lot, informed her that "those things don't matter. All Florida is good. What you are really buying is . . . the climate. Or the Gulf Stream."[37]

She began to understand the frenzy around her and to comprehend the peculiar attitudes of people like the refined young lady who shared the stifling bus ride with her down the Dixie Highway toward Miami. She was a pretty brunette with a black-edged handkerchief that signaled mourning. "Florida? Wonderful!" she burbled. "Came with a special party two weeks ago. Bought the third day. Invested everything. They guarantee I'll double by February. Madly absorbing place! My husband died three weeks ago. I nursed him over a year with cancer. Yet *I've actually forgotten I ever had a husband. And I loved him, too, at that!*"[38]

Everywhere the stories intoxicated her as they did others. "When I saw the sort of people who were making actual money," she admitted, "my hesitation appeared ridiculous." A salesman told her scornfully, "The people who have made real fortunes check their brains before leaving home. Buy anywhere. You can't lose." But when she returned home, her $13,000 profit vanished with a telegram saying, "Deal off. Title defective." Still Shelby thought the boom had "many months at least to run." The Florida fever had created, in John Kenneth Galbraith's words, "a world inhabited not by people who have to be persuaded to believe but by people who want an excuse to believe."[39]

Even during the peak year of 1925 things began to go wrong. Warnings flew about the Midwest concerning scams in Florida, prompting Ohio to pass a law forbidding certain firms from selling that state's property. During the summer a fire burned down both the Breakers and the Palm Beach hotels. In August the two major rail lines in Florida, overwhelmed by the boom traffic, declared an embargo on most traffic in order to make repairs and try to recover hundreds of freight cars being used for storage. This stoppage of supplies dealt home builders a blow from which they never recovered. In desperation attempts were made to haul supplies in by water, using any vessel that would stay afloat. However, in January 1926 one such derelict ship capsized in Miami harbor and blocked all shipping for weeks. A cold wave that winter dampened enthusiasm as frost gripped central Florida. The glut of lots in and around Miami caused prices to drop for the first time, and unemployment rose.[40]

The sunshine spokesmen tried doggedly to counter the growing chorus of anti-Florida complaints throughout the country, but the old songs no longer moved a growing audience of skeptics. Real estate sales slowed, land prices dropped, and bank deposits fell off sharply during the scorching summer of 1926. "The Florida boom has collapsed," declared a writer for *The Nation* in July. "The world's greatest poker game, played with building lots instead of chips, is over. And the players are now cashing in or paying up." To ram home the point, a major hurricane devastated the Gold Coast on September 18, 1926, killing 115 people in the Miami area and drowning another 300 at Moore Haven with flood waters from Lake Okeechobee. More than 4,000 homes were destroyed between Fort Lauderdale and Miami, with property losses in the latter alone estimated at $76 million.[41]

To most newcomers, the boom—indeed, Florida itself—had been, as writer Gloria Jahoda observed, "a romance, fanned by soft trade winds from the Atlantic and the Gulf." The killer storm demonstrated to them, in the delicious phrase of Frederick Lewis Allen, "what a Soothing Tropic Wind could do when it got a running start from the West Indies."[42]

The hurricane merely added its exclamation mark to a boom that had already expired. Two New York sophisticates gave its demise a fitting epitaph. "You know what's the matter with Florida?" asked one. Replied the other, "Who cares?"[43]

But to some observers the frenzy had revealed, as historian George Soule noted, "that large numbers of people were in a mood in which they believed that money could be made almost miraculously out of the mere growth of the country." That mood or fever had run its course in Florida, at least for a time, but it did not go away. Instead it found another promising venue in which to pan for instant gold. The fact that the collapse had scarcely ruffled the nation's economy reassured those in financial markets who recognized that stocks rather than real estate were fast becoming the best game around. As the Florida rainbow vanished, leaving as always far more losers than winners in its wake, it was no accident that yet another rainbow began taking shape at almost the same time in faraway New York City.[44]

Table 4.2   Dow Jones Industrial and Rail Averages, 1920–1926[45]

Year	Indus. High	Indus. Low	Swing	Rails High	Rails Low	Swing	Volume (000's)
1920	94.27	85.93	8.35	77.85	73.07	4.78	231,104
1921	75.77	70.97	4.80	74.72	70.81	3.91	162.433
1922	95.55	90.46	5.09	86.72	82.35	4.37	277,386
1923	97.07	92.07	5.00	84.46	80.69	3.77	245,492
1924	102.75	96.88	5.87	88.41	85.06	3.35	289,237
1925	137.95	130.48	7.48	102.63	98.81	3.82	466,615
1926	157.42	148.42	9.00	116.26	111.32	4.94	462,722

The birth of the bull market went unannounced as always, and the precise date remains the subject of debate. As historian Robert Sobel observed, "The origins of bull markets cannot be discerned in retrospect. They begin slowly, gain speed and volume irregularly, and then reach a crest at the end. Picking the first moves, however, is impossible."[46] Some analysts trace its beginnings back to 1914 despite the gyrations caused by the war and the postwar depression; others point to 1923 or 1924 as the time when the market, like the economy, started an upward march interrupted only by occasional minor reverses. Table 4.2 shows the movement of the Dow Jones averages for 1921–26.

These figures show clearly the drop in the market during the depression in 1920, the strong recovery in 1922, some uncertainty in 1923, and a steady surge upward thereafter. The sharp increase in volume during 1924-26, and the growing volatility of the market as shown by the increase in swing (which is simply the gap between high and low), reveal a market on the march after 1923. This pattern is confirmed by the high and low figures for the first and last months of each year (Table 4.3).

Prior to 1924 the stock market remained pretty much its own closed world, intruding into the headlines only on those occasions when some outrage occurred. One such episode revealed the presence of the get-rich-quick virus as early as 1919, when a former vegetable dealer named Charles Ponzi concocted a scam so popular that later versions bore his name. Lacking any background in finance or investment, Ponzi solicited funds for a plan that promised handsome returns by taking advantage of differences in exchange rates. Instead he used the money that came in from gullible investors to pay the promised returns, thereby inducing

Table 4.3　Dow Jones Industrial Averages for January and December, 1920–1926

Year	Jan. High	Jan. Low	Dec. High	Dec. Low
1920	109.88	101.90	77.63	66.75
1921	76.76	72.67	81.50	78.12
1922	82.95	78.59	99.22	95.03
1923	99.42	96.96	95.61	92.64
1924	100.66	94.88	120.51	110.44
1925	123.60	119.46	157.01	152.11
1926	159.10	153.20	161.86	156.65

more people to invest. Before his house of cards collapsed, Ponzi had taken in millions of dollars, bought control of Hanover Trust Company, and treated himself to a lavish lifestyle complete with mansion and servants. He was convicted of fraud and sent to jail; while out on bail pending an appeal (which was denied), he earned another small fortune selling Florida lots.[47]

In retrospect, Ponzi could be viewed as a preview of coming attractions, as could young Allan Ryan, son of the Wall Street giant Thomas Fortune Ryan. In May 1920 Ryan engineered a corner in Stutz Motors stock only to be ruined by the officers of the New York Stock Exchange, who first suspended trading in Stutz stock to help the trapped short sellers and then declared Ryan's contracts void. When a reporter observed that no rule or precedent sanctioned such actions, an Exchange spokesman replied loftily, "The Stock Exchange can do anything." For 20 months Ryan tried through legal action to force the Exchange to relent before succumbing to bankruptcy in July 1922. His saga made neither headlines nor a dent in the inviolable fortress of the Exchange establishment, which was not to be moved by any force short of the federal government. But only a few months later another corner did push stocks into prominence, thanks in part to Jesse Livermore.[48]

The Piggly Wiggly episode embodied much of what was to come during the 1920s. Memphis entrepreneur Clarence Saunders founded the Piggly Wiggly chain of groceries in 1919 with a unique twist: his stores were the first to feature complete self-service. Customers entered through a turnstile, made their selections, and paid the cashier on leaving. On this simple premise Saunders built an empire of more than

1,200 stores by 1922. In November, however, a bear raid on his stock so angered him that he sought revenge by hiring Livermore to engineer a corner. The bears had driven the stock from the 50s down below 40; Livermore's patient buying sent it back up past 60 by January 1923 to a high of 75¹/₂ in March. By then Saunders had also accumulated 198,872 of the 200,000 shares outstanding, but his peculiar style had made Livermore so uneasy that he quit the operation.[49]

Cornering a stock means gaining control of virtually the entire supply of it. When a stock moves upward, bear operators and some outside investors sell it short and expect to profit by buying it later when the price has dropped again. Under normal circumstances they would borrow (for a fee) the necessary shares from a broker to cover their contracts, but eventually they must go into the market to replace those borrowed. Unaware that Saunders had a corner, they assumed that plenty of shares would be available at low prices. By cornering the stock before the bears realized what had happened, Saunders could force the bears to pay an exorbitant price for enough shares to cover their contracts and thus exact revenge on them that was both sweet and profitable.

With a corner assured, Saunders asked Livermore to return long enough to spring the trap. When Livermore refused, Saunders did it himself. On March 20 he called for delivery of all the stock he had bought. As the bears scrambled to find stock to meet their obligations, they drove the price to 124 before the governors of the Exchange unexpectedly intervened to suspend trading in Piggly Wiggly stock. A few days later they struck the stock permanently from the trading list and granted the short sellers (many of whom, unlike Saunders, were thought to be members of the Exchange) five extra days to fulfill their contracts. Like Ryan before him, Saunders protested that the suspension violated the rules of the Exchange. "It is unbelievable to me," he sputtered, "that the august and all-powerful New York Stock Exchange is a welcher."[50]

When his protests went unheeded, Saunders found his position undermined. He had borrowed millions from some southern banks to buy all the Piggly Wiggly shares and counted on unloading much of the stock to the trapped bears at high prices to repay his loans. Thwarted by the Exchange, Saunders had to sell off some of his stores, turn over the rest to his creditors, and resign as president of the company. He spent three futile years trying to avenge the wrongs done him, then moved on to other ventures. In the end the episode—billed as the last corner on the Exchange—ruined Saunders while enhancing Livermore's reputation. Two years after the corner fiasco, the Exchange quietly amended its constitution by allowing the governing committee to postpone the time for deliveries on contracts. Amid the flurry of publicity generated by the fight, a revealing consequence of the deal went unnoticed: one of the most prosperous and innovative businesses in the country had been transformed into a market play, reduced to one more sordid imbroglio on the Exchange.[51]

By 1924 the stock market was attracting more attention from a wider public as well as professionals on the Street. During the early 1920s most new investors bought bonds rather than stocks. The wartime experience had made bonds familiar, and the large retailers like Charley Mitchell's National City Company specialized in them. But the action seemed to be moving toward equities. The election of Coolidge in November 1924 gave a boost to business confidence, as did the continued strength of most economic indicators. In May the *New York Times* industrial average stood at 106; it reached 134 by the end of the year and 181 by the end of 1925. The Dow Jones industrial average highs gained a mere 3 percent between 1920 and 1923 but soared 53 percent between 1924 and 1926. Even the more stolid railroad average highs moved up 32 percent, compared with 8 percent during 1920–23.[52]

Jesse Livermore had gone bullish. As early as the summer of 1922 he advised the public in an interview to "drop their wartime reasoning" and "adjust themselves to post-war conditions." His newfound prosperity allowed him once again to enjoy long winter vacations at the Breakers in Palm Beach and to indulge his passion for fishing, but even there he was seldom far from the E. F. Hutton office. The Piggly Wiggly episode and some pool operations had made him one of the market spokesmen sought out by the newspapers. During his winter sojourn in 1924, however, the rumor circulated that Livermore had again gone bearish. Richard D. Wyckoff, proprietor of the *Magazine of Wall Street*, personally saw enough to convince him that Livermore was trying to depress the market and was astonished. "We read out of the same book—the tape . . . ," Wyckoff noted. "The tape was telling me, was telling him the same thing. 'Buy, buy, buy,' it was saying. I did what the tape told me, and he did the opposite."[53]

Wyckoff thought that somebody—he never found out who—was out to get Livermore and trapped him into heavy losses on the bear side. In July 1924 Livermore denied that he had suffered serious losses and insisted that he had been active only in the grain market. Whether true or not, the admission offered a clue to his major blunder that year: getting on the bear side of wheat. This venture was to pit him against a formidable newcomer to speculative stardom, Arthur Cutten, at a time when the markets smiled much more favorably on bulls than bears.[54]

5

The

Good Life

Sell them their dreams. . . . Sell them what they longed for and hoped for and almost despaired of having. Sell them hats by splashing sunlight across them. Sell them dreams—dreams of country clubs and proms and visions of what might happen if only. After all, people don't buy things to have things. They buy things to work for them. They buy hope—hope of what your merchandise will do for them. Sell them this hope and you won't have to worry about selling them goods.

—Helen Landon Cass (1923)[1]

Since the days of the first settlements, religion had served as a bedrock for Americans, fortifying them against life's hardships and providing consolation for its sorrows. Changing times strained this role by making life easier and religion more complicated in both form and content. Church leaders and their flocks had to confront the challenge of scientific ideas and the more insidious menace of material progress that changed daily life in ways more secular than spiritual. Those who resented these forces clung fiercely to the "old-time religion" or "fundamentalism" (a name given it during the 1910s), which resisted not only newfangled ideas in religion but modernism in all its guises.[2]

This clash found its showcase in the celebrated Scopes trial of 1925, but less publicized efforts took place across the nation. Fundamentalists took the fight against evolution to the floors of half the state legislatures and tried with equal vigor to inject the Bible into education. By

1927 11 states had laws that required daily Bible readings in public schools, and more than half the states gave high school credit for Bible study done in church schools. To the hardcore like the Holy Rollers, however, education itself was a curse. "I ain't got no learnin' an' never had none . . . ," cried preacher Joe Leffew to the faithful at a revival held in Dayton, Tennessee, during the Scopes trial. "Some folks work their hands off'n . . . to give their young-uns education, and all they do is send their young-uns to hell. . . . I've got eight young-uns in the cabin and three in glory, and I know they're in glory because I never learned 'em nothin'."[3]

It was easy to make fun of the Holy Rollers and other evangelists, but the plea for a return to old-time values came from some business circles as well. "The essentially sound and more dependable elements of American citizenship . . . ," declared John E. Edgerton of the National Association of Manufacturers in 1924, "are getting tired of chasing the will-o'-wisps of radicalism in government, in religion, in art, and in social life, and are about ready to return to the God, the Bible, and the fundamental principles of their forefathers." Even some businessmen who considered themselves progressive had little tolerance for the heresies of modernism in which change had become a way of life and a blatant repudiation of older values and ideals.[4]

This outburst of fundamentalism in all its forms bore witness to the changing role of religion in American society. Although the number of Christian churches and Jewish synagogues rose from 210,000 in 1910 to 236,000 in 1926, and more than half of Americans over the age of 13 belonged to some church, the number of clergy declined and their influence diminished. More people went to church, but religion played less of a role in their lives. The most visible and vivid symbol of this change could be seen on the skylines of cities and town. For generations church spires had reigned unchallenged; in recent years, however, they had been dwarfed by skyscrapers and swallowed by other buildings. Even on Wall Street itself Trinity Church had dominated in 1900 only to be upstaged by a flurry of new construction that by 1929 had turned the street into a canyon.[5]

Fundamentalism drew its strength from rural and small-town America, but elsewhere a new and more ecumenical religion was rising. Robert and Mary Lynd found in "Middletown" (their nom de plume for Muncie, Indiana) "a strong disposition to identify the church with religion and church-going with being religious," and something more:

"Middletown is a friendly city, a heavily Christian city. . . . But money income is its personal and community blood stream." It was also becoming the medium through which social status, once the reward of familiarity acquired over generations, could be bought rather than earned. "You see," observed an older resident, "they know money and they don't know you."[6]

Henry Ford was reputed to have said that machinery was the new messiah; an even more modern version might have been "Money is the new messiah." Like religion it came in many denominations and took many forms. Its disciples took many paths to enlightenment, and their gospels often diverged, but during the 1920s many if not most Americans agreed on the core faith and worshiped the divine dollar.

Coolidge had called the factory a temple and work a form of worship, but business itself was fast becoming the new religion. "The new faith permeated the churches, the courts, the colleges, the press," wrote historian Arthur M. Schlesinger. "It created a literature of complacency, . . . an economics of success and a metaphysics of optimism. . . . For the true believer, its commandment was Service, its sacrament the weekly lunches of fellowship at Kiwanis or Rotary, its ritual the collective chanting of cheerful songs, its theologian a New York advertising man named Bruce Barton. . . . Salvation was to be measured by success; and success thus became the visible evidence of spiritual merit." Barton's most notable contribution, apart from his unflagging optimism, was a 1925 book called *The Man Nobody Knows*, which recast Jesus Christ as history's greatest executive, who had "picked up twelve men from the bottom ranks of business and forged them into an organization that conquered the world."[7]

As early as 1921 one evangelist of business sang its praise in unequivocal terms. "Thru business, properly conceived, managed and conducted," he prophesied, "the human race is finally to be redeemed. . . . The finest game is business. . . . The soundest science is business. . . . The truest art is business. . . . The fullest education is business. . . . The fairest opportunity is business. . . . The cleanest philanthropy is business. . . . The sanest religion is business. Any relationship that forces a man to follow the Golden Rule rightfully belongs amid the ceremonials of the church. A great business enterprise includes and presupposes this relationship." A few years later Silas Bent confirmed the arrival of this new religion. "The dollar is our Almighty," he observed. "Prosperity is considered a kind of morality. . . . There has been a general substitution

. . . of the religion of material progress for the political ideals which animated this republic during its first century." The scale of this transformation amazed and appalled him. "Our multimillionaires are the hierarchy of a new American faith, the religion of prosperity," he wrote. Andrew Mellon . . . is the Pope of this religion." By no means was this new creed confined to big cities and wealthy people.[8]

Just as business became a religion, so did religion become more than ever a business. "Since 1900," reported one study, "the church has been forced to compete more and more with an ever increasing number of secular agencies and activities." The tradition of strictly observing the Sabbath gave way to the Sunday drive or baseball game or movie or other pleasurable outing. A few diehard cities such as Boston, Philadelphia, and Pittsburgh clung doggedly to blue laws banning major league games on Sunday, but elsewhere the restrictions had long vanished. Even worse, the faithful had grown more perfunctory in their devotion. "Three things may bind a member to his church: money contribution, attendance at services, and church work," noted the Lynds. "Of these the last is, according to the ministers, the least common."[9]

The new gospel required new forms of worship. Some traditional churches responded by adopting the new style of business. "Come to Church," exhorted the billboard of one New York church. "Christian Worship Increases Your Efficiency." Modernist pastors adopted the adman's art; one called his sermon "Solomon, a Six-Cylinder Sport," while another billed the Trinity as "Three-in-One Oil." But advertising proved just as capable of dragging the sacred wholly into the profane. As Edith Lewis of the J. Walter Thompson agency enthused, "You can write as emotionally about ham as about Christianity." Nevertheless, advocates of the modernist movement departed from the old-time religion in several ways. They played down traditional dogma and ritual, offered an easier, more smoothly paved road to heaven, and dressed up the stark traditions of Protestant sects with more pleasing and elegant trappings.[10]

The most flamboyant recasting of religion came from a new breed of evangelists who fused elements of fundamentalism, business, and advertising into a spectacle of showmanship. No one utilized this blend of revivalism and vaudeville more expertly than Aimee Semple McPherson, who rose from obscurity to become a national icon of salvation and scandal. Once widowed and once divorced, the mother of two, McPherson honed her message by holding revival meetings up and down the eastern seaboard, across the continent, and even over the Pa-

STRETCHER DAY AT REVIVAL
MUNICIPAL AUDITORIUM
DENVER, COLORADO.

Evangelist Aimee Semple McPherson, whose career would fuse fundamentalism, celebrity, and scandal.   (Library of Congress)

cific Ocean before taking her Four Square Gospel to roost in California
in 1921. A series of revivals in San Diego, capped by a great outdoor
healing session in Balboa Park, vaulted her to fame. She moved to Los
Angeles to found the temple of her dreams in the land of dreams.[11]

Her timing proved immaculate. During the decade more than 1.2 million newcomers invaded Los Angeles County; most of those who embraced Aimee's message were "converts from the orthodox Protestant
creeds, migrants from small-town and farming areas in the Middle West."
McPherson enticed them with an irresistible blend of a simple four-point
gospel, mesmerizing showmanship, an uncanny flair for publicity, and a
striking gift for casting herself in the role of a messiah. To the faithful she
tendered not hell and damnation but a soothing, stirring brew of "flowers, music, golden trumpets, red robes, angels, incense, nonsense, and
sex appeal." On the first day of 1923 her Angelus Temple opened. A
study in ugliness valued at $1.5 million, the temple seated 5,000 in the
auditorium and featured its own radio station, a commissary, a theologi-
cal seminary for her "students," a rotating, electrified cross on top that
could be seen 50 miles away, and a "Miracle Room" for collecting the discarded crutches, trusses, and wheelchairs of the healed.[12]

Money poured in from tens of thousands of faithful, for which they received both healing and entertainment along with the Four Square Gospel. The Gospel Lighthouse featured staged rescues underscored by the theme song "Throw Out the Life Line!" At the temple she once staged a dramatization of the clash between good and evil complete with illuminated scoreboard. The audience watched breathlessly as the forces of Good scaled mountains and ravines amid gunfire and artillery to assault the citadel of Evil. As Evil withdrew before the attack, a miniature blimp floated over the terrain until a shot from a Good soldier exploded it and dumped onto the stage an ugly, grimacing Devil. While the audience cheered, a spotlight illuminated an unfurling American flag. "To visit Angelus Temple . . . ," marveled one critic, "is to go on a sensuous debauch served up in the name of religion."[13]

The religion of business was far more prosaic. Unlike McPherson's, it had no house of its own; it worshiped at the shrine of progress and preached a gospel of the good life that appealed to many more thousands than even Aimee could attract. But a common thread connected them. As one observer noted, McPherson "substituted the Gospel of Love for the Gospel of Fear. . . . The gospel she created was and is an ideal bed-time story. It has a pretty color, a sweet taste, and is easy for the patients to take. She threatens nothing; she promises everything." Much the same could be said of the emerging new consumer economy and its special ministry, the advertising industry.[14]

McPherson guaranteed the faithful access to the hereafter on a kind of "pay now, buy later" basis. The consumer economy offered even ordinary people a taste of the good life here and now on a "buy now, pay later" plan. In this sense heaven, too, was on the move, coming down to the earth in the form of a growing array of material possessions, creature comforts, technological marvels, and entertaining diversions. For those who could afford it, the good life offered an immediate gratification to masses of people that contrasted sharply with the traditional ethic of sacrifice, scrimp, and save. In the burgeoning new material civilization the pleasures of this world held far more appeal than the promise of the next. The old-time fear and dread over salvation of the soul lost its grip on those entranced by the feeding of newly awakened appetites of the body.

The scrimp-and-save generations had little choice in the ethic that shaped their habits. Most people had neither money to buy things with nor time to enjoy them, and there were far fewer goods to buy or enjoy. They were neither purer of heart nor more moral than the consumer goods generation but simply the product of their times. They cared more for the simpler things of life because those things filled far more of their life than they did for later generations. The transition from a "home-made" to a "store-bought" world of goods was an economic revolution that profoundly affected values of all kinds. Among other changes it ushered in an age of materialism with a vastly broader base of participants than had ever existed in America or anywhere else.[15]

French social philosopher Gilles Lipovetsky identified the three key features of a consumer society as "an abundance of goods and services, a cult of objects and leisure, [and] a hedonistic and materialistic morality." All three could be found broadening their influence in the American experience of the 1920s. Bernard Baruch understood the importance of desire for goods not only in terms of self-indulgence but also in terms of its critical role for the expansion of business. "The desire for more and better things—for a higher standard of living—is the real beginning of increased business," he observed. "Until people are conscious of the want for an article there can be no real market for that article."[16]

The good life of the consumer economy revolved around things— more things, better things, and the promise of still more and better things to come. "This is our proudest boast," wrote one skeptic, Samuel Strauss. " 'The American citizen has more comforts and conveniences than kings had two hundred years ago.' . . . The first condition of our civilization . . . is that we must turn out ever larger quantities of things; more this year than last year, more next year than this." This new state of things, which he called "consumptionism," posed a revolutionary new dilemma: "Through the centuries, the problem had been how to produce enough of the things men wanted; the problem now is how to make men want and use more than enough things."[17]

Mass production and the growing efficiency of American manufacturing kept widening the stream of things. "For the country as a whole . . . ," noted one survey, "even in geographically remote and socially isolated or sluggish areas, the greater availability of goods today as compared with a generation ago is marked." But things cost money, which meant that, as Stuart Chase observed, "money has become the *sine qua non* of existence." And it was for spending rather than saving: "Mass consumption has also dealt a body blow to the time honored doctrine of thrift. We are urged on the highest authority to spend rather than save. . . . This strange doctrine would have horrified our grandfathers."[18]

The basic elements of the consumer economy had been developing since the turn of the century. Rising incomes gave millions of families more money to spend, new productive miracles of American industry gave them more goods to buy, and shortened work hours gave them more time to enjoy what they bought. Bernard Baruch understood the formula better than most businessmen. "We know now," he explained, "that low wages mean low purchasing power, and that only in proportion as men and women have money to spend and hours in which to enjoy the fruits of their expenditure, can our productive capacity be kept fully employed." One advertisement linked these factors even more succinctly: "America's Greatest Discovery Was—That a millionaire cannot wear 10,000 pairs of $10 shoes. But a hundred thousand others can if they've got the $10 to pay for them, and the leisure to show them off."[19]

These factors came together after the war, driven in part by the ability of industry to provide not only more goods but a steady stream of new goods as well. The spread of residential electricity enabled people to fill their homes with appliances that made daily chores easier and life more pleasant. Radio, at first a prisoner of battery power, exploded into a major entertainment form as an electrical appliance; the 60,000 sets in use during 1922 mushroomed to 7.5 million by 1928. Rayon, a new fabric billed as "artificial silk," helped make clothes cheaper and more stylish; sales of the new material jumped from 9.2 million pounds in 1919 to 96.3 million in 1927. During the seven fat years consumer spending rose 23 percent; the outlay for durable goods increased 33 percent, and that for services 26 percent.[20]

Another basic tendency soon emerged: goods that began life as luxuries came quickly to be viewed as necessities. The automobile was the most obvious example. As expectations rose, variety became the spice of consumer life. A leading Chicago shoe retailer offered 375 styles for men in 1928 compared to 175 in 1920, and a thousand for women in 1928 compared to half that number in 1920. The Holeproof Hosiery Company's line of 480 items in 1920 soared to 6,006 items by 1927. The old pattern of seasonal changes in styles evolved into one that saw changes in merchandise occur from one month to the next. "The style expert," noted one observer, "began to be supplemented by the style forecaster." One large midwestern dry goods wholesaler estimated that 20 percent of his items became obsolete before they could be sold.[21]

The consumer economy evolved into a vast engine fueled by buyer demand, which required not only a constant desire for things but a steady supply of funds to purchase them. During the 1920s advertising fanned the flame of desire while new forms of credit—most notably installment buying—enabled people to buy more goods faster. Neither was new in American life, but they assumed innovative new forms and exerted a far greater influence than ever before. Together they transformed America into what historian William Leach has called the "Land of Desire." Their task was made easier by the fact that, as one survey noted, "people with more than their accustomed sums of money to spend do not know from past experience how they can get the most satisfaction. . . . Hence they are more than usually open to suggestions conveyed by advertising, or the examples of others."[22]

Advertising emerged as a big business during the 1920s, when total expenditures by one estimate more than doubled, and by another jumped from $2.3 billion in 1919 to $3.4 billion in 1929. President Coolidge ordained it as the official theology of the consumer economy, saying in 1926:[23]

> It informs the readers . . . of the existence and nature of commodities . . . and creates for them a wider demand. It is the most potent influence in adopting and changing the habits and modes of life, affecting what we eat, what we wear, and the work and play of the whole nation. . . . Mass production is only possible where there is mass demand. Mass demand has been created almost entirely through the development of advertising. . . . Modern business . . . constantly requires publicity. It is not enough that goods are made—a demand for them must also be made."

As the industry grew, its techniques became increasingly sophisticated. Psychology, which became the rage in many areas of American life, emerged as a major tool for reaching consumers. Ad men eagerly embraced the notions of Professor Walter Dill Scott at Northwestern, the first advocate of scientific advertising, and behaviorist John Watson, a pioneer in market research. Watson joined Scott in a consulting company and, having lost his academic position at Johns Hopkins in 1920 for sexual misconduct, turned up four years later as vice president of a major advertising agency. His work in market research helped advertisers discover, in the words of Michael Schudson, that "there are two sexes and that women, not men, are the primary consumers in American culture. . . . It was a cliché among advertisers by the 1920s that women are the 'purchasing agents' of their families." One estimate claimed that women bought 70 percent of the manufactured goods sold.[24]

The psychological approach emphasized tapping some basic human need and linking the product to it. One study conceded that that "the business of selling commercial products as substitutive reactions for more subtle forms of adjustment to job insecurity, social insecurity, monotony, loneliness, failure to marry, and other situations of tension has advanced to an effective fine art. The tendency of contemporary merchandising is to elevate more and more commodities to the class of personality buffers. At each exposed point the alert merchandiser is ready with a panacea." Products became "new therapeutic vehicles for temporary escape." In more old-fashioned terms, advertisements "set forth what our forefathers would have called temptations."[25]

For advertising people, manipulation became the new messiah. "The object of all advertising is to stimulate the desire to buy," stressed Earnest Elmo Calkins, one of the pioneer ad men who did much to bring artistic respectability to the profession. Psychology was a useful tool because, among other things, it revealed a crucial paradox of consumerism: people bought goods to gain satisfaction, but the more they bought the more dissatisfied they became. To turn goods rapidly and in great quantity, the consumer economy had to be rooted in *dissatisfaction*: however much one had, it was never enough. Calkins understood exactly what role advertising played in this paradox. "The purpose is to make the customer discontented with his old type of fountain pen, kitchen utensil or motor car," he explained, "because it is old fashioned, out-of-date. The technical term for this is obsoletism. We no longer wait for things to wear out. We displace them with others that are not more effective but more attractive."[26]

Bruce Barton echoed this insight. "The American conception of advertising," he proclaimed, "is to arouse desires and stimulate wants, to make people dissatisfied with the old and out-of-date and by constant iteration to send them to work harder to get the latest model—whether that model be an icebox or a rug, or a new home." Goods also served as a marker of social status in a nation where the old touchstones of identity were fading. This new social competition found expression in the phrase "keeping up with the Joneses," drawn from a popular comic strip. Fashion was the mechanism that kept desire churning. Already in place on the eve of the war, it "pressed people to buy, dispose of, and buy again. . . . Fashion was the thing itself—the 'new,' the heart, supposedly, of what was desired." William Leach offers this summary of its function:[27]

> Its intent was to make women (and to a lesser degree men) feel special, to give them opportunities for playacting, and to lift them into a world of luxury or pseudo-luxury, beyond work, drudgery, bills, and the humdrum of everyday. Its effect was often to stir up restlessness and anxiety, especially in a society where class lines were blurred or denied, where men and women fought for the same status and wealth, and where people feared being left out or scorned because they could not keep up with others and could not afford the same things other people had.

This new social arms race required a steady flow of money or new forms of credit like installment buying. In effect, advertisements created an appetite that installment buying made it possible to satisfy at once. The practice of buying on time had been around since the late nineteenth century, but it had been used mainly by the poor or to handle large purchases. However, even proper middle-class people who had shunned debt because it violated the Protestant ethic of saving were enticed into using the credit offered by department stores long before the war. During the 1920s people of all classes happily bought items of every kind on the installment plan. Economist Edwin R. A. Seligman estimated in 1927 that more than 75 percent of automobiles were purchased this way and that by 1925 more than 70 percent of furniture, 75 percent of radios, 90 percent of pianos, 80 percent of phonographs, and about 80 percent of household appliances were acquired by time payments.[28]

This ingenious device did more than solve the problem of providing buyers with the means of keeping up with a never-ending parade of goods and changing fashions. It also elevated credit into a sizable industry. Prior to World War I the sources of consumer credit consisted of a few banks and lending societies, pawnbrokers, department stores, some merchants, and purveyors of expensive goods like furniture, pianos, and sewing machines. During the 1920s a specialized new breed of financial institution, the sales finance company, emerged to dominate consumer credit. Fewer than a hundred such firms existed in 1920; by 1928 there were more than a thousand. Most of the early companies, like General Motors' pioneering GMAC (1919), were created by large manufacturers to handle financing of their products.[29]

As the old inhibitions against installment buying broke down and the new credit companies reaped large profits, traditional banks soon got the message. Charley Mitchell led the charge into the new era when National City Bank established in 1928 a Personal Loan Department to lend up to $1,000 "without collateral to salaried men and women" at 6 percent interest, repayable within a year. It was, Mitchell stressed, part of his plan to bring the bank closer to the people of New York City. One observer hailed it as "a new instrument of credit . . . like the install-ment purchase plan, another encouragement to average men and women to go into debt and then work themselves out again." Seligman also praised the new service. "Installment credit," he observed, "is begin-ning to do for the consumer what the gradual development of the com-mercial banking system has done for the producer."[30]

Buying on time had become respectable, but was it wise or even safe? A small-town banker disliked the way consumption chained a man to mountains of debt. "All he earns must be applied to his debts, and he now has no margin of safety at all," he noted. "Before he was sure of his ground and free from anxiety. Now, he must not only work, but he must also worry." The president of Studebaker Company wondered in the fall of 1925 whether, with 75 percent of all car sales being done on the in-stallment plan and about $1.4 billion in installment credit outstanding, a depression might not create "an awkward situation." But such concerns scarcely ruffled those eager for the good life and were more than offset by assurances that all was well. Indeed, Herbert Hoover, then secretary of commerce, talked of underconsumption as a social liability and wor-ried that Americans might be saving too much and spending too little.[31]

————

The good life involved not only new things but a variety of new plea-sures as well. Consumption itself became a kind of lifestyle steeped in small comforts and attentions once reserved for the wealthy. Depart-ment stores, merchants, hotels, and restaurants immersed customers in amenities, elegant, often stunning decors, and lavish services. This pam-pering lifted the clientele, however briefly, out of the ordinary world of toil and troubles into one of ease and blissful repose. It also underscored a major element of the good life: escape from the mundane pressures of life into a realm of fantasy or illusion that could be as restful or exciting as one chose. In this sense the good life, like Aimee Semple McPherson's brand of religion, was not of this earth although very much rooted in the things and pleasures of it.[32]

Technology drove this transformation in ways no one could have foreseen. During the late 19th century an earlier generation had learned how new technologies could profoundly change their lives by radically increasing productivity. Later generations discovered how still newer technologies could enhance their lives by providing a host of consumer goods and devices for their comfort, convenience, pleasure, and escape. Considerable attention has been given to the role of technology in the first three of these effects; little has been paid to the last. Yet in many respects it may have had the most lasting influence. The new technologies created not only new lifestyles but also new realities—or rather illusions of reality.

The automobile offered escape by giving even ordinary people mobility they had never before experienced. "Beside the elation of sheer speed and its power to determine social position," wrote Stuart Chase, the car promised "romance, adventure, and escape from the monotony which all too often characterizes modern life. . . . It has captured our psychological *interest* as nothing has ever done before, and as perhaps nothing will ever do again." It had another, less alluring effect as well. "At first I carefully set down all expenses connected with my car . . . ," admitted a small-town banker, "but the figures mounted up so fast that I dared not look the facts in the face. . . . My thrift habits were steadily giving way to spendthrift habits. . . . The result upon the individual is to break down his sense of values. Whether he will or no, he must spend money at every turn. . . . Many families live on the brink of danger all the time. They are car-poor."[33]

If cars provided physical freedom as well as thrills, motion pictures offered escape from the everyday world of routine into one of fantasy and illusion. "Go to a motion picture . . . and let yourself go," blared an ad in the *Saturday Evening Post*. "Before you know it you are *living* the story—laughing, loving, hating, struggling, winning! All the adventure, all the romance, all the excitement you lack in your daily life are in _____ Pictures. They take you completely out of yourself into a wonderful new world . . . out of the cage of everyday existence! If only for an afternoon or an evening—escape!"[34]

No new technology had a more compelling or complex impact on people. The very essence of that impact lay in a paradox that was at the heart of films: they seemed so real yet were entirely unreal. They provided, in the words of Daniel Bell, "a set of ready-made daydreams, fantasy and projection, escapism and omnipotence" that also became the most powerful classroom in America for educating the young and gradually their elders as well in everything from fashion to behavior to sex. "Our children," protested one critic as early as 1921, "are rapidly becoming what they see in the movies." Historian Robert Sklar noted that "before the movies, the art of love played almost no part in the culture's public curriculum. In movies, however, it became the major course of study."[35]

Films not only instructed people in a wide curriculum of subjects but also helped shape their attitudes and social values. Like the automobile they offered a private refuge from the pressures of the outside world; the theater was a dark cavern into which no parent, boss, spouse, or anyone else could intrude and in which the mind was free to roam wherever the picture took it. For many people the movies became a peculiar kind of "real world" with which they identified in intensely personal ways. The editors of popular motion picture magazines found themselves deluged with letters (over 80,000 a year in one case) of a deeply personal nature from people "filled with self-revelations which indicate . . . the influence of the screen upon manners, dress, codes and matters of romance."[36]

For women, who made up most of the audience, the great picture palaces in the big cities provided not only entertainment but pampering as well as fantasy. "When she goes home that evening," observed a writer, "she will perhaps clean spinach and peel onions, but for a few hours, attendants bow to her, doormen tip their hats, and a maid curtsies to her in the ladies' washroom. . . . Romantic music . . . gives her a pleasant sensation of tingling. Her husband is busy elsewhere; and on this music, as on a mildly erotic bridge, she can let her fancies slip through the darkened atmosphere to the screen, where they drift in rhapsodic amours with handsome stars. . . . The blue dusk of the 'de luxe' house has dissolved the Puritan strictures she had absorbed as a child."[37]

Movies became one of the most potent marketing forces of the era. "Few people realize how great is the power of the screen in diffusing fashion news," wrote Elizabeth Hurlock. "There are few villages of any size in America where moving pictures have not penetrated." The films were in many places "the only form of diversion from the monotony of everyday existence. . . . What is true of the small towns is equally true of the large cities. Many people form their standards of living from the pictures they see and unquestionably the styles portrayed make such an impression." Hurlock had watched the rage for Mary Pickford's curls give way to the bob popularized by Gloria Swanson along with the "robe de style type of evening dress." She also attributed the current craze for thinness to the movies. "All screen heroines are slender," she noted, "and each woman, as she watched them, decided that she must be slender, too."[38]

Commercial interests were quick to grasp the marketing possibilities in these connections. By the time a film opened, stores often had knockoff versions of the clothes worn by the stars on the racks. Although the demand for any given fashion could not be predicted, the power of movies lay in the fact that they had a captive and fast-growing audience. Attendance at movies already averaged about 40 million people a week in 1921 and doubled that number by 1929. By mid-decade the film industry had become the fourth largest in the nation, with a capital investment of more than $1.5 billion. In 1927 the country had about 20,500 theaters—half of them in towns with fewer than 5,000 inhabitants—with a seating capacity of 18 million. Movie stars achieved a level of fame and recognition unknown in history. One writer mused that a few years in films had made Charlie Chaplin "known by name and sight to more of his contemporaries in all lands than any man who has ever lived."[39]

On the heels of the movies came yet another revolution in entertainment. The motion picture gave people a place to go; radio brought pleasure and escape into the home. The phonograph and its predecessors began this process by enabling millions of people for the first time to hear music on demand without live performers. Radio topped this feat by bringing into the home not only music (live and recorded) but news, sports, lectures, political speeches, drama, comedy, interviews, and just plain talk. It began modestly on November 2, 1920, when KDKA commenced broadcasting a daily schedule with returns from the presidential election. In 1922 daily broadcasts of news, music, and Sunday sermons came to New York. That same year AT&T used its telephone lines to link several stations with WEAF in New York as the center and began to sell advertising time. By the year's end 508 stations were on the air nationwide.[40]

Growth came rapidly. Late in 1926 the National Broadcasting Company (NBC) put together the first national network of stations, followed the next year by the Columbia Broadcasting System (CBS). When Coolidge became the first president to deliver his inaugural address over the air, journalist Silas Bent caught the significance. "One did not merely read what the President *had said*," he wrote; "one *heard him say it*." Grudgingly the press conceded that, like it or not, the dawn of a new media age had arrived; by 1927 nearly a hundred papers owned or leased radio stations. William Randolph Hearst set about putting together a network of 50 stations with WHN in New York as its anchor. Rumors leaked out that he planned to broadcast not only news but eventually motion pictures as well. "Who but Hearst would have thought of it," marveled Bent.[41]

The Radio Act of 1927 created a Federal Radio Commission to oversee the industry. A reallocation plan called General Order 40, passed in 1928, sorted out the ongoing clash over frequencies in a way that ensured the triumph of a radio system dominated by networks supported by paid advertising. By 1930, when the federal census reported that more than 12 million families owned radio sets, a sponsor could reach 20 cities for $4,980 an hour on the NBC "Red" network or 11 large cities for $3,350 an hour on the "Blue" network. A nationwide hookup for 47 cities cost $10,180 for an hour of airtime. Thus did radio bring a new twist to the old adage that time was money: in 1929 NBC reported a gross income of $150 million, most of it from advertising.[42]

Complaints poured in from listeners and critics alike over the practice of selling airtime. Even Herbert Hoover objected at first, finding it inconceivable that "we should allow so great a possibility for service, for news, for entertainment, for education, and for vital commercial purposes, to be drowned in advertising chatter." Lee DeForest, a giant of radio technology, warned that "the present tendency of the broadcast chain and many individual stations to lower their bars to the greed of direct advertising will rapidly sap the lifeblood and destroy the usefulness of this magnificent new means of contact." One astute observer projected this dilemma even farther into the future. "Television is just around the corner," he predicted in 1930; "in another ten years it will be in the home. Will it bring into the home visual announcements of cigarettes and soap?"[43]

The impact of these new technologies changed American life in ways that made the consumer economy the heart of a new consumer culture.

The good life, with all its new things and pleasures along with the insatiable appetite it aroused for them, increasingly became the glue that bound otherwise diverse Americans together in a society that was becoming ever more depersonalized, standardized, and unfamiliar. Movies enabled millions of people to see the same picture. Radio allowed millions to hear the same program at the same time. It provided any speaker the largest audience ever to hear a talk and, together with the phonograph, gave any song, symphony, or opera more listeners than had heard it throughout all of history. The spread of slick national magazines brought the same material to millions of readers. The rise of this huge new national audience nurtured not only the industries that fed them entertainment products but also the advertising agencies that lived off them and the sponsors who aimed joyfully at the greatest marketing target ever created.

Thoughtful Americans tried to grasp what the emergence of this new mass society with its national audience meant. "Certain it is that the radio tends to promote cultural leveling," concluded one study. "Negroes barred from entering universities can receive instructions by radio. . . . Isolation of backward regions is lessened." Silas Bent saw quite another effect of radio. "As an entertainer it stood head and shoulders above the newspapers . . . ," he noted. "It reached the illiterate as well as the literate. If it is easier to look at pictures than read, how much easier to listen!" Others discovered that radio could be a voice reaching into a dark emotional wilderness. One early broadcaster in 1924 casually invited listeners to phone in their requests for songs to be played or sung. Immediately all three studio telephone lines were swamped as calls poured in at a rate of a thousand an hour on each line.[44]

The same station also put on an entertainer who gave talks on astrology under the name "Professor 'Radio' Wheeler." On one program he noted the date, gave the zodiac signs for people celebrating birthdays that day, and predicted what would happen to them. In closing he said playfully, "If you're in trouble or need advice . . . let me know and I'll help you out!" To his astonishment the telephone rang incessantly for more than an hour as people "sought the advice of this man who had never seen them and whom they had never seen." Like a good sport the professor dispensed canned wisdom to the callers, unaware that the seeds of a thriving new profession, indeed industry, had been planted.[45]

Sports offered their own version of escapism on a scale that elevated several of them into major industries. Like baseball, "once a national pastime, now a Big Business," college football, boxing, tennis, and golf marched toward the realm of high finance. "That college football has developed from a form of organized, spirited roughhouse to a vast national business . . . has long been obvious but seldom analyzed," noted *Time*. One writer estimated football's drawing power at about $50 million a year and concluded that "some colleges make half a million out of their teams because they get raw material, exploitation, and labor at slight cost." The big-time schools, such as the Ivy League, the Big Ten, the West Coast teams, and Notre Dame, planned schedules five years ahead and signed contracts for intersectional games "based no longer on natural rivalry or academic interest as has been the norm, but upon filling the stadium."[46]

The stadiums, which some viewed as temples to a new set of gods, were something to behold. Of the nation's 74 concrete arenas—7 of which held more than 70,000 spectators—55 had been built since 1920. By one calculation the 1928 season brought Yale a gross income topping $1 million and a net return of $543,084. Harvard fetched a gross of $845,311 and net of $420,787. In the Big Ten, Michigan, Ohio State, Illinois, and Northwestern all exceeded $500,000 in gross income from what *Time* called their "hundred yard factories roofed with sky." Former president and current chief justice William Howard Taft lamented this "menace to our whole American educational system. . . . The stadium overshadows the classroom . . . athletics have a dollar sign in front of them. . . . Most of our great universities and colleges today have professional athletic business managers, trained publicity agents, high-priced coaches."[47]

Other sports aroused the same enthusiasm on a smaller scale. The national tennis championships in 1922 filled all 15,000 available seats, the largest crowd in the sport's history. Both tennis and golf mushroomed as spectator and player sports alike. In 1916 the nation had 743 golf courses; the number jumped to 1,903 by 1923 and 5,856 by 1930. By 1928 golf represented an investment exceeding $2 billion and employed more than 3,000 workers as well as 500,000 caddies. Boxing matches and racetracks attracted huge crowds, while basketball and hockey emerged as major spectator sports. Professional football got a lift in 1925 when Red Grange turned pro after an electrifying career at Illinois.[48]

The same forms of ballyhoo that drove the consumer economy, politics, and other fields were utilized by "the merchandisers of sports in hawking their wares." Newspapers, soon followed by the immediacy of radio, gave sports fuller and more vivid coverage than ever before. Sportswriters transformed individual athletes into icons for their sports: Babe Ruth in baseball, Red Grange and the Notre Dame backfield immortalized as the Four Horseman of the Apocalypse in college football, Bill Tilden and Helen Wills in tennis, Bobby Jones in golf, Jack Dempsey and Gene Tunney in boxing. "They had something more than mere skill or competitive ability," observed Grantland Rice, a premier sportswriter. "They also had . . . that indescribable asset known as color, personality, crowd appeal, or whatever you may care to call it."[49]

More and more Americans wanted to play and to be entertained. A generation or so earlier only a tiny fraction of the people had ever seen a show or been professionally entertained, or had the leisure time for it. By the 1920s, however, there had developed what one study called "an insatiable hunger for amusement and diversion." Some businessmen registered their disapproval of this trend and clung to the old belief that "mankind does not thrive on holidays. Idle hours breed mischief." The chairman of the Philadelphia Gear Works grumbled in 1926 that the "work of the country cannot be done in forty hours a week. . . . The men of our country are becoming a race of softies and mollycoddles; it is time we stopped it and turned out some regular he-men." But others saw entertainment and recreation themselves as major growth industries and scrambled to cash in on this new El Dorado. Journalist Robert L. Duffus called it the "Age of Play," marked by "not only leisure to devote to play, but money to spend on it."[50]

And spend they did. In 1929 alone Americans bought $500 million worth of sporting goods, nearly $114 million of toys, games, and playground equipment, $75 million of phonographs and accessories, and $12 million of pool, billiards, and bowling goods. The more sedentary purchased 48 million decks of playing cards. Gate receipts for football games exceeded $21 million. One estimate placed the total cost of recreation, including travel, movies, and commercial amusements, at more than $10 billion. More than 40 million people flocked to bathing beaches in 218 cities. Thanks to the automobile, the number of visitors to national parks jumped from 198,606 in 1910 to more than 2.7 million in 1930. Even small pleasures became big business; as early as 1921 Americans paid out $448 million for soft drinks, $408 million for candy, $44 million for chewing gum, and a staggering $1.7 billion for tobacco products.[51]

Duffus found in this new appetite for leisure a remarkable change "in one of the most fundamental of folk ways[:] . . . within this generation, it has become evident that unremitting toil is not necessarily a law of human destiny." The good life seemed irresistible to most Americans in all the many forms it assumed, from Aimee Semple McPherson's version of heaven on earth to the siren's call of an automobile advertisement to the vastly different but equally alluring fantasy worlds of the department store window, movie screen, radio show, or football stadium.

Only a few Americans bothered to question the value of this materialistic notion of the good life itself. One of them, Harvard law professor Zachariah Chafee Jr., asked the question pointedly in a commencement speech at Brown University. "The United States ought to be happy," he observed. "We have long desired to be the richest nation on earth, and now we are. . . . And yet we are not particularly happy. . . . It is not enough to have prosperity. The vital question is: What are we going to do with it?"[52]

The answer came most forcefully from Wall Street. Gradually, and in its own way, the stock market joined the procession as it began improbably to combine all these ingredients in a rare and thrilling mix. As prices began to rise, playing the market provided excitement, traded increasingly in illusions, became a strange form of escapism, and more often than ever before fulfilled the fantasy of a happy ending by providing the funds to underwrite the good life.[53]

6

The

New Era

I believe that in the larger development of business and the gradual evolution of its ideals lies the best hope of the world. . . . Advertising is the spark plug on the cylinder of mass production, and essential to the continuance of the democratic process. Advertising sustains a system that has made us leaders of the free world: The American Way of Life. If advertising sometimes encourages men and women to live beyond their means, so sometimes does matrimony. If advertising is too often tedious, garrulous and redundant, so is the U.S. Senate.

—Bruce Barton (1927)[1]

Southern California had two thriving cults: that of the body and that of the spirit. Hollywood was the mecca of one, Angelus Temple of the other. For a time they merged in the bizarre disappearance of Aimee Semple McPherson.

Early on a May afternoon in 1926, Sister Aimee drove to the beach at Venice, California, near Los Angeles, donned her pea-green bathing suit, and went for a swim after sending her secretary on an errand. When Aimee did not return, thousands of the faithful swarmed to the beach to scan the horizon, sing hymns, weep, and pray for her return. Fishermen dragged and divers searched the waters in vain for the body. One diver died of exposure, a girl committed suicide, and a man flung himself into the sea, crying, "I'm going after her," and drowned. Front-page stories of her disappearance flooded every major paper. A 12-hour memorial service at Angelus Temple produced a collection totaling $36,000. For more than a month the mourning continued. Then, at 1:30 A.M. on June 23, a bedraggled Aimee appeared at the door of a cottage in Agua Prieta, Mexico, with a fantastic tale of having been kidnapped and held prisoner by "Steve," "Jake," and "Mexicali Rose" before managing to escape and stagger 18 miles across the desert without so much as a sunburn.[2]

Her return, even more sensational than her disappearance, triggered an orgy of publicity that dwarfed anything else happening in the nation. It had all the prime ingredients: mystery, sex, crime, escape, and raging controversy. Even before Aimee's reappearance, stories had begun to surface about a suspected lover named Kenneth G. Ormiston. When a frenzied search failed to find the kidnappers, attention turned increasingly to the "love nest" angle that sold even more papers than the original story. An army of detectives and reporters grilled Aimee relentlessly but could not break down her tale even though they were convinced it was fiction. The more lurid and ribald grew the stories about her, the more tenaciously she clung to her own version. "No woman ever told a more preposterous story in a balder manner or oftener," wrote one disbeliever. "She undoubtedly believes it herself now."[3]

In July a grand jury reported that evidence was lacking to indict anyone. As more juicy details of the love nest filled newspapers, a charge of conspiracy to obstruct justice was filed against Aimee on September 17. Two months of hearings produced another saga of lurid scandal versus righteous indignation. The faithful responded with $250,000 in contributions for what Sister called the "Fight-the-Devil Fund." After endless rounds of charge and countercharge in which long-awaited confessions seemed imminent, Los Angeles district attorney Asa Keyes abruptly moved to dismiss the case in January 1927. A triumphant Aimee promptly launched a 22-city "rehabilitation tour" that flopped. Soon afterward Keyes was convicted of bribery in an oil swindle while in office and sent to prison. Rumor also linked his downfall to a payoff from Aimee.

The indomitable Aimee, defiant and courageous as ever, lived to preach another day. To the faithful she resumed her siren's call to a new and better life: "Who cares about old Hell, friends? Why, we all know what Hell is. We've heard about it all our lives. A terrible place, where nobody wants to go. I think the less we hear about Hell the better, don't you? Let's forget about Hell. Lift up your hearts. What *we* are interested in, yes, Lord, is *Heaven*, and how to get *there!*"[4]

But where exactly was heaven? For Aimee, as for millions of Americans, it came increasingly to consist of earthly pleasures, which were presented to them in an ever-widening stream of colors, styles, and forms. The Four Square Gospel was at once the product of an innovative new brand of hucksterism and the purveyor of a consumer ethos. Aimee had at first sold herself to an adoring public like Ford's Model T, offering only one style and one color. But as those who followed her saga with rapt attention discovered, the new improved Aimee came in a variety of styles suitable for different needs or occasions. In the New Era, religion no less than other industries had to improve and diversify its product to expand its market share or even hold it. Especially was this true for creeds that, like Aimee's, had positioned themselves in the entertainment business.

"For seven years," wrote Frederick Lewis Allen, "the prosperity bandwagon rolled down Main Street."For many Americans it was a glorious ride, an experience exhilarating in its newness. The thrill of more and better things was driven by a rising tide of technological innovations that presented the public with a ceaseless flow of new delights while also conditioning them to expect new miracle products on a regular basis. Photographs were sent by radio from London to New York, and just over the horizon lay television; a demonstration in April 1927 sent the image of Herbert Hoover from Washington to New York. Eager forecasters imagined a not-so-distant future with talking books, lectures delivered to students by "long-running phonographs," movies transmitted wirelessly into theaters, musical instruments run by electricity, and the widespread use of artificial cooling.[5]

As the tide of marvels swelled, it diversified into endless streams of style. The advertising industry discovered that style held the key to differentiating between products and combating market saturation. Style itself became a product that could be sold through a variety of colors, designs, and packaging. "We seem to be growing in color consciousness and in the demand for color in our lives," observed one scholar, noting that the textile industry alone recognized 400 shades, a third of them in women's stockings. In 1924 the *Saturday Evening Post* confirmed the trend by adopting four-color advertisements. General Motors introduced multiple colors in its 1924 models, thanks to the creation of new Duco synthetic lacquers; by 1927 color had been crowned as "the sex appeal of business" in everything from clothing to bathrooms to towels. Clever merchandisers extended the concept of ensemble beyond its traditional realms of clothing and furniture to automobile accessories, kitchens, bedrooms, bathrooms, and even such items as clocks and galoshes. Banker Paul Mazur described the transformation:[6]

> Bathtubs appear in stylish shades. Dishpans no longer are plain Cinderellas of fire and ashes; following a wave of the hand by the fairy godmother—style—they now appear resplendent in blues and pinks. It is the vogue to have tinted linen—this year green and peach; next year, the sales manager hopes, beige and blue. . . . Automobiles change with the calendar. Last year's offerings are made social pariahs, only this year's model is desirable until it, in turn, is made out of fashion by next year's style. Furniture, clothing, radios, phonographs, tumble from the fertile minds of scientists and designers and . . . drown the sales possibilities of products that already stagger with infirmity at the age of one year.

To fuel the engine of style, General Motors spent $20 million annually on advertising. The National Retail Furniture Association raised a war chest of $1 million a year to shift consumer interest from price to style. Even Henry Ford, long a stubborn holdout against such newfangled devices as style and color changes, installment buying, and advertising, grudgingly caved in on every issue. Watching his 1921 market share of 55 percent shrivel to 30 percent by 1926, he announced the demise of the Model T in May 1927 and shut down production for more than six months to produce the new Model A. Ford advertised the new car heavily and in 1928 finally created a subsidiary finance company, but he never regained the industry leadership lost to GM.[7]

Even advertising men, the quintessential peddlers of illusion, were slow to grasp what was happening. The best of them had long taken pride in their rational and serious approach to the profession. But every modern trend showed their disbelieving minds that the public preferred "the frivolous against the serious, 'escape' as against reality, . . . the diverting against the significant." More and more, "people seemed to want escapist fantasy . . . even more than they wanted products." Secretary of Commerce Hoover understood this better than most. "In the past, wish, want, and desire were the motive forces in economic progress," he told a meeting of advertisers in 1925. "Now you have taken over the job of creating desire."[8]

By the late 1920s this grand illusion as a way of life had extended far beyond the economy to inhabit almost every area of American life. It had even taken on a name suitably slippery to mean different things to different people. Like the age itself, the term "New Era" had a chameleon quality that enabled it to change coloring whenever the occasion required.

The lineage of the phrase remains elusive. Some say it first appeared in a speech by Coolidge in November 1927 proclaiming that America was "entering upon a new era of prosperity." Whatever its origins, it slipped smoothly into the national jargon as both praise and ridicule— much as "New Economy" was to do 70 years later. In the most general sense it lauded a new economic condition grounded in continuing prosperity and freed from the old cycle of boom and bust. The authors of *Recent Social Trends* defined its characteristics as "an accelerated rate of total output; . . . more rapid expansion in the production of plant and equipment than of consumers' goods; . . . an unprecedented rise in the output of durable consumers' goods; and . . . a substantial lag in the output of the staples, food, textile and leather products."[9]

Like most clichés, however, the phrase soon expanded beyond its origins to describe a variety of changes in American life since the war's end and become a metaphor for the achievements and expectations of the fat years. It was also applied to the mood and values of a culture in transition from its fading Victorian legacy to modernism in all its varied forms. Both usages embodied the same principle that change was inevitable and nearly always for the best: today improved on yesterday, and tomorrow would be better still. One of the reigning fads of 1923 had been the infatuation of thousands of Americans with the brand of "mind cure" preached by Emil Coué with its hypnotic incantation, "Day by day, in every way, I am getting better and better." Within a remarkably short time the New Era became the application of that notion on a colossal scale long after Coué had been forgotten.[10]

John Moody, the financial analyst, gave the term cogency and dignity in 1928 when he argued that "we are living in a new era, and Wall Street, in its present condition and activity, . . . is simply reflecting this new era." According to Moody, it began around 1923 and owed its momentum to certain fundamental changes in economic and financial life. The war had made the United States a creditor nation and vastly increased production capacity and efficiency; the Federal Reserve had come into its own and stabilized the financial markets; corporations had absorbed principles of scientific management, learned to operate with thin inventories instead of overstocking, and reduced costs through use of machinery and other devices. "No one," he concluded, "can examine the panorama of business and finance in America during the past half-dozen years without realizing that . . . we have been going through an economic revolution of the profoundest character."[11]

That same revolution had reached Wall Street as well. Of the nation's nearly 122 million people, an estimated 15 million owned securities. This fact had deeply altered the public attitude toward corporate enterprise. Twenty years earlier, when big business had become a target for reformers of many stripes, only about half a million Americans owned stocks or bonds. In those days a bull market might run two or three years at best before succumbing to panic and/or depression. This one had survived for six years and showed no signs of slowing. "Most surprising of all," Moody stressed, "the incurable stock-market optimist . . . as well as the great army of innocent 'lambs,' have for several years been led, not to the proverbial slaughter, but to a continuous feast of speculative profits. For the first time within the memory of man, 'tips' galore have made good."

Would it last? Moody thought it would, even though he still believed in the old axiom that rising prices must eventually fall and that "rash stock-market speculation is as dangerous as ever." Plenty of shocks doubtless lay ahead, and with them would come "more than one massacre of the innocents in Wall Street . . . during the coming year or two . . . if only because of the vast increase in our 'lamb' population."

———————

Innovation had itself become a national pride and product, separating Americans both from their past and from other peoples. "It was the country of Lincoln," observed a visiting Frenchman; "it is now the country of Ford." The Patent Office did not issue its one-millionth patent until 1911, then took only until 1925 to complete another million. Prior to 1922, General Electric sold only one product, the incandescent electric lamp, directly to the public; by decade's end half of its enormous business came from household appliances and other products unknown before 1919. The head of GE, Gerard Swope, hailed as one of America's top business leaders, was an engineer by training, as were the chief executives of General Motors, Goodyear, Du Pont, and Singer Sewing Machine. In fact, they had all been classmates at MIT. To business they brought a new era of innovation in management as well as products. "The great monument to American industrial and commercial achievement," wrote Julius Klein, Hoover's right-hand man in the Commerce Department, "is the enormous junk heap of abandoned practices, methods, and ideals, all of which were once 'normal,' but which today are the most useless relics of antiquity."[12]

In baseball the new era of hitting over pitching reached its apogee in 1927 when Babe Ruth slugged 60 home runs and the Yankees swept the World Series. That same year the film industry opened its new era with the first "talkie," *The Jazz Singer*, and the first age of celebrity reached new heights with the nonstop adulation of Charles A. Lindbergh. For Henry Ford the new era began with the switch from the Model T to the Model A. National banks began a new era of sorts in February 1927 when passage of the McFadden Act allowed them to open branches in their home cities. Charley Mitchell responded by spreading National City Bank throughout New York City; that same year the security affiliates of National City and other banks sponsored or helped float more than $19 billion in new issues.[13]

The new era in banking blurred the traditional distinction between investment and commercial banks. By 1927 it had become apparent that the club no longer wielded the influence on Wall Street it once had. The House of Morgan still ruled with its prestige and deposits in excess of $500 million, and the club retained its aristocratic demeanor, closed membership, and air of authority in matters social and political as well as financial. The club still recruited the "right" sort of men, poised and polished specimens of the best families and Ivy League universities. Positions on Wall Street grew increasingly popular for the well connected as a way of making suitable contacts and a comfortable income with a minimum of effort. The hold of the older generation of bankers slackened as their ranks thinned and their adherence to the banker's code weakened amid the complexities and temptations of New Era finance. The sad, lonely figure of Jack Morgan personified this change as he grew ever more reclusive after his beloved wife's death in 1925, leaving management of the firm to Thomas Lamont and other senior partners.[14]

The clash of styles grew more jarring as the ranks of newcomers swelled in numbers, grew more pushy, and paid less obeisance to the club. Growing public interest in investment had flooded the financial world with large numbers of what Stuart Chase called "heavy-jowled men in immaculate sack suits and polka dot neckties" who "talked earnestly and convincingly of 'technical position,' 'sound investments,' 'gilt-edged securities,' 'attractive yields' " in "rich, creamy words" assuring investors "on the highest authority that the Republic was entering a whole new plateau of values, solid as a geological formation; the days of business cycles were gone forever." Such was the influence of Charley Mitchell, who with his boundless enthusiasm, pep talks, sales contests, and other ploys had turned banking into another branch of high-pressure salesmanship. To the club it was vulgar beyond words; to its practitioners, profitable beyond belief.[15]

Expansion in the form of branch offices throughout New York and the nation created thousands of new positions that had to be filled quickly. An earlier generation of men had migrated to Wall Street from farms and villages and learned the financial trade by starting as runners or pad-pushers and working their way up the ladder. During the 1920s, however, brokerages increasingly sought out the college men they once had scorned, looking for a veneer of polish and finesse needed to peddle securities. These recruits measured their training in weeks rather than years and knew more about selling than about the products they sold. They had no experience with the market's traditions or its fickle shifts; to the uninitiated, selling stocks and bonds differed little from selling shoes or saws or swings.[16]

Nor did the newcomers understand the market's vagaries. Old-timers like Noyes and some of the veteran brokers knew from hard experience that even in the best of times the market could not escape the law of gravity. But the younger men interpreted that law in a very different way. Stock prices had undergone several sharp retreats during the rise of the bull market, but every time it had responded by roaring upward again after a brief pause. Even those who recalled the last steep decline during the depression of 1920-21 also remembered that the market had come back in time. To both speculators and brokerage men of this breed, the law of gravity in the New Era meant only that prices could not go up in a straight uninterrupted line. But they would continue to advance.

By 1927 the product itself was shifting in emphasis. Led by Mitchell's indefatigable army, salesmen were beginning to sell not only bonds and select preferred stocks but common stocks as well. Despite the public attention given to stocks through legendary clashes on the Exchange through the years, bonds had always dominated the American financial market. Prior to 1920, the New York Stock Exchange listings contained twice as many bonds as stocks. As late as 1924 only 9 percent of new security issues took the form of common stock; in 1927 the figure actually slipped to 8 percent. The following year, however, saw a startling rise to 22 percent as promoters detected a growing public appetite for stocks and began to feed it with new issues. To a public mostly naive about finance, stocks were riskier than bonds because they fluctuated more in value and provided no assured income. But they offered something more enticing: the prospect of a possible, even spectacular rise in value.[17]

Although the war had given many people their first experience in investment with bonds, stocks were alien to all but those who worked for the growing number of large corporations with share-purchase plans. New financial vehicles arose to help newcomers put their money into stocks, the most notable being the investment trust. This early version of the modern mutual fund was designed to coax money from small investors who, lacking the capital and expertise to acquire a diversified portfolio, were invited to put their money in a company created to invest in other companies for them. One critic found this innovation curious in revealing "a widespread belief that someone else can handle your money better than you can yourself, rather a new era psychology and one not likely to endure indefinitely."[18]

Investment companies were not new; the oldest of them traced back to the 1890s. Prior to 1921, however, only 40 investment trusts came into existence. During the next five years, 139 more were created, and in 1927 alone another 140 were established. Most of the early versions were conservative "fixed" trusts, which bought blue chip securities and left their portfolios unchanged. By 1927, however, the "managed" trust was gaining popularity. In these companies the organizers or trustees actively bought and sold securities for the portfolio. For investors the focus tended to shift from the securities in the trust to the personalities operating it. When Chicago-based Dillon, Read & Co., perhaps the most active investment firm in the nation, organized the United States & Foreign Securities Corporation in 1924, it marked the first time a major private banker had identified himself personally with the management of a trust. The brilliance of Clarence Dillon had made him a legendary figure on Wall Street; the new venture was described as "an opportunity to let the public in on Dillon's investment brains."[19]

The first of what became the Founders Group of companies appeared in 1921; the Massachusetts Investors Trust (later to become the largest of them all for a quarter century), in 1924; State Street Investment Corporation, that same year. As the trend caught on, bankers, brokers, industrialists, and trust companies fashioned investment trusts of every conceivable kind: fixed and semi-fixed, open and closed end, with and without pyramided capital structures, with senior and/or junior security holdings. "The investment trust did not promote new enterprises or enlarge old ones," noted John Kenneth Galbraith. "It merely arranged that people could own stock in old companies through the medium of new ones." Their creation also greatly increased the sheer volume of stocks available to be bought and sold.[20]

It did not take imaginative founders of the less conservative investment trusts long to discover the profitability inherent in leveraged trusts. As historian Robert Sobel pointed out, investors who bought stock in investment trusts on margin "used leverage to buy shares in a leveraged company, which owned shares in other leveraged companies." No one understood the principle better than Clarence Dillon, whose firm eventually reaped a profit of between $30 and $40 million on its $5 million investment in United States & Foreign Securities Corporation. Part of those profits went to create another investment trust, International Securities Corporation; Dillon's firm garnered more than $1 million profit simply from organizing the new company. Investment bankers also discovered that investment trusts were handy vehicles for assisting in their work of purchasing, underwriting, and distributing securities.[21]

The New Era did not treat everyone as kindly as it did Dillon. For Jesse Livermore it brought yet another painful and expensive lesson, in the form of a clash with a speculator who could not have been more different from him. Arthur Cutten was a smallish, lean man with thinning silver hair, half-moon rimless glasses, a no-nonsense air, and an almost complete lack of interests or vices outside of work. At the age of 20 he had migrated to Chicago from an Ontario farm and found work as a clerk in a commodity brokerage. There he painstakingly acquired an education in commodities and diligently accumulated a stake of $1,000, which he risked in the wheat pit when he thought himself ready for the plunge. Three months later he left his job, bought a seat on the Chicago Board of Trade, and launched a spectacular career in speculation.[22]

An incurable bull, Cutten caught the rising tide of optimism in 1924 with an operation that pushed the price of wheat above $2 a bushel for the first time ever and earned him an estimated profit of $2 million. His exploits soon attracted followers and the attention of financial reporters, who were quick to promote him as the latest market maven—a practice Cutten did little to encourage. Asked his opinion of where wheat would go, he answered dryly, "Higher." Livermore thought otherwise; he was once quoted as saying, "Gravity works in the market as well as in science." Operating on one of his hunches, he began selling wheat short and persisted in the face of a market hoisted upward by Cutten and those following his lead. Rather than cut his losses, Livermore stuck obstinately to his guns until by the end of 1925 he had lost more than $3 million and was forced to surrender. By that time Cutten's profits had supposedly reached $5 million.

While Livermore retreated to repair his broken fortune and an arm broken in a fall, Cutten bid farewell to the Illinois farm he called home and moved with his wife to New York, where he opened a modest office to test a new arena—the stock market. One fabulous operation followed another as Cutten emerged as the most successful and daunting trader on Wall Street. "Cutten Cracks Whip Over the Stock Market," blared a *New York Times* headline above a feature article on the market's newest darling. "The two things a man needs most to play the market," Cutten said later, "are nerve and vision." Timing also helped; Cutten launched his market career just in time to ride the bull market to the top. A glum Jesse Livermore understood the importance of timing thoroughly and had paid dearly for ignoring it. He lapsed into obscurity again and did not emerge until the spring of 1927, when he recouped his fortune with a market pool that brought him an estimated $4 million. This time it was resolutely bullish in nature.

Ben Strong tried always to look at the big picture. His vision of global finance was as large as that of the Federal Reserve Board was small and fragmented. Herbert Hoover later called the board's members "mediocrities" except for Adolph Miller, and an even less charitable John Kenneth Galbraith dismissed them as "a body of startling incompetence." Strong filled this vacuum of direction and leadership with forceful efforts to realize the three goals of business, price, and employment stability, aiding the restoration of monetary stability abroad, and curbing excessive use of credit in the stock market. A mild recession in 1924 led him to lower the New York bank's rediscount rate in three increments that summer from 4 1/2 to 3 percent while the Federal Reserve added $500 million to its holdings of government securities through open-market purchases. This easy-money policy helped spur a recovery that was too vigorous for some observers like Hoover, but neither Coolidge nor the Federal Reserve Board opposed it.[23]

By May 1925 Strong himself had qualms about the vigor of the recovery. Three developments struck him as potentially dangerous: "overbuilding and real estate speculation, . . . too much enthusiasm in automobile production, and . . . the ever-present menace of the stock exchange speculation." The latter especially annoyed him because it seemed always to get in the way of his broader objectives. He did not believe the Federal Reserve could or should deal with anything except general economic conditions. The current situation, he wrote Montague Norman of the Bank of England that November, struck him as "an attempt to manipulate the stock market. I confess that I hate it. It is repugnant to me in every possible aspect. . . . It seems a shame that the best sort of plans can be handicapped by a speculative orgy, and yet the temper of the people of this country is such that these situations cannot be avoided."[24]

The "best sort of plans" concerned Strong's ardent desire to stabilize the international financial situation. Great Britain had returned to the gold standard in 1925, pegging the pound at its old parity of $4.86. Strong and Norman worked tirelessly to stabilize other currencies as well by helping to restore them to a gold basis, but the unwise decision to put the pound at its old rate penalized British goods in the world market and threatened serious unemployment at home. To deal with his difficult situation, Norman needed New York and other world financial centers to maintain low interest rates that would not draw gold to them from London. But the heating up of the stock market prompted the Federal Reserve banks to reverse course and raise interest rates to dampen speculation. The New York bank had hiked the rediscount rate to $3\frac{1}{2}$ percent in February 1925, and in January 1926 Strong reluctantly went to 4 percent. "We have had a dangerous speculation develop in the stock market," he explained to Norman, "with some evidence that it is extending into commodities."[25]

The power struggle between Strong and the Federal Reserve Board continued over everything from broad policy to protocol nitpicking. One board member in particular, Adolph Miller, took a dim view of open-market operations and clashed with Strong over the issue in March 1926. The following month, after testifying before a House committee, Strong left for England. Shortly after his return in October, he fell ill with influenza and then pneumonia. Forced again to leave the bank for an extended convalescence, he sojourned at Biltmore, North Carolina, until late in April 1927. Not until February of that year was he able even to resume his correspondence with Norman and other key associates. By that time events had taken yet another turn. Friction between the British and French, who had finally stabilized the franc at an undervalued level, resulted in the outflow of more gold from England and Germany.[26]

A conference hosted by Strong in July 1927 helped relieve the pressure, but he confronted a tricky dilemma. Norman still required low interest rates in England and the United States to keep gold at home, while the French insisted that England raise its rates. Concerns over speculation in the stock market had prompted Strong to increase rates rather than lower them. When he began to reassess this policy in 1927, he found mixed signals from both the government and the board. Late in March, Andrew Mellon told reporters that he saw "no evidence of over-speculation" and thought the market was "going along in very orderly fashion." Nor did he see anything to suggest that "business will not continue throughout the country. Brokers' loans give a very good insight into the stock market situation and they appear to be in a very healthy state."[27]

By late summer, however, the business outlook had lost its rosy sheen. Another mild downturn brought employment, building construction, railroad freight loadings, and commodity prices to their lowest levels in two years. The Federal Reserve Board's own production index dipped below the 1923–25 level for the first time since the mild recession of 1924. These developments, coupled with the European situation that was foremost in his mind, led Strong to urge the board to reverse course and reduce interest rates. On July 27, two weeks after the conference hosted by Strong, the Federal Reserve Board voted to ease credit. The Kansas City bank, its governor prompted by Strong, led off by reducing its rediscount rate to 3 1/2 percent. The other banks followed until by September all had gone to the new rate. The open-market committee also increased its purchases of government securities.[28]

The danger posed by easy money was that of stoking the very kind of speculative activity Strong so despised. Lower rates encouraged

banks to borrow funds cheaply from the Fed and put them in the call
loan market, where growing demand produced higher rates. It required
no great talent as a banker to borrow at 3 1/2 percent and lend at 7 percent or more. Moreover, the attractive rates in the call loan market exceeded those for regular business loans, which meant that bankers
would likely prefer to put their money into the call loan market with its
quick, safe, lucrative return than into legitimate business or agricultural
loans of longer duration, lower return, and higher risk. In this way easy
money held the potential for not only fueling more speculation in
stocks but also shifting needed funds from sectors that contributed to
real economic growth.

The new policy provoked controversy within and without the Federal Reserve system. Despite pleas from Strong, the Chicago bank refused to budge from the 4 percent rate until September 6, when the
Federal Reserve Board, by a 4 to 3 vote, ordered it to lower the rate.
Howls of protest followed this action. Although Strong favored the reduction, he opposed the board's move because he believed it had no authority to issue such an order. Privately he admitted to being "distressed
beyond my power to express it" at what he called a "silly and wholly unnecessary and . . . quite gratuitous advertising of differences of opinion."
Adolph Miller also vehemently opposed (and voted against) the order
in vain. Later he attributed the ensuing easy-money policy entirely to
Strong's influence. It was, he wrote, "the greatest and boldest operation
ever undertaken by the Federal Reserve system, and . . . resulted in one
of the most costly errors committed by it or any other banking system
in the last 75 years."[29]

But that was hindsight. At the time the policy seemed entirely reasonable even though it revealed yet again the frictions and divisions
within the Federal Reserve System. None went deeper than the
dilemma of what to do about the stock market. By one index the average of industrial stocks had gone up 34 percent between 1921 and 1924
and another 63 percent from 1924 to June 1927; another index measured the gain in industrial average as 36 percent between 1921 and
1924 and 60 percent from 1924 to June 1927. During the second half of
1927, the industrial averages responded to the new easy-money policy
by rising another 18 percent by one measure and 19 percent by the
other. The Dow Jones industrial average high, which stood at 100.66 in
January 1924, closed out 1927 at 202.40. Even the stodgy railroad average high advanced from 83.06 to 143.44 during that same period. The

volume of trading on the New York Stock Exchange had marched steadily upward from a low of 162.4 million shares in 1921 to a record 572.8 million shares in 1927.[30]

Some board members wished to impose "direct control" on the regional banks through devices to restrict use of their funds for brokers' loans without tightening credit for other business purposes. Strong adamantly opposed this notion and doubted whether even more general curbs on credit could restrain the stock market. He had never fully embraced the idea that the Fed should take responsibility for the stock market, and he saw clearly that the measures advocated by some board members would not only thwart his broader objectives but threaten general prosperity. "I think the conclusion is inescapable," he wrote in September 1927, "that any policy directed solely to forcing liquidation in the stock loan account and concurrently in the prices of securities will be found to have a widespread and somewhat similar effect in other directions, mostly to the detriment of the healthy prosperity of this country."[31]

Lest his point be missed, Strong stated it more bluntly. "Some of our critics damn us vigorously and constantly for not tackling the stock speculations," he said. "I am wondering what will be the consequences of such a policy if it is undertaken and who will assume the responsibility for it." Two years later this insightful question had grown even more urgent and still lacked even the semblance of an answer.[32]

For Billy Durant the New Era meant a new role in an old arena to which he had come reborn. The empire he had struggled to build was no longer made of stone or steel but of paper, and its product had not the palpable feel of a fine car but the smooth impersonality of a ledger entry. His new company, Durant Motors, took a backseat to his interest in the stock market and by 1926 began a steady and irreversible decline. To financial reporters he was no longer the great industrial titan but the grand bull whose market exploits put him on the front page of the *New York Times* twice within 60 days. Like Jesse Livermore, he had become hard currency for the financial press, which cheerfully found scraps of rumor to embellish about the figure they called "a silent man" who said nothing of his market maneuvers publicly and seldom even came to Wall Street.[33]

From this froth emerged a new fantasy: the "Durant markets . . . not easily pinned down . . . likely to be wild, tumultuous affairs," joining the

"Cutten markets" and "Livermore markets" as the illusions of choice on the Street. It had long been the style of the more colorful financial writers to give market movements a face by identifying them with whatever operator(s) happened to be in vogue. This device went beyond the personalizing of market machinations to instilling and sustaining the illusion that the "big operators" were capable of manipulating market movements with the help of their followers. One effect of this illusion was to foster the belief among naive investors that the trick to getting rich in such a market lay simply in discovering who was going to push what stock in which direction at what time, and then jumping aboard.

Certainly Durant was operating on a huge scale. During 1927 alone he dealt in the stocks of 75 industrial corporations (not counting investment companies), bought more than 2.6 million shares for $284.2 million, and sold 2.25 million shares for just under $270 million, realizing a profit of $7.5 million. At year's end his inventory of stocks totaled 805,012, almost double the 414,905 shares he had owned in January. He had losses as spectacular as his gains, but his bullish instincts served him well in a rising market. On the crowded ledgers of his accountants the money piled up; from dividends alone Durant garnered anywhere from $250,000 to $750,000 in income scarcely dented by Mellon's benign tax policies. In the manner of Livermore, the lion's share of that money went to sustain an increasingly lavish lifestyle centered around his showplace palace, Raymere, in the aptly named town of Deal, New Jersey. Its opulence prompted Walter Chrysler to murmur that he "had never experienced luxury to compare with Billy Durant's house."[34]

By the usual standards—and certainly by those of the New Era— Durant had crowned his life with yet another success. He saw himself as a force on Wall Street and therefore in the nation's growth, a mobilizer of capital and consultant to those seeking to build new enterprises. But he had lost the substance as well as the source of his genius. For most of his life he had rejoiced in the hard, gritty work of creating new machines and organizations, relishing the company of men who toiled happily amid grease and grime in search of new or improved designs. He had created products, erected buildings, put men to work, met payrolls, used money as one tool among many to achieve grander dreams. Now money had become the end as well as the means. "Success in the stock market," he declared, "comes from finding out a stock selling at $50 that should be selling at $100, or one selling for $100 which should be selling at $150 or $200."[35]

But neither such success, nor the profit it produced, brought him anything like the satisfaction of elevating the obscure Chevrolet into a market leader. As his biographer sagely observed, "Money in such quantities took on a shimmering, impalpable quality, lacking the literal impact of the smaller sums that he had spent his life raising and dispensing for real estate, parts, workers." On Wall Street he dealt with men who created nothing besides money. His business world grew increasingly abstract and unreal except for Durant Motors, which he tended sporadically. In March 1927 he announced a bold plan for a new combination called Consolidated Motors, but the scheme faded as quickly as it had appeared. A proposed merger of several moribund companies unveiled in November met the same fate. Durant Motors itself was in deep trouble, showing a $3.6 million loss for the first eight months of 1927.[36]

———————

"The 'New Era' had arrived," recalled Thurman Arnold. "A new school of economists argued that when you buy common stocks, you buy the future, not the present." The same economists also preached the "advantages of administered prices controlled by wise businessmen. The idea that industry must be planned by a hierarchy of corporate executives was accepted by the American people. . . . Men began to dream of a new world order in which both panics and wars could be eliminated. Panics would be impossible because all industry was regulated by sound banking houses, which would come to the rescue when danger threatened. Wars would be impossible because international business, which had everything to lose and nothing to gain by war, would prevent any powerful and civilized nation from aggression."[37]

Even to Americans still smarting from the botched outcome of the crusade to make the world safe for democracy, certain events in foreign affairs seemed to mark a new era in the quest for peace. The Dawes Plan of 1924 offered a new approach to the tangled issues of war loans and reparations. The Washington Naval Conference of 1921–22 produced the first disarmament agreement by major powers in history. The Locarno Pact of 1925 aimed to reduce tensions in Europe, while the Four Power and Nine Power treaties sought to defuse those in the Far East. Most ambitious of all, the Kellogg-Briand Pact, signed by 15 nations including the United States in August 1928, bound the participants to renounce war as an instrument of policy. Skeptics dismissed these agreements as towers of illusion, but they offered at least the hope for an enduring peace.[38]

In August 1927 the politics of the New Era took an unexpected twist. President Coolidge, vacationing in the Black Hills of South Dakota, summoned reporters to a conference and personally handed each one a slip with a single sentence: "I do not choose to run for President in nineteen twenty eight." To their entreaties he replied tersely, "There will be nothing more from this office today!" Thus did the man who had presided over the coming of prosperity prepare to ride off into the sunset, amused at how he had snookered the press and the nation with his little surprise. However useful he had been in retrieving the nation and the Republican party from the disasters of the Harding administration, Coolidge had never been a good fit for the New Era with all its ballyhoo. All his virtues and values—thrift, industry, decency, dignity, morality, understatement, simplicity—ran against the grain of the times. What use had an age of excess for a man whose worst vice was an addiction to peanuts?[39]

His desire to escape the office that was to him more burden than blessing even in the best of times seems to have been genuine. He had lost a son and, more recently, the father he had always revered, and he had no illusions about what the presidency did to men. "It is difficult for men in high office to avoid the malady of self-delusion," he wrote afterward. "They are always surrounded by worshipers. They are constantly, and for the most part sincerely, assured of their greatness. They live in an artificial atmosphere of adulation and exaltation which sooner or later impairs their judgment. They are in grave danger of becoming careless and arrogant." Some thought he acted to protect his health or that of his wife; others claimed he was merely being coy and really wanted the nomination. As usual, Coolidge offered a succinct explanation. "It's a pretty good idea," he observed, "to get out when they still want you."[40]

Critics and Democrats joked that pancake eaters would have to do without maple syrup next year because "the Vermont sap chooses not to run in 1928." For Republicans, however, the announcement set off a stampede for the nomination in which one aspirant stood above and apart from the rest. Herbert Hoover had the most impressive credentials and an effective organization already in place. He made a show of trying to persuade Coolidge to change his mind while his supporters promoted his candidacy with quiet efficiency. No one in government had a higher or more favorable profile. As early as 1925 a columnist observed "how extraordinarily extensive is his impress upon the government outside of his own Department. There is reason to doubt whether in the whole history of the American government a Cabinet officer has engaged in such wide diversity of activities or covered quite so much ground. . . . There is more Hoover in the administration than anyone else."[41]

Few men seemed better equipped for high office than Hoover. Born in 1874 in rural Iowa, he lost both parents by the age of 9 and grew up in the Oregon home of an uncle. At 17 he entered the young, tuition-free Stanford University, where he earned a degree in engineering and acquired a deep-rooted belief in the virtues of independence, hard work, ambition, and mastery over one's physical environment. A shy, awkward youth, Hoover lacked social polish and was so brusque and tactless as often to seem rude. At Stanford he also met his future wife, Lou Henry, the only woman then majoring in geology. After graduating in 1895, he launched a career in engineering that made him expert in mining technology and management, took him around the globe five times between 1902 and 1907, and earned him a fortune of about $4 million.[42]

But money alone did not slake his ambition; as early as 1907 he said that he "had all the money he wanted and wished to try something else." The something else appeared in 1914 when he got involved in the relief effort to supply occupied Belgium with food. His work in this project— the first humanitarian effort to relieve civilian suffering on so grand a scale—won him widespread praise and publicity as a man who knew how to get things done under trying circumstances. When the United States entered the war, Hoover sought and received the new post of U.S. food administrator and took charge of harnessing the nation's food supply to the needs of wartime. Here, too, his sense of organization and mission produced results that enhanced his reputation. In November 1918 President Wilson asked Hoover to convert the Food Administration into a relief and reconstruction agency for war-shattered Europe.[43]

On this larger, even more complex stage Hoover performed so admirably that economist John Maynard Keynes, a harsh critic of the postwar settlements, called him "the only man who emerged from the ordeal of Paris with an enhanced reputation." Louis Brandeis hailed him as "the biggest figure injected into Washington by the war." Hoover came home in September 1919 saying he cared never to see Europe again. Despite his lack of political experience, he was touted for the presidency in 1920 by members of both parties. "He is certainly a wonder," marveled another ambitious politician, Franklin D. Roosevelt, "and

I wish we could make him President. There couldn't be a better one."
Hoover declared himself a "progressive Republican," and his vigorous
support for the League of Nations did not endear him to party conser-
vatives. He did well in some primaries without campaigning and loyally
supported Harding during the election campaign. His reward was the
Commerce seat in Harding's cabinet, an offer he accepted reluctantly.[44]

During his seven years as secretary, Hoover transformed the Commerce Department from a low-profile assortment of disparate bureaus
into the most dynamic agency of the federal government, an efficient organization of 1,600 people dedicated to promoting and guiding American economic development while serving the needs of business. All three
of the department's organizing bureaus underwent dramatic facelifts.
Standards, which tested materials purchased by the government, became
by mid-decade the largest research laboratory in the world and lent its
expertise increasingly to assisting business with complex scientific problems. Census mushroomed beyond its original purpose to become a statistical warehouse for information useful to business. In July 1921 it
began publishing a statistical monthly *Survey of Current Business* listing industrial production and inventories. One executive called it "the most
important step in our industrial life since the inauguration of the Federal
Reserve System." To rejuvenate foreign trade, he put Julius Klein in
charge of the third bureau, Foreign and Domestic Commerce.[45]

Hoover was a whirlwind of activity, reorganizing bureaus, getting rid
of deadwood, raising salaries, adding agencies to deal with new or long-
ignored areas of concern. Everything from the health of children to
housing standards to aviation to labor relations felt the influence of the
Commerce Department. When radio burst onto the national scene,
Hoover brought it under his jurisdiction. From the first he relied on an
old but little-used device, the national conference, to attack major problems. Hoover used conferences to bring together leaders of diverse con-
stituencies to extract information on some broad economic or social
issue. His first, in August 1921, dealt with the severe unemployment re-
sulting from the depression of 1920–21. From it emerged his recom-
mendation to discard the old policy of meeting hard times by cutting
wages and instead stimulate employment through public works projects
such as building roads.[46]

The national conferences epitomized Hoover's philosophy and style.
They brought together the best minds to generate data and consider solutions through cooperative, voluntary action with the government act-

ing as something between an advisor and a midwife. Hoover was indefatigable in promoting cooperation and relentless in seeking out answers. As David Burner observed, "Hoover suffocated problems with
solutions—if one did not work, another would." Even before the title of
the "Great Engineer" was bestowed on him, he approached every issue
as a technical problem to be solved. "The world he mentally inhabited
was a little like a factory," added Burner. "When interviewed, Hoover
would answer a question curtly and then, until there was another, stop
like a machine that has run down."[47]

By mid-decade Hoover had emerged as the best-known and most publicized figure in Washington. One political cartoon depicted Coolidge
watching in amazement as an endless line of marchers, all of them
Hoover, paraded down the street. Hoover's boundless energy and impa-
tience sometimes annoyed Coolidge, the more so since he relied so
heavily on the secretary. Later, on leaving office, Coolidge is reputed to
have said of Hoover, "That man has offered me unsolicited advice for six
years, all of it bad." But Hoover, however shy and awkward he was personally, understood the value of publicity in New Era politics, and after
Coolidge's dramatic announcement he used its instruments with supreme
efficiency. "Never, perhaps," observed a columnist, "has any other person
had a personal publicity machine as powerful and effective as the one
that made Herbert Hoover President." Walter Lippmann agreed that
Hoover was "the first American President whose whole public career has
been presented through the machinery of modern publicity."[48]

One event in 1927 revealed both elements of Hoover's growing
popularity. That spring the Mississippi River overflowed its banks
across an area 1,000 miles long and as much as 40 miles wide, drowning 700,000 homes along with livestock and crops and uprooting
600,000 people. Coolidge made Hoover chairman of a special Mississippi Flood Committee, and for three months—under the glare of constant national publicity—Hoover performed an encore of his Belgian
relief effort. He wielded full authority, created an effective organization, cut through bureaucratic obstacles, and did it all with a minimum
of overhead expense. "Mr. Hoover's masterly handling of the situation,"
declared a British observer, "has aroused universal admiration. . . . He
has shown that he has lost none of his old organizing ability." It was a
virtuoso performance, and it left a lasting impression. As one pundit
noted, the great Mississippi River flood ruined the South and elected
Hoover president.[49]

Like the relief effort, the campaign to secure the Republican nomination was efficient, well oiled, and orchestrated largely by Hoover, who had learned the art of making a show out of not making a show while others made it for him. Although Coolidge never endorsed any candidate, Hoover gathered support from key Republicans, including Andrew Mellon and William Butler, head of the Republican National Committee. The convention in June 1928 handed Hoover the nomination on the first ballot. He formally accepted it at Stanford on August 11, his 54th birthday, with a speech containing his famous prediction that America was nearer to the final triumph over poverty than any nation had ever been and would soon conquer it. Here truly was the New Era writ large: the dawn of an age of perpetual prosperity from which all would ultimately benefit.[50]

Unlike many priests of the New Era, however, Hoover did not bask in the glow of the steadily rising stock market. He had long opposed what he called the "growing tide of speculation" and as early as 1925 had urged Adolph Miller of the Federal Reserve Board to restrict credit. Three times in 1926, beginning on New Year's Day, Hoover warned against "real estate and stock speculation and its possible extension into commodities with inevitable inflation; the overextension of installment buying," and similar perils. "Psychology plays a large part in business movements," he added, "and optimism can only land us on the shores of depression." But no such inflation occurred, and the tide continued to rise, slowed only by the brief business slowdown in 1927. That same year Hoover wrote, "The safety of continued prosperity will depend on caution and resistance to expansion of credit which will further stimulate speculation."[51]

These concerns, expressed repeatedly to Coolidge and Mellon, impressed neither of them. Neither did the leap in brokers' loans, which by January 1928 had risen half a billion dollars in two months to $3.81 billion. Alarmists trembled at this level, the highest since the Exchange began publishing loan figures early in 1926, and the market sputtered. Three times between January 4 and 10 the volume of trading soared past 3 million shares, a figure that had been reached only eight times since 1920. Asked his opinion by reporters, Coolidge admitted that he was no expert on the money market but dismissed the increase as "a natural expansion of business in the securities market" and said he saw "nothing unfavorable in it." His unfortunate remarks were another symptom of a new era: the oldest Wall Street veterans could not recall hearing any president comment on the market. Some of them grumbled that Coolidge would do well to keep quiet on matters he did not understand.[52]

Billy Durant was quick to second the opinion. "Why all this hue and cry about bank loans to brokers?" he scoffed. Banks existed to lend money, and to whom could the banks lend $3 billion "to better advantage or more safety than to brokers or individuals, secured by choice collateral of their own selection?" He predicted that brokers' loans would top $5 billion within another year. Ben Strong took a very different view. Too ill to participate in the meetings, he supported the Fed's decision to raise the rediscount rate back to 4 percent in February and sell government securities in the open market. During January and February the market stalled out; then, in March, having absorbed the Fed's action, it started to climb again. Both the Dow Jones and *New York Times* averages had lost some ground during the first two months of 1928; the Dow gained 19.54 points to close out March at 213.35 while the *Times* rose 14.99 points to finish at 192.42.[53]

The bull was loose and running. On March 13, 1928, the stock market moved onto the front page of the *New York Times* and other papers, where it became a frequent visitor. The headlines recorded an 18-point jump in RCA—or Radio, as it was called—stock on a day when the volume of shares traded set a new record of more than 3.8 million. The next day volume passed 4 million shares for the first time; during the last week of the month it surpassed that level four more times. Predictions of 5-million-share days could no longer be dismissed as fantasy. Average daily volume in February barely exceeded 2 million shares and never once touched 3 million. In March it *averaged* nearly 3.2 million shares a session and five times exceeded the once distant 4-million mark.[54]

Alexander Noyes shook his head at the spectacle. "Speculation on the Stock Exchange," he wrote, "reached a stage yesterday which appeared fantastic, even to seasoned Wall Street." Radio, which a week earlier had advanced 27 points, had soared 21 1/2 points overnight only to drop 20 points in a ghastly few minutes. Such a gyration "was so utterly abnormal and so completely divorced from any sane movement of investment values that it threw the rest of the market into inevitable confusion." A pattern was emerging that unsettled conservative brokers: a handful of stocks like Radio and General Motors utterly dominated the list and its swelling volume. Most of them were being manipulated by pools organized to advance the price for quick killings. The price gyrations of these "favorites" destabilized the market, and worse was in sight. The growing volume indicated that outside buyers—Jesse Liver-more's beloved "minnows"—were again flocking to the market in hopes of riding the bull to easy profits.[55]

The pool had long been the favorite vehicle for insiders seeking a quick killing. In expert hands the technique was simple but effective. A clique of high rollers put a pool of funds in the hands of a talented stock manager, who used it to acquire a large block of a chosen stock and push its price upward through the issuing of bullish information, selective buying, and other devices. When the price hit a desired level, the pool manager continued to promote the stock while quietly selling out the pool's holdings for top dollar, leaving the suckers holding their shares as the price fell. "Participation in a pool or its management by a broker," concluded a later investigation, "is more than likely to entail a violation of that elementary fiduciary relation . . . to his customers."[56]

The pool operators, backed by high-rolling investors, shifted their attention from one stock to another. When Radio stalled, they even seized on a staid blue chip like New York Central, driving it up 7 1/2 points in one day to its highest level since 1901. The buying public, clucked Noyes, "has very evidently thrown aside all concern about actual facts or conditions. It does not even watch for a general uprush of speculative stocks, but merely awaits the sign that one stock or another is about to 'move,' in order to rush after it without delay." To these buoyant boosters, the only question seemed to be how fast and how far the bull could run. A strange new mood seemed to be overtaking Wall Street. Bankers, brokers, investors, and speculators alike conceded that, like it or not, "all former yardsticks must be disregarded and that new measures, if the market is to be judged aright, must be adopted."[57]

The New Era on Wall Street was thrusting itself to center stage, and it was stealing Al Jolson's favorite line: "Brother, you ain't seen nothin' yet!"

7

The Culture

of Greed

There is no rest from the effort to make money in ever larger and larger amounts. There is no prospect of comfortable retirement in old age. . . . Our prosperity can be maintained only by making people want more, and work more, all the time. Those, and they are many, who believe that our recent prosperity has been mainly caused by the phenomenal expansion of the automobile business, tell us that it will soon be necessary to find some other article which will similarly take the public fancy and create billions in sales.

—James Truslow Adams[1]

"Wall Street's bull market collapsed with a detonation heard round the world . . . ," proclaimed the *New York Times*. "Losses ranged from . . . 23½ points in active Stock Exchange issues . . . to as much as 150 in stocks dealt over the counter. It was a day of tumultuous . . . happenings, characterized by an evident effort on the part of the general public to get out of stocks at what they could get. Individual losses were staggering. Hundreds of small traders were wiped out. The sales were countrywide. They flowed into the Stock Exchange . . . from every nook and corner of the country." Even the usually upbeat *Wall Street Journal* reported evidence of "frightened selling" amid an "avalanche of liquidation." The collapse, following a week of steady declines, saw trading volume exceed the 5-million-share mark for the first time in Exchange history. The Dow Jones industrials had hit a record high of 220.96 on June 2, then fallen 15 points in a week before dropping another 3 points that bloody Tuesday.[2]

Where Monday had seen a "violent, sharp and fiery" decline, the next day witnessed a flood of "sell at the market" orders pouring in from around the country as exposed margins forced speculators to unload. Nor was it confined to a few leading stocks; trading took place in a record 803 different stocks, and the ticker ran nearly two hours behind—another record. In the last hour alone a record 2,082,500 shares were traded. The date of this disaster was June 12, 1928, and it was the worst decline since March of 1926. The *Journal* reminded readers that "the weakness in stocks bore no relation whatever to business prospects," and the economy showed no obvious weaknesses. By month's end the Dow had climbed back past 210. After marking time through July, it surged upward again, closing August above 240. "Many old traders are more convinced than ever," quipped a *Journal* columnist, "that the longer a man is in the Street the less he seems to know about the market."[3]

Benjamin Strong had already advanced the New York bank's rate to 4½ percent in May. Two months later it joined eight other Federal Reserve banks in moving to 5 percent, but some thought the reversal of the easy-money policy of 1927 came too late. Brokers' loans, which stood at nearly $3.7 billion in March 1928, reached a record $4.56 billion by June 6. Something else was happening, though most observers did not yet grasp its significance: the proportion of total funds in the call loan market coming from sources *outside* the Federal Reserve System had risen from 24 percent at the beginning of 1928 to 41 percent by mid-June. Strong had no chance to ponder the implications of the credit situation. Ill and exhausted, he sailed for France in May only to be told by his doctor later that month that he must give up all work if he wished to live. Grudgingly he made plans to resign his position.[4]

The market itself had entered a new era as a major growth industry. New listings on the New York Stock Exchange rose from 58 million shares in 1925 to 102 million in 1928. Some analysts used this increase, coupled with the rise in share prices, to explain the growth in brokers' loans as permanent rather than a temporary aberration. The Exchange had nearly 2,000 employees for whom it provided impressive medical facilities, group life insurance, a loan fund, a savings plan, a retirement fund, and an athletic program that sponsored nine teams. Its labyrinth of communications equipment included 323 telephone lines to brokers' offices and another 80 between the floor of the Exchange and the central Quotations Room, over which more than 30,000 quotations flowed every day. The price for a seat on the Exchange, available only when an owner of one decided to sell, had been as low as $76,000 in 1923. Two years later the average price climbed to $116,971 and reached $395,283 in 1928. Nor was the action all there. Many of the newest and hottest issues were listed on the Curb Exchange or one of the out-of-town exchanges. Even the New York Produce Exchange eventually listed about a hundred stocks for trading.[5]

Speculators did not have to go near Wall Street to trade. Brokerage firms expanded their branch operations rapidly, opening 599 new offices in 1928 and 1929 alone for a total of 1,658 compared to 706 in 1925. All of them had customers' rooms, some elegantly furnished, where the outsiders flocked to watch the fluctuation of prices in the form of an illuminated reflection of the moving ticker tape projected by a device called the Translux. Other walls held huge blackboards on which scurrying "board boys" recorded changing stock prices. By the spring of 1928 these rooms, whether uptown, downtown, or in another city, were filling up with schools of "minnows" or "suckers" untutored in the market and enticed by the prospect of the quick killing. Some of them brought their life's savings as a stake. To practiced eyes they represented a new breed of gambler lured to the market more by hope than experience, like vacationers at a casino trying their luck in a game owned by professionals. They bet on tips or hunches and chased rumors and supposed leaders, making them easy prey for pool managers and brokers who knew how to earn commissions while working stocks for their own advantage rather than that of the naive customer.[6]

If the sucker lost all his money or went to another firm, the broker merely shrugged. "Suckers are born every minute," they philosophized. "One goes, two come in. Win or lose, we get our commissions." The broker's true loyalty went to his large customers, the insiders who with the collusion of the broker worked the price of a stock up or down for their own profit at the suckers' expense. If a high roller had a large line to sell, the broker tipped his smaller customers that the stock was a good buy and they gobbled it up. "We make most money from our large customers," one explained, "and we must keep them satisfied." Pool operators relied on the suckers to ride a stock upward too long while the insiders quietly unloaded at high prices and let the suckers enjoy the downward plunge.[7]

Women as well as men were invading the customers' rooms and Wall Street itself. Both the club and the Street had long ignored women or discouraged them from entering the financial world, but that discrimination had begun to soften. Just as businessmen discovered that women did most of the nation's buying, so did Wall Street realize that they also controlled a sizable chunk of its wealth—both earned and inherited. Increasingly brokers accepted women as customers and even sought them out, though most firms still relegated them to separate customers' rooms. One financial expert estimated that the proportion of women speculators had grown from less than 2 percent to more than 35 percent; others put the figure at 20 percent. Enlightened brokerages set up specially furnished rooms in uptown hotels for female clients. "The old objection . . . was based on the theory that women are 'poor losers,' " noted the *New York Times*. "Brokers who have made a specialty of women's business dispute that contention."[8]

"Primarily, of course," wrote one woman in a wry "how-to" article, "we went for the same reason that most of the other little pigs were going—that is, because we wanted to make some money quickly without working for it."[9]

A few women even found places on Wall Street, where once only weird eccentrics like the notorious miser Hetty Green had dared to go. By 1929 at least 22 Exchange firms had a woman as partner, and Ethel G. Rich headed Rich, Clark & Company. One female broker boasted a list of 300 clients, ranging from small shop owners to department store buyers to advertising writers. Some earned $15,000 a year and invested half of it; others were widows and daughters who had inherited money and wished to handle it personally. A few women found jobs as bond specialists, but those who tried to enter the brokerage business often found it tough going. Margaret E. McCann, who claimed to be the first female broker, started her own firm in 1924 but did not join any exchange. Her career came to grief in September 1928 when five indictments of grand larceny were leveled against her. No seat on the New York Stock Exchange belonged to a woman. As one writer noted, "The floor of the Exchange has been better protected against women than that of Congress."[10]

The club remained a resolutely male bastion, but even there a more modern mood or tone surfaced. One early sign came in July 1926 when Morgan partner Thomas Cochran, interviewed aboard ship prior to leaving for Europe, allowed that General Motors stock was "cheap at

the price, and it should and will sell at least one hundred points higher."
From anyone else this remark would have sounded like what the financial press called a "feedbox tip" intended to bull a stock, but Morgan
men never touted or even mentioned individual stocks. The elder Morgan had set the tone when, asked his opinion of the market, he said
curtly, "It will fluctuate." Even worse, the House of Morgan was GM's
banker, which gave the comment the flavor of an insider's tip and
seemed to violate the fiduciary relationship. GM stock promptly soared
25 points in two days, and the *Wall Street Journal* praised Cochran for
sharing his inside information with the public. Cochran tried in vain to
correct the gaffe, but the impression lingered that the mighty House of
Morgan had slipped a notch off its pedestal of rectitude.[11]

What seemed like heresy in 1926 was fast becoming a way of life by
1928. For all its exclusivity, even the club's standards were loosening
amid the waves of change washing over Wall Street. As the legion of
outside buyers grew, so did the financial services industry. To the club
and the Street was added a third sector, the outland. Unlike Wall
Street's old guard, "the specialists and floor traders . . . who actually
traded stocks face to face and knew the men they were beaten by," the
outlanders belonged to the "far-flung many-branched brokerage firms
serving the general public, most of whose members never saw the Exchange floor or made a stock trade face to face." Thanks to men like
Charley Mitchell with his salesman's approach to securities, the financial services industry had grown from a mere 250 dealers before the war
to 6,500 by 1929.[12]

The club and the street met this challenge of expansion by relying
ever more on what had always been their supreme advantage: inside information. The pool was usually their favorite vehicle provided the
right manager could be found for its operations. Few did better at this
game than Mike Meehan.

A fiery, redhaired Irishman with an equal command of wit and pro-
fanity, given to bursts of generosity and superstition, Meehan had
started as manager of a theater ticket agency. Lured to the market, he
saved enough money to buy a membership in the Curb Exchange by
1918. Two years later he anted up $90,000 for a seat on the New York
Stock Exchange, where his firm of M. J. Meehan did well enough by
1929 to own eight seats, more than any other member house. On the
floor he acted as specialist in three key stocks, most notably Radio. It
was Meehan who organized the pool that engineered the stock's spec-

tacular rise in March 1928. His carefully orchestrated campaign drove it from 90 to 109, at which point he sold out as the public watched the price slide back to 87. For this effort Meehan pocketed a fee of $500,000 while the pool divided profits of $5 million. Its members included such luminaries as Walter Chrysler, Charles M. Schwab, Mrs. David Sarnoff (the wife of Radio's president), Percy A. Rockefeller, John J. Raskob, Herbert Bayard Swope of the New York *World*, and Woodrow Wilson's former secretary Joseph Tumulty.[13]

Jesse Livermore and Arthur Cutten also excelled at managing pools. In October 1928 Harry F. Sinclair enlisted Cutten to take charge of a complicated operation in Sinclair Oil stock. For this task, which also required a secondary syndicate to assist in the buying and selling, Cutten had the help of the Chase Securities Corporation and one of Albert Wiggin's private corporations, Shermar. When the two syndicates finally closed out their work in the spring of 1929, they had realized a net profit of more than $12.6 million without the participants having actually put up a dollar of their own money. Most of the funds for purchasing stock came from a loan by the Chase National Bank to E. F. Hutton & Co., which handled the transactions. Hutton and another firm financed the remaining cash needed. Harry Sinclair and the 17 subscribers he had invited to join him collected $2.7 million of the profits.[14]

For talented managers, such maneuvers brought grand profits with little effort in a bull market, tempting them to return again and again. Gifted manipulators like Meehan had no difficulty putting together teams of investors from the ranks of the rich. Durant was ever willing, as were the seven Fisher brothers, who had reaped $280 million from the sale of their body company to General Motors and were eager to put it to good use. During 1929 no fewer than 105 stocks would be taken in hand by one or more pools on the New York Stock Exchange and another 27 on the Curb Exchange. Participants in the pools ran the gamut from the club to the street. Between 1927 and 1931, for example, even the august House of Morgan quietly took part in more than 50 stock pools. There was nothing illegal or even new about the device except for the enhanced possibilities offered by so large and willing a supply of outsider buyers.[15]

Pool operators used a variety of means to bait the minnows. They hired publicity agents to fertilize financial columns, distributed "tipster sheets," spread rumors, and paid financial journalists to boost their stock. Alexander Noyes claimed not to have known of a single instance

of a speculator buying a newspaper article, but it happened. One publicity man alone spent $286,279 on articles favorable to his pool's stock.
Another, David J. Lion, published a rag called "The Stock and Bond Reporter" which touted pool favorites in return for calls on blocks of the
stock. Lion also hired William J. McMahon to discuss the market on radio as an "impartial economist" and president of the "McMahon Institute of Financial Research," which specialized in boosting the pool
stock du jour. For his expertise, McMahon received $250 a week. Lion
did much better, engaging in as many as 30 operations at a time; the
calls he harvested from pool operators earned him a net profit of
$500,000 in three years.[16]

The bribery extended beyond the Street papers to the major dailies.
Raleigh T. Curtis, a financial columnist for the New York *Daily News*, offered his readers tips suggested by a trader who rewarded him with the
profits from a guaranteed trading account. A later investigation uncov-
ered financial writers on eight other papers who touted stocks in return
for cash or other favors. Two of the most embarrassing cases involved
daily columnists on the *Wall Street Journal*. William Gomber's "Broad Street
Gossip" and Richard E. Edmonson's "Abreast of the Market" were widely
read on Wall Street. Both were shown to have taken payoffs for stock tips
during the mid-1920s. The revelation ruined their careers and relegated
them to obscure jobs on the paper. At the time, however, only a few cyn-
ics and insiders knew or suspected how much the game was rigged.[17]

The investment trusts appeared like clouds on the distant horizon—
small, indistinct tufts attracting little attention until they increased in size
and filled the sky. In 1927 they sold the public about $400 million worth
of securities; that figure jumped to $790 million in 1928, during which
another 186 investment trusts were formed. Writer Garet Garrett divided
them into three types. One followed the original sound concept. A second group was created by "men who wished to control large properties
without the cost of owning them." They merely used investment trusts as
a vehicle for storing stocks they wanted to control for other purposes.
The third type was a different creature altogether. Garrett viewed it as
"nothing less than a pool to operate with other people's money on the
Stock Exchange. . . . The trust would play the market for you, knowing
always when to buy and what to buy. The trustees were on the inside."[18]

But who did the insiders serve? One authority, asked by a committee of the New York Stock Exchange to give his views of current investment-trust abuses, replied, "(1) dishonesty; (2) inattention and inability; (3) greed." Two glaring problems stood out: "First, that of being run for ulterior motives and not primarily for the best interest of the shareholders; second, that of being used as a depository for securities that might otherwise be unmarketable." That is, the banks or brokers running the trust seldom resisted the temptation to sell it securities they had difficulty moving. This blatant conflict of interest had yet to attract much attention or protest. No one understood what effect the investment trusts had on the overall market. One school of optimists believed they would have a stabilizing effect and, as the *Wall Street Journal* predicted, "be the main market support of the better class of stocks." Irving Fisher concluded that the trusts "made it safer to invest in common stocks than ever before."[19]

One point on which everyone agreed was that the investment trusts fed the growing public appetite for more stocks. Businessmen were not slow to grasp the possibilities offered by this trend. Instead of meeting financial needs by issuing bonds, they began to offer new stock, thereby accelerating the movement away from bonds toward stocks. Those seeking to erect business empires found stocks an irresistible scaffolding for their ambitious schemes. Since the first great merger movement of 1897–1904, the holding company had been the vehicle of choice for combining businesses on a vast scale. Standard Oil was an early example, General Motors a more recent one. Of the 573 active corporations with securities listed on the New York Stock Exchange in 1928, 92 were pure holding companies, 395 were holding and operating companies, and only 86 remained operating companies alone.[20]

Unlike operating companies, which made actual products or performed actual services, holding companies consisted of little more than an office housing the corporate and financial records of their subsidiaries. Some states, most notably Delaware, structured their laws to accommodate promoters of holding companies and became havens of residence for them. One lone building in Wilmington, for example, housed 10,000 corporations on a single floor. The merger movement during the 1920s grew as robustly as the stock market and provided fuel for it in the form of new securities. In the process it also swept away thousands of once independent firms. Between 1919 and 1928 some 1,200 mergers in mining and manufacturing eliminated more than 6,000 companies. Public utility mergers swallowed another 4,000, and an unknown number of banks were absorbed by nearly 1,800 mergers in that field.[21]

The merger movement offered choice opportunities for pyramiding that proved irresistible even to those dedicated to erecting business empires. Two of the most spectacular empires were built by men who resembled Horatio Alger far more than business pirates. To many observers Samuel Insull was nothing less than a genius and a pioneer in the organization and distribution of electric power. So too were the Van Sweringen brothers deemed innovators on a breathtaking scale. All three men had started at the bottom and worked their way to fame and fortune through bold and brilliant strokes. In the process they fashioned organizations so complex and convoluted as to defy comprehension even by the most astute business minds.

Insull cut his business teeth as secretary and financial adviser to Thomas A. Edison before moving to Chicago in 1892 as head of the Chicago Edison Company. Within fifteen years he transformed the industry by revolutionizing the economics and distribution of supplying power, which enabled him to provide ever more customers with ever cheaper electricity. To finance his growth, he shunned the New York bankers he loathed and went to London to sell bonds himself. In doing so he devised innovations in both the type of bond and the technique of selling it. By 1907, when Insull merged his company with Commonwealth Electric to form Commonwealth Edison, the utility had grown 60 times larger than when he first arrived.[22]

That same year Insull bought a farm northwest of Chicago, ran a power line to it for electricity, and gradually figured out the economics of supplying rural areas with power. While companies elsewhere shunned sparsely populated farming districts, Insull turned them into efficient, profitable markets. In 1912 he created Middle West Utilities Company, which became the parent holding company for his growing network in that region. By 1914 he had also taken charge of Chicago's elevated railways, which meant that Commonwealth Edison owned its largest customer. During the war he headed the Illinois State Council of National Defense. His gift for raising money led some people to quip that if he had run the war, he would have done so at a profit. However, his companies suffered from neglect under the duress of war and required his close attention during the painful postwar adjustment.[23]

An enlightened labor policy and two more financial innovations helped Insull weather the storm by 1923. His wartime experience sell-

ing bonds convinced him that he could peddle company securities directly to his customers. He created a security sales department in each
of his major companies, which by 1930 helped enlist a million people as
partial owners of Insull firms. To sell corporate bonds on a large scale,
he shunned Wall Street and relied instead on Harold L. Stuart of the
Chicago firm of Halsey, Stuart & Co., who recognized that a huge un-
tapped market of buyers could be reached by mass-marketing bonds
through smaller outlets. Stuart embraced utility bonds early, when most
investment bankers were wary of them. In 1922 he sold $27 million
worth of bonds at just over half the interest Insull had paid on earlier issues. This feat soon earned him all of Insull's business; in one year alone
he sold almost $200 million in bonds. Nothing pleased Insull more than
to bypass the arrogant Wall Street club. "Bankers," he once said, "will
lend you umbrellas only when it doesn't look like rain."[24]

By the mid-1920s Insull had become that peculiar American blend of
icon and celebrity, a regular cast member in both the business and society sections of the daily newspapers. His feats incurred the enmity of
the Wall Street club, which like the French Bourbons learned nothing
and remembered everything. He and Stuart had offended the club with
their marketing innovations that made the bond business more competitive. Worst of all, Insull had thumbed his nose at New York leadership.
"These New York fellows were jealous of their prerogatives," recalled
Stuart's brother, "and if you wanted to get along you had to be deferen-
tial to them and keep your opinions to yourself. Mr. Insull wouldn't, and
that made bad blood between them. Real bad blood."[25]

The bad blood was not merely personal. Utility bonds were lucrative
for bankers and had become a big business. New issues approached $1
billion by 1926, and Halsey, Stuart dominated the field along with some
smaller firms. A few minor houses created holding companies to put together combinations, while others fashioned investment trusts to raise
money for the same purpose. By 1927 the Morgan partners were pon-
dering ways to organize the utilities industry under their rule. While
they laid plans for a giant holding company, Insull invaded their domain
early in 1928 by acquiring two holding company systems that operated
in 14 eastern states, giving him a major presence there for the first time.
By then Insull's empire revolved around four major holding companies:
Commonwealth Edison, Peoples Gas, Public Service of Northern Illinois, and Middle West Utilities, the latter a $1.2 billion giant operating
in 32 states. Altogether Insull plants served more than 4 million cus-

tomers and produced an eighth of all electricity and gas consumed in the United States.[26]

Determined to preserve this empire for his son, Insull looked for ways to protect it from potential rivals such as Cyrus Eaton, who had bought large blocks of shares in all the major Insull companies. In December 1928 he formed a new holding company, Insull Utility Investments (IUI), and put all his holdings in it along with those of his brother. Never a denizen of the stock market, Insull set the initial offering price of IUI at $12 a share. To his surprise the surging market pushed it past $80 by spring, and the prices of all his other companies also soared. The bull market enriched Insull but also complicated his main task by jacking up the prices IUI had to pay for other Insull stocks. And what would happen if the bubble suddenly burst, as he assumed it must? To his chagrin Insull found himself an unwilling prisoner of the market, a role for which he had little ambition, let alone the talent to manage its fickle whims.[27]

Insull's achievement in the newly emerging power industry was paralleled by that of the Van Sweringen brothers in the nation's oldest major industry. Among the crowded gallery of enigmatic American business leaders, few even approach the strange, elusive personalities of Oris Paxton and Mantis James Van Sweringen. These two reclusive bachelors, who did everything together, could not have been more modest and unassuming in manner, yet their boldness forged the largest railroad system in the country. Born two years apart of humble origins outside Wooster, Ohio, endowed with whimsical names the origins of which even they did not know, the Vans (as they soon became known) left school after the eighth grade to go to work. Moving to Cleveland, they went into real estate and in 1900 developed Cleveland Heights. In 1906 they bought an adjacent 1,366-acre farm and gradually expanded it into a planned community called Shaker Heights, which became a landmark upper-class suburb.[28]

Aware that transportation held the key to the success of Shaker Heights, the Vans in 1910 set out to build a rapid transit system from the suburb to Public Square, the historic center of Cleveland. One of the farms they bought to expand the Heights belonged to Alfred Smith, who within a year became president of the powerful New York Central rail system. He helped finance the rapid transit line, which opened in 1920, and in 1916 sold the Vans the 523-mile Nickel Plate railroad for $8.5 million. The brothers created a holding company, the Nickel Plate

Securities Company, to buy the road, and Smith provided terms so attractive that the deal required only $520,000 cash, which the Vans bor-
rowed. Smith also recommended one of his vice presidents, John J.
Bernet, to head the Nickel Plate. Bernet soon transformed the road into
an efficient, profitable line and was to do likewise for other Van Sweringen acquisitions.[29]

From this seed of acquisition and leveraging grew a mighty rail system that exceeded 14,000 miles by 1929. Already the Vans had discovered the value of holding companies, which permitted absolute control
and quick decision making as well as vast potential for raising funds. As
one authority observed, "The control of the parent's directors over the
subsidiaries' machinery is absolute; even the information disclosed may
be so blind as to be unintelligible." The Vans lacked capital but had a
gift for making important friends to assist them in realizing their growing vision of a rail system in the East worthy of competing with the
Pennsylvania, New York Central, and Baltimore & Ohio. Smith continued his support in the belief that a competing system under the Vans
would be a friendly ally to the New York Central. In 1916 the brothers
also launched an ambitious project to revitalize downtown Cleveland
by starting work on the huge Hotel Cleveland. Construction on a majestic new terminal began in 1923 and evolved into a bold complex of
buildings with a 52-story skyscraper to be known as Terminal Tower as
its centerpiece.[30]

With Smith's help the Vans elevated the Nickel Plate into a 1,700-
mile system by acquiring two other roads and gaining control of the
Chesapeake & Ohio (C&O), Hocking Valley, Erie, and Pere Marquette
railroads. Smith's unexpected death in 1924 dealt the brothers a severe
blow, as did the Interstate Commerce Commission, which in 1926 denied their request to combine the roads into a single system. It meant
that the C&O rather than the Nickel Plate would become the core of
their system. Unable to pursue a formal consolidation, the brothers tied
their roads together in a complex series of holding companies. They
also found a new financial angel in the House of Morgan, which, explained one of the partners, George Whitney, had "great faith in their
aims of trying to build this railroad system. . . . We have believed in
them . . . and we have gone along as bankers with them."[31]

Financial backing by Morgan kept the Vans' shoestring empire afloat
while they restructured it. In 1922 they had created the Vaness Co. as a
holding company; it became the hub for a complex series of transac-

tions that relied on two loans from Morgan totaling $83 million. The Nickel Plate Securities Company was dissolved and replaced by several new entities: the Chesapeake Corporation, Special Investment Corporation, General Securities Corporation, Virginia Transportation Company, and Pere Marquette Corporation. These companies raised generous amounts of cash while keeping control of the roads securely in the Vans' hands through intertwined holdings. By 1927 the Vaness Co. controlled the key Chesapeake Corporation and had pledged all its assets against the Morgan loans. Through another complicated set of maneuvers the brothers gained control of the 530-mile Wheeling & Lake Erie early in 1929.[32]

By 1928 the Vans sat atop an impressive if convoluted rail empire buttressed by the Morgan loans and eager investors. Clevelanders lavished praise on them for the multimillion-dollar development project in the city's heart as well as their rail system. Even critics of their pyramid of holding companies found no fault with its creators. The shy, boyish brothers did not smoke or drink, had no vices except overwork, and lived modestly outside the spotlight. In an age of ballyhoo they had the trappings of simplicity that had elevated Charles A. Lindbergh into a national icon. They were also poised to launch their most ambitious undertaking: another holding company that would dwarf what had gone before. It would be done through the House of Morgan and launch that august firm for the first time down the dubious path of stock promotion through the sort of investment trust vehicle it had traditionally shunned.[33]

———

In a campaign with few live issues beyond Prohibition and Democratic candidate Al Smith's Catholicism, Hoover rode the timeless advantages of peace and prosperity to a decisive victory. Some viewed the fray as a pitched battle between urban and rural America, others as an endorsement of the New Era mentality promising still more fat years under the wise guidance of an able and sound administrator. Hoover even managed to dent the solid South, winning five former Confederate states. He had orchestrated much of the campaign himself, demonstrating yet again his gift for public relations and self-promotion that led Walter Lippmann to label his reputation a "work of art." Later, when Hoover sought a title for his collected campaign speeches, he chose *The New Day*.[34]

The cabinet he put together did not seem to merit that title. From Coolidge's crew he kept the venerable Mellon and Labor Secretary James J. Davis, a moderate who believed fervently in collective bargaining. The remaining choices, except for Secretary of State Henry L. Stimson, lacked imagination and any reputation comparable to Hoover's for progressive thinking. Most of them were millionaires; none was Catholic or Jewish or hailed from the South. As for himself, Hoover told an interviewer that he had "no dread of the ordinary work of the presidency. What I do fear is the result of the exaggerated idea the people have conceived of me. They have a conviction that I am a sort of superman, that no problem is beyond my capacity. . . . If some unprecedented calamity should come upon the nation . . . I would be sacrificed to the unreasoning disappointment of a people who expected too much."[35]

Although he would not take office for five months, Hoover had already suffered a severe blow without even realizing it. The directors of the New York bank had tried to dissuade Ben Strong from resigning in August, but fate took the matter out of their hands. On the morning of October 16 he died from a severe hemorrhage, depriving the New York bank and the Federal Reserve System of its strongest leader at a critical time. Having blamed Strong for the easy-money policy that fueled the stock market rise, Hoover did not deem him a serious loss; later he dismissed the late banker as "a mental annex to Europe." But in an age increasingly given to illusion, Strong had a clearer sense than most of what was happening. In one of his last letters he summarized the dilemma:

> I do not think the problem is necessarily one of security prices or of available volume of credit, or even of discount rates. It is really a problem of psychology. The country's state of mind has been highly speculative, advancing prices have been based upon a realization of wealth and prosperity[;] . . . consequently speculative tendencies are all the more difficult to deal with. . . . The problem now is so to shape our policy as to avoid a calamitous break in the stock market, a panicky feeling about money, a setback to business because of the change in psychology.[36]

But Strong would not be there to attempt this herculean task or mediate the unending struggle between the Federal Reserve Board and the regional banks. In his place the New York bank elected George L.

Harrison, who had been deputy governor since 1920. He was a bright young lawyer who had clerked for Oliver Wendell Holmes and served as counsel for the Federal Reserve Board from 1914 until Strong recruited him for the New York post. A capable, high-minded official, Harrison knew the Fed system thoroughly but lacked Strong's influence and force in dealing with the board and its roster of mediocrities. No one could replace Strong's leadership, and the timing of his loss could not have been worse. With Strong's death, wrote one historian, "the intimacy of the transatlantic relationship evaporated." But Harrison had more pressing problems at home. During the last weeks of Strong's life, the bull market had emerged from its summer hiatus with renewed enthusiasm.[37]

The spring rise in 1928 had lifted the market out of its winter doldrums, sending the *New York Times* average from 177.43 on March 1 to a record high of 199.53 on May 14 and the Dow Jones industrials from 194.81 to 220.88. During that run the volume exceeded 4 million shares no fewer than 22 times and twice flirted with 5 million. Prior to 1928 volume had exceeded 3 million shares only 8 times; in 1928 it did so 159 times. Wall Street and the Exchange, which had struggled to gear its equipment to handle 3-million days, staggered under this growing load. The spring bull movement also drove brokers' loans to new heights, sending them to $4.5 billion on May 16. For nearly a month the market vacillated until the collapse in mid-June that to some observers signaled the death of the bull. After its dramatic 5-million-share day on the 12th, trading wilted as it usually did in the summer months. In August the *Times* index rose nearly 13 points and the Dow Jones industrials nearly 24, but trading did not exceed 4 million shares until the last day of the month. Brokers' loans declined for most of the summer.[38]

Autumn 1928 brought a succession of good economic news including increased orders for steel, automobiles, and other industrial products, improved commodity prices, a forecast for robust fall crops, and quickening commercial activity. During September and October the *Times* average rose only 5 points and the Dow Jones 8 points, but trading picked up sharply as volume exceeded 4 million shares on 14 days in September and a dozen times in October. For the first time total volume surpassed 90 million shares in September, then ran past 97.6 million shares the following month. The election sparked a feeding frenzy that became known as the Hoover market. During November volume exceeded 114.8 million shares, demolishing all previous records. Daily trading surpassed 4 million shares no fewer than 17 times, breezed past

5 million shares 13 times, and on six days soared above the once unthinkable 6 million shares. On one frantic day, November 23, volume
reached a record 6.94 million shares.

In three whirlwind weeks the market marched into new territory,
sending the *Times* average up 17 points and the Dow up 40 points. This
was more than the Dow had gained in any entire *year* except 1927,
when it rose 47 points. As usual the gains were highly selective, concentrated among the "favorites" bulled by the growing number of pools
working the market. Even Jesse Livermore, the lover of broad trends,
conceded that the New Era had created not a stock market but a market
of stocks. "With one thousand issues, representing every industry, listed
on the Stock Exchange," he observed, "there is no such thing as a trend
anymore." Some of the favorites soared to breathless heights. Between
November 3 and 27, Radio increased 130½ points, Case Threshing
Machine 87, Wright Aeronautics (which had built Lindbergh's plane)
83, Montgomery Ward 72, International Harvester 62, and Du Pont 57,
while a dozen other stocks recorded gains of 19 points or more.[39]

"The market has over-ridden every obstacle . . . placed in its path,"
declared a *New York Times* reporter, and "mounted higher and higher, under the irresistible drive of a public participation in trading which has
never before been equaled." This heightened public buying could be
seen in the swelling business of the "odd-lot houses," which dealt only
in trades of less than a hundred shares. During the Hoover market one
such house alone handled nearly 1.2 million shares in two days. Hardly
anyone doubted that the driving force behind the surging bull was speculative. Brokers' loans followed the market upward, crossing the once
unthinkable $5 billion mark during the week of November 21. This un-
precedented level of loans disturbed many conservative observers, as
did another trend: the steadily increasing proportion of these funds
coming from corporations, individuals, foreign lenders, and other
sources outside the banking system, which by November 21 accounted
for 44 percent of call loans.[40]

An ominous pattern was developing, and no one knew what to make
of it. Traditionally large corporations kept their surplus cash in banks as
time deposits. In 101 major cities these deposits reached a peak of $6.9
billion in June 1928, then began to decline for the rest of the year. At
the same time, interest on call loans rose above 7 percent, making them
an attractive and apparently safe short-term investment for corporate
treasurers. As a result, fresh funds for the feeding frenzy on Wall Street

Calvin Coolidge with Herbert Hoover, elected his successor as president in 1928.
(Library of Congress)

flowed in not from banks but from corporations, which withdrew or withheld funds from their bank accounts to put them into the call loan market, and from other outside sources. This trend gave the Fed another serious problem apart from its internal ones: it had no control or authority over the flow of these funds coming from sources outside the banking system.[41]

On December 4 Calvin Coolidge delivered his last annual message. "No Congress . . . on surveying the state of the Union," he said proudly, "has met with a more pleasing prospect than that which appears at the present time. In the domestic field there is tranquility and contentment . . . and the highest records of years of prosperity. In the foreign field there is peace. . . . Enlarging production is consumed by an increasing demand at home and an expanding commerce abroad. The country can regard the present with satisfaction and anticipate the future with optimism." Pleased with his accomplishments, and somewhat miffed by the spate of stories filled with glowing predictions about what Hoover would achieve in the White House, Coolidge deferred action on some problems by telling his staff dryly, "We'll leave that to the wonder boy."[42]

The market had reached new high ground on November 28 as the *Times* average closed at 228.05 and the Dow Jones industrials at 295.62. For the next week it slipped downward. Alexander Noyes, tracking its upward course with growing dismay, chose Monday, December 3, to deliver one of his sermons on the dangers inherent in the "attitude of that not inconsiderable portion of the speculating public which has parted with the sense of reason or proportion." They foolishly believed that "with the irresistible forces now driving up the market, nothing can stop the rise of prices. . . . The horizon of expectation is one which merely takes for granted indefinite continuance of the existing movement throughout the future and does not trouble with arithmetic." Wall Street itself talked endlessly about how long the boom might last, but "the end is never fixed uncomfortably near." Noyes also noted shrewdly that many people "who are making no predictions, or who are possibly predicting vastly higher prices, have actually reached the conclusion that this is the time to sell."[43]

As brokers' loans climbed higher, the rate on call money reached 10 percent, sending a chill through the market. On December 6 the rate hit 12 percent, the highest since the 1920 crisis, and a wave of selling sent the market into a three-day spiral that lopped nearly 16 points (7 percent) off the *Times* average and more than 33 points (11 percent) off the Dow. The *Times* decline of 6.2 points (2.7 percent) on December 6 was the largest single day's loss ever recorded in its average. The orgy of selling overwhelmed every effort to steady prices. Not surprisingly, the speculative favorites that had led the charge upward fell the hardest. Radio, which had jumped 36 points on December 4, plummeted 72 points four days later. International Harvester dropped more than 61, National Tea 54, Federal Mining & Smelting 50, Case Threshing Machine 33, and Montgomery Ward 29. During this Saturday session, when the market was open only between 10:00 A.M. and noon, a record 3.7 million shares changed hands.[44]

Many on Wall Street had hoped for some kinder, gentler break to cool off the surging bull. "Wall Street has several comfortable euphemisms to describe such incidents without admitting that the perpetual rise of prices has been more than momentarily arrested," wrote Noyes. "Sometimes it is a 'technical adjustment.' . . . Sometimes it is a 'healthy reaction.' " The violence of this reaction prompted some to wonder whether it signaled the end of the bull market, but Noyes thought otherwise. He had seen this game played too many times, although never on this scale. "Nothing has been more familiar in our past speculative manias," he warned, "than the heavy break in prices which seems to have brought the end, but which was followed by an even greater fury of speculation, lasting until a much severer and far more effective reckoning had been invoked."[45]

On Monday and Tuesday, December 10 and 11, call loan rates fell to 7 and 8 percent, and the market responded with a solid recovery. Within another week it started yet another upward movement, and the collapse became little more than a ghastly memory. By year's end the *Times* average celebrated a new high of 230.52, and the Dow closed at exactly 300, also a record. As the Exchange closed on Monday, December 31, to prepare for its annual New Year's Eve party, investors, speculators, businessmen, financiers, and pundits alike peered anxiously into their crystal balls in search of signs for the coming year. Charley Mitchell weighed in with a buoyant forecast. "Business is entering the new year upon a high level of activity," he said, "and with confidence in the continuance of prosperity." As for the market, "No complaint regarding the level of stock prices . . . is justified except from the standpoint of credit strain. . . . When corporations and others withdraw deposits to lend at high rates, the banks are stripped of the excess funds they would normally hold for industrial needs."[46]

Businessmen generally shared the view of banker Lewis E. Pierson: "All major indications point to a prosperous coming year." Arthur Lehman of Lehman Brothers sounded a rare sour note. "When I say that the outlook for business is doubtful," he emphasized, "I mean it literally. . . . Production has been at a high rate during the past year and it is difficult to see where in many lines an expansion could arise." But Thomas J. Watson of International Business Machines noted that industrial payrolls were at their highest levels since 1920 and manufacturing employment at its highest since April 1927. He concluded that "we may look with confidence to the progress of business in 1929." Architect Henry Ives Cobb added, "All signs point to a continuance of prosperous building conditions similar to those of the past year."[47]

When Alexander Noyes sat down to compose his traditional forecast for the coming year, he found the financial horizon murky even in outline. Last year's prophecy had correctly predicted the business recovery and the continued rise in stocks but missed the growing influence of the stock market and the squeeze that produced the tightest money market since 1920. Now he noticed a troubling contradiction in conditions. On one hand he agreed with nearly everyone that the underlying economy was sound and likely to remain so. The nation was rich, the banks remained sound, production and consumption continued to expand, corporate profits were high, as were wages in many areas, and prices were stable. The stock market had survived another fall and remained a wild card, but the most ominous cloud on the horizon continued to be the credit situation.[48]

A return to the easy money and abundant bank credit of 1927 seemed unlikely because of the stock market's voracious appetite for funds. One danger was that continued tight money might begin to affect trade. Past experience, never far from Noyes's thinking, had shown a clear pattern worth remembering. A speculative market soon transformed easy money into tighter credit conditions. If speculators ignored rising rates for too long, "that inflation of credit runs beyond all possible facilities and the bubble bursts." Given this fact, so obvious to Noyes and so ignored by nearly everyone on Wall Street, "the fantastic illusions that are entertained of the economic future and the public appetite for the most reckless stock speculation, are distinctly disquieting."

Elsewhere, however, the future looked much brighter to those who didn't peer too closely at it. The New York *World* reflected this spirit with exactly the kind of braggadocio that Noyes feared and detested most. "Nothing matters as long as stocks keep going up . . . ," it brayed. "The market is now its own law. The forces behind its advance are irresistible."[49]

8

Makin'

Whoopee

The basic delusion was that we had entered a fourth-dimensional economic world. The wonderful feature of this new world was that all possibilities of increase were infinite. There was no longer any limit upon the rise of common stocks. Since this was so obvious to everyone, it followed that common stocks could not fall. How could they fall? There was no reason for people ever to sell them.

—Garet Garrett[1]

*I*n 1928 a Broadway show called *Whoopee* included a cynical little song about marriage, divorce, and alimony that Eddie Cantor turned into a hit. Its title, "Makin' Whoopee," soon became a national catch phrase for the feverish, reckless spirit of the age. "Few, during those flush years," wrote Mark Sullivan, "escaped the infection that made men act with an impulsiveness which did not sufficiently calculate the consequences." On Wall Street everyone was making whoopee, or trying to, and a record number danced happily to another popular tune called, "My God, How the Money Rolls In." Never had it seemed easier to make money. As the money market tightened, all bankers had to do was borrow from the Fed at 5 percent and lend in the call money market at 10 or 12 percent. No effort or initiative or even risk was involved. "Bankers," noted John Brooks, "like royalty in a constitutional monarchy, were in the position of being handsomely paid simply for existing."[2]

The major players grew fat from their pools, and in a rising market even the minnows could ride one of the "star" stocks upward. The brokers' bulletins, those "printed effusions of speculative houses," as Alexander Noyes called them, refined their technique of encouraging the public by going beyond mere general assurances that now was the time to buy or even recommending specific winners or sleepers. The morning letters, Noyes recalled, "had already adopted the plan of informing clients what stocks would rise that day and how far—sometimes 10 or 20 points. Now they improved the formula sufficiently to notify customers that at 2 P.M., Radio or General Motors would be 'taken in hand.' " Those hesitant to follow the leaders could always jump aboard the latest holding company or investment trust being touted as a sure thing.[3]

The holding companies, as Frederick Lewis Allen viewed them, were "like a cream-separating machine, which skimmed off the richest of the profits when these were increasing." So too were their baby brothers, the investment trusts. As the new year opened, few of those in the club or on the Street could resist becoming connoisseurs of cream. The private banking firm of Goldman, Sachs and Company did not form its first investment trust, Goldman, Sachs Trading Corporation, until December 1928, but it quickly made up lost ground. Two months later the $100 million Trading Corporation absorbed a new investment trust, Financial and Industrial Securities Corporation, raising its assets to $235 million. The stock, originally sold at 104, climbed past 222 early in February. The parent firm helped this spurt along with heavy purchases of its own, then sold a large block of the stock to Billy Durant, who doled it out to an eager public while Goldman, Sachs laid even more ambitious plans.[4]

This first major merger of investment companies set the tone for what proved a frantic year. In January 1929 another investment banking house, J. & W. Seligman & Co., launched its Tri-Continental Corporation with a capitalization of $50 million. Arthur Cutten joined the parade, as did other Chicago investors who formed the $60 million Chicago Corporation; by Labor Day the number had increased to more than 400. New holding companies also proliferated, and the line between them and the investment trusts was often nebulous at best. None had more public impact than the Alleghany Corporation, which was organized in January as the next rung on the growing ladder of Van Sweringen companies. Its significance lay not only in the scale of the venture but even more in the fact that the parent firm was the House of Morgan, which had previously remained aloof from involvement in common stock and pyramiding operations.[5]

The deal was predictably complicated. On January 29 the Van Sweringens sold to Morgan $35 million in 5 percent bonds for $32.75 million, $25 million in preferred stock, and 1.25 million of the 3.5 million common shares for $20 a share, or $25 million. In addition, Morgan paid $375,000 to obtain warrants for another 375,000 shares of common at $30 per share. The Vans also took warrants for 375,000 shares at the same price and bought 2.25 million shares of common at $20 a share. For this stock they paid not cash but 100,000 shares of Nickel Plate common and 440,286 shares of Chesapeake Corporation common. Then they sold to their own General Securities Corporation the 2.25 million shares of Alleghany and 1.725 million option warrants at $1 per warrant. Since all the directors of Alleghany were Van Sweringen associates, the deal amounted to trading with themselves. The brothers also sold Alleghany large blocks of stock in their other railroads through the Vaness Co.[6]

When the smoke cleared and the mirrors defogged, Alleghany possessed railroad securities valued at about $52 million, for which it paid $36 million in cash, 2.25 million shares of Alleghany common, and 1.725 million in option warrants on its common—a total of about $84 million—and the Van Sweringens still held more than 1.5 million shares of Alleghany. The House of Morgan had no intention of stooping to the level of mere retailer of common stock. Instead it sold 500,000 shares of Alleghany to Guaranty Trust Co. and offered the rest privately to a select group of "friends" at its own cost of $20 a share. The favored few on these "preferred lists" were prominent figures in business, politics, and banking. Although the stock was not yet available to the public, rumors abounded and would surely boost its price once it was listed on the Exchange. Those who bought at cost, therefore, stood to reap a tidy profit at virtually no risk.[7]

"We did not believe . . . it was a proper thing for us to sell those (stocks) through any hullabaloo in the general market to the general public," explained Morgan partner George Whitney. "But we . . . knew certain people who had the substantial wealth, the knowledge of their securities, and the willingness to take a risk along with us in the underwriting of these common stocks." One of the "risk takers" was John J. Raskob, who gladly accepted the 2,000 shares offered him. "Many thanks for your trouble and for so kindly remembering me . . . ," he wrote Whitney. "I appreciate deeply the many courtesies shown me by you and your partners and sincerely hope the future holds opportunities for me to reciprocate." His "risk" was amply rewarded. On February 4, when Raskob penned his letter, Alleghany was already selling above 33; it would climb to 57 that spring. Nor was this a new device. In June 1927 the House of Morgan acquired 400,000 shares of Johns-Manville common at 47$1/2$ and resold 343,750 of them at cost to its "friends." The remaining 56,250 shares went to other "friends" for 57$1/2$, a price that still fetched handsome profits since the stock was selling at 79 at the time.[8]

That same January the House of Morgan launched its counterattack against the Insull utility empire by forming the United Corporation, a super-holding company that gathered together a variety of utility companies. United's subsidiaries produced 38 percent of the electricity used in the 12 states it served and 20 percent of the nation's supply. Unlike Insull's empire, United made no attempt to integrate management or operations; the objective, as Forrest McDonald put it, was simply enough control "to capture bond accounts" with their lucrative profits. Here, too, Morgan made no public offering of United's stock but resorted to a private offering to its own list of preferred friends. Those who were invited to take units of one share each of common and preferred for $75 were pleased to find them selling at $99 when the stock went public that month. "It is not a question of altruism," said George Whitney; "it is a question of doing a legitimate, straightforward security and banking business. . . . Some of them made money. I hope most of them did. I do not know anything about that."[9]

He did know about how well the firm and its partners did. By Labor Day Morgan had sold 200,000 option warrants, for which it had paid $1 each, for a total of nearly $8.5 million. Later the partners divided another 1.5 million warrants among themselves at $1 each; within 60 days the value of these warrants rose to $40 million. Other firms also had their lists of select friends. Kuhn, Loeb relied on them, Otto Kahn explained, to "maintain the good will of individuals upon whom Kuhn, Loeb relied for advice in financial matters." When the Pennsylvania Railroad organized the Pennroad Corporation in April, Kuhn, Loeb as its bankers collected $5.84 million for its services and the resale of the new company's shares on which it had received options. The services consisted of advising the Pennsylvania to raise funds through two stock issues of common stock rather than bonds or preferred stock and assuring it that no underwriting was needed to make these stock offerings successful. "No one was more surprised than we were," said Otto Kahn of the firm's profit on options for stock that jumped 9 to 12 points above its opening quotation in a single day.[10]

The big commercial banks also had their own lists of select friends. Charley Mitchell justified one private offering by arguing that a limited distribution to "our own officers, key men, directors and special friends . . . would enable us to more easily handle further desirable mergers and . . . take away the heavy speculation that would accompany in general a public offering on our part." A later investigation concluded, however, that it had more to do with "a well-conceived plan to excite public interest in the stock so that when it was listed on a public exchange the individuals on the preferred list would be in a position to realize a substantial profit." As always the insiders, whether in the club or on the street, had every advantage, and they made it pay as never before during 1929.[11]

Mitchell's high-pitched sales approach had already drawn the National City Company into some dubious investments. During 1927 and 1928 it headed syndicates that underwrote three issues of Peruvian bonds totaling $90 million despite repeated confidential warnings from knowledgeable officers about that country's unstable government, poor history of debt repayment, shaky economy, and uncertain prospects. None of these negative reports found its way into the prospectuses given to an unwary public, which snapped up the bonds. National City did likewise with two bond issues totaling $16.5 million for the Brazilian state of Minas Gerais despite similar warnings. "It would be hard to find anywhere," reported one National City officer, "a sadder confession of inefficiency and ineptitude than that displayed by the various State officials." He summarized in detail "the complete ignorance, carelessness and negligence of the former State officials in respect to external long-term borrowing."[12]

Nevertheless, the offering went forward behind a prospectus assuring investors that "prudent and careful management of the State's finances has been characteristic of successive administrations in Minas Geraes [sic]." However, the bank was careful not to believe its own assurances. Having extended Minas Gerais $4 million in short-term credits, National City used half the proceeds from the second bond issue to repay this debt. Customers for the bonds learned nothing of these details; the prospectus said only that the funds were intended "for purposes designed to increase the economic productivity of the State."

In the realm of stocks, the National City Company took part in and financed three pools in copper shares between December 1928 and

March 1929. From these operations it earned $167,000 in profits plus about 66,000 shares of Anaconda Copper stock worth about $9 million at current prices. It helped that the pool included the president and the board chairman of Anaconda and that National City was Anaconda's banker. Dealings in Anaconda increased later in the year but paled before National City Company's vigorous campaign to peddle the stock of its own bank. It began in December 1928 and utilized the affiliate company's entire network of 350 salesmen, the investment departments of correspondent banks in the interior, and hundreds of dealers throughout the country. On February 1, 1929, managers throughout the company received a notice offering the stock to customers at a special price 5 points below market. "A premium will be allowed, of course, as usual. . . . It will result in the addition of a substantial number of new business prospects for all of us."[13]

The company pushed its salesmen not only to acquire new customers but to switch old ones into the bank's stock. To that end the company itself became the single largest buyer and seller of the bank's shares, churning them at high volume to generate public interest. During the week of February 21 alone it sold 92,709 shares, and when necessity required it did not hesitate to sell the stock short as well. That spring the company borrowed a total of 30,000 shares from Mitchell himself to fulfill deliveries on short sales, paying him $128,850 in interest. Like many bank stocks, National City was sold over the counter. The bank had removed the stock from the Exchange list in January 1928 on the pretext of protecting it from speculation; in fact the delisting enabled National City to manipulate the stock as no outside speculator could. The stock then sold at 785 per share; it climbed to 940 by June 1928 and reached 1,450 in January 1929. By then the chief speculator in the bank's stock had become its own affiliate.[14]

At the Chase National Bank, Albert Wiggin used variations on these same themes to make his own brand of whoopee. He had removed that bank's stock from the Exchange list in January 1928, explaining later that "we did not want . . . those fluctuations quoted in every paper all over the country." The bank had not only its own affiliate, Chase Securities Corporation, but also the Metpotan Securities Corporation, created in 1921 when the Chase merged with Metropolitan Bank. In addition, Wiggin used some of the six private corporations he had formed to handle his personal dealing in the bank's stock, among others. An early pool formed in September 1927, using Metpotan, Wiggin's own Shermar Corporation, and some securities dealers, earned a profit of $50,621 by the following April. During that time the bank's stock rose from 575 to 684. The same parties immediately started another pool in the bank's stock that closed out in April 1929 with a profit of $554,760. Ultimately they ran a total of eight pools in Chase stock with transactions totaling $860 million. From them Metpotan gleaned a profit of only $159,574, but Albert Wiggin did much better.[15]

To shield himself from charges of impropriety and to dodge taxes, Wiggin conducted most of his market activities through the Shermar, Murlyn, and Clingston companies, owned by himself and family members. These shells dealt primarily in Chase National Bank and Chase Securities Corporation stocks. The officers of both companies knew of this arrangement but made no objection, largely because Wiggin made many of them officers or directors in his companies and cut them in on the action. It was a cozy arrangement. Chase Securities gave Shermar and/or other Wiggin firms a subparticipation in various pools, and those companies in turn did the same for officers of Chase Securities. To finance their trading, Wiggin's corporations borrowed large sums from the Chase bank itself, as did many of the officers, sometimes on little or no collateral. During 1928–29, Shermar alone received 15 loans totaling $11.8 million.[16]

The money was put to good use. Between 1928 and 1932 Wiggin, through Chase Securities and his own firms, realized a cash profit of more than $10.4 million from dealing in Chase bank stock alone. But Shermar and its sister companies joined Chase Securities in other operations as well. One pool in Sinclair Consolidated Oil, churning 1.13 million shares, fetched a profit of $12.4 million without anyone except the brokers putting up a single dollar. Shermar's slice of this pie amounted to $891,600. Another pool brought Shermar $55,539 from dealings in a company of which Wiggin was a director. And, of course, Wiggin was on several preferred lists that enabled him to profit from operations without the slightest risk or responsibility. Small wonder that years later, with a straight face, he described what was going on as a "God-given market."[17]

––––––––––

For those on the outside, making whoopee sometimes felt and sounded more like a whoopee cushion. Edgar D. Brown of Pottsville, Pennsylvania, earned the dubious honor of serving as poster boy for the suckers. Not yet 40, he was tired and in poor health. In 1927 Brown owned $25,000 in bonds and was about to receive another $75,000 from the sale of some theaters he owned. Eager to invest this nest egg carefully and retire to California, he happened across a National City magazine ad that asked, "Are you thinking of a lengthy trip? If you are, it will pay you to get in touch with our institution, because you will be leaving the advice of your local banker and we will be able to keep you closely guided as regards your investments." Impressed by the close fit with his needs, Brown answered the ad. A representative named Fred Rummel from National City Company soon called and persuaded Brown to entrust his funds to the nation's largest, soundest institution. Brown agreed with but one stipulation: he wanted only bonds, for both safety and income purposes.[18]

Having stepped gingerly onto National City's roller coaster, Brown soon found himself hanging on for dear life. Rummel persuaded him to sell his existing bonds and buy a variety of National City offerings, including some choice Peruvian bonds. He also convinced Brown to borrow another $75,000 at $5^1/2$ percent to invest in bonds paying $7^1/2$ percent. Through 1928 National City churned the securities in Brown's account so furiously that he could not keep up with the pace or fathom its exotic mixture. By year's end only one thing was clear to him: the bonds had gone down rather than up in value. He complained to Rummel, who replied, "Well, that is your fault for insisting upon bonds. Why don't you let me sell you some stock?" The suggestion made sense to Brown in that the market had soared while the bonds just chugged along. He agreed to the change and let Rummel select the stocks for him.[19]

The trading in stocks proceeded at an even more frenzied pace than in bonds, yet Brown could see no real gain in the value of his portfolio. Even worse, he no longer had the income produced by the bonds and still had to pay interest on the money he had borrowed. In the spring of 1929 he felt desperate enough to visit National City's headquarters in New York. He would register his complaint in person and demand action.[20]

"One cannot recall when a new year was ushered in with business conditions sounder than they are today," beamed the *Wall Street Journal* on January 4. "Everything points to full production of industry and record breaking traffic for railroads." The New York Stock Exchange antici-

The exchange floor at the end of a day's trading, showing the horseshoe-shaped seats installed in 1929.   (Library of Congress)

pated a bonanza year as well. On January 11 a seat sold for $550,000, a record that lasted only until February 7, when another changed hands for $625,000. That same day the Exchange completed voting to expand the membership from 1,100 to 1,375, the first increase since 1879. To handle the swelling tide of orders, the Exchange scrambled in vain to upgrade its facilities and technologies faster than the demands made on them. On its 16,000-square-foot trading floor, recently covered with felt padding to reduce the noise, the Exchange began installing new posts, 12 of which replaced 20 older ones by year's end and accommodated 1,260 indicators as opposed to 480 on the original posts.[21]

The new posts represented an important facelift for the trading floor. Each one of the large, horseshoe-shaped posts held some clerks, file drawers, plugs for telephones, pegs for hanging hats, and member brokers who specialized in certain stocks. A broker with a sell order for United States Steel, for example, would hurry to Post Number 2 to seek a buyer and record the transaction once made. Once it was recorded on paper, a uniformed attendant sent it by pneumatic tube to the center of the floor, where a clerk put the transaction on the ticker tape. Every transaction was recorded on the tape, which became the play-by-play of the day's activities. An ability to "read" the tape referred to a talent for discerning patterns from the raw data of the trades. A new high-speed ticker machine, three times as fast as the current one, was on order but had yet to be installed. However, a new and clever reflecting device projected quotations from the ticker tape's paper onto large screens for everyone to see.[22]

Around the walls, separated from the floor by brass rails, sat an army of telephone clerks, employees of the various brokerage firms, who received orders to buy or sell and relayed them to the floor traders via call boards placed at opposite ends of the floor. To supplement the tape, floor collectors gathered quotations on transactions and reported them to clerks in the quote room upstairs, who then telephoned them to brokerage houses via rented lines. The 323 telephone lines in the quote room were rented to brokers for a fee of $75 per month. A separate ticker tape conveyed transactions in bonds, and on furiously busy days, when the pace of business swamped the ticker tape, the Exchange allowed stock prices to be transmitted over the bond ticker.[23]

As the new year opened with 1,534 bonds and 1,176 stocks listed, one brash enthusiast predicted the coming of 10-million-share trading days. Speculators hopped eagerly aboard the prosperity train, sending the Dow Jones average up $10^{1}/_{2}$ points to 317.51 and the *Times* average up nearly 12 points to 247.56 in January. The volume of trading was enormous, exceeding 110.8 million shares for the month. Prior to 1928, the Exchange had never seen a 4-million share day; in January 1929 volume *averaged* nearly 4.3 million shares a day. Then in February the market stalled out, as waves of selling erased gains and left traders more uncertain than ever about what one frustrated speculator called "a bear and a bull market at the same time." On February 20, volume dropped below 3 million shares for the first time since December 18. The month ended with the Dow down 2.27 and the *Times* average down 1.78. Some brokerages looked to capitalize on the uneasiness. "Are You Overstaying the Bull Market?" asked one house in an ad that ran for months.[24]

Much of the uncertainty centered around the Federal Reserve Board and the possibility of an interest rate hike in the face of steadily rising brokers' loans, which reached $5.5 billion by the end of February. "There are two things that can disrupt business in this country," joked Will Rogers. "One is war and the other is a meeting of the Federal Reserve

The 1929 Federal Reserve Board: left to right, Andrew Mellon, W. P. G. Harding, E. Platt, Charles S. Hamlin, Adolph C. Miller, Daniel R. Crissinger, J. R. Mitchell.   (Collection of the Museum of Financial History)

Bank." The Fed kept its deliberations secret, allowing rumor to feast on what little dribbled out. In truth it was as uncertain about what to do as Wall Street was. The old dispute between the board and the New York bank raged anew in the wake of the power vacuum created by Strong's death. George Harrison, Strong's successor, had the ability but not the influence to lead, and he inherited the board's resentment toward the leadership presumptions of the New York bank.[25]

Apart from bureaucratic infighting and petty spats, however, the board confronted a major dilemma. Should it move to restrain credit, and if so, what was the best way to do it? Two approaches could be used. The board could approve general rediscount rate increases, which would affect all other forms of business credit as well as bank funds going into the call loan market, or it could take some form of direct action such as warning banks not to borrow funds for speculative loans or risk having them refused. Raising interest rates would restrict credit to legitimate borrowers as well, while talking tough would chill the market

with uncertainty over future action. Nor could the Fed ignore the unpleasant fact that any action or statement by it would send the market
into a tailspin for which the Fed would be blamed. Increasingly the
choice came to seem one of lesser evils.[26]

No one could predict what effect either action would have on the
market, business in general, or the international scene. Underlying the
dilemma of this choice was an even more basic question that no one
could answer: was the market really too high? What was a reasonable
level for the market—and for call loans—given the current level of
prosperity and economic growth? This in turn raised the question of
how the Fed could justify any action it took—a raw nerve the *Wall Street
Journal* touched in February. "The Federal Reserve Board complains that
too much money is going into speculative loans to the detriment of
business," it observed. "But is it? The board has not produced any data
to prove this. . . . The Federal Reserve Board cannot show that business
is suffering from the stock market activity."[27]

Not surprisingly, the board split within itself and disagreed with the
New York bank on this issue as on so many others. A narrow majority,
led by Adolph Miller and Charles Hamlin, favored the narrower "direct
pressure" policy of denying rediscounting privileges to banks that put
the proceeds into the call loan market. The regional banks, led by New
York, argued that the board had no legal right to deny loans and that the
only effective remedy was hiking the rediscount rate. On February 2 the
board outlined its views in a letter to the regional banks. Three days later
an agitated George Harrison, still new to his post in New York, traveled
to Washington to remind the board that every interest rate in the open
market was above the rediscount rate, which invited borrowing from the
reserve banks and credit expansion. The best way to bring rates into line
and curb speculation, he argued, was to raise the rediscount rate.[28]

Sharply divided over the direct pressure policy, the board nevertheless
responded the next day by making public its letter to the regional banks
and expressing its dismay over the "excessive amount of the country's
credit absorbed in speculative security loans." The market promptly tumbled as the Bank of England raised its discount rate from 4¹/₂ to 5¹/₂ percent and Wall Street wondered if the Fed would follow. The board also
renewed its concern over the flow of outside funds into the call loan
market, warning that "such loans may be withdrawn without notice,
leaving a large void to be filled by the banks and threatening demoralization of the money market." Congress got into the act as the Senate

passed a resolution asking the Fed for suggestions on how to go about checking "illegitimate and harmful speculation."[29]

Like Strong before him, Harrison had no intention of backing down. On February 14 he phoned Governor Roy Young of the Federal Reserve Board to tell him that the directors of the New York bank had unanimously voted to raise the rate from 5 to 6 percent. Charley Mitchell, one of the New York directors, also spoke to Young. The board waffled, then disapproved the request. Between February 14 and May 23 the New York directors held 10 more meetings at which they voted to raise the rate only to have every vote vetoed by the board. A disgusted Harrison besieged board members with calls and letters and even enlisted Andrew Mellon's help, to no avail as the board continued to insist that the policy of direct pressure was working. Meanwhile, events caused relations between the board and the New York bank to deteriorate even further.[30]

On March 4 Herbert Hoover took office, and Wall Street looked hopefully to promote a resurgent "Hoover market." The White House had done little to dampen enthusiasm among speculators. Coolidge's parting wisdom on the subject was to hail prosperity as "absolutely sound" and stocks as "cheap at current prices." Hoover disagreed but made no public statement; his brief and general inaugural address gave Wall Street no cause for alarm. Three days later, however, a voice from an unexpected quarter denounced the rising tide of speculation and charged the Federal Reserve Board with losing its leadership "owing to its failure promptly and effectively to reverse the engines at the critical moment. . . . The rudder then passed into the hands of Stock Exchange operators, who have now for many months governed the flow of money, not only in the United States, but in the principal marts of the world."[31]

Banker Paul Warburg knew the Federal Reserve System well, having helped shape the act that created it. Currently chairman of the International Acceptance Bank, he had watched the ballooning of the market and call loans with dismay. "In aeronautics the public is generally inclined to look upon the art of rising into the air as the sole accomplishment," he noted dryly. "The layman is apt to overlook the fact that the mastery of the art of descending is of equal if not greater importance." Unlike many of his banking colleagues, Warburg did not mince his words. If the "Stock Exchange debauch" were stopped soon, the shrinkage in prices might not seriously affect business in general. "If orgies of unrestrained speculation are permitted to spread too far, however," he warned, "the ultimate collapse is certain not only to affect the speculators themselves, but also to bring about a general depression involving the entire country."[32]

Dismissing investment trusts as "incorporated stock pools," Warburg called the current rediscount rate of 5 percent "grotesque" because it had become not an index to prevailing rates or conditions but rather an exception to them. These blunt remarks set off a heated debate but provoked little action. Warburg was an authoritative voice but not an official one, and the board responded to his comments with magisterial silence. Roy Young, who had replaced the inept Daniel Crissinger as governor two years earlier, was an able but cautious banker "who sought no fame as a martyr to the broken boom." Wall Street accused Warburg of "sandbagging American prosperity," sneered that his views were "obsolete," and hinted darkly at ulterior motives on his part. When the market started upward again, his warning was lost in a cloud of contempt. Sentiment leaned more to the comments of Bethlehem Steel's Charles M. Schwab, who admitted that he had been wrong a year earlier in viewing heavy speculation with alarm. "Last year," he added, "my conclusions were based on old fashioned ideas. . . . Everyone has made money except the old timers."[33]

During March the market backed and filled as speculators tried to divine what the board would do. In a speech delivered on the 16th, Young declared that the Fed would not advance the rediscount rate unless all other efforts to untangle the credit problem had failed. "Hoss sense," he concluded, was needed most to remedy the situation. But on March 20 brokers' loans reached a record $5.79 billion, or $184 million above their level when the Fed issued its warning on February 6. Two days later George Harrison attended the board's meeting and again pressed for a rate increase. The prolonged session adjourned with no action taken and no hint given to an anxious Wall Street as to what transpired. The market, wrote a disgusted Noyes, "is getting nowhere at all. Every day a handful of issues is taken in hand and rushed violently upward under the impetus of good-sized and skillfully-placed professional orders. The body of stocks, however, do nothing at all."[34]

On March 18 the Dow started a string of declines that lasted for eight straight sessions. The losses were small at first, then reached 4.37 points on the 22nd, a market that Noyes viewed as "ruled by fear." Next day the Dow tumbled another 4.05 points amid concern over what the Fed would do. On Monday, March 25, the call rate soared to 14 percent, the highest rate since 1920, and panic seized the market. Trading exceeded 5.8 million shares as the Dow dropped 8.71 and the *Times* average 5.87. "The speculative element shivered in fear of a drastic ultimatum from the Federal Reserve Board that never came . . . ," reported the *Times*. "Many operators . . . were openly expressing the wish that the board do its worst 'and get the agony over.' "[35]

Tuesday the 26th brought an even fiercer liquidation as the call rate climbed upward until at 1:50 P.M. it reached 20 percent. The Exchange's new electrical board, which flashed current and renewal rates, blew a fuse just as the 20 percent figure appeared. Turmoil gripped the floor as many small speculators failed to meet margin calls and were sold out. A brisk rally late in the afternoon stemmed the tide but failed to save the beached minnows. Volume shattered every record, exceeding 8.2 million shares; it had never before reached even 7 million shares. The tape also set a new record for tardiness by not recording the last sale until 5:14, more than two hours after the market had closed. The bull market teetered at the brink, and some observers thought it might be dispatched with one decisive shove, but action had to come at once. "It is . . . accurate market psychology," observed Noyes amid the storm, "that the average trader . . . becomes easily panic stricken, but recovers quickly from his fright." The burning question was whether that fright should be alleviated or intensified.[36]

A pivotal moment had been reached. For nearly six years Americans had chased the rainbow of riches, aware deep down that one day it must end, but not knowing when, and unwilling in their hearts to face that fact or believe that this day might be the one. Many feared the moment had come during the December debacle, but the market had risen like a staggered boxer and fought its way back. However, this latest crisis harbored elements not present in December. A new and untested administration had taken office, brokers' loans had set yet another record, call loan rates had soared to their highest level in nine years, Federal Reserve action loomed, and the market seemed more volatile than ever—a creature of the pool operators who manipulated their pet stocks at the expense of the rest of the list. The sum of these elements was a whirlpool of uncertainty that, with luck, might suck the bull market down while disturbing the economy itself with only mild ripples of contraction.

But who would step forward at this critical juncture and smite or at least corral the groggy bull? The obvious candidate was the Federal Reserve Board. It held a prolonged session on March 26, the same day that call rates hit 20 percent, and again reached an impasse on the rate hike issue. Hoover shared the board's preference for direct action rather than a rate increase. He watched events but said nothing. In New York a frustrated George Harrison called Charley Mitchell to tell him that "in circumstances . . . bordering on the 'panicky' the Federal Reserve Bank did not want and could not be in the position of arbitrarily refusing loans on eligible paper to member banks." He added that Mitchell should not interpret these words as encouraging or discouraging him from putting National City funds into the call market, but that "the call money market was now the problem of the New York money market, that is the member banks and the private bankers." Then Harrison dutifully called Roy Young in Washington to inform him of what he had told Mitchell.[37]

This remarkable piece of ambiguity thrust the burden squarely on Charley Mitchell, who had just become a director of the New York Federal Reserve Bank on January 1. He had no obligation to do anything, but Sunshine Charley was not a man to shirk action when he thought it was necessary. Convinced that a market collapse could produce only widespread harm, he announced that National City would make $25 million available to squeezed borrowers "whatever might be the attitude of the Federal Reserve Board . . . rather than permit a complete demoralization of the money market." His action stabilized the call loan rate at 15 percent and sent the market sharply upward to recoup most of its losses before the day's end. "Hysterical selling . . . was suddenly ended . . . ," reported Noyes, "and confidence restored as quickly as it had been driven away." More important, he noted, "the industrial news continued very cheerful."[38]

When the board learned of Mitchell's action, it privately approved what he had done but professed outrage at what he was reported as saying and fired off a letter asking him if he had been quoted accurately. Senator Carter Glass lambasted Mitchell for slapping "the board squarely in the face" and treating its policy with contempt. Other senators joined Glass in demanding Mitchell's resignation from the reserve bank's board and promised an inquiry. Sunshine Charley declined to enter a war of words, saying the incident was closed and warning that "while stable conditions have been restored . . . this does not mean that the way has been cleared for a renewal of unbridled speculation." The *New York Times* reprimanded Glass for seeming "to have confused a temporary emergency with a permanent policy. The banks did not come forward with funds to promote speculation, but to prevent what threatened to be a serious crisis in the money market." Mitchell's case gained credence when the National City Bank's monthly review, which appeared on April 1, argued for an increase in the rediscount rate to 6 percent.[39]

The immediate crisis passed, but the furor over credit raged in Washington, where the board maintained its usual inscrutable silence over what it might do. One ardent bull could stand the suspense no longer and took matters into his own hands. Billy Durant first made a public show of sending telegrams asking a hundred heads of corporations if they thought their stock was overpriced in the market. Then, on April 3, he slipped unnoticed aboard a train to Washington and that evening went to the White House, where he implored Hoover to rein in the Federal Reserve Board lest it provoke a "financial disaster of unprecedented proportions." Hoover gave him no satisfaction. Next day the board resumed its jawboning with a statement warning that if its present policy did not achieve a "reversal of recent trends" by voluntary cooperation, it would resort to "other methods of influencing the situation."[40]

Undeterred, Durant bought 15 minutes of airtime for a national radio address on April 14 to urge the Fed to "keep its hands off business." He attacked the board as an "autocratic group . . . arrayed in 'battle' on the business interests of the country," praised Mitchell's act as a "patriotic offer," and urged the Fed to reduce the rediscount rate to 3 percent rather than increase it. Three days later Durant sailed with his wife for their annual vacation in Europe. For the first time reporters could recall, he left without issuing any statement on the market. The board had become his enemy because, in his biographer's words, "it threatened not only his paper wealth but his illusions, indispensable to the survival of a positive thinker and a gambler." Charley Mitchell took a different, more practical tack by urging Congress to repeal the tax on capital gains, arguing that it would cool the market by inducing liquidation among those who had large profits in stocks but hesitated to sell out because of the tax obligations they would incur.[41]

During this controversy Hoover said little. Later he admitted sharing Glass's view of Mitchell, but he kept the opinion to himself. That spring he laid the cornerstone for a new Commerce Building in Washington, using the same trowel with which George Washington had set the cornerstone for the Capitol in 1793. The new building was to be a mammoth monument filling three city blocks, the largest office structure in the world when completed in 1932 and a fitting tribute to the nation of business. Hoover had reason to be pleased. Despite the turmoil in the market, the underlying economy seemed as robust as ever. "Business never rested on a sounder foundation," proclaimed the *Wall Street Journal*. "There is no inflation anywhere. . . . Inventories are at normal or below. Corporations and individuals have more surplus money than ever before." Steel production exceeded the most optimistic predictions, and Secretary of Labor James J. Davis estimated that 200,000 more people were on payrolls than had been a year earlier. Corporate earnings were up, and combined factory output was ahead of 1928 by 8 percent. Railroad carloading returns showed record movements of freight for six consecutive weeks in April and May.[42]

The crucial automobile industry brimmed with confidence, showing more models than ever at its annual January show and predicting production of nearly 5 million cars for the year. During March, Cadillac sales set a new record in New York City. Conventional wisdom held that a bull market made investors feel flush and more willing to buy cars or other luxury items, but Charles W. Nash saw a more negative effect. "The number of small speculators has doubled since the beginning of 1928," he pointed out. "These people, of whom many are potential car buyers, bought stocks at high levels and in consequence have their money tied up." In May the *Federal Reserve Bulletin* noticed that car sales had fallen slightly behind production and that building contracts, which had been declining since November, were down 15 percent from the first quarter of 1928. But industrial production had risen 10 percent to a record level.[43]

"The stock market and business are more closely allied than at any time in history," declared the *Wall Street Journal*, "and you cannot have prosperity with a protracted decline in stocks. Neither can you have an advancing market with business on the decline." But the market seemed uncertain of its direction. Once past the March horrors, it lurched upward again as the Dow climbed nearly 19 and the *Times* average nearly 12 in April. After a strong start in May, however, it stalled out; a sharp drop on the 13th left both averages below their mark on the first of the month. Call loan rates during April fluctuated wildly between 6 and 16 percent.[44] The market itself had grown steadily more volatile as measured by the daily swings in the Dow Jones average. Table 8.1 shows the remarkable increase in both volume and volatility.

The credit controversy hung like a miasma over Wall Street. While brokers looked apprehensively toward the Fed for some sign of a rate increase, the proportion of call money coming from outside sources

Table 8.1   Dow Jones Volume and Volatility, 1920–1929[45]

Year	Volume (000's)	Average Swing
1920	321,104	8.35
1921	162,433	4.80
1922	277,386	5.09
1923	245,492	5.00
1924	289,237	5.87
1925	466,615	7.48
1926	462,722	9.00
1927	572,808	9.76
1928	922,232	18.35
1929	1,124,610	38.90

continued to rise until by mid-May it comprised 55 percent of the total. So attractive had the call loan market become that banker John H. Allen organized a new company, the First Call Loan Company of America, to operate as a kind of investment trust dealing solely in call loans. "Money is about the highest priced commodity at present," said Allen, "and I am of the opinion that the interest rates for the use of money have reached an era of new high levels." Analyst Andre Mertsanoff, in a circular called "The Golden Age," predicted that the coming decade would witness a demand for $15 to $18 billion in brokers' loans. The wags on Wall Street joked that if money went to 30 percent, it would simply split three-for-one.[46]

A columnist concluded that "there seems to be little difference between the Einstein theory and some of the theories relative to a correction of the brokers' loan situation. One is as easy to understand as the other." More cautious bankers were less amused. Colonel Leonard Ayres of Cleveland warned that the large sums being withdrawn from banks by corporations and put into the call loan market amounted to an "invisible banking system" unhampered by reserve requirements or any other restrictions. To such criticisms the Wall Street Journal countered that "big brokers' loans are here to stay . . . because they are normal. They have been created by the great growth in Stock Exchange transactions, just as Steel has grown from a 7,000,000-ton company to a 25,000,000-ton company." Yet even the Journal complained that "money rates are ridiculously high," while E. F. Hutton & Co. protested that "the artificial conditions prevailing here are nothing more nor less than a national disgrace."[47]

By May the clash between the Federal Reserve Board and the New York Reserve Bank over a rate increase had gone public. On May 1 the board sent a letter to a few reserve banks with a list of member banks that had continued to borrow from the Federal Reserve banks since the warning of February 6 but had not reduced their loans against securities. "The Board desires that it be ascertained from each of the member banks . . . ," said the letter, "why it should not bring about the adjustment expected by the Board." Roy Young was not present when the letter was composed and vainly protested its sending when he learned of it. Privately he let George Harrison know that he did not agree with it. Harrison responded in protest to the letter, and on May 10 the directors of the New York bank added their views in support of Harrison.[48]

While this dispute raged, the New York and Chicago banks voted to increase their rate to 6 percent only to be rebuffed again by the board. A few days later the board's own advisory council recommended an increase to 6 percent. "It is not easy to see how this counsel can be rejected," observed the *New York Times*, but still the board refused to budge. The uncertainty kept the market in turmoil. On May 20 the Dow dropped 8.78 and the *Times* average 3.09. "This is not to say that the great bull market . . . is over," said the *Journal*, adding that "the stock market, even in its wildest moments, is a great deal safer than it looks." It got even wilder two days later when the Dow fell 13.26 and the *Times* average 8.12, only to recover about half the loss the next day as the conviction grew that the board would not raise rates. In fact the board denied New York's request yet again on the 23rd, but four days later another wave of selling sent the Dow down 10.91 and the *Times* average 7.70.[49]

"The market is more or less a state of mind," philosophized the *Journal*. "It is a state of mind that is responsible for present low prices. Optimism has given way to pessimism because of threats by the F.R.B. and others to force drastic liquidation in stocks by tightening credit. The newspapers have been teeming with bearish propaganda. . . . Forecasters are overwhelming shareholders with predictions of a business depression and other dire happenings ahead of us."[50]

Thus was the stage set for the opening of the summer of fun.

The resurgence of the bull market crept in, like the fog, on little cat feet. Indeed, it seemed to have more lives than a cat, though few observers saw much life in it when June began. At May's end the Dow stood 9.60 points lower than it had on January 2, while the *Times* average showed an anemic gain of 0.29. The price of wheat dipped to 93¼ cents a bushel, a low unseen since September 1915. Although some healthy gains early in June cheered speculators, Noyes described the market in midmonth as "moving in a purposeless manner" with "its lately familiar uncertainty." Volume for June declined sharply to 69.5 million shares, the lowest figure since August 1928. Yet when the month ended, the Dow showed a gain of 34.67 and the *Times* average 27.77; the former had endured only six losing days all month and the latter only five. Gleeful brokerage houses filled their market letters with predictions that the bull was back.[51]

Not everyone was convinced. Edgar Brown was slow to discover that the bull assumed many forms. When he arrived from Pottsville at National City Company's headquarters in New York and made his complaint, a sympathetic officer promised to contact the Philadelphia office and see what could be done. Returning home, Brown was revisited by Fred Rummel, who persuaded him to switch his portfolio into shares of Anaconda Copper, Cannon Mills, Oliver Farm, and, of course, National City Bank. Then, said Rummel soothingly, sit still on that and see what happens. Brown was in good company. Eddie Cantor was making whoopee not only onstage but also in the stock market, where he had put most of his money. So had his friend and neighbor Groucho Marx, a cautious man with money who had amassed a nest egg of $240,000 and invested it in the market. Marx went to see Cantor's show at the Palace and afterward visited him backstage. Cantor gave him a tip to buy Goldman, Sachs, which Marx did the next morning to the tune of 200 shares on 25 percent margin.[52]

On another occasion Marx put $9,000 into United Corporation on a tip from an elevator operator and passed the advice along to brother Harpo, who sank half his savings into the stock. "Father didn't realize playing the market was so risky," recalled Groucho's son Arthur. "He was in it because, like everyone else, he was convinced that it was a sound, money-making venture." Introduced to the market in 1926, Groucho had learned the magic of buying on margin and watching prices soar like balloons. "You could close your eyes," he said, "stick your finger any place on the big board and the stock you had just

bought would start rising." Every morning after breakfast Groucho hurried to his broker's branch office in Great Neck to follow the ticker and
gloat over his good fortune. "What an easy racket," he chortled one day.
"RCA went up seven points since this morning. I just made myself seven
thousand dollars."[53]

Gradually the bullish euphoria returned to Wall Street. Call loan rates
remained high, touching 15 percent again on July 1, but the Street was
growing inured to high rates and the threat of an increase. The Fed continued to watch and wait. On June 5 the directors of the New York bank
met with the board in Washington and presented a memorandum prepared by Charley Mitchell. It proposed that the New York bank raise the
rediscount rate, ease monetary demands through open-market purchases,
continue loans to member banks regardless of how the funds were used,
and reduce the rediscount rate again as soon as conditions permitted. A
week later the board, with Roy Young again absent, rejected the program,
saying it preferred to "hold fast" to its policy of direct pressure.[54]

Nothing of what transpired at the meeting leaked out, leading one
reporter to grumble that the conference "served further to confuse the
situation." The *Times* complained editorially that "although the strange
career of economic illusion and perverted special pleading, which was
continued during nearly twelve months of stock market excitement, has
now shown signs of drawing to a close, the question as to just what the
policy of the Federal Reserve should be in combating such speculative
raids on the country's credit fund is not settled." But the excitement was
far from over. Both the Dow and the *Times* averages opened July with
record highs of 335.22 and 267.04 respectively; these turned out to be
their *lows* for the month. By July 31 the Dow had climbed to 347.70 and
the *Times* average to 281.80. The volume of nearly 93.4 million shares
obliterated the old July record of just under 40 million set in 1928. By
mid-July Alleghany's holdings had gained $60 million in value since its
founding in January, and the House of Morgan had formed another giant holding company, Standard Brands, to sweep together a number of
food companies.[55]

"We can only repeat that it is the same old market," said a *Wall Street
Journal* columnist, "a little broader . . . but still under the influence of the
same things which have shaped its course for the past several years. It
has had big reactions . . . but it always comes back . . . because general
business refuses to slump with it." But it was not the same old market. As
the *Times* observed, "Two markets are in progress most of the time, one

of them a bull market and one of them a bear market." Comparing the prices of May 27 with those of July 17, one writer found that of 522 stocks with transactions on both days, only 114 had exceeded their highest point prior to the May break while 133 were selling below their May 27 level. Another analyst found at the end of July that 150 stocks had reached new highs since June 1 while more than 175 issues had dropped below their pre-May break level.[56]

The most striking development was the extent to which the active stocks had turned into a class unto themselves. The stronger brokerages and pool operators rotated movements in these favorite few like crops and harvested them regularly as outside buyers climbed eagerly aboard for what they hoped was a nonstop ride upward to the promised land of a split. Selling at prices ranging from 150 to 400, they became known on the street as "rich men's stocks" because only the wealthy could afford to deal in them. Critics protested that these price levels were all out of proportion to their earnings. But the minnows, too, grew infatuated with them, leading some brokers to complain that "it is getting harder to interest the public in low-priced stocks." Even traders who thought them overpriced conceded that it was pointless to buck the trend since "everyone who has done that over the last year or so has lost money." As a result the larger portion of the list languished while the favorite few active stocks became in effect the bull market.[57]

In August the market went to sea, thanks to the indefatigable Mike Meehan. On the 3rd he called a press conference to announce that he had made arrangements to open a floating brokerage aboard the Cunard liner *Berengaria*. The event drew an unusually large crowd; Noyes and a host of other financial journalists attended along with some other reporters, but so did Billy Durant, John J. Raskob, Percy Rockefeller, and assistants sent by Charley Mitchell and Jesse Livermore. Meehan provided the technical details, answered questions, and listed the hundred stocks that the branch would handle. The new service meant that "the American businessman will be able to take a vacation in Europe without stopping for a single day his market transactions during the crossing." Four days later the *Berengaria* steamed out of New York with the new floating branch office open for business on the promenade deck. On the 17th the *Leviathan* departed New York with a Meehan branch ready for business in the tea room on B deck.[58]

The Fed was no less at sea. During that same first week of August brokers' loans crossed the unprecedented $6 billion threshold. "Con-

Billy Durant with his
wife aboard the S.S.
Berengaria — one of
the liners on which
Mike Meehan had
installed a floating
brokerage.
(Collection of the Museum
of Financial History)

stantly expanding loans . . . and the silence of the Federal Reserve
Board," observed Noyes, "have rather dulled the edge of Wall Street's
worry about the loan account." Roy Young had long since rejected the
direct pressure policy as useless, but other board members clung to it.
Nevertheless, the board finally approved the New York bank's request
for a rate increase to 6 percent. News of both the $6 billion figure and
the rate hike reached Wall Street after the market closed on August 8.
The market responded next day with a wave of liquidation that dropped
the Dow 14.11 and the *Times* average 9.66 on volume exceeding 5 million shares. Young hastily explained that the Fed's action had nothing to
do with the stock market but aimed to "conserve the resources of the
Federal Reserve System . . . to meet Autumn requirements." Brokers'
loans fell $68 million that week.[59]

Then the market reversed itself as both averages made up their loss
and more in three days. For the rest of the month the Dow experienced
only six losing days (four of them a decline of less than one) and the
Times average only four losses, two of them below 0.25. Brokers' loans
resumed their upward march, reaching $6.2 billion by month's end.

Managers of uptown brokerage branch offices reported a large increase in business as crowds flocked to them. Some pool operators found it more convenient to work from these uptown offices, away from the traffic and congestion on Wall Street. Many were amazed at how much stock the market would absorb without faltering; one operator boasted of unloading 60,000 shares of a high-priced favorite in an hour within a range of only 2 1/4 points. Possibly, suggested one cautious broker, "the market was working itself into a 'shock-proof condition' that might make it immune to the influences that have operated in the past."[60]

The summer of fun closed with the Dow at a record 380.33, up 29.77 for the month. The *Times* average, too, hit a new high of 303.20, up 20.25 for August. Volume of 95.6 million in August and 258.5 million for the summer months shattered all records, exceeding 1928 by 86.7 million shares during what had traditionally been the market's slow season. Rumor had it that at least a dozen new pools were organizing for fall campaigns. As eager speculators geared up for what promised to be an unprecedented autumn market, their eyes and prayers followed upward the Labor Day prophecy of Evangeline Adams that the Dow could climb to heaven. The lines forming for the journey included fully as many sinners as saints.[61]

9

The Fall

Follies

Wall Street entered the autumn financial season in a definitely optimistic frame of mind. With railroad traffic showing steady gains,
and production in the major branches of industry continuing at a
high rate, the earnings prospects of the principal corporations . . .
were looked upon as extremely promising. . . . With trade and
credit conditions favorable, buying orders accumulated in large volume over Labor Day, and the forward movement in the main body
of stocks was vigorously resumed in the early dealings.

—*Wall Street Journal*[1]

*I*t had become America's market, the rainbow that dreamers even in
remote corners of the nation hoped to ride to the pot of gold waiting at the end of its long and beguiling arc. By August the stock
market had moved to the center of American culture, displacing almost
everything else in conversations at dinner tables, meetings, social gath-
erings, even dates. No longer was it considered boorish for brokers and
others to talk shop off duty even with women. The market replaced
chatter about sex among the smart set, about books among the literati,
and about baseball in cheap restaurants. "Wherever one went," declared
a broker, "one met people who told of their stock-market winnings. At
dinner tables, at bridge, on golf links, on trolley cars, in country post
offices, in barber shops, in factories and shops of all kinds." As David
Kennedy observed, "Its sustaining oxygen was a matter not only of re-
condite market mechanisms and traders' technicalities but also of simple

atmospherics—specifically, the mood of speculative expectation that hung feverishly in the air and induced fantasies of effortless wealth that surpassed the dreams of avarice."[2]

One businessman who traveled a wide territory found the fever everywhere. "I firmly believe," he declared, "that there isn't a town of 10,000 inhabitants or over in the United States . . . that hasn't at least one night club. In the past year and a half I have been in a hundred or more of them, and I'll swear that nine-tenths of the people I saw there were having the time of their lives spending their uncashed stock-market profits." Wall Street coined a new label, "multi," for the innumerable new multimillionaires flush with market profits. On Wall Street and elsewhere the multis grew steadily in both numbers and confidence as the market continued to climb.[3]

To feed this insatiable appetite for stocks, promoters happily pushed forward mergers creating new shares and still more investment trusts. Early in August the *New York Times* noted that "hardly a week now passes but a new investment trust appears." By September the birth rate had swollen to nearly one a day, a pace that "left Wall Street in a quandary as to where the movement will halt." By year's end 265 new investment trusts had produced a staggering $3 billion in new shares; 14 of them had assets exceeding $100 million. The Founders group had evolved into a pyramided system of investment trusts and holding companies with paid-in capital exceeding $686 million. The Shenandoah Company, created by Goldman, Sachs in August as a $102 million investment trust, sold out its stock the first day; two weeks later Goldman, Sachs spawned the $127 million Blue Ridge Corporation with similar results. The $100 million Lehman Corporation, organized in September, was oversubscribed nearly 10 times. National Investors Corporation, first listed on the Curb Exchange July 3 at 11¼, soared to 345 by September 11.[4]

"We read one day of the formation of a $100,000,000 investment trust and the next day rumors have it that a $1,000,000,000 investment trust is in the course of formation," commented the *Wall Street Journal*, along with "talk of bank mergers, chemical company mergers, gas mergers, power mergers, aviation mergers, food company and asbestos-gypsum mergers." Bankers predicted that soon the investment trusts themselves would begin merging into new giants. Already 15 major banks had swallowed a total of 132 others in mergers. Amadeo P. Giannini owned the nation's fourth largest bank in San Francisco and a system that included 453 branches in California alone. Through pyramiding and mergers he had erected a banking empire topped by a holding company called Transamerica. Throughout the nation some 273 banking chains or groups controlled 1,858 banks and 18 percent of the country's banking resources.[5]

The largest bank of them all, or rather its subsidiary company, churned stocks furiously that season. Not without reason had National City's trusted advisor put Edgar Brown into Anaconda Copper and National City Bank stock. A surge in the price of copper had sent all the copper stocks soaring until April 1929, when the price dropped 25 percent. Eager to unload its 300,000 shares of Anaconda, National City Company spurred its giant sales organization with contests and prizes to induce customers like Brown to buy the stock. The same frenetic effort went into selling the bank's own stock, which hardly made for disinterested investment advice. The result, concluded a later investigation, was a "spectacle . . . where an investment affiliate of one of the largest commercial banks in the country, which . . . had accumulated . . . a substantial block of securities, was vigorously engaged, through a highly geared selling campaign, in selling securities to the investing public without any adequate disclosure of the interest of the investment affiliate in these securities." During 1929 National City sold more than 1.3 million shares of Anaconda, most of it in August and September, and 1.36 million shares of National City Bank stock.[6]

Amid the ballyhoo, brokers' loans continued to puzzle and bedevil analysts. After a drop in mid-August, they rose an average of $123.4 million a week for five straight weeks until by mid-September they reached nearly $6.57 billion. "For the time being . . . ," sighed the *New York Times*, "the speculative community seems disposed to disregard record-breaking loan figures as being of purely academic interest." The *Wall Street Journal* agreed that "there is less apprehension with brokers' loans nearing the $7,000,000,000 mark than when they were half that figure." When criticism of the loan level came from London, E.H.H. Simmons, president of the New York Stock Exchange, hastened to its defense. "None of us wishes to see credit inflation," he told a convention of Indiana bankers. "But . . . neither should we wish on purely theoretical or dogmatic grounds to kill a goose that has been laying golden eggs."[7]

Privately, however, some shrewd players thought the goose was about through laying. In July Joseph P. Kennedy, possessed of what John J. Raskob once called "a ruthless, razor-sharp mind," had met privately with Raskob, Arthur Cutten, and banker James Riordan to sound their views, then visited the heads of several brokerages to hear what they had to say. Everyone offered rosy reports, but Kennedy could not shake a nagging doubt. He stopped near 60 Wall Street to have his shoes shined by Pat Bologna, the investing shoeshine man, who promptly offered Kennedy a tip to buy oils and rails. Kennedy thanked him and returned home determined to get out of stocks. A market that anyone could play and a bootblack predict, he supposedly told his wife, Rose, was not one for him. Whether the story is true or not, Kennedy did sell out.[8]

So did David Sarnoff of high-flying RCA, Bernard Baruch, Will Rogers (on advice from Baruch), Owen Young, Paul Warburg, an uneasy Herbert Hoover, and—more quietly even than the others—Raskob. "You're sitting on a volcano," Baruch told Rogers, who was eager to put some money into the market. "That's all right for professional volcano sitters like myself, but an amateur like you ought to . . . get as far away as you can." Rogers did so and was grateful, but Baruch himself lingered near the volcano's mouth, buying nearly $500,000 in stocks on September 5 and continuing to deal through October. He got out, but not quite all the way. Samuel Insull thought the market had gone berserk and said so even though the boom inflated his own fortune on paper by $150 million. Between January and August Commonwealth Edison soared from 202 to 450 and Middle West Utilities from 169 to 529. In the 50 days ending August 23, Insull company securities mushroomed to $500 million at a rate of $7,000 a minute around the clock. Who could argue with such figures?[9]

Not Pat Bologna. The short, muscular Italian made a decent living from his shoestand at 60 Wall Street. At 19 he already had an impressive clientele of high rollers such as Charley Mitchell, Billy Durant, and Joseph Kennedy. The bankers, brokers, and other financial types who paused to let Pat brighten their appearance with a spit shine not only tipped well—Charley Mitchell, for one, was good for a dollar—but often let slip some pearl of wisdom about stocks or the market. Bright and ambitious, he kept his ears open and did not hesitate to trade market tips of his own for the tips of dimes, quarters, and dollars that came his way. For a dime shoeshine (plus tip), Bologna offered a nonstop stream of market trends and tips, and he had put his money where his mouth was. By dint of hard labor he had scraped together $5,000, and all of it was in the market on margin. "My money never leaves the Street," he said. "It's the best place in the world for it to be." And it was invested in Charley Mitchell's own National City Bank stock. If the market kept rising and the economy stayed sound, the road to the pot at the end of the rainbow would be short and sweet.[10]

The economy garnered mixed reviews, partly because no one could agree on what standard to use in measuring its performance. Many sectors had run at record-setting levels during the first half of 1929, and few observers believed they could maintain that pace. Construction still looked gloomy, automobile sales had slowed, and reports that a drought in the Northwest might slash wheat production raised concerns about railroad traffic and farmer purchasing power in that region. Steel production ranged around 90 percent of capacity, down slightly from the soaring output of June but well above averages for previous years. A downturn in the third quarter was noticeable but hardly worrisome when measured against what the *New York Times* called "a Summer of very unusual achievement." Hardly anyone expected the summer's frantic pace to continue.[11]

On September 3, the first trading day after the holiday weekend, the Dow hit 386.10 and closed at 381.17. The *Times* average did not reach its apogee until September 19, when it reached 311.90 and closed at 306.79. Although no one suspected it at the time, these figures represented a peak that would not be reached again until November 1954. On the 21st "out of a clear sky a storm of selling broke on the Stock Exchange," sending the Dow down 9.84 and the *Times* average 6.31. The turbulence struck during the final hour of trading, when 2 million shares changed hands so rapidly that the tape lagged an hour behind transactions. Pat Bologna was shaken by the sight of a man running out of a brokerage screaming that he was ruined. No one knew what to make of it. Analysts conceded that the almost unbroken gains before the holiday weekend had put the market in an "unhealthy technical condition," and fear of another large increase in brokers' loans unnerved some, but the actual figure of $137 million was not released until after the market had closed.[12]

There was one other factor. That same day statistician and self-styled prognosticator Roger Babson, in a speech at the National Business Conference, predicted that "sooner or later a crash is coming which will take in the leading stocks and cause a decline from 60 to 80 points in the Dow-Jones Barometer." He compared the coming collapse to that of the Florida land boom and added, "Fair weather cannot always continue. The economic cycle is in progress today, as it was in the past. The Federal Reserve System has put the banks in a strong position, but it has not changed human nature. More people are borrowing and speculating today more than ever in our history." He noted that 614 stocks on the Exchange stood below their levels of January 1 and that "the group of advancing stocks is continually becoming narrower and smaller. . . . Some day the time is coming when the market will begin to slide off, sellers will exceed buyers, and paper profits will begin to disappear. Then there will immediately be a stampede to save what paper profits then exist."[13]

This dark prophecy began coming over the news tickers on Wall Street around 2:00 P.M. just as the debacle of the final hour's trading got under way, but no one would admit to its having any effect. After all, Babson had delivered the same message every year since 1926, and there seemed no reason to take him more seriously now than in the past. Moreover, the news release on his forthcoming statement had circulated on the Street for several days without arousing much interest. "To many commentators," observed the *Times*, "it seemed incongruous that Wall Street . . . should have taken fright at the remarks of a statistician for whose judgment it has shown little respect in the past."[14]

But something was different: the mood on the Street. No one grasped the impact of Babson's remarks better than Alexander Noyes. "The effect on the market of such statements," he wrote, "is apt to be determined by . . . whether the ideas set forth have or have not been entertained in other quarters. . . . It cannot be disputed that the underlying sense of uneasiness . . . has become increasingly prevalent." Had Babson struck a responsive chord by saying aloud what was preying on the minds of many traders who dared not put their fears into words?[15]

That same afternoon Irving Fisher, asked for a response to Babson's prediction, denied that stock prices were too high or that a collapse was in the offing. Conceding that "none of us are infallible," he thought there might be a "recession of stock prices, but not anything in the way of a crash." Whatever the reason for the "Babson break," as it became known, the market recovered the next day, sending the Dow up 6.52 and the *Times* average 5.96 in what proved to be their largest gains of the month. "Roger Babson," noted a *Times* reporter, "was derided up and down Wall Street." The advance continued on Saturday the 7th as nearly 2.6 million shares changed hands in the short two-hour session. Once again, however, a small cluster of 10 to 15 stocks led the charge.[16]

During the next week sharp selloffs alternated with modest gains. By mid-September the Dow had lost 14.16 and the *Times* average 6.04 from their highs. Nobody could make sense of a market that seemed oblivious to all the old rules and patterns. Even Noyes conceded that "stocks continued to whirl about in confused fashion." More financial reporters detected a growing bearish mood on the street. The *Times* observed on September 15 that heavy liquidation had been taking place in many sectors of the market "under cover of the strength in fifty or more trading favorites." Three days later AT&T shares illustrated the point by gaining 14 points to a record high of 307$^1/_2$ on absolutely no news or even rumors. "A market in which some stocks can decline 5 or 10 points while a few others are advanced 10 to 50 points would once have been called distinctly erratic," scoffed Noyes, but the New Era had coined a fresh euphemism for this behavior: "selective buying."[17]

The mood in New York City had grown edgy for other reasons. The heat wave lasted a week into September, a burst water main flooded Fifth Avenue at 19th Street on the 8th, the Philadelphia Athletics formally clinched the American League pennant on the 15th, and popular Yankee manager Miller Huggins, who had left the team after Labor Day, fell seriously ill with blood poisoning and died on the 25th. His passing, coupled with the rout of the Yankees by the Athletics, marked the end of the first era of Yankee domination in baseball. The city mourned his loss as fans bemoaned the uncertainty over what lay ahead for the coming season. Mergers continued to dominate the headlines. The House of Morgan added yet another power company, Niagara Hudson, to its stable, and Charley Mitchell unveiled his plan to merge with the Corn Exchange Bank. Several major department stores announced plans for a merger, as did National Lead and some other paint manufacturers. Rail executive L. F. Loree revealed a scheme to unite 17 eastern roads around his Delaware & Hudson line.[18]

After a sharp rally on September 16, the market turned sour. For the rest of the month the Dow registered only three gains and the *Times* average four. A perplexed Noyes called one day's performance a "mystery decline" because "no one appeared capable of offering a plausible explanation for the liquidation." One columnist at the *Wall Street Journal* was content to recite his favorite litany that "It is the same kind of a market we have been having over the last year or two . . . subject to the same old influence," but doubts crept into even that normally bullish paper. "There are many bears in the financial district," it admitted on the 24th. "The so-called 'information' services are strongly advising liquidation. . . . With the buying cautious and limited . . . this pessimism has been a factor. Most observers are advising clients to remain on the sidelines for the time being. . . . As there is really no precedent for the current market situation, many in the financial district . . . are decidedly puzzled regarding the outlook."[19]

Noyes had been sounding this note for months, but for the first time others began to join him. "I have scrapped every theory I used to hold," declared one exasperated banker. "Old-time reasoning can no longer be applied—except with unhappy consequences. I don't pretend to be able to analyze the whyfor and wherefor of all that has happened. Nor do I pretend to know what the outcome is going to be. I have, however, ceased to try to go contrary to existing realities but am now governed by them and not by theory."[20]

Charley Mitchell dismissed such talk. As he stepped aboard ship on September 20 for a month's vacation in Europe, he assured reporters that "there is nothing to worry about in the financial situation" and urged their readers to "be a bull on America." That same day news broke in London of a scandal that brought down the financial empire of Clarence Hatry on charges of fraud. The story put pressure on the London exchange and then Wall Street as some British investors began liquidating their American holdings. A more ominous development in Great Britain was the steady drain of gold from the Bank of England, which forced it on September 26 to raise its discount rate from 5 1/2 to 6 1/2 percent, the highest figure in eight years. The move threatened to hasten withdrawal of British funds from the American market, although Noyes saw no immediate effect from either the Hatry debacle or the rate hike.[21]

But something had spooked the market. On the 24th heavy selling sent the Dow down 6.39 and the *Times* average 5.25 on volume of 4.4 million shares with transactions in 863 different stocks. The latter figure, a new record, lasted only until the next day, when 868 stocks changed hands in another session of violent swings called by one observer "about the most nerve-wracking day that Wall Street has experienced in many a month." Losses remained small, thanks to strong buying orders during the last hour, but earlier, noted the *Times*, "it looked to the startled watchers in commission houses as if the bottom had dropped out of the stock market, and Wall Street was in a mood of great despondency. Almost every active issue . . . was pounded." The market rallied on the 26th, but then came news that brokers' loans had jumped $192 million that week, the largest increase since July 3, to another record level of $6.76 billion.[22]

"Banking authorities have long since ceased to attach importance to the weekly swings of brokers' loan totals," sniffed the *Wall Street Journal*, but on the 27th another wave of fierce liquidation swept the market. "Prices melted away with a rapidity that astonished Wall Street," reported Noyes, as the Dow plunged 11.08 and the *Times* average 7.08. The *Journal* tried to put a cheerful face on the rout by calling it an "orderly" decline with moderate volume, no panicky selling, and no serious lag in the ticker tape. "It is not believed," added the *Journal* columnist, "the market has been forecasting a slump in business. . . . The so-called big interests continue bullish on certain stocks." But Noyes thought otherwise. "The declines . . . represent a corrective reaction of major proportions," he concluded. "The question which now confronts the financial district is just how much of a recession will be necessary to once more put the market in a healthy condition."[23]

The market's erratic behavior spooked Pat Bologna as well. The decline on the 27th had cost him "a couple hundred" but did not move him to sell. During the next few days a new phrase reached his ears, one that seemed everywhere on the street and on everyone's lips from the slowest minnow to the lordly partners at the big banking houses: "organized buying support." It insinuated the notion that if the market got into trouble, the big bankers and speculators would step forward to sustain it and keep the bull going strong. It sounded good to Pat, who promptly recycled it for the benefit of his customers. "What goes down can always come up," he said sagely. "With help."[24]

The market recovered somewhat on the 28th but fell again on the 30th. The Dow closed out September with a loss of 36.88, and the *Times* average was down 12.99 for the month. Volume exceeded 100 million shares for the first time since March and only the fourth time in history. The final week's declines had wiped out half the gains made in August and sent more than a hundred stocks to new lows for the year. The credit situation remained ominous even apart from the rarified level of brokers' loans. Autumn was normally the peak season for demands on the money market, keeping both time and call rates high. A few European nations followed the Bank of England's lead by raising their own discount rates. "Possibly one of the immediate effects . . . ," noted the *New York Times*, "will be the recall of considerable amounts of credit which have been at work in the New York money market." The most baffling mystery, however, remained the continued rise of brokers' loans in the face of a falling market.[25]

One answer lay in the sheer quantity of new securities already in the market and arriving daily from the formation of new investment trusts and holding companies. In past economic crises overproduction in industry had often been a problem; the New Era created a variation on this theme with overproduction of securities. Between January 1 and October 1 the New York Stock Exchange added more than 291 million shares to its list. The increase in September alone was 42.3 million shares with a value of $1.2 billion, $649 million of which consisted of new investment trust shares. More securities meant more collateral for brokers' loans, higher inventories for brokers, and a larger "floating supply" on the Street. Many if not most of the new investment trust securities—apart from the glamour issues that were snapped up—remained unsold and were being carried on borrowed money by the issuers or brokers. The result was what a later report called "congestion throughout the New York stock market during the early autumn" that "intensified a price decline inevitable from other causes too."[26]

As October opened, the president of the American Bankers Association warned his fellow bankers that they and not the Federal Reserve System were responsible for seeing "that not too large a proportion of the available credit of the country shall be used for the purpose of carrying stocks." Brokers, too, were concerned about the growing number of accounts with margins impaired by the fall decline. For some time many houses had demanded more margin on loans to protect them from sudden drops in so unpredictable a market. Some wondered anxiously what would happen if the corporations that had put so much money into the call market should suddenly pull their funds out. Charles Hayden of Hayden, Stone & Co. dismissed this fear, reasoning that "they would not bury it or tuck it away in a sock. They would either have to deposit it in the banks, in which case the banks would have it to lend, or they would buy stocks with it, in which case their purchases would offset the . . . calling of their loans."[27]

For every question someone had an answer, whether convincing or not. When one firm revealed that its monthly compilation of a hundred stocks showed declines in 11 of the 13 groups, the *Wall Street Journal* observed that "traders are translating moderate and seasonal recessions in some industrial lines into a business depression. This is not an unusual attitude when stocks are reactionary." To offhand remarks that "$12,000,000,000 in brokers' loans would not be unduly large," Noyes retorted that such sentiments did "not get us anywhere." Amid the sniping the level of brokers' loans continued to rise like flood waters. The next report from the Federal Reserve was due out after the market closed on October 3; that day witnessed the year's worst selloff yet on the New York Stock Exchange. Battered again by huge volume of 1.5 million shares in the final hour, the Dow plunged 14.55 and the *Times* average 11.02. The Curb Exchange suffered comparable losses, especially among utility and investment trust stocks.[28]

While the Street recovered from this blow, the report on brokers' loans showed a rise for the seventh straight week. The gain of $43 million created another record high of $6.8 billion; the market responded with a 5.6-million-share day that dropped the Dow 4.78 and the *Times* average 3.90. Then, in a startling turnabout, traders wiped out the two days of losses with two bullish sessions that boosted the Dow 20.55 and the *Times* average 15.57. After a pair of ordinary days, the Dow registered another gain of 6.20 and the *Times* average one of 4.19 on October 10, leaving the former at 352.86 and the latter at 298.21. "It is the same old market," chanted the *Wall Street Journal* columnist, "no different from the last five years or so. Stocks get a little too high and the outcome is a big smash. We have had one or two each year. . . . Since the upward movement began five years or so ago, stocks have come back and made new high records. . . . Everything will depend on the course of business. . . . Some day they won't come back; this will be when business begins to show permanent recession. No one can say that the outlook for trade and commerce is not good."[29]

The thin veneer of optimism layering the Street did not impress Noyes, whose views grew darker even as the sun appeared to peep out. "No one can have observed the market of the past eighteen months," he wrote, "and hear its story told by its faithful troubadours in print without learning that the speculating outside public was so rich and so heavily 'margined up' that nothing could shake the stability of its position. . . . Yet there always comes a day in what Wall Street cheerfully describes as 'the technical readjustment,' when the same chroniclers . . . described the agonized forced liquidation." Those days had come frequently of late as the falling market put severe pressure on the impaired accounts of small investors and wiped out many of them. "Everybody with acquaintanceship ranging from merchant princes to typewriter girls," he added, "has learned of their winnings from the stock market; none of us has heard of losses."[30]

In Noyes's view, Wall Street needed the stiff dose of reality that the past few weeks had given it. "The conviction as to the real state of affairs," he noted scornfully, "long obscured by the persistence of speculation itself and by the perverted economic judgment given out both by speculative ringleaders and . . . economic professors has been growing in Wall Street even before what seemed to the 'outside public' the thunderclap from a clear financial sky. . . . Every one seemed for once to recognize that the trouble lay in the stock market itself, and that it was serious enough." Yet scarcely had Noyes delivered these harsh words than a fresh chorus of bullish cheers rose up from several quarters. From distant Berlin vacationing Charley Mitchell repeated his belief that business was "absolutely sound and our credit situation is in no way critical." Irving Fisher uttered the words that would remain with him always: "Stocks have reached what looks like a permanently high plateau. . . . I expect to see the stock market a good deal higher than it is today within a few months."[31]

Even these notes of optimism paled before those of Ohio State professor Charles Amos Dice in his just-published book, *New Levels in the Stock Market*. The reason stocks continued to climb, Dice argued, was that "great amounts of stocks have been taken out of the market by the people as a more or less permanent investment." The day of the small investor had arrived, giving the market a broader base than it had ever possessed. For this and other reasons a new era had truly arrived; the old rules no longer applied. "Among the yardsticks for predicting the behavior of stocks which have been rendered obsolete," he declared, "are the truism that what goes up must come down, that the market will be at the end of a major advance after twenty to twenty-four months of climbing, that major declines will run from eleven to fifteen months, that stock prices cannot safely exceed ten times the net earnings."[32]

Where Dice saw new patterns, Colonel Leonard P. Ayres of the Cleveland Trust Company saw an old story. The elder J. P. Morgan once explained the so-called "rich man's panic of 1903" as the product of a market clogged by an excessive accumulation of "undigested securities." For months an outpouring of securities had rained down on the current market, said Ayres, until the public ceased to buy them "with the same avidity they had shown earlier. When this condition became apparent, a good many clear-seeing speculators began to sell their holdings." The result, he concluded in a memorable phrase, was "a sort of creeping bear market that has been hidden by the fact that many of the utility stocks and some of the rails and certain other issues have advanced so much as to carry . . . most of the well-recognized stock averages upward to new high levels . . . until the sharp decline of September began." Ayres also reminded his readers that the market had suffered "important declines" in 28 of the past 30 autumns.[33]

Charley Mitchell would have none of the bear talk. Preparing to board ship in London for the journey home on October 15, he insisted that "the last six weeks have done an immense good in shaking down prices. Many leading industrial securities are now at levels which would have been considered perfectly sound and conservative even by the standards of ten years ago. The market values have a sound basis in the general prosperity of our country." The annual trade review of the National Association of Manufacturers offered some support for Mitchell's views. Its survey of 23 basic industry groups showed 12 doing well, 3 standing about even with the previous year, and 8 falling behind the past year's level. Moreover, brokers' loans finally declined during the week of October 9 by $91 million.[34]

However, a blow to the utility stocks offset these good tidings. On October 11 the Massachusetts Department of Public Utilities rejected a request from the Edison Electric Illuminating Company of Boston to split its stock four for one and announced plans to launch an inquiry into the company's rates. Coming late on a Friday afternoon before a holiday weekend, the decision gave traders ample time to ponder its implications for other utility companies. On Tuesday the 14th stocks began to slide downward again on light volume in what one analyst called "as drab and colorless a market . . . since midsummer." The market was in the doldrums, explained one trader, because stocks were "so easy to buy and so difficult to sell." It proved to be the calm before the storm.[35]

On Wednesday the 16th another unexpectedly violent selloff drove the Dow down 11.11 and the *Times* average 7.53. The market regained about half these amounts the next day, but batterings on Friday and Saturday sent the Dow down another 17.99 and the *Times* average 11.81. Volume on the 19th totaled nearly 3.5 million shares, the second highest ever for a short Saturday session, and swamped brokerage firms lulled to sleep by the week's slow pace. The ticker tape ran an hour and 19 minutes late for a two-hour session. At week's end the Dow stood at 323.87 or 28.82 below the previous week, while the *Times* average showed a loss of 17.99 at 279.75.[36]

"No one can say that we have been in a bull market," sighed a *Wall Street Journal* columnist with vast understatement. Arthur Cutten, preparing to leave for Atlantic City, said that nothing had happened to change his opinion that good stocks would eventually go higher. Aware that market psychology played a crucial role, one wag coined a new phrase in declaring that certain stocks were now selling "ex-public imagination." A disgruntled trader complained that it was not a creeping bear market as Ayres had said, but rather "a leaping bear market." Another trader was even more curt. Asked to explain the break, he snapped, "More sellers than buyers." No one had a better answer.[37]

Not given to levity, Alexander Noyes tried to probe deeper into the rout and found one key in the fact that "business generally is lagging. . . . Compared with a year ago, the pace is yet a rapid one. Compared with the first three quarters, however, it is now evident that the slow-down has been a measurable one." It gratified him to find evidence at last that "Wall Street seemed to see the reality of things, and to discard the catch-words and newly invented maxims of an imaginary political economy," but he well knew that the Street also had a short memory. "To that large part of the present Wall Street community, whose own financial reminiscence begins with 1925," he scoffed, "comparison with 1903 by Colonel Ayres had as remote a sound as if he had cited the Grant & Ward failure of 1884 or the 'Gold conspiracy' of 1869."[38]

As Noyes pointed out, the week's stunning decline was fueled in large part by "the helpless throwing over of unwieldy speculative holdings by 'pools' and individual adventurers" and by "heavy professional sales for the decline and . . . a recurrent avalanche of forced liquidation." The growing belief that a bear pool was at work returned to the limelight a long-absent name. Rumors insisted that Jesse Livermore was the invisible hand hammering stocks, having at long last found a market that suited him. "The comeback of Mr. Livermore . . . ," gushed one reporter, "is another Wall Street wonder." Relishing the attention as always, the dapper Livermore was nevertheless quick to deny it. From his luxurious offices atop the Hecksher Building, he dismissed reports that he was head of a giant bear pool "financed by various well-known capitalists." Nor did he know of any "such combination having been formed by others. . . . It is foolish to think that an individual or combination of individuals could artificially bring about a decline in a country so large and prosperous."[39]

Livermore was not being coy; the swiftness of the fall had caught him by surprise as well. The burning question to him no less than to others was how the market would react to the Saturday fiasco on Monday the 21st. Would it show signs of recovery, or would the slide continue and accelerate under its own momentum? The balance sheet of factors was difficult to gauge. On the favorable side, business conditions remained stable if less vigorous, money rates were low and the supply ample, retail trade anticipated a record Christmas season, the bond market had revived somewhat, the large short interest in the market would have to cover sooner or later, and a reservoir of buying power lay in the investment trusts that had portfolios to replenish. On the negative side, a large aggregate of undigested securities still clogged the market, brokers' loans had started to climb again with a rise of $88 million to a total of $6.8 billion, some stocks still seemed overpriced, the dollar remained weak against the pound, gold continued to flow overseas, and agricultural commodity prices, especially wheat and cotton, remained low in the face of weak foreign demand.[40]

One other factor, much less tangible but no less important, inhabited the negative side of the ledger: the general nervousness of the market, especially speculators with impaired margin accounts or weakened pool positions. Put simply, too many people held too much stock on borrowed money. Sidney Loeb of E. F. Hutton & Co. pinpointed the threat it posed. "The great technical weakness in the market is the fact that the public is still long a tremendous amount of stock," he declared, "and that if large scale liquidation ever began, it would mean an eight-million-share day of steady selling that would bring prices down more sharply than ever in the recent few reactions."[41]

Loeb's observation appeared in the *Wall Street Journal* on Monday morning, October 21. That day the market moved back onto the front page of major papers as it took another pounding. With a record 920 stocks changing hands on a volume of nearly 6.1 million shares, a late rally held the loss in the Dow to only 2.96 and the *Times* average to 3.51. The Curb Exchange also experienced record volume of more than 3.7 million shares. The story for both was the same: heavy distress selling, little covering of shorts, and tickers running about a hundred minutes behind transactions. "Yesterday's stock market did not witness the recovery . . . even despondent Wall Street expected," reported Noyes. Rather the "character of the market left Wall Street both bewildered and frightened." Another analyst described the selling as "overwhelming and aggressive," triggering another flurry of margin calls. Many brokers admitted disappointment that the vaunted buying by investment trusts had not occurred, although one sign of organized support did appear late in the day when a broker known to act for large banking interests put in a buying order for 10,000 shares of United States Steel.[42]

The myth of "organized support," bandied about so frequently for weeks, traced back to the memorable feat of J. P. Morgan in personally directing the bankers' response that stemmed the Panic of 1907. It still comforted many on Wall Street even though the age of individual titans had long since passed. In that crisis Morgan had assumed the role of a central bank; since then the nation had acquired a central bank, but the Fed seemed to be doing little more than watching and waiting. Publicity over the feats of many financiers had elevated them to fame in the new-born age of celebrity: Mitchell, Wiggin, Cutten, Livermore, and of course the Morgan partners and other leading members of the club. But neither Jack Morgan, who was in Europe, nor Thomas Lamont nor anyone else enjoyed anything like the stature of the elder Morgan in his day, let alone his strength of character. Nevertheless, even the New Era was unwilling to let go of some prized vestiges of times gone by. When the market recovered on Tuesday, its strong opening was attributed to "the presence of organized banking support and to the optimistic remarks of Charles E. Mitchell," just returned from Europe, who said the "decline had gone too far." Roger Babson, still pessimistic, advised people to put their money into good bonds.[43]

An uneasy Herbert Hoover sent an emissary to ask Lamont about the market gyrations and whether the government should intervene. In a memo dated October 19 Lamont dismissed what he called "a great amount of exaggeration in current gossip about speculation," reiterated the gospel of the marketplace as self-correcting, spoke glowingly of the remarkable era of expansion and prosperity since the war, and assured the president that "the future appears brilliant." On Monday morning the 21st, Hoover and Andrew Mellon arrived in Dearborn, Michigan, to participate in a grand celebration organized by Henry Ford to honor his friend Thomas A. Edison on the 50th anniversary of the invention of the incandescent lamp. Ford had lavished millions of dollars on a unique museum that included painstaking reconstructions of the rural village of his own youth and of Edison's original laboratory in Menlo Park, New Jersey. Such diverse luminaries as Owen Young and Gerard Swope of General Electric, Otto Kahn of Kuhn, Loeb, Charles Schwab of Bethlehem

Steel, John D. Rockefeller Jr., Marie Curie, and Orville Wright gathered to praise the 82-year-old inventor in the culminating gala banquet. Greetings also came via shortwave from Albert Einstein in Germany.[44]

In a touching ceremony, Edison reenacted the invention for a national radio audience and shortwave listeners overseas. As Edison turned up the old lamp, special replicas blazed to life throughout Dearborn, Detroit, and other cities across the country. At the banquet Hoover paid tribute to the work of the old inventor, who was so exhausted that he barely made it through the event. Rain poured down during the day and continued as Hoover traveled to Louisville, where on the evening of the 23rd he gave a major speech on the development of inland waterways. The stock market was still very much on his mind; the day before he had dispatched a messenger to inform Lamont of his concern about the "speculative situation which seemed to him to be running very wild." Lamont passed the message on to Jack Morgan. On that same October 22 a worried General John J. Pershing cabled his friend Bernard Baruch from Paris about the market situation. "WOULD YOU HOLD SELL OR BUY ANACONDA," he asked. "IF SELL WHAT WOULD YOU BUY." Baruch replied promptly: "I WOULD STAND PAT." Personally, the financier picked up 1,800 shares of American Smelting and 1,400 of Warner Brothers that day.[45]

In the Midwest the drenching rain that had plagued Hoover's trip changed suddenly to snow, knocking down telephone and telegraph wires. For the many people interested in America's market, the loss of communication with the East could not have come on a worse day.

10

Rainbow's

End

Rock-a-bye, trader, on the tip top.

When the Board meets, the market will rock.

When the rate rises, quotations will fall.

And down will come trader, margins and all.

—*Wall Street Journal*[1]

What came to be known as the Great Crash was not one but a series of events stretched across the last week in October. John Brooks described it as coming "with a kind of surrealistic slowness—so gradually that, on the one hand, it was possible to live through a good part of it without realizing that it was happening, and, on the other hand, it was possible to believe that one had experienced and survived it when in fact it had no more than just begun." In broad terms it was the climax of seven weeks of market convolutions, the last bumpy ride of illusion on its way to the rainbow's end. Like a giant storm, its violence and intensity stunned even those who thought they saw some such disturbance looming on the horizon. With parts of the Midwest unable to follow events because the snow and sleet had disrupted communications, it began in earnest on Wednesday, October 23.[2]

The day opened calmly enough as many stocks rose on quiet trading. Then a sharp selloff of automobile stocks sent the market downward by early afternoon, and once again a hurricane of liquidation struck during the final hour, when nearly 2.6 million shares changed hands. Brokerage offices filled up with tense, anxious people watching their holdings and their dreams melt away. The usual chatter and joking gave way to a pall of silence, and no more talk was heard of mysterious bear operators. Something larger than individual players had engulfed not only the Exchange but the Curb and every other stock market, and no one knew what to make of it. The tape lagged 104 minutes behind closing as volume reached nearly 6.4 million shares; the rate of trading during the final hour would have created a day of more than twice that figure. At day's end the Dow had dropped 20.66 points and the *Times* average 18.24, the largest losses in history. Frederick Lewis Allen called it "a perfect Niagara of liquidation." It was, said Noyes dryly, "plain enough reckoning" for those who had assumed that prices would keep "rushing forward into previously unimagined heights."[3]

Nothing had been heard of organized support during the day. One banker explained that selling had been "too aggressive" to intervene directly, though support was likely when things quieted down. The larger investment trusts were reported to have between $750 million and $1 billion poised to invest in the better stocks, but no one knew when or if they would begin to buy. One benefit of the decline, said a banker, was that "it will send back to work many people who have been sitting around brokerage offices for a year or so on the trail of easy money. . . . I have heard thousands of reports of merchants, farmers and men and women in all walks of life literally giving up their businesses to watch the stock market."[4]

That evening in Washington, Irving Fisher explained to a gathering of bankers why stock prices had gone so high and would remain so despite the current buffeting caused by what he termed a "lunatic fringe of reckless speculators." On Wall Street and elsewhere, however, sharks and minnows alike cowered at the thought of what tomorrow would bring. The late selling frenzy had caught hundreds of stop orders and impaired thousands of margin accounts, as well as frightening investors across the nation. Large flocks of margin calls flew out of brokerages that night. What would happen when all those foreclosed shares hit the market? And what about the legion of investors in the Midwest who had lost touch with the market and could not respond to the late afternoon liquidation? Or pool operators and other professionals who had lost heart or could not sustain their lines of stock under such pressure?[5]

Grimly the Street prepared for the worst. A strange and strained silence fell across Wall Street. "People just stood there," recalled Pat Bologna, "stopped talking, and looked towards the Stock Exchange. It was like the silence before the . . . big race." Police wagons arrived and

choked the narrow entrance to Wall Street from Broadway. A large
number of policemen alighted from them and posted themselves
throughout the financial district. A messenger asked why they were
there. "In case there's trouble," came the curt reply. In their offices
Mitchell, Durant, Livermore, Raskob, Kennedy, Cutten, and other high
rollers stood tensely by their stock tickers, poised to act on whatever
signal it sent. "I was up to *here* in the market," Raskob said later. "My life,
my future and that of my family depended on what the ticker told."[6]

Where Wednesday's wave of liquidation had caught the Exchange by
surprise, Thursday morning found nearly all the trading members at
their posts along with full complements of clerks, runners, telephone
operators, and other staff. Every available employee was on hand when
Superintendent William R. Crawford, who admitted to feeling "electricity in the air so thick you could cut it," sounded the gong to open the
floor for trading at 10:00 A.M. The market opened, said one broker, "like
a bolt out of hell." The dreaded tsunami of selling crashed down at
once. Never had so many orders poured in so fast from so many places;
1.6 million shares changed hands in the first half hour alone, and the
pace never slowed. No sooner was a phone hung up than it rang again.
It was not fear that drove prices downward but rather the thousands of
shares dumped on the market as a result of accounts wiped out by margin calls overnight. As Allen put it, "The gigantic edifice of prices was
honeycombed with speculative credit and was now breaking under its
own weight."[7]

The annunciator boards at both ends of the floor flapped wildly as
they struggled to keep up with the calls for orders. The selling wave
seemed irresistible, catching thousands of stop orders and frightening
holders into "selling at the market"—dumping the stock for whatever
price it would bring. But few buyers appeared, creating what the Street
called "air pockets," or gaps formed when large blocks of stock went begging for buyers at any price. Like seasoned troops confronted by overwhelming numbers, the brokers absorbed wave after wave of sell orders
until their ranks staggered and pandemonium engulfed the floor. By
11:30 A.M. panic had seized the market, throwing the floor into turmoil
and swamping the trading posts in confusion. "I can't get them," cried a
usually unflappable telephone clerk when asked for some quotations by a
broker. "I can't get any information. The whole place is falling apart!"[8]

The ticker was already 48 minutes late and falling ever farther behind
transactions. From his balcony position Crawford watched in dismay as

The first wave of the Crash broke on October 23, 1929. Here, brokerage house employees telephone for more margin. (Breuer, Ebbs, Daily News L. P.)

the rule that traders should not "run, curse, push or go coatless" was trampled underfoot. At Post 2, where General Oliver Bridgeman served as specialist for United States Steel, the mob surrounding him was "bellowing like a lunatic." At Post 4 Crawford watched a fat, sweating man grow hysterical and scream orders that made no sense until some friends grabbed his arms and led him away. Wild rumors spread of failures and suicides. Dazed and bewildered, their faces wreathed in sweat and their collars torn open, the financial troops stumbled about, unable to fathom the chaos around them.[9]

Shortly before 11:00 A.M. Pat Bologna, after a difficult struggle, managed to squeeze into a customers' room near his stand. In the crowd he spotted a "Chinaman wearing a hat which rests on his ears," chewing "a dead cigar in a mouth of dead teeth." The man stood on tiptoes to peer over the shoulder of a woman in a large fancy hat, who clutched her wedding ring and cried, "You want more margin—you can't have more margin." Everyone was shouting and trying to reach the glass booth that encased the clerks. Their efforts frightened the boy manning the green

As news of the disaster on the Stock Exchange spread, crowds collected on Wall and Nassau Streets.   (Library of Congress)

quotation board, who couldn't keep pace with the speed of falling prices. The Irishman who ran the room stood at the back, his ear glued to a telephone. Bologna couldn't hear what he was saying, but a man closer to Pat shouted above the din, "The sonofabitch has sold me out!"[10]

The cry gave Bologna pause. On this mad day, far from offering advice, he had come to get it, but amid the uproar in the customers' room he saw no chance for that. He wondered whether to sell his precious holding, then recalled some advice Charley Mitchell had once given him along with his tip. "A wise man," said Mitchell, "never sells out at the first sign of trouble. That's for the pikers." It made sense to Pat. Gingerly he worked his way out of the customers' room and returned to his stand, having decided to stand pat for a while.[11]

On the Exchange a loud, unceasing roar spread upward and spilled into the street outside. As word spread of the excitement, enormous crowds poured into the financial district, jamming the narrow streets. Most of them simply stood and stared at the Exchange building. One reporter expressed surprise at the number of women in the milling throng; he thought them mostly stenographers anxious about their small accounts in the market. The police already there were quickly reinforced with 10 men on foot, 20 on horseback, and 20 detectives to keep order. At 12:30 Exchange officials closed the Broad Street visitors' gallery; one interested spectator that morning had been Winston Churchill. While police struggled to keep control of the huge crowd on the street, motion picture crews set up cameras on the steps of the Sub-Treasury Building to record the scene. News photographers were there, too, capturing for posterity what in the city of show business had become the wildest show in town.[12]

Throughout Wall Street and uptown, hundreds of people wedged into the customer's rooms of brokerages intended to hold only dozens. Hundreds more stood outside, straining for a glimpse of the Translux flashing transactions. Edwin Lefevre visited a dozen of them and found not a trace of hysteria; the ashen faces showed "not so much suffering as a sort of horrified incredulity — the dazed unbelief of men who have been robbed of their all by their dearest and most trusted friend." This eerie sense of unreality swelled as the ticker tape fell farther behind. "The untickered truth meant much more than the end of hope," wrote Lefevre. "It meant poverty, debt, a fresh start under heavier handicaps." In many customers' rooms the victims sat long after the market had closed, staring vacantly at the "illuminated strips of opaque glass" as darkness fell. In one speculative firm's room a lone white-haired woman with a dazed expression sat quietly in the corner behind clusters of veteran players as she waited to meet with her broker.[13]

That afternoon banker Edgar Speyer, a wealthy partner in one of the Street's most aristocratic Jewish houses, welcomed Claud Cockburn, a visiting British journalist, among other guests to luncheon at his gracious rose-colored home on Washington Square. In a genteel atmosphere of "elegant calm" amid a gorgeous collection of Chinese paintings and porcelain, they talked of recent poets, of whom Mrs. Speyer was one, until interrupted by odd thumping behind the closed door leading to the kitchen. When the English butler and footman entered with a saddle of lamb, Cockburn noticed behind the door four or five maids in an angry, excited cluster. After the butler and footmen withdrew, the noise grew louder and a woman's voice cried, "Go on — or else!" Suddenly the door was flung open and unseen hands launched the red-faced butler back into the room. In apologetic tones he begged Speyer to come with him.[14]

The perplexed Speyer hesitated, then followed the butler to the kitchen only to return with a look of dismay. The staff, he explained distractedly, had their own ticker tape in the kitchen, being heavily invested in the market, and it was telling them quite incredible things. With scarcely an excuse, Speyer hurried away, leaving his wife and guests to finish their meals alone "under conditions of confusion and makeshift which probably had never been seen in the Speyer household before." Not even the financier's deeply embedded code of civility could prevent this breach of decorum with the market collapsing. In more ways than one, something quite out of the ordinary was occurring.

Never had organized support been more urgently needed, and at midday it seemed actually to be organizing. Shortly after noon a shirt-sleeved Charley Mitchell pushed his way through the crowd and entered the House of Morgan; a few minutes later Albert Wiggin arrived, followed soon afterward by Seward Prosser of Bankers Trust and William Potter of Guaranty Trust. For twenty minutes they conferred with Thomas Lamont in a meeting of which, like the partners' meetings, no notes were taken or record kept. When they had finished, the four visitors hurried out of the elevator and departed, leaving Lamont to face the shouting throng of reporters. In his cool, unflappable manner, using his pince-nez to gesture with the finesse of a conductor, he gave them five minutes of explanation. "There has been a little distress selling on the Stock Exchange," he said in one of the grand understatements of all time, "and we have held a meeting . . . to discuss the situation." Reports indicated that no houses were in danger of failing and that margins were being maintained. "It is the consensus of the group," he added, "that many of the quotations on the Stock Exchange do not fairly represent the situation."[15]

Word had already raced to the floor of the Exchange that "they" had met and were about to support stock prices. At 1:30 Richard Whitney, vice president of the Exchange and brother of Morgan partner George Whitney, stepped onto the floor and went to the post where United States Steel was traded. Steel was not only the market leader but a stock long associated with the House of Morgan, which had given birth to the company. It had fallen below 200 despite efforts to maintain the price. With all eyes upon him, Whitney bid 205 for a reported 25,000 shares, then moved on to place conspicuous bids for more stocks at other posts. The mood on the floor transformed at once. Organized support had arrived! The cavalry had come over the ridge to rescue the

The inner sanctum of the House of Morgan. Here, under the stern likeness of founder J. P. Morgan, who had quelled Wall Street panics before, key bankers from several firms held an emergency meeting on the 24th to organize support for the collapsing market.   (Collection of the Museum of Financial History)

beleaguered troops! Prices rallied almost at once and cut deeply into the day's losses. When trading ceased at 3:00 P.M., the Dow was down only 6.38 and the *Times* average 6.58—a far cry from earlier quotations.[16]

"Lately," conceded the *Wall Street Journal*'s resident pundit at last, "it hasn't been 'the same old market.'" That day two stocks made new highs while 441 registered new lows.[17]

Never had Wall Street seen a day like what came to be known as Black Thursday. An astonishing volume of nearly 12.9 million shares smashed the previous record by 4.6 million and kept the ticker tape running past 7:08 that evening. Floor traders, support staff, and office workers alike were exhausted, but the estimated 50,000 people who worked on the Street would get little rest. Every exchange in the country had been swamped with record business, and the shock waves hit the Canadian, London, and other markets as well. The Curb Exchange set its own record of more than 6.3 million shares; its day had commenced with a whopping 150,000-share block of Cities Service being thrown onto the market. Chicago's exchange topped the million mark for the first time. Wild trading also engulfed the Board of Trade, where the price of wheat crashed 12 cents to a new low before regaining 7 cents of the loss by day's end. The madness extended even to the liner *Berengaria* at sea, where Mike Meehan's floating brokerage was almost as busy as he was on the Exchange floor.[18]

In Chicago, too, the major banks came to the aid of the stock market. Bankers in both cities looked expectantly toward Washington in hopes of a rate cut from the Federal Reserve. The board met twice that Thursday, heard reports from Thomas Lamont and other sources, and followed the record-breaking events of the day. At 5:00 P.M. Roy Young informed reporters that the board had taken no action and that he had no comment. While the Fed remained silent, several senators vented their views on "stock market gambling" and talked again of an investigation into the use of credit for speculation. Carter Glass savaged his target of choice. "The present trouble is due largely to Charles E. Mitchell's activities," he growled. "That man more than forty others is responsible for the present trouble." The target himself reiterated his earlier views that the break was "purely technical" and nothing in the general situation worried him.[19]

Wall Street received the news of the Fed's inaction with silent disgust. At 4:30 the five bankers, joined by George F. Baker Jr. of the First National Bank, met again and agreed to form a pool with each member putting in $20 million to meet future emergencies. Their intent was not to boost prices so much as support them. As one banker put it, they were "not back of the market, but under the market." Other banks were thought to have pledged their support as well, but it was the elite, the members of the club, who remained firmly in charge. That same afternoon Colonel John W. Prentiss of Hornblower & Weeks summoned representatives of 35 major brokerages to a meeting at which it was agreed that the selling had been greatly overdone and that the market was in sound condition. The overnight circulars regularly dispatched by the firms to their customers carried a uniform tone of optimism. Hornblower & Weeks revived and published in 85 newspapers a 1926 advertisement boosting the purchase of sound securities. "We believe," it exhorted, "that present conditions are favorable for advantageous investment in standard American securities."[20]

Prominent figures across the country hastened to add their voices to the chorus of optimism. President Hoover, back in Washington, assured the nation that "the fundamental business of the country . . . is on a sound and prosperous basis." Business leaders of every stripe insisted that the reaction had been overdone and that the problem was confined to the stock market. Odd-lot houses reported an unusually large number of orders coming in from small buyers. The consensus was overwhelming that the storm, however violent or freakish, had passed, and an editorial writer for the *New York Times* was quick to draw the proper moral. "We shall hear considerably less in the future of those newly invented conceptions of finance which revised the principles of political economy with a view solely to fitting the stock market's vagaries," he wrote. "It will not be easy after this week's occurrences to dismiss contemptuously the teachings of past financial experience."[21]

That Thursday evening astrologer Evangeline Adams found her studio over Carnegie Hall still swamped with waiting clients despite the fact that the Dow seemed headed in the opposite direction from heaven. The reason for her popularity was simple: with almost uncanny precision she had predicted the crash 24 hours before it happened. Unable to hold private consultations with the horde of clients, she set up mass meetings in her waiting room. Noting that the movements of certain planets were creating "spheres of influence over susceptible groups, who in turn will continue to influence the market," she predicted that Friday and Saturday would witness a clear turnaround. Reassured, her followers hurried away to spread the word.[22]

Wearily the people who worked the Street prepared to meet the coming day. The tsunami had left in its wake a pile of debris in the form of unrecorded sales, transfers of stock, and a mountain of other paperwork. The telephone, telegraph, and cable services had done a record business, leaving the operators numb with fatigue. The day's mad pace had exhausted everyone, but there was no time to rest. Through the night the staffs plugged doggedly away in offices throughout the financial district. Firms booked blocks of hotel rooms for their employees or brought cots into the office and food from restaurants that had done little business for much of the day. Workers got paid well during the crisis, some earning nearly a month's salary that week alone, but they stayed at their posts because it was expected of them and, like good soldiers, they did their duty. Some firms kept a nurse on duty, and workers who felt ill or weak were sent home or to a hotel.[23]

Taking no chances, Police Commissioner Grover Whelan dispatched an extra 400 men and 100 detectives to patrol the financial district on Friday. Sightseeing lines diverted some of their buses for special tours of

THE WEATHER.
TODAY—Fair, Fresh southwest to west winds.

AMERICA FIRST!

New York American

MIDNIGHT EDITION

No. 16,506.—DAILY. FRIDAY, OCTOBER 25, 1929—30 PAGES ★R

MANY STOCKS DOWN DESPITE RALLY AFTER 12,894,650 SHARE PANIC! SENATE TO PROBE FINANCIAL SYSTEM

| REDS HUNTED AFTER ITALY'S | 52 Lost as Lake Michigan Ferry Sinks in Storm | GRUNDY RAISED $1,300,000 FOR G O P ELECTION | MAYOR HEARS PLANS TO CURE DOPE ADDICTS | Losses 3 Billion More; Morgan Stems Stampede |

Newspaper headline after Thursday's panic selling. (Collection of the Museum of Financial History)

Wall Street, hoping to profit from another day of excitement. Like many traders, they were a day late and a dollar short. To the relief of red-eyed brokers, the market opened strong and remained orderly all day, the Dow gaining 1.75 and the *Times* average 0.79 on a hefty volume of 5.9 million shares. That day 3 stocks hit new highs and 118 new lows. During the short Saturday session the Dow slipped back 2.25 and the *Times* average 2.63 in a 2-million-share day, but nothing seemed out of the ordinary. The excitement was over, but the cleaning up went on through the weekend. For the first time ever, the Exchange's governors summoned all specialists to their offices on Sunday to make their books available. The staffs in every brokerage on Wall Street also kept at their work on Sunday, giving it an air of bustle and activity when normally it was abandoned to tourists, strollers, and guards.[24]

What to make of it all? Never had the weekend respite from trading called forth a greater flood of opinion and speculation on what had been and what was to come. "Wall Street is allowing its imagination full rein in explaining the recent debacle," noted one reporter, and the gist of its response was an almost penitential reversal. Bankers, brokers, even economists agreed solemnly that the crash had been occurred because "speculation . . . had been carried beyond all limits of safety," and that the market had been "'overbulled' for a long period." Many bankers and businessmen applauded the shaking out as beneficial.

The *New York Investment News*'s optimistic report that the crisis was "over" on the 25th proved less than prescient.   (Collection of the Museum of Financial History)

From London Alfred P. Sloan of General Motors termed it "a healthy thing. . . . It had to come sooner or later and it is better over. . . . Now everyone will get back to work instead of cherishing the idea that it is possible to get rich overnight."[25]

Most observers concurred that the worst was over and the storm had passed. No one expected a quick recovery or return to some fresh version of "normalcy"; nearly everyone conceded that, as one analyst put it, "the back of the bull market has definitely been broken." Alexander Noyes was even more explicit on its demise. "The philosophy . . . that a rise in prices can go on forever," he wrote, "that the speculative 'outside public' is the best judge of intrinsic values, . . . that buying of stocks on margin is really nothing but investment on the installment plan, that 'bull leaders' buy stocks always and . . . never sell, that stocks may just as well be valued at 'thirty times earnings' as ten—this carefully cultivated philosophy of the past two years has been . . . irreparably damaged."[26]

There was general agreement, too, that the unqualified statements of so many key figures from the president on down had done much to stabilize the market, as had the fact that no banks or brokerages had gone under in the crisis. In 1907 J. P. Morgan had organized efforts to keep key banks and trust companies from failing amid a panic. In this case, however, it was the market rather than the banks that required help. The *Wall Street Journal* saw this as the key to recovery. "It was a panic, a purely stock market panic, of a new brand . . . ," noted one columnist. "Panics of the past were brought about by something fundamentally wrong with finance or business, crop failures, earthquakes, strained international relations, prohibitive rates for money, inflated inventories and the like. The recent break was due to the position of the market itself. . . . The storm has left no wreckage except marginal traders forced to sell at a loss."[27]

That wreckage was considerable. No one knew how many thousands of small traders (and some large ones) had been wiped out when they could not meet margin calls and their brokers were forced to sell them out—to dump their stock on a falling market. In many cases the process was impersonal, but often it involved a relationship as well. "I was obliged to sell out one of my best friends," sighed one broker, "for my protection and his. It was the toughest job I ever had to do." In the heat of battle the customer could not get answers from his broker or the broker from the specialists. "You ask me what I think you ought to do?" said one exasperated broker to a client. "I'll tell you the only thing you can do: Wait—wait and pray!" The broker who recounted this story paused, then mused, "If that man is praying, he is not praying for the broker."[28]

Everyone heard stories about or knew firsthand ordinary people devastated by the sudden fall from riches to rags. A broker told Edwin Lefevre of a customer who lost everything and went home despondent. Next day the man's brother told the broker that he had killed himself. "He [the brother] couldn't blame us," added the broker, "because he heard me beg his brother more than once to take his profit." Noyes had an acquaintance who, unable to place a call from his hotel room, went downstairs and found the operator in tears while talking on the phone. After hanging up she said, "That was my broker. I'm ruined. All I have left in the world is my sealskin coat." The story was apt in more ways than one. The seal had lost its skin, and so had thousands of small investors who had waded into the market over their heads. Too late they had learned the most obvious lesson of the market: "Beginner's luck is short lived in Wall Street."[29]

One of the few winners of sorts from the calamity was a man who kept smiling as the prices sank like stones into water. For nearly two years, he told Lefevre, his wife had been making his life miserable, telling him how much her brother had made in Radio or a friend's husband in Steel, and how she could have a new car instead of a "second-hand flivver" if only he had the nerve. "I was a hopeless pill, and worse," he said with a rueful smile. But no longer. "Last night I ate my dinner in comfort—you know, in silence," he added. "Tonight I expect to be told that I am not so dumb as I look. Tomorrow, when she gets the reports of the casualties in our set, I will be restored to the esteem in which I was held before the bull market."[30]

Praise was heaped on the bankers' pool for providing organized support while the Fed stood on the sidelines and did nothing. Since Morgan's dramatic intervention in 1907, the myth of organized support had hovered over Wall Street like a reassuring fairy tale, but never before had it sprung to life in the form of identifiable participants known to have come together for the explicit purpose of shoring up the market. The bankers said nothing to the public about a pool; indeed, they made a point of *not* saying anything about "concerted action." Once their presence was known and their views about the market were made clear, rumor and supposition did most of the work for them. As one reporter concluded, "The decision of the group of powerful bankers to state their position did more toward stopping the smash than all of the money they could have used."[31]

As the weekend wound down, the economic horizon looked favorable. Broker Charles E. Merrill asked a wide variety of industries and 26 major chain stores whether they had noticed any sudden change in business conditions that might be attributed to the market break. A large majority replied that no obvious change had occurred; the chain stores reported "volumes of business greater than at any time in their history, with prospects excellent for expansion." But weekends have always been a peculiar time for Wall Street, the one halt in the frantic, pulsating rhythm of the Exchange when reflection on the course of events and future prospects is possible without being under immediate fire. During that brief interlude optimism and pessimism had waged many a titanic battle in the hearts of speculators over the years, with victory going more often than not to the dark side. As Galbraith so aptly expressed it, "The Sabbath pause had a marked tendency to breed uneasiness and doubts and pessimism and a decision to get out on Monday."[32]

That Sunday evening the Jewish Theatrical Guild welcomed Eddie Cantor as master of ceremonies for its annual celebration. The audience at the Commodore Hotel included Police Commissioner Whelan and Mayor Jimmy Walker, who was locked in a campaign for reelection against a dogged Fiorello La Guardia. Cantor had the stock market very much in mind when he opened his monologue. "If the stock market goes any lower," he cracked, "I know thousands of married men who are going to leave their sweethearts and go back to their wives. As for myself, I am not worried. My broker is going to carry me; he and three other pall bearers."[33]

Shortly after dawn on Monday morning, October 28, a remarkable spectacle greeted those few people out at that early hour. An immense cloud of blackbirds and starlings, gathered for their winter migration, filled up City Hall Plaza to rest and forage for food. A policeman walking his beat saw the sky raining birds and took shelter in a doorway. For a brief time Fourth Avenue was impassable until the enormous flock departed, leaving behind about a hundred of their number that had died of exhaustion or starvation. The superstitious might well have taken the sight as an omen for the day to come.[34]

When the gong sounded on Monday morning, traders watched apprehensively as the first orders poured in. To their horror the vast majority were selling orders, and fresh batches came surging in behind them. Once again the floor dissolved into frantic confusion as it became clear that another huge wave of liquidation was sweeping over it. By 11:00 A.M. the market seemed plunged back into the nightmare of Black Thursday as prices dropped "almost perpendicularly" with spreads of 2, 3, 5, even 10 points between transactions on individual stocks. Another swirl of ugly rumors about failures and suicides—all of them false— swept through the surging, shoving mob of traders. And at 1:10 P.M. the cavalry seemed just over the horizon when the news ticker reported that Charley Mitchell had just entered the House of Morgan, raising hopes for organized support. The floor calmed and prices steadied briefly. United States Steel was selling at 193½ when a Morgan broker on the floor started bidding for it. The stock rallied fitfully but within 10 minutes fell back to 190 and kept falling as it became clear that the cavalry was nowhere in sight.[35]

Amid the turmoil, however, could be found some key differences from the earlier debacle. The huge wave of sales was somehow being absorbed albeit at plummeting prices; no "air holes" developed. To the floor's surprise, much of the action had moved from the speculative favorites to the blue chip stocks, which took a pounding no one thought

Brokers' messengers sharing a newspaper at the height of the panic. (Breuer, Ebbs, Daily News L. P.)

possible. Evidently Thursday's tsunami had carried out to sea most of the minnows on margin accounts, leaving larger operators to withstand this onslaught, and many of them were reaching deep into their strong-boxes either to raise needed cash or get out of the market at all costs. The Curb was also being pounded, as were the Chicago and other out-of-town exchanges. Nor did the over-the-counter market escape; there the bank stocks took a beating. The message was as chilling as it was clear. In the words of one reporter, "It was not so much the little trader or speculator who was struck[;] . . . it was the rich men of the country, the institutions which have purchased common stocks, the investment trusts and investors of all kinds."

The selling surge hit every kind of stock as well. Speculative favorites, blue chips, banks, utilities, investment trusts—all dropped through low levels no one dreamed they would break. Once again the last hour of trading turned into a nightmare as 3 million shares changed hands, rendering the ticker useless as it fell more than two hours behind. Frantic traders looked instead to the bond, Dow, and New York News Bureau tickers, which began carrying running flows of quotations from the floor. Once again the telephone and telegraph lines carried record traffic. Most brokerages abandoned all pretense of keeping their quotation boards current, leaving customers helpless to learn what was going on at the Exchange. The crowds had thinned considerably in most of the rooms, thanks to the heavy casualties suffered from margin calls. They waited quietly and in vain for the organized support to appear. In Washington the Federal Reserve Board met and decided no action was needed.

When the closing gong sounded, the Dow had plummeted a record 38.33 points to close at 260.64 while the *Times* average plunged 29.22 to a closing figure of 224.33 on a volume of more than 9.2 million shares—a figure second only to that of Black Thursday. The ticker did not record its last transaction until nearly 5:48 P.M. The Exchange floor was in shambles along with those who worked it. The carnage among blue chips had been fearful. General Electric lost 47^1/2, Eastman Kodak nearly 42, Westinghouse 34^1/2, AT&T 34, Columbia Gas & Electric 22, Union Carbide 20, and even staid New York Central nearly 23. United States Steel, the bellwether stock of the bull market, lost 17^1/2 on the day. On the Curb, Andrew Mellon's Alcoa dropped more than 50 and Samuel Insull's Middle West Utilities a whopping 119. Among the banks George F. Baker's First National went down $500, and bankers worried that the drop in their stocks might give people the erroneous impression that the banks themselves were in trouble.

Late that afternoon, the cavalry in the form of the six distinguished bankers gathered again at the Morgan offices to discuss the situation. When they emerged around 6:00 P.M., Thomas Lamont again took on the clamoring reporters along with fellow Morgan partner George Whitney. Patiently Lamont reminded them that the group's purpose was to prevent demoralization in the market, not to prop up prices. No demoralization had occurred, no air pockets had developed, so the bankers did not intervene. The break in prices was not unexpected, he explained. Once the brokerages brought their books up to date, investors knew their positions, and many were either forced to liquidate or decided to get out of the market. Lamont would not predict what would happen next, but he did suggest that at current prices some investment buying would surely occur. Rumors from other sources elaborated this theme to such an extent that a headline in next morning's *Times* read, "BANKERS MOBILIZE FOR BUYING TODAY."

Two of the bankers mobilized in ways that they did not care to see in headlines. On returning to his office from the meeting, Charley Mitchell learned to his chagrin that National City Company had bought 71,000 shares of National City Bank stock for $32 million in a vain attempt to support the price. The decline posed a major threat to the pending merger with the Corn Exchange Bank, for which National City needed to maintain its own stock at a level above $450 a share. Next morning before the market opened, Mitchell visited the House of Morgan to obtain a $12 million line of credit, pledging his own 30,000 shares of National City as collateral. With these funds Mitchell personally relieved National City Company of 28,300 shares of the bank's stock for $10.6 million. In effect he had used his own fortune to preserve the financial integrity of National City Company. Albert Wiggin chose a quite different method of dealing with Chase Bank stock: since September he had been quietly selling it short through his private corporations and reaping large profits on the fall.[36]

Where had the flood of stock come from? Large blocks had been dumped by foreign investors, especially German and Dutch interests. Another source of liquidation came from out-of-town banks that had bought stock on behalf of their customers, made loans against the stock—the proceeds of which often went right back into the market for margin purchases—and been forced to sell out the overextended owners. A puzzled Alexander Noyes saw something more than "outside liquidation" in the collapse of "stocks of the highest value and the soundest rating," which was "in no respect occasioned by a bad turn in the news." Some of the selling may have come from frightened holders, but another possible source occurred to him: "It must have signified the surrender of professional 'pools' which, with all their reckless operations, had believed their own position to be impregnable." Whatever the cause, he concluded grimly, "the extreme severity of these successive convulsions of readjustment has been only proportioned to the duration and extravagance of the period of illusion."

Even veteran players, the smartest of the smart, bled freely during the day. The so-called Big Ten, which included the Fisher brothers, were reported to have lost heavily. Billy Durant watched his portfolio shrivel by the hour, forcing his brokers to unload parts of his heavily margined holdings as they did those of lesser lights. The not-so-smart suffered equally. In August, Edgar Brown had finally moved to Los Angeles. His unease with the market's gyrations led him on October 4 to visit the National City office there and tell them "to sell out everything." Salesmen flocked around him at once and warned him that it was a foolish thing to do, especially with National City Bank stock. A telegram arrived from Rummel, whom Brown had never told of his whereabouts, informing him that "National City Bank now 525. Sit tight." Again he allowed himself to be persuaded, but after Monday's debacle sitting tight had ceased to be an option.[37]

Bernard Baruch, too, had been hurt by the collapse but lost neither his nerve nor his perspective. That Monday night he hosted a dinner party in honor of Winston Churchill, the distinguished visitor who had himself lost heavily in the fall. The gathering was a glittering one. Thomas Lamont was there along with Charley Mitchell, Albert Wiggin, Eugene Meyer, Charles Schwab, John D. Ryan of Anaconda Copper, and Gerard Swope and his brother Herbert. After dinner Mitchell brought smiles by offering a toast to "my fellow former millionaires." After leaving the party, Herbert Swope wired a fellow speculator, "CONSENSUS OF OPINION . . . AT BARUCH'S . . . WAS THAT THOSE WHO STAND PRESSURE WOULD NOT ALONE BE DISCHARGING PUBLIC DUTY BUT WOULD BE CONFERRING BIG FAVOR UPON THEMSELVES WITH CERTAINTY OF RECOVERY OF STOCKS." Arrangements were being made, he added, for operations of a big pool in Western Union stock that might begin on Tuesday.[38]

That Monday evening a wealthy midwestern industrialist checked into his regular hotel, where he had a standing order for a call girl and a bottle of champagne. The champagne arrived but the girl did not. After calling the night manager to remind him, the guest was rewarded with a knock at the door a few minutes later. Eyeing the lovely blonde outside his door, he told her gruffly to get inside and undress. In steely tones the woman informed him that she was his broker's secretary, handed him a margin call for $400,000, and stalked out. A few minutes later the deflated guest checked out.[39]

That same Monday night Edgar Brown got an equally discouraging message in a phone call from an officer of National City's Los Angeles branch. "Brown," he said, "things are looking terrible. I think the market might bust wide open tomorrow morning and let you out. You'd better come down and watch it. If they move off you get out from under." Brown, who had never even been in a customers' room, hurried with his wife to the National City office shortly after 6:00 A.M. Tuesday to catch the opening sales from the East at 7:00 A.M. The first transaction in Anaconda Copper was a huge 45,000-share block at 80; it had closed Monday at 96. "Now if this thing strengthens up the first hour," said his broker, "everything will be all right. But if it does not, look out."[40]

It did not. The opening gong Tuesday morning unleashed a frenzy of selling that dwarfed even those of previous days. The difference lay not in the number of orders but in their size: blocks of 5,000 to 50,000 shares of blue chip stocks were thrown onto the market "as if they were so much junk" for whatever price they would bring. More than 3.2 million shares changed hands in the first half hour with 630,000 of them going in the first 26 transactions. No fewer than 58 different stocks opened the day with sales of 10,000 or more shares, many of 50,000 or more, and always at prices shockingly lower than those at Monday's close. Standard Oil was down 7³/₄, United Corporation 7¹/₂, General Motors 2¹/₄, and International Telephone & Telegraph 17 points—all on opening trades of 50,000 shares. Radio opened down 30 on a sale of 30,000 shares, Westinghouse down 14¹/₂ on 25,000 shares. On the Curb Exchange, Transamerica opened down 42¹/₂ from Monday's close and Electric Bond & Share down 34³/₄.[41]

Confusion again swept the floor as no buyers could be found for even the best stocks. As one reporter noted, "All considerations other than to get rid of the stock at any price were brushed aside." Clearly these were not the desperate sales of ruined margin traders but the frantic heaving overboard of holdings by the wealthy, institutions, investment trusts, and others who dealt in stocks on a large scale. Once again prices plummeted steadily, the ticker fell farther and farther behind, the dreaded air pockets developed, and a sense of panic overtook the besieged traders. Cries of "Sell at the market!" and "Sell at any price!" filled the air from throats already hoarse from a week of shouting. Telephone, telegraph, and cable wires burned with record traffic all day. On a whimsy one messenger boy put in a bid for 100 shares of White Sewing Machine at $1 a share and got it; the stock had sold at 48 at its peak and closed at 11¹/₈ on Monday. Pat Bologna's National City stock went on the block because he could no longer afford to cover the margin. From his $5,000 investment he managed to salvage $1,700.[42]

What Robert Shiller has called "irrational exuberance" had turned swiftly into irrational hysteria. The bankers met again at noon and agreed that even their buying could not deflect the enormous wave of selling. Any attempt to support the market was, as an analyst said, "like trying to stem the falls of Niagara." As Galbraith put it, "Support, organized or otherwise, could not contend with the overwhelming, pathological desire to sell." The Federal Reserve Board met at 10:00 A.M. and remained in session for six hours, but no word or deed came from its inner sanctum. Meanwhile, a serious problem had developed like an undertow behind the tsunami: money was rushing out of the call loan market even faster than it had flowed in. The "other" lenders—corporations, individuals, and out-of-town banks, which by October 23 provided 58 percent of the funds in call loans—were pulling their money out, leaving a credit vacuum that could spell disaster in a sinking market unless it was filled.[43]

George Harrison understood the danger and moved to deflect it with a decisiveness that would have impressed Benjamin Strong. At 3:00 A.M. on that Tuesday he conferred with a few of the directors of the New York Federal Reserve Bank, who agreed with his plan. Before the market opened that fateful morning, he let it be known that the bank would purchase $100 million in government securities to ease the strain in the money market. Harrison did this without approval from the Federal Reserve Board and outside the system's regular Open Market Investment Committee account. Roy Young was startled and Adolph Miller indignant when the news reached them, but grudgingly they agreed that the emergency justified the action. In all, the New York bank bought $132 million in government securities, thereby pumping funds into the vacuum created by the wholesale withdrawals from the call loan market.[44]

Harrison's courageous move may have been the pivotal moment of the crash. By making these funds available to banks for lending during the severe credit crunch, he probably saved many individuals and institutions from failing. No single act did more to stave off even worse disaster on this disastrous day. The board was slow to appreciate its importance, and few outside Wall Street even realized what he had done, let alone understood it. On a day destined to live in financial infamy he emerged as a genuine if invisible hero. To Young's criticism that he lacked authority for any such action, Harrison later replied, "Had we not bought governments so freely . . . the stock exchange might have had to yield to the tremendous pressure brought to bear upon it to close."[45]

The New York banks, too, did their part in filling the credit vacuum and trying to stem the tide of liquidation. Some reportedly took over undermargined accounts and held them for later sale rather than throw them into the market, or in other cases simply ignored the need for more margin because the drastic fall in stock prices made it unrealistic. Whether in the banks or on the floor of the Exchange, few felt obliged to play strictly by the rules with such huge waves crashing over them. Orders to sell were held up rather than executed, in hopes that better conditions would develop; so great was the torrent of orders that they could not all be dealt with promptly anyway. One exhausted broker later discovered a wastebasket he had stuffed full of orders to be executed but had forgotten in the heat of battle.[46]

This day of duress, coming on the heels of so many before it, forced the governing committee to consider the dreaded possibility of closing the Exchange. Around noon, the 40 members began discreetly leaving the bedlam on the floor and slipping away not to their regular meeting room but to another small, narrow office below the trading floor. There, cramped together and wreathed in cigarette smoke, they debated whether to close the Exchange. Doing so might create such apprehension as to trigger an even worse panic when the Exchange reopened; for that matter, they had tried to keep their meeting secret lest it affect an already frightened market. Richard Whitney, acting president while the president, E. H. H. Simmons, honeymooned in Hawaii at this most inopportune of times, recalled the nervousness of the members in "continually lighting cigarettes, taking a puff or two, putting them out and lighting new ones." Reluctant to act, they put off the decision and agreed to meet that evening.[47]

Outside the Exchange, crowds again jammed Wall and Broad streets. The visitors' gallery remained closed, but people flocked to customers' rooms to follow events as best they could on a badly lagging ticker tape. Some were still players; others who had been sold out had, like the curiosity seekers, turned the crisis into a spectator sport. The mood in many customers' rooms was that of fellow sufferers, each one eager to tell the others how much he or she had lost. In one crowded office an elderly woman puffing a succession of gold-tipped cigarettes announced loudly that she had lost $10,000. Four other women turned the day into a social event by going from one broker's office to another in a chauffeured car. At one stop they marched in regally, looked around, and left after one of them sniffed, "This place is depressing me."

The sense of depression on the Exchange floor grew steadily steeper until the final half hour, when the mood began abruptly to lighten. Suddenly, inexplicably, the crush of sell orders turned into buying orders. A vigorous rally during the last 15 minutes before the gong raised hopes that the worst had passed and that the orgy of liquidation had finally touched bottom. Good news came over the wires in the form of extra dividend declarations by United States Steel and American Can, adding to the relief brought earlier by the cutting of margins on loans. "There is no money problem involved in the present situation," read a statement issued by the House of Morgan. "There is plenty of money and it will be loaned freely." Although the Fed had taken no action, rumor insisted that a rate cut was imminent. Despite an utterly disastrous day, concluded a reporter, "there was no denying the increased optimism with which leaders of the financial district viewed the situation."[48]

When the gong sounded and the floor slowed to a mild roar, the figures for the day staggered even those already numbed by a week of record setting. The Dow plummeted another 30.57 points and the *Times* average 24.66; both would have done worse except for the late rally. Since Black Thursday the Dow had lost 96.44 points, or 30 percent of its value, and the *Times* average 80.54, or 40 percent. At the close of Bloody Tuesday the Dow stood at 230.07, its lowest mark since June 27, and the *Times* average at 199.67, a figure it had not touched since August 28, 1928. Volume totaled an incredible 16.4 million shares, dwarfing even the enormous record set on Black Thursday by 27 percent. It was a record as formidable as Babe Ruth's 60 home runs and lasted even longer; it would not be surpassed until April 1, 1968. More shares changed hands that one day than in all but three whole months of 1921.

The same pattern prevailed on every other exchange throughout the country. The Curb recorded its largest decline in history on an unprecedented volume of more than 7 million shares. Large losses also plagued the Boston, Chicago, Philadelphia, San Francisco, Montreal, and Toronto exchanges. The London exchange, which had greeted the first tsunami of selling with a smug "I told you so" attitude, dissolved into pandemonium at this second wave of violent selling. Bank stocks took another big tumble, with National City falling as low as 300 at one point. Yet amid the chaos not a single firm on the New York Stock Exchange failed, and only one small Curb brokerage was forced to suspend. The banks, too, remained solid despite the enormous drain on them throughout the day. The tsunami had inflicted enormous damage, but the financial system survived its passing intact. That fact brought comfort to beleaguered brokers.

After the close, the Exchange's governing committee met again and, buoyed by the late rally, issued a statement that the floor would open for its usual hours on Wednesday. The banking group also gathered at 4:30 and conferred for two hours. When a weary Thomas Lamont emerged to face the reporters, he had to fend off an awkward question about rumors that the bankers had not only failed to support the market but had actually sold stock. Once again he explained that "it was not the intention of the group to attempt to maintain prices, but to maintain a free market. . . . The group . . . will continue in a cooperative way to support the market and has not been a seller of stocks."[49]

For the Exchange to open on Wednesday, another massive effort had to be made to clean up the debris of a record-setting day. The exhausted staffs of banks, brokerages, and other financial houses braced for another lengthy session. Deep into the night the financial district looked as busy as during the day, its narrow streets crowded with cars and cabs. Restaurants remained open until midnight and enjoyed full tables all evening. Brokers scrambled to get hold of the day's transactions. "We did more than 1,000,000 shares," moaned one, "but we don't know yet how much we really made because the machine broke down. I can't tell you how many orders we received, executed, and then reported to the customer. Later, we could not find who bought the stock from us. Lost in the shuffle! . . . The number and character of mistakes that could not be avoided are beyond computing."[50]

The record total of 16.4 million shares covered only the New York Stock Exchange. Adding the 7 million traded on the Curb and those dealt over the counter and in odd-lot houses, one broker estimated the actual figure at 25 million shares—for which there were both buyers and sellers. "The telegraph operators handling our out-of-town business went without sleep for thirty and thirty-five hours," recalled a broker. "Trays with sandwiches and coffee were passed around every two hours. None of our clerks went home at all during the worst. My brother didn't sleep a wink in twenty-seven hours. He had been working eight hours a day for weeks, and he was only one of hundreds of clerks. Girls at the adding machines and typewriters fainted at their work. In one odd-lot house thirty-four keeled over in one afternoon from sheer exhaustion. In another, nineteen had to be sent home."[51]

That night, while Wall Street toiled to put its house in order, the forces of sunshine and optimism regrouped in hopes of rallying crushed spirits. Again the nightly brokers' letters expressed their strong belief/wish/hope that the bottom had been reached. "Now, at last," read one, "stocks may be safely recommended both as investments and for the speculative turn." John J. Raskob, himself largely clear of the market, issued a statement that many stocks were now at bargain levels. "The pendulum has swung too far," he said. "The list is filled with bargains and my friends and I are all buying stocks." Julius Klein, assistant secretary of commerce and a close confidant of President Hoover, went on radio to declare that business was sound and that the crash was "not a major barometer of business." He viewed the problem as one of attitude. "Many of the business depressions of past decades have been primarily psychological," he asserted, "and could have been avoided or minimized if the business men and the masses of the people had had the proper confidence in themselves."[52]

Klein dared to mention the dreaded "depression" word lurking behind so much of the immediate apprehension. Many newspapers picked up the same theme. "The sagging of stocks," stressed the New York *Daily News*, "has not destroyed a single factory, wiped out a single farm or city lot or real estate development, decreased the productive powers of a single workman or machine in the United States." The *Times* found a useful solace in the whole affair. "Painful as the experience has been . . . ," an editorial moralized, "the longer result of it will be restoration of the community's mental health and vision." Mayor Jimmy Walker attacked the problem in his own unique style. That afternoon, while the crash was raging, he attended a luncheon of 75 motion picture exhibitors at the Astor Hotel and urged them to "show pictures that will reinstate courage and hope in the hearts of the people. Give them a chance to forget their financial losses . . . and look with hope to the future."[53]

Many of those licking their financial wounds could not have their grief assuaged by a cheerful movie. Groucho Marx saw his holdings first battered by waves of margin calls, which he struggled mightily to meet, and then swept away by the wave of selling. "All I lost was two hundred and forty thousand dollars . . . ," he quipped later. "I would have lost more but that was all the money I had." It was no joke at the time; at a salary of $2,000 a week, he figured the loss at 120 weeks of work. That Monday the Marx Brothers opened a week's run of *Animal Crackers* in Pittsburgh. A devastated Groucho refused to go onstage for two of the performances; brother Harpo went on with the show even though he, too, had been wiped out. Eddie Cantor walked away with $60 in his pockets, not yet aware that he owed his bank $285,000 for covered margin calls. Harpo did not have even that much. To meet margin calls, he recalled, "I had scraped the bottom of the barrel . . . liquidated every asset I owned except my harp and my croquet set . . . borrowed as far in advance as I could against my salary. My market holdings . . . were probably worth a medium-sized bag of jelly beans."[54]

Elsewhere a grateful Will Rogers said a silent prayer of thanks to Bernard Baruch, while Edgar Brown prayed in vain for salvation from the disaster that had befallen him. An hour or so after the market opened, his broker told him, "My God, Brown, City Bank is crashing. The banks are in on this thing and the market is actually way under what it is quoted out here." He advised Brown to sell his National City stock, saying it had fallen to 350. Brown figured that at worst he could walk away with $25,000 of his original investment and agreed to sell. He walked out of the office and told his wife what he had done. She was furious that he even thought of selling on a falling market. "You go back in there and tell him not to sell the stock," she insisted. He did so, only to be told that the order had gone in and could not be stopped. "Anyway," added his broker, "the way they are busting this thing open you'll be able to buy back all the Anaconda you want at 65, and anyhow, the bank is calling your loan."[55]

Perplexed, Brown walked over to the bank, "and they just gave me hell," he said later. "They said they were not even thinking of calling me." Next morning he got a confirmation slip saying that his National City stock had been sold not for 350 but for 320. The $25,000 he had hoped to salvage had shriveled to barely $6,000. Dejected, tubercular, almost totally deaf, and wiser in the ways of chasing rainbows, he prepared gloomily to move his family back to Pottsville. Unlike the Marxes or Eddie Cantor, he had no way of recouping his lost fortune or even earning a living. Within a few years his only employment was clerking for the poor board in Pottsville.

No one captured the moment better than Max Gordon, the man Groucho Marx called his "friend, sometime financial adviser and shrewd trader." On Bloody Tuesday he called Groucho and said only five words before hanging up: "Marx, the jig is up!"[56]

To the relief of everyone, the opening gong on Wednesday brought a steady rush of buying orders. One reporter called it "a vigorous, buoyant rally that lasted from bell to bell." Around 2:00 P.M. news came over the ticker that the 90-year-old John D. Rockefeller Sr., who rarely spoke for public consumption, had issued a statement. "Believing that fundamental conditions of the country are sound," it read, "and that there is nothing in the business situation to warrant the destruction of values that has taken place . . . my son and I have for some days been purchasing sound common stocks." The news spurred the buying impetus. The day's steady gains enabled the governing committee to proclaim that the Exchange would open only for three hours on Thursday and close all day Friday and Saturday to give everyone rest and a chance to catch up. Worn-out brokers, staff, and customers alike greeted the announcement with cheers. Other exchanges quickly followed suit.[57]

"Everybody in Wall Street . . . was talking about psychology," observed a reporter at day's end. "Psychology, it seemed, was the all-important element in buying and selling. It was psychology that sent stocks tumbling into a seemingly bottomless pit and it was psychology, of a quite different brand, that sent them upward yesterday." The Dow climbed back 28.40 and the *Times* average 17.66 on another huge volume of 10.7 million shares. More good news greeted traders on Thursday when the Federal Reserve Board finally cut the rediscount rate from 6 to 5 percent after the Bank of England reduced its rate to 6 percent. Brokers' loans showed an unprecedented drop of nearly $1.1 billion, and Henry Ford added to the good cheer by announcing price cuts on his cars and trucks.[58]

When the Exchange opened at noon on Thursday for its shortened session, a backlog of buying orders sent prices soaring again as nearly 2.5 million shares changed hands in the first half hour. So strong was demand that analysts talked happily of air pockets above stocks rather than below them. By the closing gong, the Dow had registered an impressive gain of 15.04 and the *Times* average 12.67 on an enormous volume of 7.1 million shares in only three hours of trading. In all the Dow recovered about 63 percent of its losses for the previous two days, and the *Times* average 56 percent.[59]

With a profound sense of relief the Exchange closed for a long weekend to absorb the fallout from the busiest and most eventful week in its history. The volume of trading in October set a record that would not be surpassed until 1965; its total of 142.1 million shares exceeded by more than 27 million shares the next busiest month, November 1928. The frantic week of October 24 to 31 alone produced a volume of 64.4 million shares, a figure far exceeding that of any *month* prior to March 1928. For the month the Dow lost 69.06 and the *Times* average 57.70. On October 31 the Dow closed at 273.51, or 33.50 below where it stood on January 2; the *Times* average finished the month at 230, or 4.80 below its price when the year began. The huge gains of 1929 had been wiped out, but both averages still stood above where they had been prior to late 1928.

The bull market seemed clearly to be dead; the question was whether it could hang on to the earlier gains made before 1929. The *Wall Street*

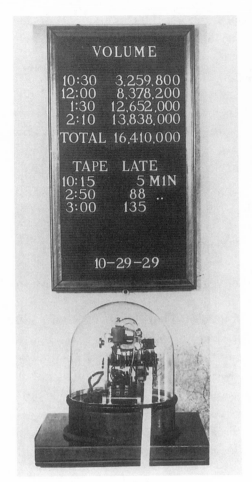

VOLUME

10:30	3,259,800
12:00	8,378,200
1:30	12,652,000
2:10	13,838,000
TOTAL	16,410,000

TAPE LATE

10:15	5 MIN
2:50	88 ..
3:00	135

10-29-29

The stock ticker, photographed
for posterity on October 29,
when it fell hours behind the
torrent of selling.   (Collection of
the Museum of Financial History)

Journal said again that the panic "was not due to anything fundamentally
weak in either business or finance. It was confined to the market itself."
Alexander Noyes, as usual, looked deeper. "There is an old-time tradition
(fulfilled no further back than 1921)," he observed, "that . . . a Stock Exchange panic foreshadows business depression, unemployment and hard
times." He also acknowledged more recent thinking that "trade prosperity has in the recent past been bulwarked in a very different way from the
boom in stocks." Which to believe? "It is always rash to adopt unre-
servedly either kind of inference. . . . At the present moment business
men may be described as hopeful even though perplexed."[60]

A more immediate and pressing question was what the market would
do when it reopened on Monday, November 4. Every sign, to say noth-

ing of every public forecast, pointed to a strong, orderly market with plenty of reserve buying power behind it. The odd-lot houses had a large backlog of orders from all over the country waiting to be filled. The rate cut and dramatic drop in brokers' loans eased fears of a credit strain, and leading figures filled the air with bullish or at least hopeful sentiments. Here, too, however, Noyes sounded a cautionary note. "Markets invariably forget . . . ," he wrote in his professorial tone, "that every such financial crisis leaves in the hands of banks or fellow-brokers great masses of stock taken over to relieve or save the larger victims. . . . Stock held on such a basis is invariably sold again as soon as the market is in shape to take it."[61]

11

Over

the Rainbow

When the history of the present phase of the stock market is written, we believe it will be referred to as the "era of projected inflation," . . . the period when enthusiasm for future profits obscured actual earnings to an excessive degree. We are on the way towards returning to the age of reason of several years ago when stocks had to show substantial earning power, reasonable book value, and dividend returns comparable to the cost of carry.

—Baar, Cohen & Co.[1]

*E*verything possible was done to make ready for Monday's market, not only in cleaning up the books, the Exchange floor, and the loose ends of a chaotic week but also in restoring that most critical and fragile of factors, public confidence. From all sides came a chorus of affirmation that the storm had passed, the skies were clearing, little damage had been left in its wake, the cleanup had begun, and conditions would return to normal in a short time. "We are deluged with optimistic statements from banks, Washington, heads of big industrial and railroad enterprises and men of great wealth," observed the *Wall Street Journal*. The "prosperity chorus," as Stuart Chase called it, worked overtime to detach the market's collapse from the broader business picture. On this point Chase agreed. Wrapping up a six-month survey on the structure of American prosperity, he dismissed the crash as a factor in the broader picture. "We probably have three more years of prosperity ahead of us," he told a reporter, "before we enter the cyclic tailspin

236

which has occurred in the eleventh year of each of the four great previous periods of commercial prosperity."[2]

HUGE BUSINESS IN STOCKS READY FOR MONDAY OPENING, blared the headline of the Sunday *New York Times*. Two other papers echoed this belief, but doubt filled the minds of many brokers, and the *Wall Street Journal* dismissed it as a "cock and bull story." A flood of buying orders had poured in, but many were hedged as to price and some were canceled before the market opened. Anticipating another enormous volume, the governing committee of the Exchange met early that morning and decided to confine trading to the hours of 10:00 A.M. to 1:00 P.M. for the rest of the week and close on Saturday to give exhausted brokers and staff more time to rest and catch up on the paperwork. The wisdom of their decision soon became evident. To the dismay of everyone, the market opened with a steady wave of selling that continued all day, drowning what little buying had accumulated. Even with a volume of 6.2 million shares the market remained orderly, although selling grew more intense at the close.[3]

By day's end the Dow had lost 15.83 and the *Times* average 12.41 to close at 257.68 and 217.59 respectively. Although no one suspected it at the time, these figures proved to be the *highs* for both averages in November. At his usual late afternoon meeting with reporters, Thomas Lamont found himself obliged to confront rumors that the banking group had been heavy sellers of the stocks purchased during Black Thursday. He deflected the question by saying that he had no knowledge of what the others had done. Since Tuesday was election day, the markets remained closed while Jimmy Walker swept to a landslide victory over Fiorello La Guardia. Next day the landslide moved to the market as heavy, relentless selling sent the Dow plunging another 25.55 and the *Times* average 22.96. After a decent rally on Thursday, the market absorbed a small loss on Friday before closing for another long weekend of catching up.[4]

Wall Street agreed that a cascade effect was driving the market down. As the brokerage houses sorted out the week's paperwork and brought their books up to date, they sent out a steady stream of belated margin calls that forced further liquidation. Even with reduced trading days it would take most firms several more weeks to bring their records current; until they did, the cascade effect would continue to feed each day's decline on the margin calls of the previous one. The Exchange's governing committee extended the shortened trading sessions and did not reinstate the normal schedule until November 26. Everyone longed for a return to some semblance of normalcy; one pundit declared that the best thing the market could do was to get itself off the front pages of newspapers. But on Monday the 11th, stocks began a disheartening three-day slide that carried the Dow down 37.84 and the *Times* average 31.96. There was no panic but rather a steady drumbeat of selling punctuated by brief, ineffectual rallies.[5]

On Wednesday, November 13, the averages finally bottomed out at 198.69 and 166.15 respectively. The Dow had not seen that figure since February 1928; the *Times* average had not gone lower than 174.12 in all of 1928. When a mild earthquake rattled New York City on November 18, the joke ran that it was too little too late. "In less than three months," moaned the *Wall Street Journal*, "the financial community has seen the greatest bear market in the history of the Dow-Jones compilation." Rumors that the latest drop had been spurred by a "well-timed bear raid" prompted Exchange officials to ask members for disclosures on all stock being borrowed and loaned—an action last taken in 1917. Even Jesse Livermore, the most likely bear suspect, was moved to tell reporters that stocks had been "driven down too far" and that the market had bargains galore.[6]

The slide finally stopped on Thursday the 14th, thanks in part to a flurry of favorable news. Late Wednesday afternoon the Rockefeller interests moved to peg the price of Standard Oil by entering a bid for a million shares at 50. Secretary Mellon announced plans to ask Congress for quick action on a 1 percent reduction of personal and corporate income taxes. The Federal Reserve Board cut the rediscount rate from 5 percent to $4^{1}/_2$ percent, the second reduction in two weeks. Already some corporations, such as Standard Oil and United States Steel, and individuals, notably Julius Rosenwald of Sears, Roebuck and Samuel Insull, had bailed out employees caught in the market crash with emergency loans. Brokers' loans continued to fall like a pierced balloon, dropping another $710 million to their lowest level since April 1928. In four weeks the loan total plummeted nearly $3.1 billion until by November 20 it stood at less than $3.6 billion, a figure not seen since December 14, 1927.[7]

Buoyed by good tidings, the Dow and the *Times* average closed out the week with increases of 30.04 and 24.55 respectively over two days. After suffering small losses on Monday the 18th, the Dow rose another 20.93 and the *Times* average 17.20 in three days of solid gains before losing about half that amount during the last days of November. While Wall Street heaved a sigh of relief, Noyes offered his opinion that "the real cause for the sharp change . . . was the financial community's return to common sense." With the losses stemmed and volume shrinking, brokers dared believe that normal times had returned. On the 20th the *Wall Street Journal* commented that "dullness in the general list strengthened the impression that urgent liquidation was no longer overhanging the market." Never had the Street wished more ardently for dullness to return.[8]

The fallout from the crash had other effects that nurtured the "atmosphere of gloom" on Wall Street. It killed Charley Mitchell's cherished merger with the Corn Exchange Bank and spurred rumors that Mitchell would leave National City. Insurance companies reported record borrowings against policies; the reason was thought to be raising cash to cover margins. Investment trusts incurred a barrage of criticism for proving to be a source of weakness rather than strength during the crisis. Too late investors discovered that here, as elsewhere, leverage worked in both directions. No amount of explanation by trust executives could atone for their poor performance or falling prices. As Barrie Wigmore observed, "They prospered in the market's optimism and suffered in its pessimism." Reports of suicides and embezzlements attributed to the crash began to crop up in the papers. The most shocking suicide was that of banker James J. Riordan, a confidant of Al Smith, who shot himself on November 8. No embezzlement was more spectacular than the theft of nearly $3.6 million by officers of the Union Industrial Bank in Flint, Michigan, to underwrite their market adventures.[9]

For some the crash signified the end of a wild party, the time to clean up, tote up the bill, and figure out who would pay. "Life would no longer be, ever again, all fun and games," mourned Harpo Marx. "The bam-bang-sock-and-pow part was over, and so was the permanent, floating New Year's Eve party. Our million-dollar playground had been condemned." Others saw in it a return to sounder old-fashioned values that had been scorned by devotees of New Era thinking. The *New York Times* moralized that "what has happened was insistently declared, a very short time ago, to be utterly impossible in our new economic era. Now that the sequel has proved that sudden and disastrous collapse was as possible in 1929 as in 1920, the truth thus established lends peculiar interest to the policy of cautious conservatism long maintained by trade and industry." Some bankers also hastened to denounce the folly of New Era ideas and ridiculed what they labeled "jazz economists." Ministers, too, lost no opportunity to condemn "the mad desire to get rich quickly and easily."[10]

For a morality play the crash made a perfect ending, but the end was not yet in sight. As the market edged off the front pages, a no less burning question took its place. "We shall soon have entered a period of quiet and normal markets . . . ," observed Noyes. "There is still left to us to be discovered the sequel in the country's general trade." This sequel was in many respects the second of two doctrines in the gospel of New Era thinking. The first decreed that the market could never dive as it had in the past, the second that the economy could never follow it downward into a depression as usually happened after past crashes. Did the discrediting of the first law apply equally to the second? One trade journal, *Iron Age*, argued that however mythical the new era in the stock market, it truly existed in industry. "Mass production depends on mass demand," it stressed, "and the sources of mass demand must be protected." *Time* put the case more succinctly: "Behind the shadow of Speculation there was still the substance of Prosperity."[11]

Noyes agreed that "there has been no shutting down of business houses, no crash in prices of manufactured products, no sweeping reduction of working forces such as occurred in immediate sequence to nearly all of the older Wall Street panics." An early report showed no effect on employment from the crash. The luxury trades already suffered declines from buyers abruptly stripped of their market profits, the Christmas season suddenly looked more bleak, automobile dealers noticed a fall in sales along with cancellation of orders, and dealers reported a glut of used cars, but none of this signaled depression. Although the steel, automobile, and copper sectors continued to lag, some sectors of trade had good news to report. Clearly businessmen had grown more conservative; the question was whether they might become too cautious.[12]

But something else had changed—something less tangible but more basic. "Prosperity is more than an economic condition," noted Frederick Lewis Allen; "it is a state of mind. The Big Bull Market had been more than the climax of a business cycle; it had been the climax of a cycle in American mass thinking and mass emotion. There was hardly a man or woman in the country whose attitude toward life had not been affected by it in some degree and was not now affected by the sudden and brutal shattering of hope. . . . Americans were soon to find themselves living in an altered world which called for new adjustments, new ideas, new

habits of thought, and a new order of values. . . . An era had ended."
Stuart Chase agreed that the "prosperity chorus" had been overdone
and thought he had caught a glimpse of this new state of mind. "There
is, in New York, at least," he wrote, "a widespread feeling of uncertainty
tinged with fear. This is not an atmosphere in which business turnover
can flourish."[13]

Fear and uncertainty: increasingly these words crept into the vocabu-
lary of analysts and ordinary people alike. The fear was not of what had
happened but of what might result. Noyes was right: after the crash, the
economy was still solid if slumping somewhat, the banks seemed in
good shape, credit was ample and cheap, and no permanent damage
had been done except to an unknown number of investors. The real
problem lay where it could not be seen—in the minds and hearts of the
American people. The crash had struck a deadly, perhaps fatal blow at
the key to the whole edifice, the foundation that held the rainbow
aloft—the American psyche. Belief in the rainbow itself, in a future
where all was well, anything was possible, and endings were always
happy, had suffered damage that might be irreparable.

The change was neither immediate nor pervasive, but as the sense of
fear and uncertainty spread, it fed the uneasiness of those who had already grown apprehensive about the economy. For an increasing number of people the mood evolved into one of hoping for better numbers
and a brighter outlook but anticipating the worst and bracing themselves for it. A classic reversal of what an older generation liked to call
"tone" occurred. Where the New Era had inclined people always to see
a glass half full, their mounting apprehension after the crash led them
more and more to view it as half empty. Publicly, everyone who was
supposed to know something blared assurances that all was well and
that New Era prosperity still lived, however much they might be wringing their hands in private. Illusion begot illusion and acquired its own
momentum. To an intriguing but unmeasurable degree, the fear became
father to the fact.

No one understood the potential dangers of this shifting mood better
than Herbert Hoover. He had spent the past decade exhorting businessmen to abandon their old ways and adopt more modern ways of
thinking and doing things. Their traditional response to impending
hard times was to retrench by cutting orders and inventories, slashing
prices, slowing production, and laying off workers. As Albert Romasco
put it, "They liquidated in anticipation of a severe deflation, thereby

making a reality the very state of affairs they feared. . . . Confidence would not revive until businessmen somehow decided that the downward spiral had reached bottom." During this working out of the "natural" process of the business cycle, the president and the federal government kept largely out of the way. The chief executive might exhort or admonish, but aside from cheerleading he had no particular role to play other than to echo the stern tenet uttered by Grover Cleveland that it was the duty of the people to support the government, not the duty of the government to support the people.[14]

Andrew Mellon was the strongest advocate of this traditional approach within the administration. His formula for dealing with the situation was simple: "Liquidate labor, liquidate stocks, liquidate the farmers, liquidate real estate." Letting events run their course, he argued, would "purge the rottenness out of the system. High costs of living and high living will come down. People will work harder, live a more moral life. Values will be adjusted, and enterprising people will pick up the wrecks from less competent people." Any interference with this natural cycle of things would only disrupt the process and delay recovery.[15]

But Hoover was not one to sit back and merely observe. He believed ardently that government too had entered a new era—however much he came to despise that term—and that he must lead vigorously in any crisis. The people expected it of him, and he expected as much of himself; the "Great Engineer" had to engineer some way out of the enveloping gloom unleashed by the crash. As a first step he must display not an inkling of the fear and uncertainty felt by others. Throughout these months, regardless of his inner feelings, he radiated outwardly a sense of hopefulness and good cheer so unwavering that it became a caricature. But sunshine and smiles were merely the surface response. Hoover also determined to become the most active president ever in dealing with a financial or economic crisis. In that goal he succeeded.[16]

He began with his favorite vehicle for action, the conference. After meeting with business and government officials, Hoover announced on November 15 that he was summoning a "small preliminary conference of representatives of industry, agriculture and labor" to develop an agenda for action. "In market booms we develop over-optimism with a corresponding reverse into over-pessimism," he declared. "They are equally unjustified. . . . Any lack of confidence in the economic future or the basic strength of business in the United States is foolish. Our national capacity for hard work and intelligent cooperation is ample guarantee of the future." But he also emphasized that "words are not of any great importance in times of economic disturbance. It is action that counts."[17]

Action took the form of Mellon's proposed tax cut and a plan to speed up public works construction projects, many of them long deferred. The purpose of the conferences was to get industry, utilities, railroads, and state governments to spend vigorously on improvements and expansion as well. "The situation is further assured," he added, "by the exceptionally strong cash position of the large manufacturing industries of the country." The Federal Reserve had already cut rates, making credit cheaper and easier to get. Hoover also called for the "stimulation of exports," which reached a near record level of $530 million in October, but that goal lay at the mercy of the interminable battle over the tariff raging in Congress. So muddled had the fight grown that an exasperated Senator Hiram Johnson of California muttered, "I don't know where we're at," before Congress finally adjourned its special session on November 22.[18]

Hoover's statement, declared *Time*, "stirred the business world." Dutifully a steady procession of leaders filed into the White House for their meetings. On November 19 Hoover met with railroad executives, who pledged to expend $1 billion in capital improvements during the next year. Two days later he welcomed a gaggle of industrial titans, led by Henry Ford, Owen Young, Julius Rosenwald, Pierre du Pont, and Alfred P. Sloan, in the morning and a group of labor leaders in the afternoon. Representatives of the building and construction industry arrived on the 22nd, followed by state governors on the 24th, farm leaders the next day, and utilities executives on the 27th. Everyone pledged cooperation and assistance. The industrialists agreed not to lay off workers, the labor leaders not to strike or seek higher wages. The utilities men projected expenditures of $1.8 billion; the governors vowed to keep public works at a level that would sustain employment. In New York City Mayor Walker announced that work would go forward on $1 billion in public works projects.[19]

In every case, noted a reporter, the object of the conference was "not so much a promise of an orgy of unusual spending as a pledge not to curtail ordinary spending." Hoover wanted no repetition of past patterns of cutbacks and layoffs. Henry Ford walked out of the industrialists' meeting and told waiting reporters that the crash had been caused by "a serious withdrawal [because of speculative activity] of brains from business" and the fact that "American production has come to equal and

even surpass not our people's power to consume, but their power to purchase." As a step toward remedying that defect, Ford declared that he
would raise the wages of all his workers. His theories struck a bemused
Noyes as typical of "that amateur economist's economic eccentricities,"
but he marveled that the nation's largest manufacturer frankly admitted
that "the often-disputed 'saturation point' was a reality."[20]

The flurry of activity continued into early December. On the 2nd
Hoover greeted the reconvened Congress with an upbeat State of the
Union message described by one reporter as "crowded with recommen-
dations and suggestions that will furnish the foundation of much controversy during the regular legislative session." He reviewed the recent
conferences and declared his conviction that "through these measures
we have re-established confidence," but he had no intention of stopping
there. "In my message . . . ," Hoover wrote later, "I did not wish to add
alarms to the already rising fears. Therefore, I gave a guarded discussion
of the economic situation arising out of the crash." The call to action,
however, was clear and unmistakable. He asked Congress to reduce the
income tax, expedite railroad consolidation, complete the tariff in ac-
cordance with his notion of a "limited revision," and revise the banking
laws to deal with chain banking, along with a host of other requests.[21]

Two days later, before Congress could catch its breath, Hoover presented the members with his first budget message. It projected a surplus
of more than $225 million for 1930, enough to absorb the proposed in-
come tax cut and still continue Mellon's policy of paying down the debt.
On December 5 the president welcomed a gathering of 400 "key men"—
business leaders summoned for a conference to devise practical means
for stimulating and stabilizing business. It was, said one impressed reporter, "the greatest cross section of American industry that has ever
been gathered together." Hoover told them the country was regaining its
confidence and required their leadership and planning to make recovery
possible. "You have been invited to create a temporary organization," he
said, "to counteract the effect of the recent panic in the stockmarket. . . .
The cure for such storms is action. . . . I have no desire to preach. I may,
however, mention one good old word—work."[22]

The executives cheered Hoover loudly as he departed with a broad
smile of satisfaction. Julius Klein followed with a speech reminding them
that "the only sound that counts is the clang of shovels and cash register
bells" and urging them to "get out of the huddle of 'conferences' and play
ball. . . . A goodly number of citizens are inclined to be almost disre-

spectfully skeptical as to the value of committees and resolutions. . . . They are looking for action." Commerce Secretary Robert P. Lamont informed the executives that projected expenditures of $2.5 billion for public works meant jobs for 600,000 people. James A. Farrell of United States Steel led off a series of reports by industry spokesmen that were uniformly optimistic. By day's end the group had created an executive committee of 72 headed by Julius Barnes, chairman of the U.S. Chamber of Commerce. That same day the House passed the tax-reduction bill.

It was an impressive performance. The spectacle of an activist president was new to Americans, who had long tended to look for leadership less to politicians than to businessmen. Many liked what they saw in Hoover's energetic response and in his style, which "exuded the laconic assurance of a highly successful executive." Hoover blended the two realms nicely; as president he was all business and, as writer Sherwood Anderson noted, he was a man who had never known failure. "Too much praise cannot be given the President for the prompt and resolute and skillful way in which he set about reassuring the country after the financial collapse," declared a *New York Times* editorial. "The President's course in this troublous time has been all that could be desired. No one in his place could have done more; very few of his predecessors could have done as much." The "noble experiment" he had undertaken was nothing less than "attempting to change the mental attitude of a whole people."[23]

Hoover had taken conspicuous steps to nudge the federal government toward a new role as caretaker of the economy. This was a far cry from the old economic orthodoxy, with its view of downturns as a natural and inevitable part of the business cycle that could neither be avoided nor interfered with by government. As Senator Thomas P. Gore of Oklahoma put it, depressions were "an economic disease. You might just as well try to prevent the human race from having a disease as to prevent economic grief of this sort." The notion that government might intervene in some constructive way never occurred to many people and seemed absurd to businessmen like one who described government and taxation as "necessary nuisances—forever costing something, or in the way of doing something." Calvin Coolidge might have applauded that sentiment, but Hoover thought otherwise. As he wrote later, he "determined that the Federal government should use all of its powers."[24]

But those powers were limited to a degree hardly imaginable to a modern generation. In 1929 federal expenditures comprised a mere 2.5 percent of the gross national product, compared with 22 percent in

1990. Federal purchases of goods and services totaled about 1.3 percent of GNP and federal construction a tiny. 2 percent, hardly enough to serve as a prime stimulant. The federal government spent only about $200 million on construction projects in 1929, while the states spent $2 billion, or 10 times as much, and private industry $9 billion. It employed only 579,559 people and operated no social welfare programs, unless one put veterans' benefits or grants made by the Children's Bureau in that category. Nor could the administration control the credit markets, since the law made the Federal Reserve System independent of its control if not its influence. It was, in short, a dwarf by modern standards, though at the time some regarded it as a bureaucratic labyrinth. Hoover pitched his appeal so vigorously to the private sector not only because he believed ardently in voluntarism but because real recovery could only come from there.[25]

A promising start had been made. The conferences accomplished some novel results in the form of agreements to maintain wages and avoid strikes or lockouts. The Federal Farm Board moved to support the prices of commodities that had declined sharply, notably wheat and cotton. It was hoped the tax cut, when passed by Congress, would increase investment and consumption while public works projects would put more people to work. But, as Hoover well knew, public works projects took time to plan, design, and get organized, and, as the *New York Times* pointed out, "it will be some time before the projected outlays by the great corporations can be made concrete in actual employment." He had taken the pulse of the economy and prescribed various tonics to restore its vigor; the crucial question was how well the patient would respond to the treatment.[26]

———

While Charley Mitchell labored to repair the damage to his bank and his own reputation, Albert Wiggin followed an artfully designed and superbly executed path of deceit through these turbulent months. Where Mitchell borrowed heavily in a vain effort to shore up the price of National City Bank stock, Wiggin saw a rare opportunity for profit in selling short the shares of Chase National Bank. That he was chief executive of the institution in which he was dealing seemed to bother him not at all. He began going short in Chase as early as September 23 and continued right through the crash. By November 4 his Shermar

Corporation had sold 42,506 shares of the bank's stock for nearly $10.6 million. During November and December he borrowed $8 million from the Chase to help cover these short sales even though he and his family owned enough shares to have served that purpose.[27]

By the time Wiggin closed out this operation on December 11, he had amassed profits exceeding $4 million. Through an elaborate series of transactions utilizing his Canadian as well as American companies, he managed to avoid paying any income tax on this windfall. Some of his sales had been to the bank itself, which had obligingly loaned him both stock to cover his short sales and then funds to buy the stock. Asked later whether he thought such dealings were sound or ethical, he replied in his wonderfully cryptic way, "I think it is highly desirable that the officers of the bank should be interested in the stock of the bank." Compared to this venality, concluded Ferdinand Pecora, "Mr. Mitchell looms up as an heroic and laudable figure."[28]

Wiggin at least had been shrewd enough to be on the right side of a collapsing market. No such luck favored Billy Durant. Although an occasional rumor still had him directing the latest operation in RCA stock, the "king of the bulls" watched helplessly as his assets shriveled and his brokers sold him out. It was a blow from which he never recovered; a year later he admitted to one of his oldest friends, "I'm wiped out." By 1933 his once enormous income had dwindled to a mere $9,478; bankruptcy followed three years later. Jesse Livermore survived the crash but struggled to track both a fickle market and an unraveling marriage. This same uncertainty about the future plagued everyone on Wall Street, where operators large and small, their pockets emptied by the crash, looked for ways and means to get back into the game and recoup their losses.[29]

The market itself offered few clues as to what the future held. It opened December with solid gains on five of the first six days, stalled out for four days, and then suffered a painful drop of 15.30 in the Dow and 10.38 in the *Times* average on the 12th. Over the next two days it recovered two-thirds of that loss but bounced up and down for the rest of the month. Volume remained high by pre-1928 standards but dropped back to what had in the past two years come to be considered normal trading days, exceeding 5 million shares only twice. For the month the Dow gained a modest 7.18 and the *Times* average 3.57. The Dow closed this most tumultuous of years at 248.48, or 58.53 below its average on January 2, while the *Times* average finished at 206.40, down 28.40 for the year. At those levels the Dow still stood 45.13 and the *Times* average 23.95 above where they had opened 1928.[30]

As always, the players cared less about where the market had been than where it was heading. "The dominating business fact of 1929," declared Colonel Leonard Ayres, "is that the great bull market of the past five years has terminated." It had been "unique in its magnitude," he added, "and . . . may also prove to be unique in . . . its consequences. . . . Speculation comes out of business slowly, but it comes out of the stock market rapidly." Some bankers and brokers argued that the market had already discounted a moderate recession but agreed that no new bull market was possible "until there are signs that the business recession has touched bottom or is close to it." An analyst agreed that "it would be unfortunate at this time if the impression became spread throughout the country that the bull market . . . had been resumed."[31]

The sharp declines in mid-December took care of that problem, serving to remind operators, in Noyes's words, "that ideas of a 'new bull market,' to be based on forgetting everything that has happened since September, may be a little premature." It amused Noyes to observe how the "promoters of the lately collapsed speculation crept from their cyclone-cellars to inform the public that the panic had been a wholly unnecessary incident for which someone else than they had been to blame. . . . One of the college professors who, as recently as October, had predicted indefinite continuance of the 'boom,' now explains to an admiring audience how the whole thing happened because some buccaneers of European high finance betrayed the confidence of trustful American multi-millionaires and broke down the market out of sheer malignity."[32]

Scanning the economic horizon, Noyes found little to encourage him. Steel production continued to sag; United States Steel was operating at 64 percent of capacity compared with 83 percent a year earlier. Trade continued to slacken, car loadings were down, and, most surprising of all, exports dropped to their smallest November total since 1925. Noyes recalled that after the Panic of 1907 exports had shot upward while imports declined, creating the second largest trade surplus ever. He pondered the meaning of the drop, as he did the broader "shrinkage in productive activity." The trade journals had an explanation: the fall in orders signaled not hard times coming but a drop in inventories that would spur "an equivalently sharp recovery in trade orders and trade activity" next year. Well, it was the holiday season, a splendid time for wishful thinking, and even Noyes had to concede that "the underlying consideration, after all, is the immense economic power of the country, which nobody believes to have been permanently shaken."[33]

As the most fateful year in its history drew down, Wall Street tried to don a cheerful holiday face. A huge Christmas tree went up on Broad Street opposite the Exchange, and its lighting on the afternoon of December 23 formally opened the festive season. Trading died down as usual, having to do at this time of year less with speculation than with tax maneuvering, and the bonuses awarded brokerage staffs equaled or bettered those of 1928 thanks to the year's huge flood of business. Adding to its large collection of new records, the New York Stock Exchange rang up its first billion-share year, with total volume exceeding 1.12 billion. The other exchanges also set new records, all of which meant handsome profits for the houses and sizable bonuses all around. Employees of the Exchange itself received amounts equal to 10 percent of their salaries, the same figure awarded the year before.[34]

The glow of seasonal good cheer extended beyond Wall Street to leaders of business as well. Asked as usual for their views on business prospects for the coming year, they responded with almost uniform optimism. The old "prosperity chorus" retuned itself into a "revival chorus" that could not have sounded more harmonious if Herbert Hoover himself had rehearsed it. Industrial leaders sang amen to the prediction of United States Steel's James A. Farrell that "after the turn of the year operations . . . will substantially improve." Even the automobile executives joined in; John J. Raskob foresaw "in the course of a few months a larger output of motor cars than ever before." Utility leaders projected record outlays that would hasten the revival of trade, while bankers thought the immediate future looked uncertain and recovery would come gradually.[35]

Leonard Ayres outdid all other forecasters in specificity. The year 1930, he predicted, would start badly and end well. Car and truck production would fall short of 1929 by half a million to a million units. Total construction value would differ from 1929 by no more than 5 percent. Short-term interest rates would fall early in the year, and stock prices would rise by year's end to a higher level but one still below the summer's peak. Iron and steel output would decline sharply. Average wholesale prices of nonagricultural commodities would fall but not by more than 5 percent. Unemployment would rise but improve later in the year. Industrial wages would deviate less than 3 percent. Building

costs would probably decline slightly, and net profits of industrial corporations considerably.[36]

Nor was the chorus limited to businessmen. "All the factors which
make for a quick and speedy industrial recovery are present and evident," declared William Green, head of the American Federation of Labor. Later he added, "We are going to move forward until I think in a
few months we will be back to a normal state in the industrial and economic life of our nation." Secretary of Commerce Lamont conceded
that it was "impossible to forecast what temporary ups and downs may
occur . . . but one may predict for the long run a continuance of prosperity and progress." The American Economic Association predicted recovery by June 1930, while the *Journal of Commerce* stressed that "there is
nothing fundamentally unsound as far as can be learned in our present
situation." The *New York Times* reported that "a distinct change of sentiment on the outlook for business in 1930 . . . is apparent. . . . Lack of
widespread commercial failures, the absence of serious unemployment,
and robust recovery in the stock market have been factors calculated to
dispel the gloominess." Dispatches from the various Federal Reserve districts shared this uniform belief that "normal prosperity" loomed ahead
after a sluggish first quarter or two.[37]

Never one to join a chorus, inclined always to scrutinize dispassion-
ately with an eye unclouded by cant, Alexander Noyes took a different
tack in preparing his annual financial outlook for the New Year's Day
edition of the *Times*. In his prim, methodical manner he itemized the arguments on both sides of the ledger, noting first the caveat that such
forecasts tended to be more accurate "in years when the financial tide
was setting strongly in one direction and when no convincing reason
for a turn was visible." Such had been the case from 1925 through 1928.
But when "the economic trend had been suddenly reversed and new
forces were at work whose scope was difficult to determine, prediction
usually went astray," as it had from 1919 to 1921. Rather than guess
which of these categories best described 1930, or simply sing the re-
vivalist hymn, Noyes put down the following alternative scenarios for
the coming year.[38]

PRO: Optimists argued that "an orgy of reckless speculation" had
caused the stock market crash, but "no such excesses had been practiced
in business and industry." The latter had no unduly high prices or
swollen inventories, and business methods had promoted greater efficiency rather than chicanery or a craze for quick profits. In short, the

collapse brought the market back to a reality that business had never left. CON: Skeptics replied that even if industry had not indulged in "unwarranted use of credit and excessive accumulation of supplies," consumers certainly had done so. Through investing in the market of the good life, Americans had put an estimated $2 billion to $3 billion worth of "finance paper" into circulation, and no one knew how much the economy could absorb. Henry Ford's startling admission of overproduction in the automobile industry offered an ominous clue, since the largest share of installment buying took place there.

PRO: President Hoover had taken vigorous, positive steps to prevent the economy from backsliding. The conferences had yielded pledged expenditures of more than $2 billion in construction for 1930, which Hoover emphasized would do much to avert general unemployment and encourage industrial activity. CON: The very existence of these unusual measures "amounted to recognition of a critical situation." Moreover, the programs submitted by the various private sectors were not really pledges but projections that depended more or less on later developments. Some were cast forward a number of years rather than for 1930 alone and might be jettisoned if conditions changed. And many industries had yet to make their plans, or lack of them, known.

PRO: In broader terms, argued the optimists, nothing could stop industrial expansion given the continued growth of the nation's population and wealth. By one estimate total income had risen from $69.6 billion in 1924 to $81 billion in 1928. Production had to increase to meet "this rapidly increasing power to purchase." CON: The estimates of increased annual income did not carry with them estimates of expenditures. Moreover, "no one can be sure . . . how far the yearly increment of wealth and buying power will have been affected by last Autumn's losses in stock speculation." After all, income fell from $65.5 billion in 1920 to $55.8 billion the next year during that slump. Then, too, it was always possible that in a consumer economy people would spend more than they earned until it was no longer possible for them to do so.

PRO: The drastic reduction in brokers' loans ended the credit crunch and ensured that general business and trade would have ample supplies of credit at cheap rates. Easy money would promote not only commercial stability but industrial expansion as well. CON: Easy money after a financial crisis could signal not only industrial revival but its opposite of reduced industrial activity as well. Historically, cheaper credit followed the panics of 1893, 1907, and 1920 but did not spur trade revival in any of these cases. Moreover, bank portfolios were still clogged with stocks taken over during the crash, which limited their ability to lend freely. In short, cheaper credit did little good unless there were borrowers eager to use it for business purposes.

PRO: In prior Wall Street crises, national or international politics had often complicated trade recovery. Recent settlements, especially the Young plan, would come on line in 1930 and stabilize international finance, while a conservative, enlightened Republican administration in Washington would pursue prudent public policies to maintain stability. CON: Certain kinds of stability have had a negative rather than positive effect on prosperity. Since 1926 American business activity had increased "when European politics were in a dangerous condition" and receded as efforts to stabilize the international scene seemed to be succeeding. Conspicuously missing from this discussion was any consideration of the role of the tariff on exports, even though Congress was still wrangling bitterly over the issue with no end in sight.

What conclusions to draw from these opposing views? Noyes pointed to three other, larger considerations. "The quite indomitable spirit of confidence in the longer trend of American prosperity," he predicted, "is bound to restrict, as it always has restricted, the scope of a trade reaction." Long experience had also taught that the foundation for a new and greater era of prosperity was always laid in such periods of reaction. Finally: "the position of overshadowing economic power in the United States since 1914, exists in its important aspects now, as it existed . . . before the ill-fated stock market 'boom' began." Noyes hoped, and perhaps even believed, that these traditional factors would in the coming year tip the balance in favor of the positive side of the ledger.

For the present, however, Americans shared only one unanimous sentiment as they welcomed the new year with the usual celebrations: how far away the summer of fun already seemed.

Epilogue: The Winter
of Discontent, 1930

Let's not forget that millions upon millions of regular folks throughout this *grand, greatly-desiring, gorgeously-spending America* need power,
heat, light, food, transportation, recreation and adornment, same as
always. . . . They'll go on dreaming, and earning, and *buying*—in
that lavish fashion that has always characterized the shortest-mem-
oried and longest-confidenced people that ever lived.

—Erwin, Wasey & Company (advertising firm)[1]

A s winter came on, the market once again belonged to the professionals. Outside buying dried up, volume dropped sharply, and
stocks vanished from the front pages. On 1930's second day of
trading, the ticker paused at times for full minutes "out of sheer lack of
something to print. . . . Few houses were able to pay their overhead
with the commissions collected." Brokers complained that the crash had
reduced the number of their accounts 50 to 75 percent, with many of
those remaining still frozen or simply inactive. One short Saturday session in January saw volume drop below the million-share mark for the
first time since the summer of 1928. Two days later the market produced its smallest volume for a five-hour day since July 1928. For the
month volume totaled only 62.3 million shares, more than 7 million
fewer than the slowest month of 1929.[2]

Yet for all its inertia, the market crept sluggishly upward, especially
during the last two weeks of January. In a month where the largest trading day reached only 3.7 million shares, the Dow gained 22.94 and the

Times average 14.03, putting them back to where they had been in December 1928 prior to the takeoff. On February 6 the Federal Reserve
Bank of New York made credit even cheaper by again lowering the rediscount rate from 4¹/₂ to 4 percent. A few days later the *Wall Street Journal* declared that the "well-known Dow theory as elaborated by the late
William Peter Hamilton" signified clearly that "the worst of the current
industrial recession had passed and that stock prices have started on an
upward trend of major proportions." The theory had proven a useful
guide for three decades; never had observers wished more ardently for it
to be accurate.[3]

No one pretended that it was the same old market or that any of the
brash optimism from 1929 still lingered. Even the *Wall Street Journal*, in a
startling reversal of tone, thumbed its nose at the New Era theories on
which it had once lavished praise. "It is fitting that it should have passed
from the stage unwept, unhonored and unsung," the paper declared,
"because the prominence once given it was a threat to safe and stable
business conditions. Under different names this idea has been here before and, unless human nature changes, it is sure to appear again. . . .
That idea ignores the essential basis of values in earnings and rushes far
beyond the point where values are tested by any tangible thing. . . .
With the confidence of youth it ridicules as old-fashioned and out-of-
date the time-tried truth that values are the real underpinning of market
movements. Farewell has been said to an illusion. . . . The place it occupied . . . is being taken by principles that are as old as the stock and investment markets."[4]

Alexander Noyes couldn't have put it any better.

———————

For Herbert Hoover 1929 ended on a particularly sour note. On Christmas Eve, while he and his wife hosted a party for the children of his secretaries, an aide rushed in with news that his office was on fire. Hoover
threw on an overcoat and tramped through the biting snow to watch
firemen battle the blaze for three hours. "Save my files!" he cried as his
secretaries and his son Allan dashed into the office to retrieve papers
and the drawers of Hoover's desk. The fire, smoke, and water gutted the
Executive Office Building next to the White House and destroyed
many of the records it held. For two days Hoover worked out of the
Lincoln study on the second floor of the White House; then he moved

into the ornate office of General John J. Pershing down the block in the State, War, and Navy Building. Even before the new year began, he had become a displaced person.[5]

Less than two weeks later a fire broke out in a document storage room in the Capitol but was extinguished in less than an hour. Senator Arthur Vandenberg of Michigan was not alone in viewing it as "more than a coincidence," but in fact both fires seemed purely accidental even though darker minds suspected that someone was trying to light a fire under the government in these trying times. The excitement stirred up by the fires passed quickly and did not attract anything like the attention devoted to the annual automobile show in New York. With the economic outlook so uncertain, all eyes scanned the public response to the new year's models. "Not since 1921 has the . . . show centered the hopes and anxieties of the industry or attracted the interest of the business world generally," reported the *Wall Street Journal*. The reason was obvious: "It is widely and no doubt correctly assumed that the measure in which people curtail their purchases of cars this year will be a fairly accurate gauge of the extent to which consumption of all but the most necessary staples will be reduced."[6]

The models showcased throughout the Grand Central Palace represented 44 American and 2 foreign manufacturers. The most conspicuous absentee was Henry Ford, who displayed only in his own showrooms. Cadillac unveiled a new 16-cylinder model; elsewhere front-wheel drive made its first appearance. Everyone understood the importance of new models for the industry. "Our chief job in research," said Charles F. Kettering of General Motors, "is to keep the customer reasonably dissatisfied with what he has." Salesmen on the floor had more than the usual edge of eagerness to promote the level of dissatisfaction among visitors. Presidents and vice presidents of automobile firms also spent more time than usual in the booths scanning public response. The demand for cars had slumped since April, many manufacturers had overproduced, and a business recession had set in—all of which meant, in the words of one reporter, "that without popular fancy 1930 may well be a disastrous year for any company." That same week a firm that had produced one of the era's flashiest cars, Stutz Motors, saw its creditors file a bankruptcy petition even as its latest model went on display at the show.[7]

Far more was at stake than the automobile industry alone. "At the wheel of the automobile," declared *Standard Statistics*, "rides America's industrial destiny." Motorcars consumed 85 percent of the rubber, 80 percent of the gasoline, 75 percent of the plate glass, 25 percent of the lead, and 18 percent of the steel produced in the nation. They were also the lifeblood for 320,000 filling stations, 51,200 public garages, and 56,300 car and truck dealers. In projecting a future annual production of about 5.2 million cars over a five-year period, *Standard Statistics* conceded that the industry's future depended upon "the disposition of the American automobile users . . . to continue to be the most 'wasteful' class of human beings that has ever inhabited this planet." Stuart Chase conceded that some 4 million jobs depended on automobiles, "but it still escapes me why a prosperity founded on forcing people to consume what they do not need, and often do not want, is, or can be, a healthy and permanent growth."[8]

Never had the vital signs of the economy been scanned so closely by so many people in so many ways as during this winter of growing discontent. The problem was that hardly anyone agreed on what the signs actually revealed or which ones mattered most. Past experience offered several ready formulas. One held that normal investing and consuming power was so great that any slowdown or recession would soon generate heavy remedial buying. "There is nothing normal in business but change," snorted the *Wall Street Journal*, which dismissed "normal" as "a convenient refuge for the mentally indolent, who apparently use it to stand for some dim conception of an average condition." Noyes offered a scenario that few cared to contemplate: "continuance for a period more or less prolonged, of uninterrupted stagnation in trade and on the markets. That happened after our older panics."[9]

Certain signs were deemed vital because they supposedly conveyed the core activities of the economy. Steel production was a staple in the two key industries, automobiles and construction. Railroad loadings signaled the extent of trade through movements of crops, merchandise, and other goods. Automobile production had become central to the consumer economy, and exports showed whether overseas markets were growing or shrinking. One crucial area was conspicuous for the inadequacy of its signs. As David Kennedy noted, "Reliable data on unemployment simply did not exist." No agency, public or private, had the means or the mechanism to gather comprehensive data on national unemployment. Nor was there any way to measure partial employment—the number of people whose hours had been reduced, and with them their income. Yet nothing was more important to the health of a consumer economy than knowing how many people were working how long to earn how much for spending on goods.[10]

In January the Department of Labor issued a monthly report on employment in industry, which showed a rise in layoffs during December. Secretary of Labor James J. Davis tried to put a happy face on the report and informed Hoover that unemployment had improved with the new year. However, Frances Perkins, the industrial commissioner for New York, dismissed the report's comments on that state as unduly optimistic and cited data showing a much darker picture. By her estimates, more than 100,000 factory workers had been laid off in New York since October 1929—an alarming figure since the state employed nearly 13 percent of the nation's factory workers. The next Labor Department report, covering January, disclosed data that supported those of Perkins; it indicated that manufacturing employment in the nation had dropped another 2 percent, making a total decline since September of 12 percent. A churlish Davis responded by charging that people in some quarters, who happened to be Democrats, were trying to "make politics out of the unemployment situation."[11]

Unemployment was not the only sector where uncertainty reigned. The flow of economic data seemed far more full than it was. Among the traditional signs of economic health, for example, only data on railroad car loadings appeared on a weekly rather than a monthly basis. Some mercantile journals produced weekly surveys of wholesale and retail trade, and trade journals tracked developments in their own field. The Federal Reserve issued a monthly bulletin on the state of finance and the economy, as did private banks such as National City and Cleveland Trust, but collating the available information into a coherent overview remained fiendishly difficult, if not impossible—especially at a time when the economy seemed to be behaving so erratically. "Conditions throughout the country remain extremely spotty," admitted the *New York Times* in mid-February, "making it difficult to get a picture of the whole."[12]

None of the traditional signs looked either favorable or prophetic that winter. Steel production, which *Time* had called "the best index of U.S. prosperity" during the summer of fun, continued its bumpy slide. Having ended 1929 operating below 64 percent of capacity, it rebounded to 67 percent in January, but output remained well below the previous year. Railroad loadings fell consistently below the marks of 1929 and 1928 week after week. Automobile production offered a stark example of the "normal" dilemma: it fell 32 percent short of 1929's record output in both January and February but outperformed 1928 in both months. Since production had increased 20 percent in 1928 from 1927, the former was hardly a slack year. How, then, should such figures be interpreted?[13]

For that matter, what standard should be used to measure the overall business recession? "Some call what we are going through a severe trade depression," scoffed the *Wall Street Journal*. "But they do not remember the trade depressions . . . years ago when things were not as stable as they are now. . . . One does not have to go back more than a quarter of a century to recall depressions that closed mills and factories for months at a time and made soup kitchens a thriving industry. . . . It was hard to get work. . . . Recovery was slow, and some depressions continued for two years or more." Hardly anyone confessed to foreseeing conditions so dire on the horizon; the problem was the difficulty in divining anything at all. Most observers shared Noyes's cautious assessment that "there is evidently not yet anything to determine the trend of things in the very near future."[14]

Irving Fisher was among the few who offered a darker prophecy. The badly burned bull revealed in January that he had changed outlooks radically. "The U.S. is headed toward a business depression," he warned a joint New York legislative committee, "probably beginning within the next two years, which may exceed that which preceded the War." The only way to avert disaster, he added, was "a new gold policy or the discovery of a new process or additional gold fields. If the fall [of gold production] is not prevented by design or accident we shall throttle business, wringing out all profits and experiencing all the evils of deflation." Few took him seriously, given his track record on prediction. Roger Babson, for one, dismissed the gold supply as "only one of the many factors which bear upon the business situation."[15]

Although Fisher's warning went unheeded, he had identified a major threat that received little attention at first. Past experience, especially that of the postwar years, had spawned a deep fear of inflation as the prime enemy. Nothing had gladdened businessmen and economists alike more than the fact that the great expansion of the 1920s had been accomplished with virtually no inflation except in security prices. Since the crash, however, the opposite problem had begun to surface. In January the *New York Times* noted that average commodity prices had opened the year at their lowest level on that date since 1922. Falling prices created their own problems, especially in a sluggish economy. As Noyes explained, they caused "postponement of orders except in small lots for immediate needs." Buyers hesitated to restock or order materials and supplies when it appeared that prices for them might go still lower the next week. Falling prices also reduced the income of sellers, cutting into corporate profits and thereby affecting both dividend income and efforts to maintain wages at existing levels. Consumers hesitated to buy if they thought prices would soon move lower.[16]

Alarm bells did not sound immediately because classic economic theory and conventional wisdom alike viewed falling prices as stimulants rather than threats to a lagging economy. Henry Ford had followed this credo in cutting the prices of his cars to spur sales, as savvy businessmen had long done in the belief that rising prices discouraged buyers while falling prices attracted them. The precise role of prices in a consumer economy was still an enigma to economists, as was the exact effect of installment buying. It was painfully clear that the health of the economy depended on installment buying, which by one estimate totaled $8 billion in 1929 and gave employment to several million people. A banker estimated that 95 percent of the nation's business was done on credit. "Do away with installment buying suddenly," declared the *Wall Street Journal*, "and the country might face a real industrial depression."[17]

A clear consensus of opinion on the economy emerged that winter, marked by what Noyes called an overall attitude of "increasing hopefulness but also of increasing perplexity." Businessmen, bankers, brokers, barbers, butchers, and bureaucrats agreed that recovery would be slow but solid and that its first signs would sprout with the spring flowers. Traditionally spring had always signaled a quickening pace of trade and production, but seldom had it been looked for more eagerly than in 1930. "As to the course of business over the next six months," declared the *Wall Street Journal* in early February, "a majority believe the trend will be upward, but . . . do not hold that there is to be a quick comeback." Julius Klein foresaw "a slight lull for the first three months . . . followed by a return to normal economic trends." The stock market echoed this conviction; after its strong performance in January, it plodded through February with a modest gain of 2.70 in the Dow and 4.29 in the *Times* average, then added 12.86 and 11.51 respectively in March.[18]

Hoover felt confident enough about impending recovery to leave for a 10-day Florida vacation in mid-February. The employment picture seemed to have brightened; the Labor Department index, which had fallen from 93.3 in October 1929 to 86.0 by year's end, climbed back to 92.8 by February 18. Reassuring reports came from state governors and independent surveys. Once back in Washington, he warned Congress to economize or face a tax hike of as much as 40 percent and drew an angry salvo from several senators led by Carter Glass, who growled that "nothing more shameless has ever emanated from the White House" in his thirty years in Congress. Tempers had begun to climb with the thermometer as a record-breaking heat wave hit the East Coast late in February. On the 25th the temperature reached 73 in New York and 83 in Washington, the highest reading for any winter day in major eastern cities.[19]

The political heat was ratcheting up as well. In Congress the interminable battle over the tariff seemed at last to be nearing an end. Hoover's vaunted Federal Farm Board drew severe criticism for pouring millions into a vain effort to halt the slide of wheat prices. As the blast from Carter Glass suggested, Hoover himself had become a more frequent target for many people who had once praised him. He had early begun to curtail his public exposure by eliminating the traditional noontime receptions at the White House and informing congressmen not to send their constituents there to shake his hand on a routine basis. Speaking engagements were cut back and callers shunted to secretaries who screened him from intruders. Above all, his once close relationship with the press deteriorated steadily after the inauguration.[20]

It had started off brilliantly. At his first press conference Hoover, smiling and cordial, had announced a new set of rules to replace the stilted Coolidge procedures that had frustrated reporters. Reporters would continue to submit written questions in advance, but in some instances they could quote him directly—a welcome departure from the past. In other cases they could attribute information to the White House or use it as background as in the past. Hoover promised more press conferences with less canned information. By early 1930, however, the promised reforms had turned sour. Paul Y. Anderson of the *St. Louis Post-Dispatch*, who had welcomed the new rules, declared sadly that "the working of this plan has steadily been narrowed and restricted until now less reliable and printable information comes from the White House than at any time while Coolidge was President."[21]

The disillusioned Anderson itemized his complaint. Hoover so consistently ignored written questions that many reporters stopped submitting them. The heralded direct-quotation policy had "degenerated into a system of Presidential 'hand-outs,' palpably propagandist in character and seldom responsive to any inquiry." Worst of all, "the practice of having 'fair-haired boys' " had been revived, "whereby the President gives private audiences to correspondents who have demonstrated their willingness and ability to publish stories that he particularly desires published." Anne O'Hare McCormick echoed this feeling that the "mood for magic" she and others had felt at the inauguration had faded into disappointment. Her complaint was precise and unsparing:

> President Hoover's procedure so far is that of the administrator rather than the executive, of the technical advisor rather than of the leader. There is hardly a single instance in which he has come out boldly for his own ideas, rallied the people in support of a cause, or given any indication that he considers such crusading the function of the Chief Magistrate. Rather he has taken the problems he found waiting for him on the Executive desk, gathered all the available data on each subject and passed it on to the regular agency to deal with on the basis of the facts.[22]

For Hoover personally, nothing could have been more ominous than to have the press, which had lavished praise on his every move since his days in Commerce, turn suddenly and sharply against him. Like the economy and the market, the press was a fickle entity, prone to playing favorites and to dropping them as abruptly as it adopted them. The fault for this change lay on both sides. Hoover had mastered the art of public relations and allowed his image to be oversold to the public at a level that escalated as steadily as the stock market. "All of these 'sell jobs,' " observed historian Joan Hoff-Wilson, "evolved into the superhuman image of 'some great impersonal force' capable of solving any and all problems the country might encounter."[23]

Walter Lippmann described the "Hoover legend, the public stereotype of an ideal Hoover" as "consciously contrived" and thought the result inevitable: "By arousing certain expectations, the legend has established a standard by which the public judgment has estimated him. . . . The ideal picture presents him as the master organizer, the irresistible engineer, the supreme economist." No one could live up to such expectations, but, as Lippmann observed, Hoover also suffered from flaws that proved fatal in the political arena:

In the realm of reason he is an unusually bold man; in the realm of un-
reason he is, for a statesman, an exceptionally thin-skinned and easily
bewildered man. . . . He can face with equanimity almost any of the
difficulties of statesmanship except an open conflict of wills. . . . The
political art deals with matters peculiar to politics, with a complex of circumstances, of historic deposit, of human passion, for which the problems of business or engineering as such do not provide an analogy.[24]

Politics was a contact sport, and Hoover loathed hard contact with
either Congress or the press. Nor did the zeal with which he and his
wife shielded their private lives from public view endear him to reporters. Negative accounts in the papers wounded him easily; he lacked
the toughness of the flinty Coolidge, who followed the credo "If you
don't like it, don't read it." For their part reporters, fed by a growing
sense of their own importance, punished Hoover for his lack of cooperation by puncturing his overblown reputation as vigorously as they had
inflated it. As the market plummeted, Hoover's stock followed it. "The
great engineer," wrote historian Albert Romasco, "had become the
newsmen's great fall-guy." Hoover had the misfortune to be the wrong
man in the wrong place at the wrong time. He had become president
during the first age of images, of mass-media human-interest sagas, and
the image he projected worked almost entirely against him.[25]

A man of sunshine engulfed by clouds that would not dissipate,
Hoover could not and would not change his style. While the economic
signs remained mixed early in March, the president declared on the 7th
that "all the evidences indicate that the worst effects of the crash upon
employment will have been passed during the next sixty days." A survey
revealed that unemployment appeared to be normal and improving in
36 states and "distressed" in only 12, which Hoover steadfastly refused
to name because he did not wish to single them out. Ten days later the
New York Board of Trade assured Governor Franklin D. Roosevelt that,
although unemployment was above normal, its peak had been reached
in February.[26]

Senator Robert F. Wagner of New York disagreed. At a hearing on
three bills he had presented on unemployment, he argued that "no more
serious employment situation than the present has ever existed in the
United States." As part of his testimony he showed a news photograph
of a breadline two blocks long at a dispensary on the Lower East Side.
The director of the Illinois state employment agency testified that un-

employment in Chicago was the "most acute in ten years" and added that conditions were the same in other industrial cities. Pittsburgh also reported long lines at local soup kitchens. A few days later Frances Perkins rebuked the rosy picture given of New York by calling unemployment there the worst since 1914.[27]

As steel production dipped again, Roy Young of the Federal Reserve Board urged businessmen to use the cheap credit available and show "more initiative and less hesitancy" in their operations. The Fed had done its part on March 13 when the New York Reserve Bank lowered its rediscount rate yet again from 4 to 3½ percent. A *Wall Street Journal* columnist read a double meaning into the reduction. "It spells easy money," he wrote, "and at the same time it denotes a depressed condition of business. The rate is to all intents and purposes at the irreducible minimum (only once has it been lower) and this naturally raises the question of how poor business really is and how instrumental such a low money level will be in bringing about a revival." The economic signals remained maddeningly mixed even though most business leaders remained upbeat. On March 23 Julius Barnes, head of the National Business Survey Conference created by Hoover in December 1929, reported that the signs of recovery were encouraging and the factors retarding business were fading. Two days later the Senate passed a pair of bills to underwrite construction and road building—the first congressional action on Hoover's requests of the past autumn.[28]

The most encouraging sign came from, of all places, the stock market. Its March rise saw volume move back into the 3- and 4-million share range and top 5 million shares three times during the final week. To Wall Street's relief the market was also broadening; on the 28th trading involved 859 different stocks. Brokerage houses that had reduced their staffs found themselves swamped with orders, and the long-snoozing ticker began running late again. The surge continued into April, when volume exceeded 111 million shares—a monthly figure surpassed only by those of October 1929 and November 1928. Prices moved steadily but not sharply upward. On April 15 the *Times* average reached a high for the year of 242.66; two days later the Dow followed suit at 294.07. Since the first of the year the two averages had gained 37.73 and 49.87 respectively and stood 76.51 and 95.38 higher than their November lows.[29]

A hint of the old bullish attitude returned to the Street, what Noyes called "a bold pretense . . . of returning to last Summer's speculation." It featured the same careless handling of facts or twisting of them to suit immediate needs and the same "hostility and dislike . . . toward any one who cited unfavorable news." But one analyst pointed out that no less than 40 percent of one week's heavy volume involved only the 20 most active stocks, while another noticed that the many market letters mentioned fewer than 50 stocks as likely to move "considerably higher." "One might wonder," he mused, "what the other 1,150 stocks or so . . . are going to do while the 50 selected issues are advancing." The outpouring of first-quarter earnings reports proved as disappointing as expected for industrial firms and railroads, but the utilities showed encouraging strength. Retail buying remained stronger than output, and some automobile companies registered impressive reductions in overhead expenses.[30]

Still, the overall economic picture remained unimpressive, and as usual Noyes was among the few to say so in blunt terms. "The beginning of Springtime has made evident what had in fact been plainly enough foreshadowed by the course of general trade in March," he wrote, "that the year's earlier predictions of emphatic revival of industry on the arrival of that season are not to be fulfilled. Markets will hereafter be engaged in conjecture as to what special influence can be reckoned on to change the picture in the later Summer months or in the Autumn." Deeper forces were at work not only in the American but also in the world economy. Noyes did not pretend to know or even guess what lay behind the derangement, but its presence could no longer be doubted or denied. "The past three months," he said flatly, "have shown quite indisputably that something else was wrong with the economic situation a year ago than a mere outburst of mania on the Stock Exchange."[31]

Yet Noyes was no alarmist. "Belief in the country's power to surmount the present difficulties is held by every competent reader of our history," he added. "Most of them hold that full recovery will not be as long deferred as in the sequel to our prewar panics. All of them agree that, in the long run, renewed industrial expansion in this country will carry its business activities and achievements to a higher plane even than was reached in 1928 and 1929."[32]

But how long was the long run? It was clear that the market had rushed ahead of the business picture as it had done in 1929 under very different circumstances, and equally clear that it would not long stay on higher ground if business conditions did not improve. But the signals grew even more mixed. *Time* noticed two contradictory currents on the unemployment question. One ran "uphill to large headlines proclaiming a quickening return to Prosperity. The other ran downhill to accounts of breadlines and jobless distress." Politics lay behind both efforts: Republicans were as eager to gloss over the unemployment issue as Democrats were to blame them for it. "I'm no believer in empty optimism," insisted Labor Secretary James J. Davis. "At the same time one doesn't improve the condition of a sick man by constantly telling him how ill he is. . . . Business is staging a record recovery."[33]

Official optimism paled before the 10,000 jobless men rioting outside the gates of the Ford Motor Co. plant at Dearborn, Michigan, or the lengthening breadlines in New York City, or the 1,156 skilled workmen (a third of the total) laid off at the Brooklyn Navy Yard, or the five applicants vying for every two jobs in Chicago. William Green, the staid, conservative leader of the American Federation of Labor, startled a Senate committee with his union's estimates of 3,700,000 jobless men in February, a loss of $1 billion in wages since the first of the year, and one worker in four seeking work. "Workers are simply turned adrift," he said. "Men should earn money, not have it doled out to them. But unless employers change their tactics toward the Unions, we shall face either Federal unemployment insurance . . . or have a revolution on our hands. The country cannot stand these continual shocks."[34]

Green's admonition received support from Senator James Couzens of Michigan, who warned that if industry did not move to stabilize the income of workers the government would do so through unemployment and old age insurance. The *New York Times* complained anew that "the unsatisfactory nature of the government estimates of unemployment is notorious. There is no adequate knowledge of how much has actually been done to relieve the situation." Preliminary census statistics showed that only about 6 percent of New York workers were unemployed, a much lower figure than expected. However, the Department of Agriculture found farm wages to be the lowest since it began collecting figures in 1923. And prices continued to fall. By April's end wheat had dropped 15 percent, silver 16 percent, and lead 13 percent since January 1. Copper plummeted 22 percent in only a few days.[35]

Spring had come, life was reborn, and with it fresh hope and renewal, but the economy remained dormant. The *New York Times* was not alone in asking why, with the economic indicators falling and business failures the highest since 1922, "the stock market has been rising continuously." Leonard Ayres viewed the market's strength as a sign of better times coming. "There is not much actual statistical evidence of improvement," he admitted, "but there are some symptoms of betterment which are hopeful." However, another erstwhile bull joined Irving Fisher in changing sides. "With keen regret," said a disillusioned Billy Durant, "I make the prediction that we will see next winter business conditions unimproved, longer breadlines, more soup kitchens, continued uneasiness and distress and a more pronounced tendency to Socialism and Communism — this regardless of assurance from Washington that everything is all right."[36]

Some omens came from arenas far removed from Wall Street. On April 14 Hoover cheerfully followed the tradition of attending the opening game of the baseball season and throwing out the first ball. It was a wild pitch.[37]

The stock market responded to these mixed messages by closing out April with a string of losses. After peaking on the 17th, the Dow fell 14.84 to finish the month down 7.88. The *Times* average declined 10.48 from its April 15 high to 5.58 below its April 1 level. During that drop Durant hurled another broadside at the Federal Reserve Board, but his voice had grown too shrill in recent months. The *Wall Street Journal* dismissed his charges as "too suggestive of animus to carry much weight, even among those who may once have been impressed by the public utterances of this automobile builder, market operator and economist." But even the *Journal* conceded that recovery had been disappointingly slow in coming. "That the market until recently had been advancing faster than business improvement, every one seems to know," it said at month's end. "Earlier in the year, it was believed business conditions would be much better before the end of spring. Now the opinion prevails that business improvement will be slower than expected. Some say it will be several months before business begins to approach normal. Others take a less optimistic view."[38]

Hoover, as always, tried to make the best of things. He signed a bill authorizing $125 million annually for a three-year road-building program, continued to lecture Congress about the need for curbing expenditures, and ordered the first house-to-house census of unemployment ever undertaken. At the end of April he welcomed the U.S. Chamber of Commerce to Washington for its annual meeting. Its chairman, Julius Barnes, joined Secretary of Commerce Robert P. Lamont in praising Hoover's "quick action toward stemming the business slump last Fall." On May Day evening Hoover himself addressed the delegates. "We have been passing through one of these great economic storms which periodically bring hardship and suffering to our people," he began. "While the crash only took place six months ago, I am convinced we have now passed the worst and with continued unity of effort we shall rapidly recover." The remainder of his speech was a hymn to the courage and perseverance of the American people coupled with a recitation of the steps taken to banish the business recession.[39]

On the eve of the convention Barnes issued the long-awaited report of the National Business Survey Conference. It was predictably upbeat and even more predictably ambiguous at key points. "Some of the reports," complained *Time*, "seemed extremely vague" and tended to conclude with what had come to be the mantra of optimists within and without the administration: "Underlying economic factors show slow but steady improvement." To that chant the venerable *Commercial & Financial Chronicle* countered, "Verily, trade and business in this country have undergone great shrinkage." First-quarter earnings had been dismal; exports were down 24 percent and imports 28 percent from 1929; car loadings showed the worst March figures since 1924, pushing railroad net earnings down 22.4 percent; manufacturing output in March fell 10.7 percent and steel production 22.6 percent below that of 1929. As for prices, compared with March 1929 commodities had dropped 6.7 percent, raw materials 9.6 percent, farm products 12.4 percent, and chemicals and drugs 4.2 percent.[40]

Like other analysts, Noyes still found the industrial scene "as mixed as the market itself has been" and the overall picture "perplexing even to those who watch it at close range. All that can be positively said of the trade position is that the reaction in consumers' demands . . . has apparently not 'been checked.' But comparison with other seasons and with other years differs so widely in different industries, and so many visible phenomenon seem so inconsistent with one another, that the attempt to determine dominant underlying causes finds itself blocked at every turn."[41]

The merry month of May opened with not only Hoover's dose of official optimism to the Chamber of Commerce but also a stunning simultaneous cut in the rediscount rate in New York, London, and Paris. The New York Federal Reserve Bank dropped its rate from 3 1/2 to 3 percent, the lowest since February 1925. Instead of cheering this news as they would in better times, traders responded by hammering the Dow down 20.92 and the *Times* average 16.09 in three days of hectic trading with volumes reminiscent of the previous autumn. On Monday the 5th volume surged to nearly 8.3 million shares, a level not matched since the four panic days of October. Next day the Dow jumped 9.13 and the *Times* average 6.44 as volume subsided, leaving only confusion in its wake.[42]

It was the professionals driving this market, not the public, Noyes concluded. Some had come back in after the fall and bet heavily on the anticipated upturn; others had formed pools for the same reason and in the recent selloff had "wound up their affairs not too brilliantly." As the market treaded water during the next week, Noyes believed that the decline in recent weeks "was a consequence not of an alarming turn in the business situation but of necessary readjustment on the Stock Exchange itself. . . . When the turn for the better actually comes, it is apt to take even Wall Street by surprise, the idea having by that time grown that it will never come. But we are still making financial history." A *Times* editorial agreed that "nobody interpreted the break as necessarily foreshadowing an equivalent decline of business activities."[43]

For the rest of May the market sank back into apathy and went nowhere on modest volumes. The Dow closed that volatile month with a miniscule gain of 0.48, while the *Times* average rose 1.60. Amid the confusion and clamor of conflicting voices one point at least became clear. As the *Times* put it, "The explicit prophecies from official Washington regarding an early return to trade activity were falling entirely flat on the stock market. The intimations from the Department of Commerce that trade would be 'normal again' within 60 or 90 days were followed by falling prices. . . . Wall Street appeared to have grown somewhat weary of the cocksure attitude of Washington." Noyes echoed this sentiment, while Senator Joe Robinson, the Democratic floor leader, denounced the "Pollyana statements of the administration" and charged that Hoover had "persistently colored real conditions."[44]

What a later generation would call a "credibility gap" had arisen and was widening steadily, leaving Hoover at a loss to understand or counter it. To make matters worse, the never-ending saga of the tariff bill was winding its tortuous way to completion in a form quite unlike what Hoover had desired. It promised not reform or flexibility but the highest rates in history at a time when exports were already falling sharply. As it neared final action, 1,028 economists, including Irving Fisher, Wesley C. Mitchell, and other leading lights, issued a statement urging Hoover to veto the bill if passed. On May 7 Roy Young of the Federal Reserve Board admitted in passing that the nation was in "what appears to be a business depression," which seemed to contradict Hoover's rosy assessment given to the Chamber of Commerce.[45]

The credibility gap owed its existence partly to Hoover's inability to choose among conflicting paths to follow and policies to pursue. He wanted the federal government to do more but not to become more, to lead rather than perform. In the perfect world of his philosophy, the government spurred the private sector into voluntary action and cooperated with it. An enlarged role for Washington meant expanding the federal bureaucracy, and Hoover hated bureaucracy above all else. It was, he said, "ever desirous of spreading its influence and its power. You cannot extend the mastery of the government over the daily working life of a people without at the same time making it the master of the people's souls and thoughts." The whole point of the fall conferences had been to organize the private sector into a vast voluntary army to respond vigorously to the crisis and work together rather than follow separate paths that led to collective doom.[46]

The public works program and the Federal Farm Board had stretched that premise by providing more direct relief, but the first was slow to get under way and the second had drawn harsh criticism for its costly yet futile efforts to support the price of wheat that winter.[47] Both cost a great deal of money and impinged on Hoover's ardent desire to keep the federal budget in surplus. Increasingly that spring Hoover talked less of spending and more of curtailing expenditures. As Arthur M. Schlesinger Jr. put it, "The public works theory was fighting a losing battle in Hoover's mind against his mounting concern for the budget." In all the federal government would spend only $210 million for construction in 1930, a pittance compared to the level of private spending, which declined from $9 billion in 1929 to $6.3 billion in 1930. Hoover had also moved to curb immigration and increase the funds available for the federal employment service, but these actions barely scratched the surface of unemployment.[48]

This dilemma gave Hoover the worst of both worlds: he could neither spend fast enough to stimulate recovery nor goad the private sector into reversing its contraction of investment. The presence of cheap, ample credit, normally a boon in such times, was helpful but not sufficient in this case. A large infusion of official good cheer had done nothing to slow the relentless decline in prices, consumption, exports (further threatened by the looming tariff bill), or railway traffic, which Noyes called "the most striking phenomenon of the period." The figures for

March revealed a shocking drop in net railroad earnings of nearly 40 percent from 1929, which reflected a "great reduction either in consumers' purchasing capacity or in their willingness to purchase." On June 1 the *New York Times* unveiled a new "Weekly Index of Business Activities" that showed a combined average of 92.4 on May 24 compared with 94.6 on January 4 and a 1929 high of 107.0 on April 27.[49]

If there had also been an index of the national mood, it would have revealed a marked shift toward pessimism that spring. The spreading sense of unease was obvious even to casual observers. The National City Bank's monthly review for June felt obliged to admonish readers that the thing most to be guarded against was "an excess of pessimism, just as an excess of optimism was the basis of danger a year ago." Senator William Borah added his voice to a growing chorus warning against "premature pessimism." Even the *New York Times* felt obliged to remind Americans and the rest of the world of the need to "incline to hope rather than fear." No one preached the gospel of hope more fervently than Hoover. In June a delegation from the National Unemployment League visited Hoover to urge creation of a $3 billion public works program. Hoover listened to their argument patiently, then interjected, "Gentlemen, you have come sixty days too late. The depression is over."[50]

The market thought otherwise. On June 2 an investment company published a full-page ad in *Time* with a bold headline asking, "Will Stocks Break Their November Lows?" That same day stocks began a slide that saw the Dow suffer losses on 12 and the *Times* average on 11 of 15 days. Most observers attributed the decline to the work of professional bears; volume remained moderate, and the hammering of key stocks was relentless. Once again the market moved back onto front pages. By Wednesday, June 11, prices were cascading so badly that Richard Whitney repeated his performance of October by stepping conspicuously onto the floor to bid for 60,000 shares of United States Steel, which had hit a new low for the year. His appearance sparked a brief rally but could not stem the downward trend. At week's end the Dow had lost 30.20 and the *Times* average 21.06 for the month.[51]

"Sentiment rules the market, and is about as low as it has been in a number of months," admitted the *Wall Street Journal*. "Ask any broker, and he will tell you that the main reason for the market's weakness is the failure of business to improve as predicted." With steel and automobile production, construction, and railroad traffic all down, "Wall Street resigned itself to a series of poor earnings statements for the second quarter." Few signs of cheer penetrated the spreading gloom. "What the country needs at present," said the *Journal*, "is one good 'break' of luck, according to some Wall Street diagnosticians." The best break, these sources added, would be "defeat of the pending tariff bill in the Senate."[52]

At this critical juncture the breaks turned out to be all bad. Despite fierce opposition, the Smoot-Hawley tariff bill went to Hoover, who surprised reporters with a typed statement that weekend explaining why he would sign it. The market responded on Monday with a massive selloff that lasted three days. A heavy volume above 5 million shares and exceeding 6.4 million shares on the 18th signaled heavy outside selling as well. Commodity prices also plummeted as criticism of the new tariff poured in from Europe along with threats of retaliation. The conventional wisdom on Wall Street blamed the fall on the tariff, and certainly bear operators used it to club prices down. Billy Durant had his own scapegoat: he demanded an investigation of the Federal Reserve Board, which he claimed "had interfered with the stock market and had brought about the present depression."[53]

For Hoover the market rout amounted to a Bronx cheer, another sign that the credibility gap was fast becoming a chasm. "No expert in reading public opinion is required," observed the *New York Times*, "to report it is turning rather heavily against the Hoover Administration." It could be seen in the frustration born of high expectations gone sour and in "remarks . . . about the break-down of a supposed 'expert' in government." Democrats moved in eagerly for the political kill, while some Republicans, aghast at the extent to which their party's stock had fallen, blamed Hoover for the party's drop in public esteem. Even Andrew Mellon, the darling of the business community, had lost his charmed touch. When he tried to reassure Wall Street that the tariff would not interfere with business recovery, the market thumbed its nose with another ghastly decline in prices. This "heretical disregard for the statement," in the *Times*'s opinion, "emphasized the present disillusionment of Wall Street on the score of reassuring pronouncements from Washington."[54]

The disillusionment extended far beyond Wall Street. When the market collapsed, Alexander Noyes happened to be aboard a ship heading for England along with a number of financial men going on vacation. The mood was jovial, buoyed by the market's recent performance. Then came a series of daily dispatches informing them of the selloff, which in midocean hit with even more devastating impact than in a broker's office. "Everyone realized at once," Noyes recalled, "that the market's previous recovery had been fallacious, that reaction and depression, instead of being ended, had in reality only begun. . . . On land as at sea, illusion disappeared. The harsh realities of the whole situation began to present themselves." Glumly the Wall Street men began canceling the expensive tours they had planned and booked passage for a quick return.[55]

They were at sea as was the country itself, helpless to prevent the stripping away of the last fond illusions that had caught even those shrewd speculators who had pulled out of the market before the crash and then come back to cash in on the anticipated rise. Hoover, too, was at sea, caught in the same thick fog that engulfed Charley Mitchell. They were men of sunshine who thought they had done everything right and could not figure out why it had all turned out so badly. For Hoover it was an especially bitter pill to swallow because he had acted quickly and vigorously to ward off the very conditions that now surrounded him. In David Kennedy's apt phrase, he had scraped against "the boundaries of available intelligence" as well as those of inherited institutions. However, he found himself restrained not only by these boundaries but by his own deeply ingrained unwillingness to venture beyond them for reasons he deemed entirely sound. The fault, Hoover would always insist, lay not in himself but in the stars.[56]

"He is not to blame for what has happened to him," agreed the *New York Times*, "except as he had identified himself with a party which undertakes to make everybody rich and happy, and stupidly headed itself for the very disaster which has at last overtaken it; but he has to face the political consequences just as if they were wholly of his own creating. His only hope, like that of his party, lies in the changes for the better which the next year or two may bring."[57]

By the end of June no glimmer of change was in sight. The market continued its downward course, finishing the month with the Dow down 48.11 at 226.34 and the *Times* average down 34.30 at 193.00. The New York Reserve Bank had tried to stem the tide on June 19 with still another rate cut to an unprecedented 2 1/2 percent, but the move proved wholly ineffective. Hundreds of stocks stood at new lows for the year, many of them at levels comparable to their November 1929 bottoms. Volume shrank almost as fast as prices as public interest in the market waned. More pressing matters had moved to center stage, most notably the continuing fall in prices. On June 22, 14 commodities, including copper, zinc, lead, tin, silk, and rubber, reached new lows for the year.

Some sold at levels not seen since 1921, others at prices unknown since early in the century. A few, such as silk, silver, sugar, rubber, and zinc, had never known lower prices. In Chicago rye was cheaper than sawdust.[58]

Unemployment remained a bone of bitter contention. Secretary Lamont's estimate for the entire country of just under 2.3 million contrasted sharply with that of the National Unemployment League's Darwin J. Meserole, who calculated the minimum at 6.6 million. One point alone commanded wide agreement. "With the end of the half year considered by many to have been the most critical period in the process of business readjustment," declared the *New York Times*, "evidence of any significant change in the condition of trade and industry is wholly lacking. . . . There is still no sign of the long-expected revival." Nevertheless, the newspaper's publisher, Adolph S. Ochs, had not lost faith, as he made clear in a speech to the American Club of Paris:

I am an optimist. . . . I think the day is not far distant when there will be little or no excuse for unemployment, when the reward for industry, inventive genius and political wisdom will far surpass anything heretofore known in the history of the human race. We are on the threshold of a new world and the utilization of natural forces that were unthought of and undreamed of a few years ago. A new epoch of man, a conquest of nature, is just beginning. . . . We no longer think in millions but in billions. . . . Disease is being conquered. . . . International questions have nearly all been settled, and the problems of government have now become social and economic within the confines of the State. . . . Dictators are weakening. Democracy is triumphant.[59]

It would be easy to make fun of Ochs's remarks, yet the real irony is not how wrong he was about the immediate future but how right he was about several aspects of the more distant future. The brighter world Ochs envisioned did not begin to emerge until after World War II. At the time, what the crash did above all else was to transform the "irrational exuberance" of Americans into a grimmer, more sober outlook. The rainbow had vanished, and with it the enticing pot of gold that shimmered just beyond the horizon. The New Era became a figment of someone's imagination as once again it became painfully clear that good times do not last forever. As Noyes observed, the real "new era" came in with the New Deal and the profound changes it wrought, not all of them welcome, but nobody in their darkest visions imagined that ahead lay ten years of the longest, deepest depression in American history followed by four years of bloody global war.[60]

The Great Crash turned into the Great Slide as prices on the stock market declined relentlessly for three years. When they finally touched bottom on July 8, 1932, the Dow stood at 41.22 and the *Times* average at 34.43. Among the market favorites of 1929, Alleghany Corporation sold for 3⅝, Anaconda Copper for 4, General Electric for 9⅜, General Motors for 7¾, Montgomery Ward for 4⅜, RCA for 3⅝, and United States Steel for 21½.[61]

After this roller-coaster ride of change many Americans doubtless shared the exasperation of W. W. Kiplinger, who declared that "the amazing lesson from this depression is that no one knows much about the real causes and effects of ANYTHING." Then something even more amazing happened. Whoever said that there are no second acts in American life could not have been more wrong. This one came at the end of World War II, when the rainbow reappeared in colors that gleamed more brightly and vividly than ever. As the scars of depression and war healed, the rush toward the rainbow's end resumed with more vigor than ever before, and with brief interruptions it has not stopped since.[62]

Only a few of the major figures of the 1920s lived to see the rainbow's return. Alexander Noyes remained dutifully at the post of financial editor for the *New York Times* until his death on April 22, 1945. When World War II broke out, he predicted that "if the war is long-continued the world which emerges from it will be another world. But judging by the last few months it could not, politically and diplomatically, be a worse one." Irving Fisher suffered no less than the most naive investor from the crash. At the market's peak his holdings in Remington Rand, then selling at $58 a share, would have paid off his bank loans for his large margin purchases and left him a fortune of around $9 million for the foundation he hoped to establish and other good works. But instead of selling he waited for the rise that was sure to come and found himself holding shares eventually worth about $1 each. Financially ruined, he lived to catch only a glimmer of the postwar rainbow before his death on April 29, 1947.[63]

After the crash, Samuel Insull watched his empire and his own life crumble into ruins. During 1930 he boldly expanded his operations, bought out his arch rival Cyrus Eaton at too high a price, and plunged heavily into debt to accomplish these goals. By 1932 his major companies had gone into receivership, and Insull was pushed out of the management as Durant had been from General Motors. Two years later he was indicted for mail fraud but was found innocent; a year later the state of Illinois tried him on embezzlement charges but also failed to get a conviction. To a large extent Insull had been punished more by the profound change in the public mood than by any wrongdoing on his part. As his biographer wrote, "For his fifty-three years of labor to make electric power universally cheap and abundant, Insull had his reward from a grateful people: He was allowed to die outside prison."[64]

The depression treated harshly businessmen in general and Republican politicians in particular. Those who had proclaimed the new era loudest were excoriated for bringing on the disaster that had befallen the economy. None endured more unrelenting criticism than Hoover, whose presidency turned into a personal nightmare leaving emotional scars that lasted until his death in October 1964. It was his fate not only to preside over the worst depression in American history but also to live longer than any other president except John Adams. During those long, lonely years he was remembered chiefly not for his many accomplishments but for his inability to end the depression. Andrew Mellon finally left the Treasury Department in 1932 to become ambassador to Great Britain. A year later, at age 78, he returned to the Mellon National Bank and occupied his remaining years with philanthropy as well as some ugly fights with the government over income taxes and an antitrust suit against the Aluminum Company of America. He died in 1937, shortly after the latter legal battle had begun.[65]

In the financial district the club and the street alike found themselves tarnished first by neglect and then by scandal. An investigation launched by the Senate Banking Committee in 1932 plodded on until 1934, by which time it had piled up 10,000 pages of testimony that blackened the reputation of Wall Street and many of its leading citizens. Its revelations begat legislation that ended the era of self-regulation by the exchange in favor of government supervision of securities markets. Neither the club nor the street would ever be the same again. Jack Morgan lived on until March 1943, Thomas Lamont until February 1948. By that time the House of Morgan was well on its way to becoming a quite different institution—a public corporation and a member of the Federal Reserve System. A more modest Wall Street figure, Pat Bologna, could be found there 50 years after the crash, still shining shoes at the age of 69.[66]

The Senate committee investigation unearthed the private dealings of Albert Wiggin but never got him to admit wrongdoing of any kind. In December 1932 he retired from the Chase and was rewarded by the board with an annual pension of $100,000. However, the new management of the Chase, led by Nelson W. Aldrich, repudiated both Wiggin and his policies, and in October 1933 Wiggin renounced his pension. That same month a group of Chase stockholders sued him, the bank, and its officers for $100 million; Wiggin assumed personal responsibility for any losses the plaintiffs had suffered and settled with them for $2 million. He lived in uneventful retirement until his death in May 1951.[67]

Charley Mitchell fared no better at first. Lambasted by the investigating committee as no less a "bankster" than Wiggin, he was indicted in March 1933 for income tax evasion, was acquitted of criminal charges, and finally settled with the government on civil charges in December 1938. He left National City Bank unwillingly in February 1933, refused bankruptcy because it was not the "square thing," and worked tirelessly to repay all his debts. In 1934 he opened his own financial consulting firm, then became chairman of the banking house of Blythe & Co. the next year. Despite repeated tangles with the government, he rebuilt his fortune and died in 1955 a respected man on Wall Street. Sunshine Charley thus lived long enough not only to witness the rainbow's return but to bask once more in its glow. Nothing through these turbulent years quite succeeded in dimming the warmth of his personality or the driving energy behind his ambition.[68]

No such good fortune befell Jesse Livermore. He made money in the market of 1930 only to lose most of it the next year. His wife, a hopeless alcoholic, plunged into an affair with a Prohibition agent. After their divorce in September 1932, the 58-year-old Jesse wed a concert pianist 20 years his junior and promptly borrowed $136,000 of her securities to use as collateral. She never saw them again. Dogged by market losses, creditors, and lawsuits, he finally declared bankruptcy in March 1934 and spent the next five years trying to pay off his debts. He returned to the market only as a financial advisor but never regained a footing in life. In desperation he pinned his hopes on a new book, *How to Trade in Stocks*, but it went nowhere after publication in March 1940. On November 28, 1940, at the men's bar in the Sherry-Netherland Hotel, Livermore scribbled a rambling eight-page note to his wife dominated by one theme: "My life has been a failure." After signing it, he walked into the cloakroom near the men's room, sat down on a chair, pulled out a pistol, and shot himself.[69]

The greatest and most persistent dreamer of them all, Billy Durant, lived on until March 18, 1947. After enduring the humiliation of bankruptcy, he returned to Flint, where he had begun his climb toward greatness, and started in business anew as proprietor of a bowling alley. Ever expansive, he soon added a lunchroom with a drive-in window. "After all," he told a reporter, "money is only loaned to a man. He comes into the world with nothing, and he goes out with nothing." As his biographer observed, "Durant believed, like Gatsby, like an entire American generation, in the orgiastic future, the green light, the morning toward which one ran with arms ever outstretched in expectation."[70]

To the end he remained not only a dreamer but an embodiment of the American Dream itself, the fiery faith that had driven so many people in quest of the ever elusive rainbow.

Notes

List of Abbreviations

ANB	*American National Biography*
DAB	*Dictionary of American Biography*
NCAB	*National Cyclopedia of American Biography*
NYSE29	New York Stock Exchange, *Annual Report for 1929* (New York, 1930)
NYT	*New York Times*
RST	President's Research Committee on Social Trends, *Recent Social Trends in the United States*, 2 vols. (New York, 1933)
SEP	"Stock Exchange Practices," *Report of the Committee on Banking and Currency*, 73d Cong., 2d Sess., no. 1455 (Washington, D.C., 1934)
WSJ	*Wall Street Journal*

Introduction

1. David M. Kennedy, *Freedom from Fear: The American People in Depression and War, 1929–1945* (New York, 1999), 39.

2. Throughout this book, all figures for the Dow are taken from Phyllis S. Pierce, ed., *The Dow Jones Averages, 1885–1995* (Chicago, 1996), which has no page numbers. The *NYT* figures have been compiled by me from the newspaper itself; the combined average is used because it included 25 industrials and 25 railroads, giving it a broader range than the Dow.

3. The New York Stock Exchange's board of governors shortened daily trading sessions from five to three hours and eliminated the Saturday short session to allow brokerages and others to catch up on the immense backlog of paperwork generated by the crash. Normal trading hours and days resumed on November 26. The Exchange also closed on Tuesday, November 5, for election day.

4. Quoted in Christina D. Romer, "The Great Crash and the Onset of the Great Depression," *Quarterly Journal of Economics* 105 (August 1990), 597.

5. Maury Klein, *Days of Defiance: Sumter, Secession, and the Coming of the Civil War* (New York, 1997).

6. One recent book, Thomas Frank, *One Market Under God* (New York, 2000), amasses an impressive list of quotations illuminating the widespread belief in the New Economy. Many bear an uncanny resemblance to those trumpeting the New Era in the 1920s.

7. John Kenneth Galbraith, *The Great Crash* (Boston, 1955), 83.

8. Frederick Lewis Allen, *Only Yesterday* (New York, 1931), 281.

9. *WSJ*, February 12, 1929.

10. *Newsweek*, December 18, 2000, 52.

Prologue

1. All information is taken from various articles in *NYT*, September 1, 1929.

2. Ibid.

3. Ibid., September 3, 1929.

4. Ibid.

5. John Brooks, *Once in Golconda* (New York, 1969), 90.

6. *Time*, July 19, 1929.

7. Preston W. Slosson, *The Great Crusade and After, 1914–1928* (New York, 1930), 151.

8. *NYT*, July 7, August 18, and August 20–29, 1929; *Time*, July 29, August 19, and September 9, 1929.

9. *NYT*, August 18, 1929; *Time*, July 22 and July 29, 1929.

10. *WSJ*, July 18, 1929.

11. Ibid., August 21, 1929.

12. Ibid., July 17, 1929; *Time*, June 10, 1929; *NYT*, July 18, 1929.

13. *NYT*, August 25, 1929; Albert U. Romasco, *The Poverty of Abundance* (New York, 1965), 102–7.

14. *NYT*, August 18 and September 3, 1929.

15. Alexander Dana Noyes, *The Market Place: Reminiscences of a Financial Editor* (New York, 1969), 311–12. The original edition appeared in 1938.

16. David Burner, *Herbert Hoover: A Public Life* (New York, 1979), 201; Anne O'Hare McCormick, "A Year of the Hoover Method," *New York Times Magazine*, March 2, 1930, 1.

17. *NYT*, June 15, June 16, July 25, August 16, and August 30, 1929; *Time*, August 19, 1929. Young was chairman of the board for both companies; GE controlled RCA until forced to sell its shares in 1932.

18. William K. Klingaman, *1929: The Year of the Great Crash* (New York, 1989), 159–64; Ron Chernow, *The House of Morgan* (New York, 1990), 310–12.

19. *NYT*, June 14, July 10, July 18, July 19, August 25–30, and September 10, 1929.

20. Ibid., September 1 and September 4, 1929; *Time*, July 29, 1929.

21. Sarah Bradford Landau and Carl W. Condit, *Rise of the New York Skyscraper, 1865–1913* (New Haven, 1996), 394–95; Norbert Messler, *The Art Deco Skyscraper in New York* (New York, 1986), 73; *The 1929 World Almanac and Book of Facts* (New York, 1971), 500. This is a facsimile edition of the original New York *World* almanac. Eight of the buildings in the list were still under construction.

22. *Time*, January 7, 1929; Slosson, *Great Crusade*, 408–9; Klingaman, *Year of the Great Crash*, 210–11; *NYT*, May 3 and August 19, 1929.

23. Peter L. Skolnik, *Fads: America's Crazes, Fevers, and Fancies* (New York, 1978), 40–41.

24. *Time*, August 19, 1929; Frederic Nelson, "The Child Stylites of Baltimore," *New Republic*, August 28, 1929, 37–38; George E. Mowry, ed., *The Twenties: Fords, Flappers, and Fanatics* (Englewood Cliffs, N.J., 1963), 69, 73–74. The following paragraphs are drawn from the same sources.

25. Klingaman, *Year of the Great Crash*, 221.

26. Elizabeth B. Hurlock, *The Psychology of Dress: An Analysis of Fashion and Its Motive* (New York, 1929), 10; Stuart Chase, *Prosperity: Fact or Myth* (New York, 1929), 29–30; Stuart Ewen and Elizabeth Ewen, *Channels of Desire: Mass Images and the Shaping of American Consciousness* (New York, 1982), 203–4.

27. Chase, *Prosperity: Fact or Myth*, 65; Hurlock, *Psychology of Dress*, 3, 40–41.

28. *NYT*, August 21, 1929; *Time*, August 26, 1929.

29. *NYT*, May 7, 1929; Samuel Crowther, "Everybody Ought to Be Rich: An Interview with John J. Raskob," *Ladies' Home Journal*, August 1929, 9. Klingaman, *Year of the Great Crash*, 211, errs in saying Raskob suggested saving $15 per *week*.

30. *NYT*, May 7, 1929; Klingaman, *Year of the Great Crash*, 187, 211.

31. Brooks, *Once in Golconda*, 90; Allen, *Only Yesterday*, 257.

32. *Time*, August 5 and 10, 1929.

33. Ibid., August 19, 1929.

34. Ibid.

35. Brooks, *Once in Golconda*, 97; Thomas F. Huertas and Joan L. Silverman, "Charles E. Mitchell: Scapegoat of the Crash?" *Business History Review* (Spring 1986), 87; Klingaman, *Year of the Crash*, 215.

36. James Grant, *Bernard M. Baruch: The Adventures of a Wall Street Legend* (New York, 1997), 221; *NYT*, August 21, 1929; Gordon Thomas and Max Morgan-Witts, *The Day the Bubble Burst* (Garden City, N.Y., 1979), 274.

37. *WSJ*, January 25, 1929; Robert Sobel, *Panic on Wall Street* (New York, 1968), 354; Irving Fisher, *The Stock Market Crash—and After* (New York, 1930), 69; Charles Amos Dice, *New Levels in the Stock Market* (New York, 1929), 75–82.

38. George Soule, *Prosperity Decade* (New York, 1947), 294.

39. Klingaman, *Year of the Great Crash*, 109, 219; Allen, *Only Yesterday*, 260.

40. Arthur Marx, *Life with Groucho* (New York, 1954), 108.

41. Noyes, *Market Place*, 325; Edwin Lefevre, "The Little Fellow in Wall Street," *Saturday Evening Post*, January 4, 1930, 102.

42. *NYT*, April 23, 1945; Noyes, *Market Place*, 49, 74, 306.

43. Noyes, *Market Place*, 321–25.

44. Ibid., 22–23, 62, 322–23.

45. *NYT*, September 1–3, 1929.

46. Klingaman, *Year of the Great Crash*, 215.

Chapter 1

1. Mark Sullivan, *Our Times: The Twenties* (New York, 1935), 2–3.

2. Quoted in Harold Seymour, *Baseball: The Early Years* (New York, 1989), vii. This is the later paperback edition; the original book appeared in 1960.

3. For the Black Sox scandal, see David Quentin Voigt, *American Baseball: From the Commissioners to Continental Expansion* (University Park, Pa., 1983), 124–33.

4. Slosson, *Great Crusade*, 31.

5. Ibid., 370–71; Sullivan, *Our Times*, 12–13; Maury Klein, *The Flowering of the Third America* (Chicago, 1993), 188–89; Soule, *Prosperity Decade*, 32; Edward L. Bernays, *Crystallizing Public Opinion* (New York, 1923), xxxiii–iv.

6. Soule, *Prosperity Decade*, 43; Ellis W. Hawley, *The Great War and the Search for a Modern Order* (New York, 1979), 24–27; David M. Kennedy, *Over Here: The First World War and American Society* (New York, 1982), 93–143; Walker D. Hines, *War History of American Railroads* (New Haven, 1928), passim.

7. Slosson, *Great Crusade*, 54–55; Soule, *Prosperity Decade*, 41, 60; David F. Noble, *America by Design* (New York, 1977), 16–17.

8. Sullivan, *Our Times*, 13; Klein, *Flowering of the Third America*, 188–89; U.S. Bureau of the Census, *Historical Statistics of the United States, Colonial Times to 1970* (Washington, 1975), 511, 517. Average manufacturing wages rose from $580 annually in 1914 to $1,358 in 1920.

9. Soule, *Prosperity Decade*, 47; NYSE29, 52; Robert Sobel, *The Big Board: A History of the New York Stock Market* (New York, 1965), 216–17; *Historical Statistics*, 1117; Robert T. Patterson, *The Great Boom and Panic, 1921–1929* (Chicago, 1965), 9; Alexander D. Noyes, *The War Period of American Finance, 1908–1925* (New York, 1926), 193–97; Vincent P. Carosso, *Investment Banking in America: A History* (Cambridge, Mass., 1970), 250.

10. Soule, *Prosperity Decade*, 5; Kennedy, *Over Here*, 279–80; Klein, *Flowering of the Third America*, 186–87.

11. For the influenza pandemic, see Alfred W. Crosby, *America's Forgotten Pandemic* (New York, 1989).

12. Kennedy, *Freedom from Fear*, 1; Sullivan, *Our Times*, 3–9.

13. Harris Gaylord Warren, *Herbert Hoover and the Great Depression* (New York, 1959), 11. For a detailed analysis of the disruptions to the European systems, see Barry Eichengreen, *Golden Fetters: The Gold Standard and the Great Depression, 1919–1939* (New York, 1992).

14. Warren, *Hoover and the Great Depression*, 11; Soule, *Prosperity Decade*, 252–55.

15. Joseph Nathan Kane, *Facts About the Presidents* (New York, 1989), 159, 173. Theodore Roosevelt was the first to visit a foreign country, going to Panama in 1906.

16. Kennedy, *Freedom from Fear*, 8.

17. Hawley, *Great War*, 43–45; Kennedy, *Over Here*, 356–62; Sullivan, *Our Times*, 179.

18. Charles Kindleberger, *The World in Depression, 1929–1930* (London, 1973), 15; Kennedy, *Over Here*, 251–52; Klein, *Flowering of the Third America*, 189–90.

19. Lester V. Chandler, *Benjamin Strong: Central Banker* (Washington, D.C., 1958), 136; Soule, *Prosperity Decade*, 104.

20. Noyes, *Market Place*, 286–90.

21. Chandler, *Benjamin Strong*, 168; Soule, *Prosperity Decade*, 104–5; Klein, *Flowering of the Third America*, 190, 202; Noyes, *War Period of American Finance*, 382–98.

22. Kennedy, *Over Here*, 45–92.

23. Robert K. Murray, *Red Scare* (New York, 1955), passim; Klein, *Flowering of the Third America*, 200.

24. Chernow, *House of Morgan*, 212–14; Brooks, *Once in Golconda*, 1–3, 6–11.

25. Brooks, *Once in Golconda*, 7.

26. Sullivan, *Our Times*, 1.

27. Brooks, *Once in Golconda*, 41; Frederick Lewis Allen, *The Lords of Creation* (New York, 1935), 222. For analysis of the sudden shift from depression to prosperity, see Soule, *Prosperity Decade*, 108–14.

28. Hawley, *The Great War*, 80–81.

29. Chase, *Prosperity: Fact or Myth*, 48.

30. Soule, *Prosperity Decade*, 128, 182; Slosson, *Great Crusade*, 136.

31. Soule, *Prosperity Decade*, 113–14; *RST*, 222–23.

32. *Historical Statistics*, 716; Robert S. Lynd and Helen M. Lynd, *Middletown: A Study in Contemporary American Culture* (London, 1929), 256–57; William Ashdown, "Confessions of an Automobilist," *Atlantic Monthly*, June 1925, 789; Bernard A. Weisberger, *The Dream Maker: William C. Durant, Founder of General Motors* (Boston, 1979), 184.

33. *Time*, January 13, 1930.

34. *RST*, 457.

35. Ibid., 175; Kenneth Jackson, *Crabgrass Frontier: Suburbanization of the United States* (New York, 1985), 167.

36. Quoted in Richard Tedlow, *New and Improved: The Story of Mass Marketing in America* (New York, 1990), 120.

37. Ibid., 120–30; David A. Hounshell, *From the American System to Mass Production, 1800–1932* (Baltimore, 1984), 217–62; Slosson, *Great Crusade*, 229–30. For a detailed account of Ford's rise, see Allan Nevins, *Ford: The Times, the Man, the Company* (New York, 1954), 2 vols.

38. Soule, *Prosperity Decade*, 166.

39. The profile of Durant is drawn largely from Weisberger's superb biography, *The Dream Maker*, passim.

40. Ibid., 59–61, 74, 78–80, 101.

41. Ibid., xvii, 93–109.

42. Ibid., 112, 197, 200, 234.

43. Ibid., xvii, 69–73, 121–26.

44. Ibid., 131–38.

45. Ibid., 139–42; Alfred P. Sloan Jr., *My Years with General Motors* (New York, 1963), 5–9.

46. Weisberger, *Dream Maker*, 147–51.

47. Ibid., xix, 153, 159, 177–85.

48. Ibid., 160–74.

49. Ibid., 174–77, 185–201; Sloan, *My Years with General Motors*, 12–16; Alfred D. Chandler Jr. and Stephen Salsbury, *Pierre S. du Pont and the Making of the Modern Corporation* (New York, 1971), 435–43.

50. Weisberger, *Dream Maker*, 209–14.

51. Ibid., 215–17, 233–35.

52. Ibid., 217–21; Sloan, *My Years with General Motors*, 46–47. For a fuller portrait of Pierre du Pont, see Chandler and Salsbury, *Pierre S. du Pont*, passim, and Joseph Frazier Wall, *Alfred I. du Pont: The Man and His Family* (New York, 1990).

53. Weisberger, *Dream Maker*, 221–28; Chandler and Salsbury, *Pierre S. du Pont*, 444–49.

54. Weisberger, *Dream Maker*, 228–31; Chandler and Salsbury, *Pierre S. du Pont*, 450–56.

55. Weisberger, *Dream Maker*, 231–32, 237; Chandler and Salsbury, *Pierre S. du Pont*, 450–60.

56. Weisberger, *Dream Maker*, 237–41; Chandler and Salsbury, *Pierre S. du Pont*, 460–62.

57. Weisberger, *Dream Maker*, 238–41; Chandler and Salsbury, *Pierre S. du Pont*, 462–66.

58. Weisberger, *Dream Maker*, 241–46; Chandler and Salsbury, *Pierre S. du Pont*, 456–70.

59. Weisberger, *Dream Maker*, 248–49, 252–54.

60. Ibid., 255–58; Chandler and Salsbury, *Pierre S. du Pont*, 475–80.

61. Weisberger, *Dream Maker*, 259–61; Chandler and Salsbury, *Pierre S. du Pont*, 480–82; Sloan, *My Years with General Motors*, 34.

62. Weisberger, *Dream Maker*, 261–65; Chandler and Salsbury, *Pierre S. du Pont*, 482–85. Durant had used 3 million of his own shares of GM and 1.3 million shares owned by "others" as collateral.

63. Weisberger, *Dream Maker*, 266–73; Chandler and Salsbury, *Pierre S. du Pont*, 484–91. More detail on the new company can be found in these sources. The primary source for these events is a letter written by Pierre to his brother. The full text is in Sloan, *My Years with General Motors*, 37–43. Of the new company's 100,000 shares, 40 percent went to the Du Pont Company, 40 percent to Durant, and 20 percent to the House of Morgan.

64. Weisberger, *Dream Maker*, 272–74; Chandler and Salsbury, *Pierre S. du Pont*, 489–91.

65. Weisberger, *Dream Maker*, 263–64, 287–93.

66. Sloan, *My Years with General Motors*, 4.

67. Weisberger, *Dream Maker*, 300, 302.

Chapter 2

1. Ferdinand Pecora, *Wall Street Under Oath* (New York, 1939), 6.

2. Chernow, *House of Morgan*, 161, 166–68. For a fuller portrait of J. P. Morgan and his relationship with Jack, see Jean Strouse, *Morgan: American Banker* (New York, 1999).

3. Chernow, *House of Morgan*, 168–71, 186–88, 200.

4. Ibid., 203, 205, 249–53; Chandler, *Benjamin Strong*, 31–32, 152.

5. Chernow, *House of Morgan*, 217–21.

6. Brooks, *Once in Golconda*, 45–46.

7. Ibid., 50–51; SEP, 223.

8. Brooks, *Once in Golconda*, 53–54; Chernow, *House of Morgan*, 196–97.

9. Allen, *Lords of Creation*, 364–75; Brooks, *Once in Golconda*, 56–57. The list contained 16 investment bankers (including 10 Morgan partners), 11 commercial bankers, and "a scattering of insurance company heads, powerful private investors, brokers, market operators, industrialists, utility executives, etc." Allen, *Lords of Creation*, 368.

10. Chernow, *House of Morgan*, 24.

11. S. Marshall Kempner, *Inside Wall Street, 1920–1942* (New York, 1973), 16–17.

12. Ibid., 17–23.

13. NYSE29, 61; Pecora, *Wall Street Under Oath*, 258–59; Brooks, *Once in Golconda*, 22.

14. Brooks, *Once in Golconda*, 22–23.

15. Robert Sobel, *The Great Bull Market* (New York, 1968), 31; *NYT*, June 13 and July 21, 1929. In 1953 the Curb Exchange became the American Stock Exchange.

16. Thomas and Morgan-Witts, *Day the Bubble Burst*, 11–12.

17. Noyes, *Market Place*, 50.

18. *Time*, November 18, 1929; Huertas and Silverman, "Charles E. Mitchell," 82–83.

19. Harold van B. Cleveland and Thomas F. Huertas, *Citibank, 1812–1970* (Cambridge, Mass., 1985), 58–63.

20. Ibid., 63–75. For more detail on affiliated companies, see Carosso, *Investment Banking in America*, 271–73.

21. SEP, 155–56.

22. Cleveland and Huertas, *Citibank*, 32–59, 75–84.

23. Ibid., 84–87.

24. Ibid., 88–104.

25. Ibid., 104–7.

26. Ibid., 107–12; Huertas and Silverman, "Charles E. Mitchell," 86–87; SEP, 206.

27. Cleveland and Huertas, *Citibank*, 114–15; Huertas and Silverman, "Charles E. Mitchell," 83–84.

28. Cleveland and Huertas, *Citibank*, 115–16; Huertas and Silverman, "Charles E. Mitchell," 83.

29. Cleveland and Huertas, *Citibank*, 116–20; Huertas and Silverman, "Charles E. Mitchell," 85–86, 93–94.

30. Cleveland and Huertas, *Citibank*, 121–28.

31. Ibid., 128–30, 135–36.

32. Ibid., 135–36.

33. Ibid., 136–37; Huertas and Silverman, "Charles E. Mitchell," 83–84; Pecora, *Wall Street Under Oath*, 72; SEP, 165.

34. Huertas and Silverman, "Charles E. Mitchell," 81; Allen, *Lords of Creation*, 304.

35. Cleveland and Huertas, *Citibank*, 136–50; Pecora, *Wall Street Under Oath*, 76.

36. Cleveland and Huertas, *Citibank*, 153–56.

37. Ibid., 134; Carosso, *Investment Banking in America*, 274.

38. Pecora, *Wall Street Under Oath*, 96.

39. *DAB* Supp. 5:744–45; *NCAB* 39:502–3; Brooks, *Once in Golconda*, 103.

40. *DAB* Supp. 5:744–45; Pecora, *Wall Street Under Oath*, 131–33, 137–38.

41. Pecora, *Wall Street Under Oath*, 147–49; SEP, 187, 325.

Chapter 3

1. Quoted in Brooks, *Once in Golconda*, 21.

2. For a brief description of short selling, see SEP, 50–52.

3. Ibid., 74, 76; *NYT*, October 20, 1929.

4. Paul Sarnoff, *Jesse Livermore: Speculator King* (Palisades Park, N.J., 1967), 12–20; Edwin Lefevre, *Reminiscences of a Stock Operator* (Garden City, N.Y., 1923), 9–12. There is no satisfactory biography of Livermore. The Sarnoff is short and prone to error and exaggeration. Lefevre's book is cast in the form of an autobiography but is clearly drawn from interviews with Livermore and dedicated to him. Shortly before his suicide in 1940, Livermore revealed that he had actually done the book with Lefevre as his "editor and coach." Sarnoff, *Livermore*, 22. However, its format evidently fooled Charles Geisst, *Wall Street: A History* (New York, 1997), 178, 182, 375, who erroneously describes Lefevre as one of the legendary operators of the era. He was rather one of its better-known writers, especially on Wall Street topics. See Lefevre's obituary in *NYT*, February 24, 1943.

5. Lefevre, *Reminiscences*, 12–21.

6. Ibid., 21–37.

7. Ibid., 36–63.

8. Ibid., 64.

9. Ibid., 169.

10. Ibid., 172–87.

11. Sobel, *Great Bull Market*, 70–71.

12. Burner, *Herbert Hoover*, 44.

13. Sullivan, *Our Times*, 242; Kennedy, *Freedom from Fear*, 33; James Prothro, *The Dollar Decade* (New York, 1954), 223, 225.

14. John D. Hicks, *Republican Ascendancy* (New York, 1960), 50–59.

15. Ibid., 51–53; Hawley, *Great War*, 66; *DAB* Supp. 2:448. Mellon lacks a good biography. Philip H. Love, *Andrew W. Mellon: The Man and His Work* (Baltimore, 1929) is lavish in its praise; Harvey O'Connor, *Mellon's Millions: The Biography of a Fortune* (New York, 1933) is detailed but caustic. The short summary of his life in *DAB* is by Allan Nevins.

16. Mellon announced the gift in 1937 along with $15 million for construction of a building and $5 million for an endowment. He stipulated that the building not bear his name.

17. *DAB* Supp. 2:448; Love, *Mellon*, 15. For a less favorable view of Mellon's "greatness," see Walter Lippmann, *Men of Destiny* (New York, 1928), 184–95.

18. Silas Bent, *Strange Bedfellows: A Review of Politics, Personalities, and the Press* (New York, 1928), 81; Noyes, *Market Place*, 300.

19. O'Connor, *Mellon's Millions*, 126–37; Hicks, *Republican Ascendancy*, 53–54; *DAB* Supp. 2:449; William E. Leuchtenburg, *The Perils of Prosperity* (New York, 1958), 98. The first act also raised the level of exemptions for some low-bracket taxpayers and eliminated several "nuisance" taxes. Details on the second plan are in Andrew W. Mellon, *Taxation: The People's Business* (New York, 1924), 54–62.

20. O'Connor, *Mellon's Millions*, 140–41; Hicks, *Republican Ascendancy*, 106. For Mellon's own explanation of the surcharge, see Mellon, *Taxation*, 69–89.

21. *Historical Statistics*, 1104, 1106. During the 1920s interest payments and veterans' benefits absorbed more than half the federal budget, with the military taking most of the remainder. See Kennedy, *Freedom from Fear*, 29–30.

22. Robert Sobel, *Coolidge: An American Enigma* (Washington, D. C., 1998); O'Connor, *Mellon's Millions*, 229–30, 272–79.

23. Donald F. Kettl, *Leadership at the Fed* (New Haven, 1986), 18.

24. For background to the Federal Reserve Act, see Robert Craig West, *Banking Reform and the Federal Reserve, 1863–1923* (Ithaca, 1977), 15–154.

25. Unless otherwise indicated, details on the Federal Reserve System are drawn from Soule, *Prosperity Decade*, 50–51; West, *Banking Reform*, 113–35, 209–13; Chandler, *Benjamin Strong*, 6–15. The twelve regional banks were set up in Boston, New York, Philadelphia, Richmond, Atlanta, Dallas, Kansas City, St. Louis, Chicago, Cleveland, Minneapolis, and San Francisco. State banks were chartered by individual states and possessed whatever powers or limitations their charters contained. New or existing banks seeking to become national banks had to abide by the more stringent regulations of the National Banking Act of 1863 and later legislation. They also served as depositories for government funds.

26. The rediscount rate is also known as the discount rate. Although the two terms are used interchangeably now, the former was most often used during the 1920s.

27. Chandler, *Benjamin Strong*, 6–15.

28. West, *Banking Reform*, 213–15.

29. Ibid., 216–17; Chandler, *Benjamin Strong*, 15–17, 99–134; Elmus R. Wicker, *Federal Reserve Monetary Policy, 1917–1933* (New York, 1966), 3–24.

30. Chandler, *Benjamin Strong*, 17. For the gold standard and the overall financial situation, see Eichengreen, *Golden Fetters*, 3–124.

31. Chandler, *Benjamin Strong*, 38–45.

32. Ibid., 20–24.

33. Ibid., 25–30.

34. Ibid., 30–31, 52.

35. Ibid., 46–50.

36. Ibid., 140–52; Milton Friedman and Anna Jacobson Schwartz, *A Monetary History of the United States, 1867–1960* (Princeton, 1963), 225–26; Wicker, *Federal Reserve Monetary Policy*, 25–43.

37. Chandler, *Benjamin Strong*, 52, 153–75; Soule, *Prosperity Decade*, 98–99; Friedman and Schwartz, *Monetary History*, 231–35; Wicker, *Federal Reserve Monetary Policy*, 43–56.

38. Friedman and Schwartz, *Monetary History*, 239, 241; Wicker, *Federal Reserve Monetary Policy*, 57–76.

39. Chandler, *Benjamin Strong*, 191–99. Chandler details the devices used by Strong to keep gold holdings from promoting inflation.

40. Ibid., 133, 204–6.

41. Ibid., 208–20, 238–39; West, *Banking Reform*, 225. Chandler, 238–39, offers the best short explanation of how open-market operations affected lending by member banks.

42. Chandler, *Benjamin Strong*, 52, 221–28.

Chapter 4

1. Chase, *Prosperity: Fact or Myth*, 40.

2. Samuel Hopkins Adams, "The Timely Death of President Harding," in Isabel Leighton, ed., *The Aspirin Age, 1919–1941* (New York, 1949), 89; Sullivan, *Our Times*, 181. The Adams article is a useful summary from his longer biography, *Incredible Era* (New York, 1939). A slightly different version of the quotations is in William Allen White, *The Autobiography of William Allen White* (New York, 1946), 616. The fullest account of Harding's life and affairs is Francis Russell, *The Shadow of Blooming Grove* (New York, 1968). See also Andrew Sinclair, *The Available Man* (New York, 1965) and Robert K. Murray, *The Harding Years: Warren G. Harding and His Administration* (Minneapolis, 1969).

3. Adams, *Incredible Era*, 336–37.

4. White, *Autobiography*, 619; Adams, "Timely Death of President Harding," 101–2. For the oil scandal, see Burl Noggle, *Teapot Dome* (Baton Rouge, 1962).

5. William Allen White, *A Puritan in Babylon* (New York, 1938), 240–43; Sobel, *Coolidge*, 232–33. Other biographies of Coolidge include Claude M. Fuess, *Calvin Coolidge: The Man from Vermont* (Boston, 1940) and Donald R. McCoy, *Calvin Coolidge: The Quiet President* (New York, 1967).

6. White, *Puritan in Babylon*, 250–55; Alice Roosevelt Longworth, *Crowded Hours* (New York, 1933), 337. The "pickle" image comes from Longworth, who makes it clear that she got it from her doctor, who heard it from a patient, but the friends she told about it soon attributed it to her. Many historians and writers continue to make that same mistake.

7. Noyes, *Market Place*, 299; Irving Stone, "Calvin Coolidge: A Study in Inertia," in Leighton, *Aspirin Age*, 144; Ronald Steel, *Walter Lippmann and the American Century* (Boston, 1980), 204; Sobel, *Coolidge*, 236–39; White, *Puritan in Babylon*, 256–57.

8. White, *Puritan in Babylon*, 252.

9. Ibid., 260; Lippmann, *Men of Destiny*, 12–13.

10. White, *Puritan in Babylon*, 253; Prothro, *Dollar Decade*, 224.

11. Sobel, *Coolidge*, 295–98; Calvin Coolidge, *Autobiography of Calvin Coolidge* (New York, 1929), 189–90, 196.

12. Peter Temin, *Did Monetary Forces Cause the Great Depression?* (New York, 1976), 4; *RST*, 232; Eugene N. White, ed., *Crashes and Panics: The Lessons from History* (Homewood, Ill., 1990), 146; *Historical Statistics*, 162, 950; Soule, *Prosperity Decade*, 107–8, 117, 120; Kindleberger, *World in Depression*, 46; Kennedy, *Freedom from Fear*, 20.

13. *Historical Statistics*, 618–21, 640, 821, 825, 827–28; Soule, *Prosperity Decade*, 128, 164, 170–74, 182; Chase, *Prosperity: Fact or Myth*, 138. In 1899 Americans spent only 7 percent of their outlay for durable goods on transportation; by 1929 the figure had increased to 36 percent. Martha L. Olney, *Buy Now, Pay Later: Advertising, Credit, and Consumer Durables in the 1920s* (Chapel Hill, 1991), 33.

14. The income figures are in *Time*, February 10, 1930, and cover reported income. A total of 4,050,959 persons reported income, of whom 2,434,640 paid taxes. The average net income was $6,078.93.

15. Harold Barger, *Outlay and Income in the United States, 1921–1938* (New York, 1942), 58–59; Soule, *Prosperity Decade*, 107; Chase, *Prosperity: Fact or Myth*, 35–36, 101. In 1925 the average worker took home $1,384 a year. Bank clerks led the list at $2,179, followed by government employees at $1,585, construction workers at $1,574, transportation and utility workers at $1,554, and factory workers at $1,362. Miners earned $1,318, only $3 more than clerks and shop girls. Farm laborers trailed badly at $537.

16. Warren, *Herbert Hoover and the Great Depression*, 6; Soule, *Prosperity Decade*, 206–7; *RST*, xxxv. One survey found that increased purchasing power had raised the standard of living for average workers 25 percent since 1900; another measured the increase in real earnings at about 19 percent since 1914.

17. Chase, *Prosperity: Fact or Myth*, 122–25; Slosson, *Great Crusade and After*, 169; *WSJ*, July 22, 1929.

18. This sketch of Fisher is drawn chiefly from the biography by Irving Norton Fisher, *My Father Irving Fisher* (New York, 1956). See also the sketch by Theodore M. Porter in *ANB* 8:12–15. Fisher's portrait of his father is fairly detailed and balanced.

19. Fisher, *My Father*, 223.

20. Ibid., 154, 160–61, 222–23.

21. Sobel, *Big Board*, 207.

22. Robert Sklar, *Movie-Made America* (New York, 1994), 67.

23. *Historical Statistics*, 26; Mowry, *Twenties*, 51. Galbraith, *Great Crash*, 8, called it "an inordinate desire to get rich quickly with a minimum of physical effort."

24. Allen, *Lords of Creation*, 327; Charlton W. Tebeau, *A History of Florida* (Coral Gables, Fla., 1971), 383–84. Tebeau has a good photograph of a line of developers' buses carrying land seekers. He dates it October 1921.

25. Tebeau, *History of Florida*, 384.

26. Slosson, *Great Crusade*, 243–47; Edward N. Akin, *Flagler: Rockefeller Partner and Florida Baron* (Kent, Ohio, 1988), 116–66.

27. George B. Tindall, "The Bubble in the Sun," *American Heritage*, August 1965, 78–79; Polly Redford, *Billion-Dollar Sandbar: A Biography of Miami Beach* (New York, 1970), 79. Tindall offers a more condensed version with footnotes in George B. Tindall, *The Emergence of the New South, 1913–1945* (Baton Rouge, 1967), 104–8. Ultimately Flagler built his Florida East Coast line down to Key West.

28. Redford, *Billion-Dollar Sandbar*, 80–134.

29. Ibid., 149; Tindall, "Bubble in the Sun," 78–80.

30. Tindall, "Bubble in the Sun," 79–80, 83, 109; Redford, *Billion-Dollar Sandbar*, 149–50; Lawrence W. Levine, *Defender of the Faith: William Jennings Bryan, the Last Decade* (New York, 1965), 238. There is wild disagreement on Bryan's role and fees. Levine, who is somewhat reticent on the subject, says Bryan received $250 per lecture. Tindall says he got "an annual salary of more than fifty thousand dollars." Redford ups the ante to "a fee of $100,000 a year, half in cash, the other half in land."

31. Tindall, "Bubble in the Sun," 80, 83; Allen, *Only Yesterday*, 227. For the boom in St. Petersburg, see Walter P. Fuller, *This Was Florida's Boom* (St. Petersburg, Fla., 1954).

32. Tebeau, *History of Florida*, 384; Tindall, "Bubble in the Sun," 80–83, 109.

33. Allen, *Only Yesterday*, 226; Gertrude Mathews Shelby, "Florida Frenzy," *Harper's Monthly Magazine*, January 1926, 177; C. P. Russell, "The Pneumatic Hegira," *Outlook*, December 9, 1925, 559–60. For another firsthand account of the boom, see Theyre H. Weigall, *Boom in Paradise* (New York, 1932).

34. Russell, "Pneumatic Hegira," 560.

35. Shelby, "Florida Frenzy," 177.

36. Ibid., 178–79.

37. Ibid., 178–81.

38. Ibid., 179. Italics are in the original.

39. Ibid., 180–86; Galbraith, *Great Crash*, 8.

40. Tindall, "Bubble in the Sun," 110; Tebeau, *History of Florida*, 385–86; Gloria Jahoda, *Florida: A Bicentennial History* (New York, 1976), 124–25. The embargo on most goods was lifted February 26, 1926, but on some items it lasted until May 15.

41. Tindall, "Bubble in the Sun," 111; Tebeau, *History of Florida*, 386–87.

42. Jahoda, *Florida*, 123; Allen, *Only Yesterday*, 233.

43. Jahoda, *Florida*, 127.

44. Soule, *Prosperity Decade*, 126.

45. These computations are based on figures in Pierce, *Dow Jones Averages*. The highest and lowest closing figure was taken for each month of every year; the number in the table is the average for the twelve months.

46. Sobel, *Great Bull Market*, 97.

47. Sobel, *Great Bull Market*, 17–21.

48. Brooks, *Once in Golconda*, 23–40.

49. Slosson, *Great Crusade*, 184; Tedlow, *New and Improved*, 234–35; Sobel, *Great Bull Market*, 70–71; Sarnoff, *Jesse Livermore*, 67–68; Sobel, *Big Board*, 263–64; John Brooks, "A Corner in Piggly Wiggly," *New Yorker*, June 6, 1959, 128–36. Brooks has the most detailed account of the corner.

50. Brooks, "Corner in Piggly Wiggly," 138–42.

51. Ibid., 143–50.

52. Galbraith, *Great Crash*, 12–13. The Dow Jones figures are computed from tables 4.2 and 4.3.

53. Richard D. Wyckoff, *Wall Street Ventures and Adventures Through Forty Years* (New York, 1930), 269, 275–76.

54. Ibid., 277–79; Sarnoff, *Jesse Livermore*, 71–74.

Chapter 5

1. Quoted in William Leach, *Land of Desire: Merchants, Power, and the Rise of a New American Culture* (New York, 1993), 298.

2. The origins of fundamentalism are outlined in *RST*, 1010–11.

3. Ibid., 1012, 1036; Mowry, *Twenties*, 155–56.

4. Prothro, *Dollar Decade*, 4.

5. *RST*, 1019–40.

6. Lynd and Lynd, *Middletown*, 34, 322, 481; Robert S. Lynd and Helen M. Lynd, *Middletown in Transition: A Study in Cultural Conflicts* (London, 1937), 242.

7. Arthur M. Schlesinger Jr., *The Crisis of the Old Order* (Boston, 1957), 71–72; Leuchtenburg, *Perils of Prosperity*, 189. As the alert reader will doubtless notice, many elements of the 1920s resonate strikingly in American life at present. For one such example compare Barton's book with Laurie Beth Jones, *Jesus, CEO* (New York, 1995).

8. Edward Earle Purinton, "Big Ideas from Big Business," *Independent*, April 16, 1921, 395–96; Bent, *Strange Bedfellows*, xi–xiii; Lynd and Lynd, *Middletown*, 242, 481.

9. *RST*, 1012; Voigt, *American Baseball*, 89; Lynd and Lynd *Middletown*, 356.

10. Prothro, *Dollar Decade*, 229; Leuchtenburg, *Perils of Prosperity*, 189; Jackson Lears, *Fables of Abundance: A Cultural History of Advertising in America* (New York, 1994), 227; Mowry, *Twenties*, 154.

11. Carey McWilliams, "Aimee Semple McPherson: 'Sunlight in My Soul,' " in Leighton, *Aspirin Age*, 50–57; Morrow Mayo, "Aimee Rises from the Sea," *New Republic*, December 25, 1929, 136–37; Lately Thomas [Robert V. Steele], *Storming Heaven: The Lives and Turmoils of Minnie Kennedy and Aimee Semple McPherson* (New York, 1970), 1–24. The Thomas book has an excellent selection of photographs.

12. McWilliams, "Aimee Semple McPherson," 58–59; Mayo, "Aimee Rises from the Sea," 137; Thomas, *Storming Heaven*, 25–37.

13. McWilliams, "Aimee Semple McPherson," 59–60; Mayo, "Aimee Rises from the Sea," 137–38; Shelton Bissell, "Vaudeville at Angelus Temple," *Outlook*, May 23, 1928, 1258.

14. Mayo, "Aimee Rises from the Sea," 137.

15. "It is doubtful whether any earlier decade in the country's history had seen the wholesale adoption of so many new goods, such considerable changes in the habits of consumers, as the years 1920–1929." *RST*, xxxvii.

16. Gilles Lipovetsky, *The Empire of Fashion* (Princeton, 1994), 134; Bruce Barton, "Bernard M. Baruch Discusses the Future of American Business," *American Magazine*, June 1929, 134.

17. Samuel Strauss, "Things Are in the Saddle," *Atlantic Monthly*, November 1924, 578.

18. *RST*, 871; Chase, *Prosperity: Fact or Myth*, 78, 177. For an excellent study into the origins of the consumer economy, see Leach, *Land of Desire*.

19. *RST*, xxxvi–vii; Chase, *Prosperity: Fact or Myth*, 23; Barton, "Bernard M. Baruch Discusses," 26.

20. Soule, *Prosperity Decade*, 324, 330; Slosson, *Great Crusade and After*, 368.

21. *RST*, 878–80.

22. Ibid., xxxvii.

23. Olney, *Buy Now, Pay Later*, 136–39, 170; Silas Bent, *Ballyhoo: The Voice of the Press* (New York, 1927), 224.

24. Slosson, *Great Crusade and After*, 382–83; Roland Marchand, *Advertising the American Dream: Making Way for Modernity, 1920–1940* (Berkeley, 1985), 69; Susan Strasser, *Satisfaction Guaranteed: The Making of the American Mass Market* (New York, 1989), 155–56; Michael Schudson, *Advertising, the Uneasy Persuasion: Its Dubious Impact on American Society* (New York, 1984), 173; Bent, *Ballyhoo*, 235–36.

25. *RST*, li, 867–68; Lears, *Fables of Abundance*, 181.

26. Earnest Elmo Calkins, *The Business of Advertising* (New York, 1915), 202–3; Juliet B. Schor, *The Overworked American: The Unexpected Decline of Leisure* (New York, 1992), 122; Stuart Ewen, *All Consuming Images: The Politics of Style in Contemporary Culture* (New York, 1988), 243.

27. Lears, *Fables of Abundance*, 227; Slosson, *Great Crusade and After*, 366; Leach, *Land of Desire*, 91–92.

28. Daniel Bell, *The Cultural Contradictions of Capitalism* (New York, 1973), 69; Slosson, *Great Crusade and After*, 181; Olney, *Buy Now, Pay Later*, 95. For prewar developments in consumer credit, see Leach, *Land of Desire*, 123–30.

29. Olney, *Buy Now, Pay Later*, 106–9, 126–27, 130–31.

30. *Outlook*, May 23, 1928, 150.

31. Mowry, *Twenties*, 50; Noyes, *Market Place*, 319; Garet Garrett, *The American Omen* (New York, 1928), 210.

32. For the role of elegant surroundings, amenities, and service, see Leach, *Land of Desire*, 112–50.

33. Chase, *Prosperity: Fact or Myth*, 45–46; Ashdown, "Confessions of an Automobilist," 787–88. Italics are in the original.

34. Lynd and Lynd, *Middletown*, 265. Italics and blank space are in the original.

35. Bell, *Contradictions of Capitalism*, 67; Sklar, *Movie-Made America*, 125, 137.

36. *RST*, 209.

37. Quoted in Klingaman, *Year of the Great Crash*, 184–85.

38. Hurlock, *Psychology of Dress*, 115–16, 142.

39. *Historical Statistics*, 400; *RST*, 209; Slosson, *Great Crusade and After*, 393–95.

40. Slosson, *Great Crusade and After*, 389–90; Sullivan, *Our Times*, 548, 574; James Lincoln Collier, *The Rise of Selfishness in America* (New York, 1991), 170–72; George W. Gray, "Signing Off on the First Ten Years," *World's Work*, December 1930, 47–48.

41. Robert W. McChesney, *Telecommunications, Mass Media, and Democracy: The Battle for the Control of U.S. Broadcasting, 1928–1935* (New York, 1993), 14; Bent, *Ballyhoo*, 297, 304; Bent, *Strange Bedfellows*, 226.

42. McChesney, *Telecommunications, Mass Media, and Democracy*, 3–5, 17–18, 25–31; Daniel Czitrom, *Media and the American Mind from Morse to McLuhan* (Chapel Hill, 1982), 78–79; *RST*, 211; Gray, "Signing Off on the First Ten Years," 48.

43. Gray, "Signing Off on the First Ten Years," 86; Susan Smulyan, *Selling Radio* (Washington, D.C., 1994), 68–70.

44. *RST*, 215; Bent, *Ballyhoo*, 296; Mowry, *Twenties*, 65–66.

45. Mowry, *Twenties*, 67.

46. *Time*, April 15 and October 7, 1929; Francis Wallace, "This Football Business," *Saturday Evening Post*, September 28, 1929, 10.

47. *RST*, 928–31; *Time*, October 7, 1929; Frazier Hunt, "Million-Dollar Football: An Interview with W. H. Taft, Chief Justice," *Cosmopolitan*, November 1929, 30–31.

48. Sullivan, *Our Times*, 589, 649; *RST*, 926; *NYT*, October 19, 1924; Slosson, *Great Crusade and After*, 280.

49. Slosson, *Great Crusade and After*, 271; Warren I. Susman, *Culture as History* (New York, 1984), 142. For Rice, see Charles Fountain, *Sportswriter: The Life and Times of Grantland Rice* (New York, 1993).

50. Collier, *Rise of Selfishness in America*, 103; *RST*, lii; Prothro, *Dollar Decade*, 7, 10; Robert L. Duffus, "The Age of Play," *Independent*, December 20, 1924, 539.

51. *RST*, 920, 952; Soule, *Prosperity Decade*, 150–51; Duffus, "Age of Play," 540.

52. Klingaman, *Year of the Great Crash*, 216.

53. Duffus, "Age of Play," 540.

Chapter 6

1. Quoted in Susman, *Culture as History*, 127–28.

2. The McPherson episode is taken from Mayo, "Aimee Rises from the Sea," 138–40; McWilliams, "Aimee Semple McPherson," 66–72; and Thomas, *Storming Heaven*, 38–122.

3. Mayo, "Aimee Semple McPherson," 139.

4. Ibid., 140. Italics are in original.

5. Allen, *Only Yesterday*, 133; Sullivan, *Our Times*, 552, 623; *RST*, xxvi, 134; Warren, *Hoover and the Great Depression*, 4; *Outlook*, January 5, 1928, 139, and February 29, 1928, 323.

6. Marchand, *Advertising the American Dream*, 121–32; *RST*, 979–80; Truman Moore, *Nouveaumania: The American Passion for Novelty and How It Led Us Astray* (New York, 1975), 25.

7. Kennedy, *Freedom from Fear*, 22; *RST*, 878; David A. Hounshell, *From the American System to Mass Production, 1800–1932* (Baltimore, 1984), 263–93; Marchand, *Advertising the American Dream*, 7; Olney, *Buy Now, Pay Later*, 127.

8. Marchand, *Advertising the American Dream*, 115; Leach, *Land of Desire*, 375.

9. Brooks, *Once in Golconda*, 90; *RST*, 234.

10. Sullivan, *Our Times*, 593–94; Mowry, *Twenties*, 159. The term "mind cure" comes from Leach, *Land of Desire*, 225–62.

11. John Moody, "The New Era in Wall Street," *Atlantic Monthly*, August 1928, 255–62.

12. André Siegfried, "The Gulf Between," *Atlantic Monthly*, March 1928, 293; Noble, *America by Design*, 103, 279–80, 310; Charles A. Beard, ed., *Whither Mankind* (New York, 1928), 99.

13. Soule, *Prosperity Decade*, 153, 156.

14. Pecora, *Wall Street Under Oath*, 14–15; Allen, *Lords of Creation*, 376; Chernow, *House of Morgan*, 254–301.

15. Chase, *Prosperity: Fact or Myth*, 10–11.

16. Sobel, *Great Bull Market*, 64–65, and *Big Board*, 240–41.

17. Allen, *Lords of Creation*, 317; Barrie A. Wigmore, *The Crash and Its Aftermath: A History of Securities Markets in the United States, 1929–1933* (Westport, Conn., 1985), 106–7.

18. White, *Crashes and Panics*, 147; *NYT*, September 14, 1929.

19. Hugh Bullock, *The Story of Investment Companies* (New York, 1959), 15, 19–20; Carosso, *Investment Banking in America*, 287; White, *Crashes and Panics*, 147.

20. Bullock, *Story of Investment Companies*, 21–22, 28–29; Galbraith, *Great Crash*, 51–52.

21. Sobel, *Big Board*, 258–59; Pecora, *Wall Street Under Oath*, 207–13; White, *Crashes and Panics*, 147. Leveraging means basically using borrowed money to buy securities that earn more profit than the cost of the loan. In effect the transaction involves little or no use of the borrower's own money.

22. *Time*, July 22, 1929; Sarnoff, *Jesse Livermore*, 75–82.

23. Herbert Hoover, *The Memoirs of Herbert Hoover: The Great Depression, 1929–1941* (New York, 1941), 9; Galbraith, *Great Crash*, 32; Chandler, *Benjamin*

Strong, 199, 241–42, 255; Friedman and Schwartz, *Monetary History*, 288; Wicker, *Federal Reserve Monetary Policy*, 77–94.

24. Chandler, *Benjamin Strong*, 328–29, 423, 427–28.

25. Ibid., 291–331; Sobel, *Great Bull Market*, 56–57.

26. Chandler, *Benjamin Strong*, 351–59. For details on the complex European situation, see ibid., 360–80, and Eichengreen, *Golden Fetters*, 187–216.

27. Ibid., 375–80; O'Connor, *Mellon's Millions*, 308. The conference included Montague Norman of England, Hjalmar Schacht of Germany, and Charles Rist of France.

28. Chandler, *Benjamin Strong*, 377, 438–41; Noyes, *Market Place*, 315.

29. Chandler, *Benjamin Strong*, 435–49. Wicker, *Federal Reserve Monetary Policy*, 95–116, takes issue with Chandler on several points and offers some useful detail.

30. The first set of figures, based on Standard & Poor indexes, is taken from Chandler, *Benjamin Strong*, 425; the second set, reflecting the average highs for the Dow Jones industrials, is calculated from the figures in Pierce, *Dow Jones Averages*.

31. Chandler, *Benjamin Strong*, 427–33; Friedman and Schwartz, *Monetary History*, 254.

32. Chandler, *Benjamin Strong*, 427.

33. Weisberger, *Dream Maker*, 303–7.

34. Ibid., 304–5, 308–12. Weisberger includes some examples of specific gains and losses in 1927 and a detailed description of Raymere.

35. Ibid., 305–6.

36. Ibid., 305, 317–21.

37. Thurman Arnold, "The Crash—And What It Meant," in Leighton, *Aspirin Age*, 216, 220.

38. Leuchtenburg, *Perils of Prosperity*, 113–18; Hicks, *Republican Ascendancy*, 33–49.

39. White, *Puritan in Babylon*, 359–61; Fuess, *Calvin Coolidge*, 370, 378, 392–95.

40. Coolidge, *Autobiography*, 241; Fuess, *Calvin Coolidge*, 395–97.

41. McCoy, *Calvin Coolidge*, 384–87; Burner, *Herbert Hoover*, 192.

42. Burner, *Herbert Hoover*, 3–62. For Hoover's early life and career, see also George H. Nash, *The Life of Herbert Hoover: The Engineer, 1874–1914* (New York, 1983) and *The Life of Herbert Hoover: The Humanitarian, 1914–1917* (New York, 1988).

43. Burner, *Herbert Hoover*, 72–114.

44. Ibid., 115–58.

45. Ibid., 159–62; Warren, *Hoover and the Great Depression*, 27.

46. Warren, *Hoover and the Great Depression*, 26–29; Burner, *Herbert Hoover*, 160–67; Kennedy, *Freedom from Fear*, 48.

47. Burner, *Herbert Hoover*, 58, 64.

48. Ibid., 192–93; Kennedy, *Freedom from Fear*, 34; Warren, *Hoover and the Great Depression*, 30; Romasco, *Poverty of Abundance*, 207.

49. Burner, *Herbert Hoover*, 193–95.

50. Ibid., 197–201.

51. Ibid., 245–46; Hoover, *Memoirs*, 5–6, 11.

52. Noyes, *Market Place*, 320–21; NYT, January 5–7, 1928; *Literary Digest*, January 21, 1928, 70–71; White, *Puritan in Babylon*, 388–92.

53. Sobel, *Coolidge*, 379; Chandler, *Benjamin Strong*, 454–55. The Dow Jones figures are for industrial stocks; the *Times* quotations embrace a combination of 50 industrial and rail stocks.

54. *NYT*, March 13 and 14, 1928; Allen, *Only Yesterday*, 244–47.

55. *NYT*, March 13 and 14, 1928.

56. SEP, 36–38.

57. *NYT*, March 13 and 17, 1928.

Chapter 7

1. Quoted in Chase, *Prosperity: Fact or Myth*, 24–25.

2. *NYT*, June 12 and 13, 1928; *WSJ*, June 12 and 13, 1928. Here and throughout the remaining chapters, unless otherwise indicated, all figures for stock prices are taken and/or computed from the *NYT* for 1928–30 and Pierce, *Dow Jones Averages*.

3. *NYT*, June 12 and 13, 1928; *WSJ*, June 12–22, 1928. Both Allen, *Only Yesterday*, 249, and Brooks, *Once in Golconda*, 95, err in stating that the market recovered within a few days and surged upward.

4. Chandler, *Benjamin Strong*, 455, 471–72; Wicker, *Federal Reserve Monetary Policy*, 117–28. Unless otherwise indicated, all data on brokers' loans are taken from tables published regularly in the *NYT* and the *WSJ* for 1928–30, and all calculations are derived from this data.

5. NYSE 29, 35, 37, 70–3, 109; Sobel, *Big Board*, 264; Galbraith, *Great Crash*, 71–72; Patterson, *Great Boom and Panic*, 14.

6. Wigmore, *Crash and Its Aftermath*, 26; Patterson, *Great Boom and Panic*, 15; Robert Ryan, "Brokers and 'Suckers,' " *Nation* 127 (August 15, 1928), 154–55. Ryan gives several examples of ways brokers maximized profits at the expense of such customers. For a list of branch offices in New York, see *NYT*, July 2, 1929.

7. Ryan, "Brokers and 'Suckers' " 155–56.

8. *NYT*, August 6, 1929; Eunice Fuller Barnard, "Ladies of the Ticker," *North American Review* (April 1929), 405–7; Patterson, *Great Boom and Panic*, 17.

9. Katharine Dayton, "This Little Pig Went to Market," *Saturday Evening Post*, March 23, 1929, 29.

10. Patterson, *Great Boom and Panic*, 17; Barnard, "Ladies of the Ticker," 408–10; *Time*, March 24, 1930. McCann was convicted of all charges in 1930. See also Barnard's feature article in *NYT*, June 23, 1929.

11. Brooks, *Once in Golconda*, 87–89.

12. Ibid., 199–200; Chernow, *House of Morgan*, 303.

13. Patterson, *Great Boom and Panic*, 50; Thomas and Morgan-Witts, *Day the Bubble Burst*, 6–7; Brooks, *Once in Golconda*, 65–66.

14. SEP, 63–66; Pecora, *Wall Street Under Oath*, 169–83.

15. Patterson, *Great Boom and Panic*, 38; SEP, 32–33; Chernow, *House of Morgan*, 307.

16. Noyes, *Market Place*, 220; SEP, 44–45.

17. SEP, 44; Lloyd Wendt, *The Wall Street Journal* (Chicago, 1982), 222–23; Edward E. Scharff, *Worldly Power: The Making of the Wall Street Journal* (New York, 1986), 37–38. I am grateful to Angela Santoro of the *Wall Street Journal* for providing me with employment records and other information on Edmonson and Gomber.

18. Galbraith, *Great Crash*, 54–55; Carosso, *Investment Banking in America*, 287; Wigmore, *Crash and Its Aftermath*, 40; Garet Garrett, "Wall Street and Washington," *Saturday Evening Post*, December 28, 1929, 80–81.

19. Paul C. Cabot, "The Investment Trust," *Atlantic Monthly*, March 1929, 404–5; *WSJ*, January 26, 1929; Fisher, *Stock Market Crash—and After*, 268.

20. Adolf A. Berle and Gardiner C. Means, *The Modern Corporation and Private Property* (New York, 1968), 184. This is the revised edition of the 1932 classic.

21. Allen, *Lords of Creation*, 255; *RST*, 241.

22. Forrest McDonald, *Insull* (Chicago, 1962), 1–103.

23. Ibid., 104–213.

24. Ibid., 203–5, 210; Carosso, *Investment Banking in America*, 259.

25. McDonald, *Insull*, 247.

26. Ibid., 248–53, 275.

27. Ibid., 276–82.

28. This profile is taken from the biographical sketch of the brothers by Herbert W. Harwood Jr. in Keith L. Bryant Jr., *Encyclopedia of Business History and Biography: Railroads in the Age of Regulation, 1900–1980* (New York, 1988), 450–58, hereafter referred to as Harwood, Van Sweringens. See also Allen, *Lords of Creation*, 293–94.

29. Harwood, Van Sweringens, 455; SEP, 364–65; Pecora, *Wall Street Under Oath*, 214–17. All three sources detail the complex transaction. The New York Central had to sell the Nickel Plate because the 1914 Clayton Antitrust Act made possession of a directly competing line illegal.

30. Berle and Means, *Modern Corporation and Private Property*, 183; Harwood, Van Sweringens, 455.

31. Harwood, Van Sweringens, 454–56; SEP, 366–69; Pecora, *Wall Street Under Oath*, 218–21.

32. SEP, 370–73; Pecora, *Wall Street Under Oath*, 221–22; Harwood, Van Sweringens, 456.

33. Allen, *Lords of Creation*, 296–97.

34. Kennedy, *Freedom from Fear*, 31; Burner, *Herbert Hoover*, 197, 204; Romasco, *Poverty of Abundance*, 202.

35. Burner, *Herbert Hoover*, 208–11.

36. Chandler, *Benjamin Strong*, 460–61, 473; Hoover, *Memoirs*, 9.

37. Chandler, *Benjamin Strong*, 179; NCAB 53:563; Eichengreen, *Golden Fetters*, 209.

38. *NYT*, December 2, 1928. This feature article, written not by Noyes but by W. F. Wamsley, contains some errors, such as declaring that the first 4-million-share days occurred in September.

39. Ibid.; Sobel, *Big Board*, 247.

40. *NYT*, December 2, 1928.

41. Wigmore, *Crash and Its Aftermath*, 94. The other sources included foreign investors and wealthy American individuals seeking safe, short-term havens that paid well.

42. McCoy, *Calvin Coolidge*, 392–94.

43. *NYT*, December 3, 1928.

44. Ibid., December 4–9, 1928.

45. Ibid., December 9, 1928.

46. Ibid., January 1, 1929.

47. Ibid.

48. Ibid.

49. Klingaman, *Year of the Great Crash*, 54.

Chapter 8

1. Garet Garrett, "Wall Street and Washington," 80.

2. Sullivan, *Our Times*, 448; Brooks, *Once in Golconda*, 99.

3. Noyes, *Market Place*, 328.

4. Allen, *Lords of Creation*, 273; SEP, 566–67; Galbraith, *Great Crash*, 65–66; Bullock, *Story of Investment Companies*, 33.

5. *WSJ*, February 9, 1929; Bullock, *Story of Investment Companies*, 37; *Time*, February 25, 1929; *NYT*, September 14, 1929; SEP, 363.

6. SEP, 374–76, details these complicated transactions. See also Berle and Means, *Modern Corporation and Private Property*, 69–71.

7. SEP, 101–2, 376; Pecora, *Wall Street Under Oath*, 25–34. Alleghany also assumed a Van Sweringen liability of slightly over $1 million. Pecora lists many of the prominent individuals on the "preferred list." These early buyers purchased the stock on a "when issued" basis.

8. Pecora, *Wall Street Under Oath*, 31–33; SEP, 101–2, 105. Chernow, *House of Morgan*, 309, called the Alleghany offering the "master boondoggle of 1929."

9. Pecora, *Wall Street Under Oath*, 21–24; SEP, 104–6; McDonald, *Insull*, 248–51.

10. SEP, 104, 106, 110–15.

11. Ibid., 107–10.

12. Ibid., 126–33. Cleveland and Huertas, *Citibank*, 177–80, offer a vigorous defense of the bank's Peruvian loans but say nothing about Minas Gerais.

13. Ibid., 166–69; Pecora, *Wall Street Under Oath*, 92–93, 105–11.

14. SEP, 168–73; Pecora, *Wall Street Under Oath*, 110–12.

15. SEP, 173–79. Three of the six private corporations were Canadian and used chiefly for the purpose of tax evasion.

16. SEP, 183–99.

17. Ibid. The quotation is on 179.

18. Brown's story is in ibid., 2170–82.

19. The complete transaction, as explained by Brown, was to buy bonds selling below par and use the difference to pay off the loans when the bonds came back to par, as (he was told) they surely would. A list of the securities bought for Brown's portfolio is in SEP, 2174–75.

20. Brown produced the confirmation slips for all the purchases while testifying before the Senate committee on banking and currency. Ferdinand Pecora, the committee counsel, noted that they were "so numerous . . . that I do not think it necessary to spread them all on the record." SEP, 2176.

21. *WSJ*, January 4, 1929; *NYT*, January 26, February 7, and February 8, 1929; NYSE29, 33, 60–61, 77, 79; Thomas and Morgan-Witts, *Day the Bubble Burst*, 1.

22. Tom Schachtman, *The Day America Crashed* (New York, 1979), 90–91; Thomas and Morgan-Witts, *Day the Bubble Burst*, 2–3.

23. Ibid., 89–91.

24. *NYT*, January 31 and March 3, 1929. The average volume for January included Saturday half days, when trading took place from 10:00 A.M. to noon. The drop in volume below 3 million shares does not include Saturdays but only full days of trading. Galbraith, *Great Crash*, 96–97, notes this same "arresting headline" in the New York papers on September 22, but it had appeared with some regularity at least since February, as noted above.

25. Klingaman, *Year of the Great Crash*, 152; Chandler, *Benjamin Strong*, 465.

26. Chandler, *Benjamin Strong*, 424–25.

27. Ibid.; *WSJ*, February 20, 1929.

28. Chandler, *Benjamin Strong*, 466; Friedman and Schwartz, *Monetary History*, 254–57; Wicker, *Federal Reserve Monetary Policy*, 129–37; Eichengreen, *Golden Fetters*, 216–21.

29. *NYT*, February 7–12, 1929; *WSJ*, February 2, 4, and 14, 1929; *Time*, February 25, 1929. Galbraith, *Great Crash*, 39–40, said of this letter, "It is impossible

to imagine a milder, more tentative, more palpably panic-stricken communiqué than that issued by the Board. . . . Clearly the Federal Reserve was less interested in checking speculation than in detaching itself from responsibility for the speculation that was going on." However, Wicker, *Federal Reserve Monetary Policy*, 136, properly labels Galbraith's account "seriously misleading."

30. *NYT*, February 15–17, 1929; Chandler, *Benjamin Strong*, 466; Friedman and Schwartz, *Monetary History*, 258–60; Wicker, *Federal Reserve Monetary Policy*, 137–39.

31. *NYT*, March 1–3 and 8, 1929; Hoover, *Memoirs*, 16; *Commercial and Financial Chronicle*, March 9, 1929, 1444.

32. *NYT*, March 8, 1929; *Commercial and Financial Chronicle*, March 9, 1929, 1444. Warburg made his remarks in the Acceptance Bank's annual report.

33. *Time*, March 18, 1929; Galbraith, *Great Crash*, 32–33; Noyes, *Market Place*, 324; *WSJ*, March 8, 1929. The description of Young is from Galbraith, who is one of the harshest critics of the board. "The Federal Reserve," he added, "was helpless only because it wanted to be." Galbraith, *Great Crash*, 37.

34. *NYT*, March 15, 17, and 23, 1929. Kindleberger, *World in Depression*, 96–97, explains the board's refusal to approve the rate increase by noting that "it was too soon after the completion of the Treasury's financing at 4.5 percent." That reasoning would not account for the later denials.

35. *NYT*, March 23–27, 1929.

36. Ibid., March 27 and 28, 1929; *WSJ*, October 21, 1929.

37. *NYT*, March 27, 1929; Friedman and Schwartz, *Monetary History*, 260–61; Huertas and Silverman, "Charles E. Mitchell," 99–100. Curiously, Wicker, *Federal Reserve Monetary Policy*, having taken Galbraith to task, says nothing at all about this crucial episode.

38. *NYT*, March 28 and 29, 1929; Galbraith, *Great Crash*, 34; Friedman and Schwartz, *Monetary History*, 260–61.

39. *NYT*, March 29–April 1, 1929; Friedman and Schwartz, *Monetary History*, 260–61; Huertas and Silverman, "Charles E. Mitchell," 100. Historians have been equally divided over Mitchell's actions. Most earlier accounts are strongly critical. For example, Brooks, *Once in Golconda*, 100, depicts Mitchell as "coolly and brazenly defying the Fed's warning. . . . Government interference was humiliated and discredited; now anything went." Galbraith, *Great Crash*, 42–43, called Mitchell's action "the Wall Street counterpart of Mayor Hague's famous manifesto, 'I am the law in Jersey City.' "

40. Weisberger, *Dream Maker*, 327; *NYT*, April 3 and 5, 1929.

41. Weisberger, *Dream Maker*, 327–28; *NYT*, April 15, 18, and 19, 1929. To elaborate on Mitchell's point: the capital gains tax dissuaded many individuals from selling their stocks and taking their profits, because stocks had already risen so much in value that the tax on the gain would be prohibitive. The effect was to curtail an important selling force that normally dampened a rising market.

42. Hoover, *Memoirs*, 18; Leach, *Land of Desire*, 349–50; *WSJ*, February 12, February 21, April 9, April 16, May 8, and May 23, 1929; *NYT*, March 21, 1929.

43. *Time*, January 7, 1929; Brooks, *Once in Golconda*, 94; *WSJ*, May 15 and 21, 1929.

44. *WSJ*, February 14, 1929; *NYT*, May 1, 1929.

45. Volume given in thousands of shares. The average swing is the average of the 12 monthly averages for each year.

46. *NYT*, April 6 and May 1, 1929; *WSJ*, April 5, 1929. Galbraith, *Great Crash*, 45, says that "after the defeat by Mitchell in March, the Federal Reserve retired from the field. There continued to be some slight anxiety as to what it might do." The evidence indicates that the anxiety was far more than slight and continued well into the summer.

47. *WSJ*, April 22, April 23, April 27, and May 18, 1929; *NYT*, May 4, 1929.

48. Friedman and Schwartz, *Monetary History*, 261–63.

49. *NYT*, May 18–28, 1929; *WSJ*, May 21, 1929; Wicker, *Federal Reserve Monetary Policy*, 139.

50. *WSJ*, May 29, 1929.

51. *NYT*, June 13, 15, and 30, 1929.

52. SEP, 2176–77; Groucho Marx, *Groucho and Me* (New York, 1974), 193–94; A. Marx, *Life with Groucho*, 120–21.

53. A. Marx, *Life with Groucho*, 120–22; G. Marx, *Groucho and Me*, 188–94. The accounts of father and son differ in some details on these episodes.

54. Friedman and Schwartz, *Monetary History*, 262–64; Wicker, *Federal Reserve Monetary Policy*, 140–41; *NYT*, June 6 and July 2, 1929. Young was present at the June 5 meeting.

55. *NYT*, June 6, July 14, and August 2, 1929; *WSJ*, July 4 and 18, 1929.

56. *WSJ*, July 16 and 20, 1929; *NYT*, July 24 and 30, 1929.

57. *NYT*, August 4 and 6, 1929; *WSJ*, August 7, 1929.

58. Thomas and Morgan-Witts, *Day the Bubble Burst*, 229–31; *NYT*, August 4, 8, and 18, 1929.

59. *NYT*, August 2–4, 9–10, and 16, 1929; Wicker, *Federal Reserve Monetary Policy*, 141–42.

60. *NYT*, August 22, 25, and 30, 1929.

61. Ibid., August 28, 1929.

Chapter 9

1. *WSJ*, September 4, 1929.

2. Brooks, *Once in Golconda*, 81–82; Lefevre, "Little Fellow in Wall Street," 100; Kennedy, *Freedom from Fear*, 37.

3. Lefevre, "Little Fellow in Wall Street," 7.

4. *NYT*, August 11, August 20–22, and September 12, 1929; *Time*, August 5, 1929; Fisher, *Stock Market Crash—and After*, 5; Bullock, *Story of Investment Companies*, 33–40; *WSJ*, September 19, 1929.

5. *WSJ*, September 20, 1929; *NYT*, September 1, 1929; Allen, *Lords of Creation*, 319–25. A list of the bank mergers is in *NYT*, September 1, 1929.

6. SEP, 167–70; Pecora, *Wall Street Under Oath*, 92–96. See the sales contest "flash," dated September 27, 1929, in Pecora, *Wall Street Under Oath*, 91–92.

7. *NYT*, September 2, 4, 12, and September 20, 1929; *WSJ*, September 17, 1929.

8. Thomas and Morgan-Witts, *Day the Bubble Burst*, 219–23. This book has possibly the worst method of citing sources ever devised, making it difficult if not impossible to trace the sources used for specific episodes. In this case, however, the authors did interview a much older Pat Bologna, and doubtless most of his story derives from his telling of it.

9. Klingaman, *Year of the Great Crash*, 188, 211; Bernard M. Baruch, *Baruch: The Public Years* (New York, 1960), 222–25; Grant, *Bernard Baruch*, 218–23; Burner, *Herbert Hoover*, 247; McDonald, *Insull*, 282. Grant itemizes the transactions contradicting Baruch's assertion that he sold out of the market.

10. Thomas and Morgan-Witts, *Day the Bubble Burst*, 143, 250, 356.

11. *WSJ*, July 22 and August 21, 1929; *NYT*, August 1, 8, 11, 27, and 29, 1929. Later writers tend to support this view of the economy. Chase, *Prosperity: Fact or Myth*, 15, argues that "the underlying structure of prosperity was proceeding at par, or a little better than par, when the stock market collapsed. Declining business was not responsible for declining security prices." Galbraith, *Great Crash*, 95, agrees that "there were no reasons for expecting disaster. . . . The crash did not come—as some have suggested—because the market suddenly became aware that a serious depression was in the offing." Eugene N. White, *Crashes and Panics*, 177, adds that "the decline in all indices came only when the October figures were published after the crash." See also Wigmore, *Crash and Its Aftermath*, 101–2.

12. *NYT*, September 6, 1929; Thomas and Morgan-Witts, *Day the Bubble Burst*, 283.

13. *NYT*, September 6, 1929; New York *Herald-Tribune*, September 6, 1929.

14. *NYT*, September 6, 1929. Thomas and Morgan-Witts, *Day the Bubble Burst*, 282–83, have the news arriving about 12:30 P.M. and describe the reactions of Raskob, Durant, and others as being to a sudden panic. The *Times* account, however, is very specific about the time of 2:00 P.M.

15. *NYT*, September 6, 1929; Patterson, *Great Boom and Panic*, 89; *WSJ*, September 6, 1929. *WSJ* includes some excerpts from Babson's prophecy made on September 11, 1926.

16. *NYT*, September 6–8, 1929; Patterson, *Great Boom and Panic*, 90.

17. *NYT*, September 11, 15, and 19, 1929.

18. Ibid., September 4–26, 1929.

19. Ibid., September 25, 1929; *WSJ*, September 17 and 24, 1929.

20. *Forbes*, October 1, 1929, 11, quoted in Harold Bierman Jr., *The Great Myths of 1929 and the Lessons to Be Learned* (Westport, Conn., 1991), 177–78.

21. Thomas and Morgan-Witts, *Day the Bubble Burst*, 290–94; *WSJ*, September 23, 1929; *NYT*, September 26 and 27, 1929.

22. *NYT*, September 25–27, 1929.

23. Ibid., September 28, 1929; *WSJ*, September 28, 1929.

24. Thomas and Morgan-Witts, *Day the Bubble Burst*, 312–14.

25. *NYT*, September 29, 1929.

26. NYSE29, 9, 45–50, 95; *Commercial and Financial Chronicle*, October 12, 1929; Fisher, *The Stock Market Crash—and After*, 5. The Exchange report concluded that "undoubtedly the expansion of these [brokers'] loans during the first three-quarters of 1929 was largely due to increased listing of shares." NYSE29, 45. *WSJ*, October 8, 1929, noted that "of late there has been more or less 'backing up' of excess production. . . . A practical result . . . is a net increase in the volume of all securities seeking buyers."

27. *NYT*, October 2, 1929; *WSJ*, October 1, 1929. Since stocks bought on margin served as collateral for the loans that bought them, every drop in the stocks' price reduced their worth as collateral, i.e. impaired their margin. This required the holder to put up more cash to cover the difference.

28. *WSJ*, October 3, 1929; *NYT*, October 1 and 4, 1929.

29. *NYT*, October 4–11, 1929; *WSJ*, October 8, 1929.

30. *NYT*, October 6, 1929.

31. Ibid., October 7 and 9, 1929; Edward Angly, *Oh Yeah?* (New York, 1931), 38.

32. *NYT*, October 13, 1929; Dice, *New Levels in the Stock Market*, passim. Some recent scholars have defended Dice's and Fisher's views. See, for example, Gerald Sirkin, "The Stock Market of 1929 Revisited: A Note," *Business History Review* (Summer 1975), 223–31, and Eugene N. White, "When the Ticker Ran Late: The Stock Market Boom and Crash of 1929," in White, *Crashes and Panics*, 150–54. For a critical reaction, see the editorial in *NYT*, October 20, 1929.

33. *NYT*, October 16, 1929. Ayres's comments appeared in the monthly bulletin published by the Cleveland Trust Company.

34. Ibid.; *WSJ*, October 17, 1929.

35. *WSJ*, October 12 and 17, 1929; Patterson, *Great Boom and Panic*, 105–6; *NYT*, October 15, 1929.

36. NYT, October 16–20, 1929; *WSJ*, October 18–21, 1929.

37. *WSJ*, October 18 and 21, 1929; *NYT*, October 18 and 19, 1929. Both papers picked up the "leaping bear" remark.

38. *NYT*, October 17–21, 1929.

39. Ibid., October 20 and 21, 1929; *WSJ*, October 22, 1929; *Time*, October 28, 1929.

40. *NYT*, October 21, 1929.

41. *WSJ*, October 21, 1929.

42. Ibid., October 22, 1929; *NYT*, October 22, 1929.

43. *WSJ*, October 23, 1929; *NYT*, October 23, 1929.

44. Chernow, *House of Morgan*, 314–15. Later an embittered Hoover wrote that Lamont's memorandum "makes curious reading today." Hoover, *Memoirs*, 17.

45. *NYT*, October 22–24, 1929; Matthew Josephson, *Edison: A Biography* (New York, 1959), 476–81; Chernow, *House of Morgan*, 315; Grant, *Bernard Baruch*, 223.

Chapter 10

1. *WSJ*, March 29, 1929.

2. Brooks, *Once in Golconda*, 109.

3. *NYT*, October 24, 1929; *WSJ*, October 24, 1929; Allen, *Only Yesterday*, 270.

4. *NYT*, October 24, 1929.

5. Ibid.

6. Thomas and Morgan-Witts, *Day the Bubble Burst*, 352–53.

7. Ibid., 355; Allen, *Only Yesterday*, 271.

8. *NYT*, October 25, 1929; *WSJ*, October 25, 1929; Thomas and Morgan-Witts, *Day the Bubble Burst*, 358. Unless otherwise indicated, the events of Black Thursday are drawn from these sources.

9. Thomas and Morgan-Witts, *Day the Bubble Burst*, 358.

10. Ibid., 356.

11. Ibid., 356–57.

12. Apropos of this point, Soule, *Prosperity Decade*, 290–91, observed that "the course of affairs was a logical and natural development of what had gone before. . . . The delusions that prevailed were shared by the leaders of finance, business, government, and even many academic experts in economics. Indeed, they were not only shared but loudly proclaimed. . . . The outcome was . . . comic enough to furnish material for a musical extravaganza."

13. Lefevre, "Little Fellow in Wall Street," 6; *NYT*, October 25, 1929.

14. Claud Cockburn, *A Discord of Trumpets* (New York, 1956), 191–94.

15. Ibid., 190.

16. The *Times* reported the bid to be for 25,000 shares. Later accounts reduced it to 10,000.

17. *WSJ*, October 25, 1929.

18. *NYT*, October 25 and 26, 1929. Volume on the ship that day reached nearly 20,000 shares.

19. Ibid., October 25, 1929; *WSJ*, October 25, 1929.

20. *NYT*, October 25 and 26, 1929; Wigmore, *Crash and Its Aftermath*, 10–11. Later the Guggenheim brothers joined the pool but did not attend any of the meetings.

21. *NYT*, October 26, 1929, contains Hoover's statement and a sampling of comments from businessmen and brokerage firms.

22. Thomas and Morgan-Witts, *Day the Bubble Burst*, 370.

23. Ibid.; Patterson, *Great Boom and Panic*, 130–32.

24. *NYT*, October 26 and 27, 1929.

25. Ibid., October 27, 1929.

26. Ibid., October 27 and 28, 1929.

27. *WSJ*, October 28, 1929.

28. *NYT*, October 26, 1929; Lefevre, "Little Fellow in Wall Street," 100.

29. Lefevre, "Little Fellow in Wall Street," 97; Noyes, *Market Place*, 335; Edwin Lefevre, "The Bigger They Are—," *Saturday Evening Post*, January 11, 1930, 123.

30. Lefevre, "Little Fellow in Wall Street," 7.

31. *NYT*, October 27, 1929.

32. Ibid.; Galbraith, *Great Crash*, 101. The *Times* article includes excerpts from the replies of several chain stores.

33. Klingaman, *Year of the Great Crash*, 276–77.

34. *NYT*, October 29, 1929.

35. Unless otherwise indicated, the events of Monday are drawn from ibid.

36. Huertas and Silverman, "Charles E. Mitchell," 93–94; Pecora, *Wall Street Under Oath*, 153–54. Huertas and Silverman provide more detail on how the falling price of National City threatened the merger with the Corn Exchange Bank.

37. SEP, 2177–78.

38. Grant, *Bernard Baruch*, 225–26.

39. Thomas and Morgan-Witts, *Day the Bubble Burst*, 384.

40. SEP, 2178–79.

41. *NYT*, October 30, 1929; Patterson, *Great Boom and Panic*, 146; *Time*, November 4, 1929. Unless otherwise indicated, the day's events are drawn from *NYT*, October 30, 1929.

42. Patterson, *Great Boom and Panic*, 148; Allen, *Only Yesterday*, 277; Thomas and Morgan-Witts, *Day the Bubble Burst*, 392.

43. Robert J. Shiller, *Irrational Exuberance* (Princeton, 2000); Galbraith, *Great Crash*, 115. Shiller's useful concept for explaining market behavior is poorly served in his shallow discussion of the crash of 1929, which almost completely ignores the complexity of the context in which it occurred. He borrowed the phrase "irrational exuberance" from Alan Greenspan, who used it in a 1996 speech.

44. Wicker, *Federal Reserve Monetary Policy*, 144–45; NYSE29, 43.

45. Sobel, *Panic on Wall Street*, 387–88. Sobel observed that "had recovery followed, Harrison would be remembered today as one of the heroes of the pe-

riod. But there was no full-scale recovery. . . . As a result, Harrison is an all-but-forgotten figure."

46. *NYT*, October 30, 1929; Wigmore, *Crash and Its Aftermath*, 96–98; Allen, *Only Yesterday*, 277. Put another way, the banks took over accounts where individuals could not meet margin calls but held the stock they acquired rather than throwing it on the market for whatever it would bring; in some cases they let people go without meeting margin requirements.

47. Galbraith, *Great Crash*, 122–23.

48. *NYT*, October 30, 1929.

49. Ibid.

50. Lefevre, "Little Fellow in Wall Street," 97.

51. Ibid.

52. *NYT*, October 30, 1929.

53. Ibid.

54. A. Marx, *Life with Groucho*, 124–25; G. Marx, *Groucho and Me*, 197; Harpo Marx, *Harpo Speaks!* (New York, 1976), 262.

55. SEP, 2178–82.

56. G. Marx, *Groucho and Me*, 197.

57. *NYT*, October 31, 1929.

58. Ibid., October 31 and November 1, 1929; *WSJ*, October 31 and November 1, 1929.

59. Ibid.

60. *WSJ*, October 31, 1929; *NYT*, November 3, 1929.

61. *NYT*, November 1, 1929.

Chapter 11

1. *WSJ*, October 21, 1929.

2. *NYT*, November 1, 1929; *WSJ*, November 2, 1929. For the "prosperity chorus" phrase, see Chase, *Prosperity: Fact or Myth*, 43.

3. *NYT*, November 3–5, 1929; *WSJ*, November 7, 1929. "Why is it," asked the *Journal*, "that a general newspaper, usually with a fairly intelligent financial editor, completely loses its head when the stock market becomes general news?"

4. *NYT*, November 5–10, 1929.

5. Ibid., November 7–14, 1929; *WSJ*, November 7–14, 1929.

6. *NYT*, November 13, 14, and 19, 1929; *WSJ*, November 13 and 14, 1929.

7. *NYT*, November 14, 15, and 22, 1929; *WSJ*, November 14 and 15, 1929; *Time*, November 11, 1929.

8. *NYT*, November 15, 1929; *WSJ*, November 20, 1929.

9. *NYT*, November 8–13 and 17, 1929; Wigmore, *Crash and Its Aftermath*, 44; *Time*, November 18 and 25, 1929. *Time*, November 25, 1929, noted that "to con-

tradict rumors of a suicide wave New York authorities showed that in Manhattan there were only 44 from Oct. 13–Nov. 15, as compared to 53 last year." A detailed version of the Flint embezzlement is scattered through Thomas and Morgan-Witts, *Day the Bubble Burst*.

10. *NYT*, November 10, 11, 17, and 18, 1929; H. Marx, *Harpo Speaks!*, 266.

11. *NYT*, November 18, 1929; *Time*, November 18, 1929.

12. *NYT*, November 4, 11, 15, 17, and 18, 1929.

13. Allen, *Only Yesterday*, 280–81; Chase, *Prosperity: Fact or Myth*, 16, 43.

14. Romasco, *Poverty of Abundance*, 34–35; Hoover, *Memoirs*, 29.

15. Hoover, *Memoirs*, 30.

16. Burner, *Herbert Hoover*, 250. Hoover later wrote the wife of Sinclair Lewis, "*Please* do not use me as a whipping boy for the 'New Era.' I was neither the inventor nor the promoter nor the supporter of the destructive currents of that period. I was the 'receiver' of it when it went into collapse." Burner, *Herbert Hoover*, 330. Burner, 248, also notes that "so earnestly did Hoover believe in the importance of confidence that he later attended a World Series game in Philadelphia simply to make an example of his own serenity." But the game Hoover saw took place on October 14, well before the crash.

17. *NYT*, November 16, 1929.

18. Ibid.. November 16 and 21, 1929; *Time*, November 11 and 25, 1929.

19. *Time*, November 25, 1929; *NYT*, November 20–28, 1929. A summary of Hoover's message to the industrial leaders is in Hoover, *Memoirs*, 43–44.

20. *Time*, December 2, 1929; *NYT*, November 25, 1929.

21. *NYT*, December 4, 1929; Hoover, *Memoirs*, 57.

22. *NYT*, December 5 and 6, 1929; *Time*, December 16, 1929.

23. Romasco, *Poverty of Abundance*, 39; Kennedy, *Freedom from Fear*, 11; *NYT*, November 23 and December 1, 1929.

24. Kennedy, *Freedom from Fear*, 51; Prothro, *Dollar Decade*, 111; Hoover, *Memoirs*, 31.

25. Herbert Stein, *The Fiscal Revolution in America* (Chicago, 1969), 14; U.S. Bureau of the Census, *Statistical Abstract of the United States: 1997* (Washington, 1997), 335; Kennedy, *Freedom from Fear*, 56–57; *Historical Statistics*, 1102; *RST*, 764. Galbraith, *Great Crash*, 145, wrote that "the modest tax cut apart, the President was clearly averse to any large-scale government action to counter the developing depression." But Galbraith offers no suggestions as to what Hoover or the government might have done; indeed, he admitted in his very next sentence, "Nor was it very certain at the time what could be done."

26. Hoover, *Memoirs*, 45, 50; Stein, *Fiscal Revolution in America*, 9; *NYT*, December 1, 1929. For the farm board, see Romasco, *Poverty of Abundance*, 106–15, and Warren, *Herbert Hoover and the Great Depression*, 171–77.

27. SEP, 325–28; Pecora, *Wall Street Under Oath*, 152–58.

28. Pecora, *Wall Street Under Oath*, 154, 161. Pecora was counsel for the Senate investigating committee that produced the SEP report.

29. Weisberger, *Dream Maker*, 331–41; *NYT*, December 13, 1929.

30. *WSJ*, January 4, 1930. The *Journal* calculated that during 1929 the Dow declined 183 points from its high and regained about 50 by year's end. Railroads dropped about 61 points and regained 16, while utilities fell 80 points and recovered 24 of them.

31. Ibid., December 16 and 19, 1929; *NYT*, December 10, 1929.

32. *NYT*, December 15, 1929.

33. Ibid., December 17–26, 1929.

34. Ibid., December 22, 1929.

35. Ibid., December 16, 1929, and January 1, 1930.

36. *WSJ*, December 11, 1929.

37. William Starr Myers and Walter H. Newton, *The Hoover Administration: A Documented Narrative* (New York, 1936), 22; Burner, *Herbert Hoover*, 250; *NYT*, December 8, 1929, and January 1, 1930.

38. *NYT*, January 1, 1930. Of this prediction the *Wall Street Journal* said, "That is, a forecast is most likely to be sound when it is least useful or informing." *WSJ*, January 6, 1930.

Epilogue

1. Klingaman, *Year of the Great Crash*, 290. Italics are in the original.

2. *NYT*, January 3, 5, and 19, 1930.

3. *WSJ*, February 7 and 10, 1930.

4. Ibid., January 10, 1930.

5. *Time*, January 6, 1930.

6. Ibid., January 13, 1930; *WSJ*, January 8, 1930.

7. *NYT*, January 5, 1930; *Time*, January 13, 1930.

8. Ibid.; Chase, *Prosperity: Fact or Myth*, 17.

9. *NYT*, January 13, 1930; *WSJ*, January 13, 1930.

10. Kennedy, *Freedom from Fear*, 57.

11. *NYT*, January 21 and 24, February 12 and 20, 1930.

12. Ibid., February 16 and June 1, 1930.

13. *Time*, July 29, 1929; *NYT*, December 25, 1929, and January 23, 1930; *WSJ*, March 20, 1930. *Time* added that "as steel goes, so goes the country." The figures on automobile production are calculated from data in *WSJ*, April 22, 1930.

14. *WSJ*, January 23, 1930; *NYT*, January 11, 1930.

15. *Time*, January 20, 1930. Much later, some economists and economic historians would elaborate on Fisher's argument. For the fullest example, see

Eichengreen, *Golden Fetters*, who attributed the length and depth of the depression to an unwise and prolonged clinging to the gold standard.

16. *NYT*, January 12 and March 1, 1930. Eichengreen, *Golden Fetters*, 24, observed that "there is no little irony in the fact that inflation was the dominant fear in the depths of the Great Depression, when deflation was the real and present danger."

17. *WSJ*, February 19, 1930.

18. Ibid., February 6, 1930; *NYT*, January 11 and February 2, 10, and 22, 1930.

19. *Time*, February 17, 1930; Myers and Newton, *Hoover Administration*, 35; *NYT*, February 22, 25, and 26, 1930.

20. *NYT*, February 25 and 27, 1930; Klingaman, *Year of the Great Crash*, 178.

21. Romasco, *Poverty of Abundance*, 204; Burner, *Herbert Hoover*, 253; Paul Y. Anderson, "A Cross-Section of Washington," *Nation*, April 9, 1930, 420.

22. McCormick, "Year of the Hoover Method," 2.

23. Joan Hoff-Wilson, "Herbert Hoover: The Popular Image of an Unpopular President," in Lee Nash, ed., *Understanding Herbert Hoover* (Stanford, 1987), 5.

24. Walter Lippmann, "The Peculiar Weakness of Mr. Hoover," *Harper's Magazine*, June 1930, 1–7.

25. Nash, *Understanding Herbert Hoover*, 5; Burner, *Herbert Hoover*, 255; Romasco, *Poverty of Abundance*, 208.

26. *NYT*, March 2, 8, 16, and 17, 1930.

27. Ibid., March 19 and 22, 1930. The gist of Wagner's bills is given in the March 19 issue.

28. Ibid., March 14, 19, 21, 24, and 26, 1930; *WSJ*, March 17, 1930.

29. *NYT*, March 23, 27, and 30 and April 6, 1930.

30. *NYT*, April 15, 21, and 27, 1930; *WSJ*, April 18 and 21, 1930.

31. *NYT*, April 14 and 21, 1930.

32. Ibid., April 21, 1930.

33. *Time*, March 31 and April 14, 1930. The March 31 article includes some sample headlines.

34. Ibid., April 14, 1930.

35. *NYT*, April 6, 10, and 11, 1930; *Time*, April 28, 1930.

36. *NYT*, April 6 and 15, 1930; *Time*, May 5, 1930.

37. Ibid., April 15, 1930.

38. *WSJ*, April 25 and 30, 1930.

39. *NYT*, April 5, 22, 23, and 30 and May 1, 1930; Hoover, *Memoirs*, 48–49.

40. *Time*, May 5, 1930.

41. *NYT*, May 1, 1930.

42. Ibid., May 2–6, 1930.

43. Ibid., May 6, 7, and 12, 1930; Noyes, *Market Place*, 342.

44. *NYT*, May 9, 25, and 26, 1930.

45. Ibid., May 5, 8, 9, and 24, 1930. Allen, *Only Yesterday*, 284, erroneously gives the date of Young's talk as May 8.

46. Romasco, *Poverty of Abundance*, 14.

47. Hoover himself defined federal and state programs as indirect relief. Direct relief was that "given directly to individuals or families through charitable, local, county, municipal, or state action." Hoover, *Memoirs*, 42.

48. Schlesinger, *Crisis of the Old Order*, 231; Stein, *Fiscal Revolution in America*, 22–23; Hoover, *Memoirs*, 47. Of the total private expenditure, nonresidential construction dropped from $5 billion to $4 billion and residential construction from $4 billion to $2.3 billion.

49. *NYT*, June 1, 1930; *Time*, May 12, 1930. The new *Times* index measured steel production, freight car loadings, automobile production, and electric power production.

50. *NYT*, June 3, 1930; Schlesinger, *Crisis of the Old Order*, 231; Stein, *Fiscal Revolution in America*, 21.

51. *Time*, June 2, 1930; *NYT*, June 8–13, 1930.

52. *WSJ*, June 9–11, 1930.

53. Ibid., June 17–19, 1930; *NYT*, June 17–19 and 22, 1930; *Time*, June 23, 1930.

54. *NYT*, June 22, 1930; *WSJ*, June 22, 1930. The *Wall Street Journal* echoed this sentiment: "As depression in the basic industries continues long past the time when so many expected it to yield to trade revival, the voices of exasperation over the alleged failure of the President's 'prosperity conferences' of last November have become a chorus." *WSJ*, June 26, 1930.

55. Noyes, *Market Place*, 343.

56. Kennedy, *Freedom from Fear*, 56.

57. *NYT*, June 22, 1930.

58. Ibid., June 20–30, 1930; *Time*, June 30, 1930.

59. *NYT*, June 29, 1930; *Time*, June 23, 1930.

60. Noyes, *Market Place*, 49, 361.

61. *NYT*, July 8, 1932.

62. Burner, *Herbert Hoover*, 248.

63. *NYT*, April 23, 1945; Fisher, *My Father*, 264; *DAB* 8:14–15.

64. McDonald, *Insull*, 284–333. The quotation is on 333.

65. Burner, *Herbert Hoover*, 338; *DAB* Supp. 2:451–52.

66. Chernow, *House of Morgan*, 359–60, 469–81; Thomas and Morgan-Witts, *Day the Bubble Burst*, 424.

67. *DAB* Supp. 5:744–45.

68. Huertas and Silverman, "Charles E. Mitchell," 82–83, 91–93; *NYT*, December 15, 1955.

69. *NYT*, November 29, 1940.

70. Weisberger, *Dream Maker*, 335–63.

Selected Bibliography

Books

Adams, Samuel Hopkins. *Incredible Era* (New York, 1939).

Adamson, Joe. *Groucho, Harpo, Chico, and Sometimes Zeppo* (New York, 1973).

Alexander, David. *Panic! The Day the Money Stopped* (Evanston, Ill., 1962).

Allen, Frederick Lewis. *The Lords of Creation* (New York, 1935).

———. *Only Yesterday* (New York, 1931).

Angly, Edward. *Oh Yeah?* (New York, 1931).

Arce, Hector. *Groucho* (New York, 1979).

Ayer, N. W., and Son. *In Behalf of Advertising* (Philadelphia, 1929).

Barger, Harold. *Outlay and Income in the United States, 1921–1938* (New York, 1942).

Barnouw, Erik. *A Tower of Babel: A History of Broadcasting in the United States* (New York, 1966).

Baruch, Bernard M. *Baruch:The Public Years* (New York, 1960).

Beard, Charles A., ed. *Whither Mankind* (New York, 1928).

Bent, Silas. *Ballyhoo: The Voice of the Press* (New York, 1927).

———. *Strange Bedfellows: A Review of Politics, Personalities, and the Press* (New York, 1928).

Berle, Adolf A., and Gardiner C. Means. *The Modern Corporation and Private Property*, rev. ed. (New York, 1968).

Bernays, Edward L. *Crystallizing Public Opinion* (New York, 1923).

Bernstein, Michael A. *The Great Depression: Delayed Recovery and Economic Change in America, 1929–1939* (New York, 1987).

Bierman, Harold Jr. *The Causes of the 1929 Stock Market Crash: A Speculative Orgy or a New Era?* (Westport, Conn., 1998).

———. *The Great Myths of 1929 and the Lessons to Be Learned* (Westport, Conn., 1991).

Boyle, Andrew. *Montagu Norman* (London, 1967).

Brooks, John. *The Go-Go Years* (New York, 1973).

———. *Once in Golconda* (New York, 1969).

Brown, William R. *Imagemaker: Will Rogers and the American Dream* (St. Louis, 1970).

Bullock, Hugh. *The Story of Investment Companies* (New York, 1959).

Burner, David. *Herbert Hoover: A Public Life* (New York, 1979).

Cannon, James Jr. *Bishop Cannon's Own Story* (Durham, N.C., 1955).

Cantor, Eddie. *Caught Short! A Saga of Wailing Wall Street* (New York, 1929).

Carosso, Vincent P. *Investment Banking in America: A History* (Cambridge, Mass., 1970).

Carver, T. N. *The Present Economic Revolution in the United States* (Boston, 1925).

Chandler, Alfred D., Jr., and Stephen Salsbury. *Pierre S. du Pont and the Making of the Modern Corporation* (New York, 1971).

Chandler, Lester V. *Benjamin Strong: Central Banker* (Washington, D.C., 1958).

Chase, Stuart. *Men and Machines* (New York, 1929).

———. *Prosperity: Fact or Myth* (New York, 1929).

———. *The Tragedy of Waste* (New York, 1925).

———. and F. J. Schlink. *Your Money's Worth* (New York, 1927).

Chernow, Ron. *The House of Morgan* (New York, 1990).

Churchill, Allen. *The Incredible Ivar Krueger* (New York, 1957).

Cleveland, Harold van B., and Thomas F. Huertas. *Citibank, 1812–1970* (Cambridge, Mass., 1985).

Cockburn, Claud. *A Discord of Trumpets* (New York, 1956).

Coit, Margaret. *Mr. Baruch* (Boston, 1957).

Collier, James Lincoln. *The Rise of Selfishness in America* (New York, 1991).

Coolidge, Calvin. *Autobiography of Calvin Coolidge* (New York, 1929).

Dana, Julian. *A. P. Giannini—Giant in the West* (New York, 1947).

Davis, John H. *The Bouviers* (New York, 1969).

Dice, Charles Amos. *New Levels in the Stock Market* (New York, 1929).

———. *The Stock Market* (New York, 1926)

Edwards, George. *The Evolution of Finance Capitalism* (New York, 1938).

Edwards, R. H., et al. *Undergraduates: A Study of Morals in Twenty-three American Colleges and Universities* (New York, 1928).

Eichengreen, Barry. *Golden Fetters: The Gold Standard and the Great Depression, 1919–1939* (New York, 1992).

Epstein, Ralph C. *The Automobile Industry* (Chicago, 1928).

Ewen, Stuart, and Elizabeth Ewen. *Channels of Desire: Mass Images and the Shaping of American Consciousness* (New York, 1982).

Fabricant, Solomon. *Employment in Manufacturing, 1899–1939* (New York, 1942).

———. *The Output of Manufacturing Industries, 1899–1937* (New York, 1940).

Fass, Paula S. *The Damned and the Beautiful: American Youth in the 1920s* (New York, 1977).

Fausold, Martin L. *The Presidency of Herbert C. Hoover* (Lawrence, Kan., 1985).

Fisher, Irving. *The Stock Market Crash—and After* (New York, 1930).

Fisher, Irving Norton. *My Father Irving Fisher* (New York, 1956).

Frederick, Christine. *Selling Mrs. Consumer* (New York, 1929).

Friedman, Milton, and Anna Jacobson Schwartz. *A Monetary History of the United States, 1867–1960* (Princeton, 1963).

Fuess, Claude M. *Calvin Coolidge: The Man from Vermont* (Boston, 1940).

Galbraith, John Kenneth. *The Great Crash* (Boston, 1955).

Garrett, Garet. *The American Omen* (New York, 1928).

Geisst, Charles R. *Wall Street: A History* (New York, 1997).

Grant, James. *Bernard M. Baruch: The Adventures of a Wall Street Legend* (New York, 1997).

Gustin, Lawrence R. *Billy Durant* (Grand Rapids, Mich., 1973).

Harris, Seymour E. *Twenty Years of Federal Reserve Policy* (Cambridge, Mass., 1933).

Hawley, Ellis W. *The Great War and the Search for a Modern Order* (New York, 1979).

Hicks, John D. *Republican Ascendancy* (New York, 1960).

Hirst, Francis Wrigley. *Wall Street and Lombard Street* (New York, 1931).

Hodson, Henry V. *Slump and Recovery, 1929–1937* (London, 1938).

Hoover, Herbert. *The Memoirs of Herbert Hoover: The Great Depression, 1929–1941* (New York, 1941).

Hounshell, David A. *From the American System to Mass Production, 1800–1932* (Baltimore, 1984).

Hurlock, Elizabeth B. *The Psychology of Dress: An Analysis of Fashion and Its Motive* (New York, 1929).

Johnston, Alva. *The Legendary Mizners* (New York, 1953).

Jones, Joseph M. Jr. *Tariff Retaliation: Repercussions of the Smoot-Hawley Bill* (Philadelphia, 1934).

Josephson, Matthew. *Infidel in the Temple* (New York, 1967).

Kempner, S. Marshall. *Inside Wall Street, 1920–1942* (New York, 1973).

Kennedy, David M. *Freedom from Fear: The American People in Depression and War, 1929–1945* (New York, 1999).

————. *Over Here: The First World War and American Society* (New York, 1982).

Kettl, Donald F. *Leadership at the Fed* (New Haven, 1986).

Kindleberger, Charles P. *Manias, Panics, and Crashes*, 4th ed. (New York, 2000).

————. *The World in Depression, 1929–1939* (London, 1973).

Klingaman, William K. *1929: The Year of the Great Crash* (New York, 1989).

Knapp, Paul. *The Berengaria Exchange* (New York, 1972).

Kuznets, Simon. *National Income and Its Composition, 1919–1938* (New York, 1941).

Landau, Sarah Bradford, and Carl W. Condit. *Rise of the New York Skyscraper, 1865–1913* (New Haven, 1996).

Lawrence, Joseph Stagg. *Wall Street and Washington* (Princeton, 1929).

Leach, William. *Land of Desire: Merchants, Power, and the Rise of a New American Culture* (New York, 1993).

Lee, Maurice. *Economic Fluctuations: Growth and Stability* (Homewood, Ill., 1959).

Lefevre, Edwin. *Reminiscences of a Stock Operator* (Garden City, N.Y., 1923).
———. *Stock Market Manipulator* (New York, 1967).
Leighton, Isabel, ed. *The Aspirin Age, 1919–1941* (New York, 1949).
Leuchtenburg, William. *The Perils of Prosperity* (New York, 1958).
Lichtenberg, Bernard. *Advertising Campaigns* (New York, 1926).
Lippmann, Walter. *Men of Destiny* (New York, 1928).
Livermore, Jesse Lauriston. *How to Trade in Stocks* (New York, 1940).
Livingston, J. A. *The American Stockholder* (New York, 1958).
Lundberg, Ferdinand. *America's 60 Families* (New York, 1937).
Lynd, Robert S., and Helen M. Lynd. *Middletown: A Study in Contemporary American Culture* (London, 1929).
———. *Middletown in Transition: A Study in Cultural Conflicts* (London, 1937).
McCoy, Donald R. *Calvin Coolidge: The Quiet President* (New York, 1967).
McDonald, Forrest. *Insull* (Chicago, 1962).
MacManus, T. F., and Norman Beasley. *Men, Money, and Motors* (New York, 1929).
Marchand, Roland. *Advertising the American Dream: Making Way for Modernity, 1920–1940* (Berkeley, 1985).
Marx, Arthur. *Life with Groucho* (New York, 1954).
Marx, Groucho. *Groucho and Me* (New York, 1974).
Marx, Harpo. *Harpo Speaks!* (New York, 1976).
Mazur, Paul M. *American Prosperity: Its Causes and Consequences* (New York, 1928).
Meikle, Jeffrey L. *Twentieth Century Limited: Industrial Design in America, 1925–1939* (Philadelphia, 1979).
Mellon, Andrew W. *Taxation: The People's Business* (New York, 1924).
Messler, Norbert. *The Art Deco Skyscraper in New York* (New York, 1986).
Moggridge, D. E. *British Monetary Policy, 1924–1931* (Cambridge, Eng., 1972).
Mowry, George E. *The Urban Nation* (New York, 1965).
———, ed. *The Twenties: Fords, Flappers, and Fanatics* (Englewood Cliffs, N.J., 1963).
Myers, William Starr, and Walter H. Newton. *The Hoover Administration: A Documented Narrative* (New York, 1936).
Nash, Lee, ed. *Understanding Herbert Hoover* (Stanford, Cal., 1987).
Nash, Roderick. *The Nervous Generation: American Thought, 1917–1930* (Chicago, 1969).
The 1929 World Almanac and Book of Facts (New York, 1971).
Noggle, Burl. *Teapot Dome* (Baton Rouge, 1962).
Noyes, Alexander Dana. *The Market Place: Reminiscences of a Financial Editor* (Boston, 1938; New York, 1969).
———. *The War Period of American Finance, 1908–1925* (New York, 1926).
Nystrom, Paul H. *Economics of Fashion* (New York, 1928).
O'Connor, Harvey. *Mellon's Millions: The Biography of a Fortune* (New York, 1933).

Olney, Martha L. *Buy Now, Pay Later: Advertising, Credit, and Consumer Durables in the 1920s* (Chapel Hill, 1991).

Parker, John L. *Unmasking Wall Street* (Boston, 1932).

Patterson, Robert T. *The Great Boom and Panic, 1921–1929* (Chicago, 1965).

Pecora, Ferdinand. *Wall Street Under Oath* (New York, 1939).

Pierce, Phyllis S., ed. *The Dow Jones Averages, 1885–1995* (Chicago, 1996).

Poffenberger, Albert T. *Psychology in Advertising* (Chicago, 1925).

President's Research Committee on Social Trends. *Recent Social Trends in the United States*, 2 vols. (New York, 1933).

Prothro, James. *The Dollar Decade* (New York, 1954).

Redford, Polly. *Billion-Dollar Sandbar: A Biography of Miami Beach* (New York, 1970).

Rheinstrom, Carroll. *Psyching the Ads: The Case Book of Advertising* (New York, 1929).

Ripley, William Z. *Main Street and Wall Street* (Boston, 1927).

Robbins, Lionel. *The Great Depression* (New York, 1934).

Robinson, Edgar Eugene, and Vaughn D. Bornet. *Herbert Hoover, President of the United States* (Stanford, Cal., 1975).

Rogers, Will. *The Autobiography of Will Rogers* (Boston, 1949).

Romasco, Albert U. *The Poverty of Abundance: Hoover, the Nation, the Depression* (New York, 1965).

Rothbard, Murray N. *America's Great Depression* (Princeton, 1963).

Russell, Francis. *The Shadow of Blooming Grove* (New York, 1968).

Ryant, Carl. *Profit's Prophet: Garet Garrett (1878–1954)* (Cranbury, N. J., 1989).

Sarnoff, Paul. *Jesse Livermore: Speculator King* (Palisades Park, N. J., 1967).

Schachtman, Tom. *The Day America Crashed* (New York, 1979).

Scharff, Edward E. *Worldly Power: The Making of the Wall Street Journal* (New York, 1986).

Schlesinger, Arthur M. Jr. *The Crisis of the Old Order* (Boston, 1957).

Schwartz, Jordan A. *The Interregnum of Despair: Hoover, Congress, and the Depression* (Urbana, Ill., 1970).

Sears, John. *The New Place of the Stockholder* (New York, 1929).

Seldes, Gilbert. *The Seven Lively Arts* (New York, 1924).

Seligman, E.R.A. *The Economics of Farm Relief* (New York, 1929).

Simmons, E.H.H. *The Principal Causes of the Stock Market Crisis of 1929* (pamphlet).

Sinclair, Andrew. *The Available Man* (New York, 1965).

Skolnik, Peter L. *Fads: America's Crazes, Fevers, and Fancies* (New York, 1978).

Sloan, Alfred P. Jr. *My Years with General Motors* (New York, 1963).

Slosson, Preston W. *The Great Crusade and After, 1914–1928* (New York, 1930).

Smulyan, Susan. *Selling Radio* (Washington, D.C., 1994).

Sobel, Robert. *The Big Board: A History of the New York Stock Market* (New York, 1965).

————. *Coolidge: An American Enigma* (Washington, D.C., 1998).

————. *The Great Bull Market* (New York, 1968).

————. *Panic on Wall Street* (New York, 1968).

Soule, George. *Prosperity Decade* (New York, 1947).

Sparling, Earl. *Mystery Men of Wall Street* (New York, 1930).

Starrett, W. A. *Skyscrapers and the Men Who Build Them* (New York, 1928).

Stein, Herbert. *The Fiscal Revolution in America* (Chicago, 1969).

Strasser, Susan. *Satisfaction Guaranteed: The Making of the American Mass Market* (New York, 1989).

Sullivan, Mark. *Our Times: The Twenties* (New York, 1935).

Tallmadge, T. E. *The Story of Architecture in America* (New York, 1927).

Tedlow, Richard. *New and Improved: The Story of Mass Marketing in America* (New York, 1990).

Temin, Peter. *Did Monetary Forces Cause the Great Depression?* (New York, 1976).

Thomas, Gordon, and Max Morgan-Witts. *The Day the Bubble Burst* (Garden City, N.Y., 1979).

Tindall, George B. *The Emergence of the New South, 1913–1945* (Baton Rouge, 1967).

Warburg, Paul M. *The Federal Reserve System—Its Origins and Growth* (New York, 1930).

Warren, Harris Gaylord. *Herbert Hoover and the Great Depression* (New York, 1959).

Weisberger, Bernard A. *The Dream Maker: William C. Durant, Founder of General Motors* (Boston, 1979).

Weissman, Rudolph. *The New Wall Street* (New York, 1933).

West, Robert Craig. *Banking Reform and the Federal Reserve, 1863–1923* (Ithaca, 1977).

White, Eugene N., ed. *Crashes and Panics: The Lessons from History* (Homewood, Ill., 1990).

White, William Allen. *A Puritan in Babylon* (New York, 1938).

Wicker, Elmus R. *Federal Reserve Monetary Policy, 1917–1933* (New York, 1966).

Wickwire, Arthur. *The Weeds of Wall Street* (New York, 1933).

Wigmore, Barrie A. *The Crash and Its Aftermath: A History of Securities Markets in the United States, 1929–1933* (Westport, Conn., 1985).

Wilson, Joan Hoff. *Herbert Hoover: Forgotten Progressive* (Boston, 1975).

Wilson, Thomas. *Fluctuations in Income and Employment* (New York, 1948).

Winkelman, Barnie F. *Ten Years of Wall Street* (Philadelphia, 1932).

Wyckoff, Richard D. *Wall Street Ventures and Adventures Through Forty Years* (New York, 1930).

Scholarly Articles

Brown, E. Cary. "Fiscal Policy in the Thirties: A Reappraisal." *American Economic Review* 46 (December 1956), 857–79.

Huertas, Thomas F., and Joan L. Silverman. "Charles E. Mitchell: Scapegoat of the Crash?" *Business History Review* (Spring 1986), 81–103.

Marchand, Roland. "The Corporation Nobody Knew: Bruce Barton, Alfred Sloan, and the Founding of the General Motors 'Family.' " *Business History Review* (Winter 1991), 825–75.

Pontecorvo, Giulio. "Investment Banking and Security Speculation in the Late 1920's." *Business History Review* (Summer 1958), 166–91.

Raff, Daniel M. G. "Making Cars and Making Money in the Interwar Automobile Industry: Economies of Scale and Scope and the Manufacturing behind the Marketing." *Business History Review* (Winter 1991), 721–53.

Romer, Christina D. "The Great Crash and the Onset of the Great Depression." *Quarterly Journal of Economics* 105 (August 1990), 597–624.

Sirkin, Gerald. "The Stock Market of 1929 Revisited: A Note." *Business History Review* (Summer 1975), 223–31.

Magazine Articles

Ashdown, William. "Confessions of an Automobilist." *Atlantic Monthly* (June 1925).

Atwood, Albert. "The Appetite for Stock." *Saturday Evening Post* (April 19, 1930).

———. "Company Craze." *Saturday Evening Post* (March 1, 1930).

———. "The Future of Stock Speculation." *Saturday Evening Post* (September 13, 1930).

———. "Giants of Finance." *Saturday Evening Post* (June 29, 1929).

———. "The Great Bull Market." *Saturday Evening Post* (January 12, 1929).

———. "Investment and Speculation." *Saturday Evening Post* (December 7, 1929).

———. "Men and Markets." *Saturday Evening Post* (April 27, 1929).

———. "The Merger Movement." *Saturday Evening Post* (August 17, 1929).

———. "Money and the Market." *Saturday Evening Post* (February 23, 1929).

Barnard, Eunice Fuller. "Ladies of the Ticker." *North American Review* (April 1929).

Barton, Bruce. "Bernard M. Baruch Discusses the Future of American Business." *American Magazine* (June 1929).

Bissell, Shelton. "Vaudeville at Angelus Temple." *Outlook* (May 23, 1928).

Brooks, John. "A Corner in Piggly Wiggly." *New Yorker* (June 6, 1959).

Cabot, Paul C. "The Investment Trust." *Atlantic Monthly* (March 1929).

Child, Richard Washburn. "Hoover—or Some Other?" *Saturday Evening Post* (March 16, 1929).

Coolbaugh, Kenneth. "Unemployment Statistics." *Saturday Evening Post* (February 16, 1929).

Corey, Lewis. "Who Gains by Speculation?" *New Republic* (April 17, 1929).

Crowther, Samuel. "Everybody Ought to Be Rich" (interview with John J. Raskob). *Ladies' Home Journal* (August 1929).

———. "How Do They Get Their Money?" *Saturday Evening Post* (March 9, 1929).

———. "Supersalesmanship and the Consumer's Dollar." *Saturday Evening Post* (June 8, 1929).

———. "Who Has the Money?" *Saturday Evening Post* (May 31, 1930).

Dayton, Katharine. "This Little Pig Went to Market." *Saturday Evening Post* (March 23, 1929).

Duffus, Robert L. "The Age of Play." *Independent* (December 20, 1924).

Ellsworth, D. W. "Causes of the Stock Market Boom." *Current History* (December 1928).

Evans, W. Carl. "Why Banks Fail." *Saturday Evening Post* (April 20, 1929).

Florance, Howard. "What Really Happened?" *Review of Reviews* (January 1930).

Flynn, John T. "The Birthday of the Slump." *Forum* (November 1930).

———. "How to Make Money in Wall Street." *Woman's Home Companion* (January 1930).

———. "Riders of the Whirlwind." *Collier's* (January 9, 1929).

———. "Speculation and Gambling." *Harper's Magazine* (January 1930).

———. "Taming the Great Bull." *Forum* (February, 1929).

Fraser, Elizabeth. "The Lady and the Ticker." *Saturday Evening Post* (March 8, 1930).

Gammack, Thomas H. "Six Million Share Days." *Outlook* (December 5, 1928).

Garrett, Garet. "The Seven Sound Years." *Saturday Evening Post* (April 13, 1929).

———. "Speculation." *Saturday Evening Post* (May 4, 1929).

———. "Wall Street and Washington." *Saturday Evening Post* (December 28, 1929).

———. "The Wild Wheel in the Business Machine." *Saturday Evening Post* (January 18, 1930).

Garrett, Paul W. "The Forces Behind the Fever." *Outlook* (December 26, 1928).

———. "The Jazz Age in Finance." *North American Review* (February 1930).

Gray, George W. "Signing Off on the First Ten Years." *World's Work* (December 1930).

Hall, Henry. "The Money Market." *Nation* (June 19, 1929).

Haney, Lewis H. "Who Gets the Money?" *North American Review* (January 1930).

Hunt, Frazier. "Million-Dollar Football: An Interview with W. H. Taft, Chief Justice." *Cosmopolitan* (November 1929).

Jordan, Virgil. "The Era of Mad Illusions." *North American Review* (January 1930).

Kieran, John. "Big-League Business." *Saturday Evening Post* (May 31, 1930).

Kulas, E. J. "The Whip of Prosperity." *Saturday Evening Post* (June 29, 1929).

Lefevre, Edwin. "The Bigger They Are—." *Saturday Evening Post* (January 11, 1930).

———. "Bulls on America," *Saturday Evening Post* (February 16, 1929).

———. "The Little Fellow in Wall Street." *Saturday Evening Post* (January 4, 1930).

———. "The Long and the Short of It." *Saturday Evening Post* (December 13, 1930).

———. "Running Past the Signal." *Saturday Evening Post* (February 9, 1929).

———. "So Says the Bond." *Saturday Evening Post* (May 17, 1930).

———. "A Trip on the Magic Carpet." *Saturday Evening Post* (February 1, 1930).

———. "With Blue Chips This Time." *Saturday Evening Post* (February 2, 1929).

McCormick, Anne O'Hare. "A Year of the Hoover Method." *New York Times Magazine* (March 2, 1930).

McFadden, Louis T. "Convalescent Finance." *Saturday Evening Post* (February 15, 1930).

———. "Investment Trusts." *Saturday Evening Post* (April 12, 1930).

McMullen, Frances D. "Women and Ticker Tape—A Year after the Crash." *Woman's Journal* (November 1930).

Marcosson, Isaac F. "The Alien and Unemployment." *Saturday Evening Post* (June 14, 1930).

Mayo, Morrow. "Aimee Rises from the Sea." *New Republic* (December 25, 1929).

Merz, Charles. "Bull Market." *Harper's Magazine* (April 1929).

Moody, John. "The New Era in Wall Street." *Atlantic Monthly* (August 1928).

Murphy, Charles J. V. "Wall Street Branches Out." *Outlook* (September 18, 1929).

Nelson, Frederic. "The Child Stylites of Baltimore." *New Republic* (August 28, 1929).

Noyes, Alexander Dana. "The Conflict over Credit Reaches a Climax." *Scribner's Magazine* (May 1929).

———. "The Stock Market Panic." *Current History* (December 1929).

Payne, Will. "Deflation." *Saturday Evening Post* (May 3, 1930).

———. "Greatest of Bull Markets." *World's Work* (January 1929).

———. "No Par." *Saturday Evening Post* (February 2, 1929).

———. "A Reformed Speculator." *Saturday Evening Post* (August 10, 1929).

———. "Stocks or Bonds." *Saturday Evening Post* (May 18, 1929).

Phillips, H. I. "My Stock Market Operations." *American Magazine* (March 1929).

Purinton, Edward Earle. "Big Ideas from Big Business." *Independent* (April 16, 1921).

Rascoe, Burton. "The Grim Anniversary." *New Republic* (October 29, 1930).

Roberts, George E. "Lessons of the Stock Panic." *Outlook* (January 8, 1930).

Rosenwald, Julius. "The Burden of Wealth." *Saturday Evening Post* (January 5, 1929).

Russell, C. P. "The Pneumatic Hegira." *Outlook* (December 9, 1925).

Scroggs, William O. "By-products of the Bull Market." *Outlook* (May 8, 1929).

————. "We Have Changed All That." *Outlook* (December 25, 1929).

Shelby, Gertrude Mathews. "Florida Frenzy." *Harper's Monthly Magazine* (January 1926).

Siegfried, André. "The Gulf Between." *Atlantic Monthly* (March 1928).

Sparkes, Boyden. "A Career in Wall Street." *Saturday Evening Post* (March 8, 1930).

Strauss, Samuel. "Things Are in the Saddle." *Atlantic Monthly* (November 1924).

Tindall, George B. "The Bubble in the Sun." *American Heritage* (August 1965).

Uncle Henry. "The Shock Market." *Collier's* (May 4, 1929).

Wallace, Francis. "This Football Business." *Saturday Evening Post* (September 28, 1929).

Willis, H. Parker. "Who Caused the Panic of 1929?" *North American Review* (February 1930).

Winkler, Max. "Paying the Piper." *North American Review* (January 1930).

Documents

"Stock Exchange Practices," *Report of the Committee on Banking and Currency*, 73d Cong., 2d Sess., no. 1455 (Washington, D.C., 1934).

New York Stock Exchange, *Annual Report for 1929* (New York, 1930).

Acknowledgments

For many authors, writing is a collaborative act in which every chapter is shared with colleagues to gain their input and insight. This process makes perfect sense, especially for scholars seeking to avoid errors of fact and flaws in reasoning. For other writers, however—myself included—the conception and execution of a work is a solitary business in which the final product is prepared and cooked almost entirely in one's own mind, with many ingredients added by the host of books and other works that are part of the research behind the final recipe. The difference between these two approaches has less to do with the question of which one is superior than with the practical issue of which one works better for a given writer.

Given my preference for working solo, I have no long list of colleagues to thank for their time and suggestions. However, many other people have given generously of their time and expertise in assisting my work. The library staff at the University of Rhode Island has, as usual, been uniformly helpful in responding to the many problems and puzzles presented to them. Angela Santoro of Dow Jones & Company provided me with useful material from the archives of that firm. Theresa Collins shared with me chapters from her forthcoming book on Otto Kahn of Kuhn, Loeb. Kristin Richard expedited my use of photographs from the Musuem of American Financial History. Steven Wheeler of the New York Stock Exchange archives provided photographs from that collection.

The careful scrutiny and thoughtful suggestions of my editor, Peter Ginna, did much to improve the manuscript. I am grateful too for the helpful advice of David Hackett Fischer and James M. McPherson, editors of the Pivotal Moments series at Oxford. Copyeditor India Cooper gave the manuscript a deft and sensitive combing. No one has been more supportive of my work over the years than my agent, Marian Young, who stood as firmly behind this book as she has previous endeavors. For her efforts and friendship I give special thanks. Finally, even more special thanks go as always to my wife, Kathy, who has always sustained the singer regardless of the song.

East Greenwich, Rhode Island   MAURY KLEIN

Index